OBSERVATION IN MODERN ASTRONOMY

By the same author

FRONTIERS OF ASTRONOMY

TEACH YOURSELF ASTRONOMY

To my masters in Britain and
South Africa who taught me
my trade, this work is
gratefully dedicated

OBSERVATION IN MODERN ASTRONOMY

DAVID S. EVANS

Chief Assistant, Royal Observatory
Cape of Good Hope

This book is published and distribute
in the United States by
S. AMERICAN ELSEVIER PUBLISHING COM
52 Vanderbilt Avenue, New York, N.Y

LTD
E C 4

78369

First printed 1968

SBN 340 05069 1
PRINTED IN ENGLAND FOR THE ENGLISH UNIVERSITIES PRESS LTD
BY C. TINLING AND CO. LTD, LIVERPOOL, LONDON AND PRESCOT

Author's Preface

I T WOULD BE idle to pretend that prefaces are written as they are printed, at the beginnings of books. When the preface comes to be written, the author at last knows what his book is about and what it can hope to achieve. His mood is such that he feels he may permit himself a personal or even sententious note. This book is very different from what either the author or the publishers contemplated when the work was first proposed. Twenty years ago I found myself responsible for launching a popular science magazine and compelled to develop in a few days a policy for the magazine itself and a system of advice to potential contributors. One cardinal rule was "Write about what you know, and not what you think you ought to know". In nearly two decades of continuous work as an observational astronomer I have found myself struggling at first hand, or have been privileged to have a ringside seat, in most departments of astronomical observation in the optical field. I have tried to write of this, and to explain how and why these things are done: in the writing I have found out how incomplete my knowledge was. Such a book may fill a need: the Mrs. Beeton of astronomy which will contain all recipes and may be held in one hand while any conceivable operation of astronomy is carried out, has yet to be written. So far as it goes, the present work may provide the directions for the preparation of some good plain fare with a few frills. There is no such thing as an average observatory: always, somewhere, there is practised a more sophisticated method of carrying out a given operation, but this may require instrumental resources, such as the largest telescope in the world, which the average astronomer does not possess. Highly-educated readers will at most points be able to cite instances of equipment and techniques which surpass those I have mentioned, and the headlong progress of some departments of modern astronomy will make this, or any book, obsolescent before it is published.

There is, it appears to me, a need for a kind of manual for the student who aspires to be a working astronomer, or the physicist who wants to know what goes on in observatories which will give indications of standard methods and standard topics of discussion. It should assume a knowledge of physics but not of astronomy. It is hoped that this is it. Astronomy is an academic science (but in this space-minded age with more practical applications than would have been imagined a few years ago). In countries where the climate is indifferent, observational astronomy suffers relative neglect in the academic world because it is difficult to fit into the strait jacket of the academic curriculum with its stress on the award of a research degree such as the

Ph.D. as a mark of originality. How can a professor gamble with a student's future by running the risk that no useful body of observations will be obtained because there may be a run of hopeless weather during the first half of the three years needed for the degree? Even if successful, wherein would the essental quality of originality lie? It is safer to stick to the development of some new observational technique, most of which can be done in the laboratory: then a few observations can be obtained to show that the method is good, which usually means demonstrating that the "right" answer is obtained for a number of previously well observed astronomical objects. All requirements are satisfied: the method is original: the work is sound: the student gets his degree—and the equipment is probably never used again because the next student would not be original if he used it. Astronomy as a science is hardly advanced at all. This is a serious deficiency which afflicts optical astronomy, but not radio astronomy: for the latter, good climates exist almost everywhere—even Manchester is one of the world's leading observational centres. Optical astronomy is a kind of industry: apart from restricted flashes of genius, most advances in the science depend on lengthy programmes of observation. The astronomer who spends some years at the meridian circle, or produces a thousand stellar magnitudes in clusters or the general field, or engages in such work as the Cape Photographic Catalogue of the southern sky which took more than twenty-five years to complete, does far more good to astronomy than the development of most innovations of method. Such a man becomes immensely experienced, but it is difficult to express this in a form of currency acceptable in the academic world. This is not to say that new methods should not be developed. A worth-while new method is one that can be extensively applied afterwards. If we consider the important new developments in observational techniques (the majority of which have come from France in recent years) we see that they all require many years, perhaps a decade, of the most sophisticated development work before they are brought into use. The electronic camera and the impersonal astrolabe provide examples.

So it is that many recruits to the astronomical profession have a very limited experience of optical observational practice: they do not know how to carry out the standard operations of their trade, and are quite inexperienced in the highly skilled and demanding task of drafting programmes which will make the most productive use of that priceless commodity, time at the telescope. It is hard to think of any other profession in which any substitute would be accepted for skill in its rudiments.

The philosophy of this book is that the Universe is not divisible into thesis-size fragments, that there is no substitute for clear skies, and that assiduous systematic observation can alone discover what problems there are to be solved in astronomy.

Royal Observatory,
Cape of Good Hope

Acknowledgements

My deepest thanks are due to numerous colleagues who have read this work in manuscript or proof, in whole or in part, and particularly to Dr. S. V. M. Clube, Dr. A. W. J. Cousins, Mr. G. A. Harding, Dr. P. W. Hill, Dr. Harlan J. Smith, Dr. R. H. Stoy, Dr. D. V. Thomas, Dr. A. J. Wesselink, Dr. P. A. T. Wild, Dr. N. J. Woolf, and, most painstaking and pungent of all, Dr. Andrew T. Young. Their criticisms have always been welcome, even if not always met by textual changes. Any responsibility for residual errors rests with the author and not with them. I am also vastly indebted to many colleagues, who have permitted me to use diagrams and photographs, some produced only by the expenditure of much time and trouble on their part, and to the editors of journals who have so readily permitted me to reproduce material. The acknowledgements in the text express a sincere gratitude.

D. S. E.

Contents

page

AUTHOR'S PREFACE   v

ACKNOWLEDGEMENTS   vii

INTRODUCTION   xiii

I. ASTRONOMY OF POSITION   1
    1.1. The Celestial Sphere; 1.2. The Effects of Latitude; 1.3. The Earth's
Rotation; 1.4. Celestial Coordinates: Declination; 1.5. Hour Angle and
Sidereal Time; 1.6. The Ecliptic and Equinoxes; 1.7. Local Sidereal Time
and Right Ascension; 1.8. Equatorial Mounting of Telescopes; 1.9. Other
Systems of Coordinates; 1.10. Changes in Astronomical Coordinates; Aber-
ration; 1.11. Precession and Nutation; 1.12. The Transit Circle; 1.13. The
Variation of Latitude (Polar Movement); 1.14. Nadir Observations; 1.15. The
Determination of Declinations; 1.16. Atmospheric Refraction; 1.17. Instru-
mental Errors and Right Ascensions; 1.18. Observational Determination of
Right Ascensions; 1.19. Summary of Transit Circle Procedure; 1.20. Time
and Timekeeping; 1.21. The Caesium Clock; 1.22. Astronomical Aspects of
Time; 1.23. The Relation between Mean and Sidereal Time; 1.24. Ephemeris
Time; 1.25. Universal Time; 1.26. The Determination of Time: The Photographic Zenith Tube; 1.27. The Impersonal Astrolabe of Danjon; 1.28. The
Mirror Transit; 1.29. Mean and Apparent Places of Stars; 1.30. Astronomical Causes of Positional Changes: Annual Parallax; 1.31. Proper Motions;
1.32. Orbital Motion; 1.33. Astronomical Photography; 1.34. Star Nomenclature; 1.35. Star Catalogues; 1.36. Proper Motions by Photography;
1.37. The Measurement of Trigonometrical Parallaxes. References.

II. THE MEASUREMENT AND ANALYSIS OF STELLAR RADIATION   47
    2.1. The Laws of Radiation: Effective Temperature; 2.2. Deviations from
Black-Body Radiation; 2.3. Limb Darkening; 2.4. Stellar Spectra; 2.5.
Interstellar Effects; 2.6. Effects of the Earth's Atmosphere; 2.7. Stellar
Magnitudes; 2.8. Photographic and Photovisual Magnitudes; 2.9. The
Objective Grating; 2.10. Magnitude Sequences; 2.11. The Photometric
System of W. W. Morgan and H. L. Johnson; 2.12. Developments in the
Southern Hemisphere; 2.13. Photoelectric Equipment; 2.14. Observations
and Reductions; 2.15. A Technical Miscellany; 2.16. Photographic Photo-

metry; 2.17. Direct Photography; 2.18. The Effects of Focal Ratio; 2.19. The Measurement of Radial Velocities; 2.20. Observational Procedure; 2.21. Measurement and Reduction of Spectra; 2.22. Radial Velocities from Objective Prism Spectra; 2.23. The Diversity of Stellar Spectra; 2.24. The Definition of Spectral Types; 2.25. Spectrophotometry and Spectral Types. References.

III. INTERRELATIONS BETWEEN OBSERVED QUANTITIES   91
3.1. Introduction; 3.2. Absolute Magnitudes; 3.3. Extinction and Reddening; 3.4. The Hertzsprung-Russell Diagram; 3.5. The Main Sequence; 3.6. Observational Selection; 3.7. The Giant Stars; 3.8. The Supergiant Stars; 3.9. The Subgiants; 3.10 The Subdwarfs; 3.11. Line Blanketing; 3.12. The White Dwarfs; 3.13. Magnitudes and Colours in Clusters; 3.14. Galactic Clusters; 3.15. The Hyades; 3.16. Interstellar Absorption and Reddening in more Distant Clusters; 3.17. The Globular Clusters; 3.18. The Hertzsprung-Russell Diagrams of Globular Clusters; 3.19. Stellar Structure; 3.20. The Generation of Stellar Energy; 3.21. Stellar Evolution; 3.22. Stellar Evolution and Globular Clusters; 3.23. The Origin and Evolution of Individual Stars; 3.24. Stellar Associations; 3.25. Age Parameters in Astronomy. References.

IV. THE MOTIONS OF THE STARS   126
4.1. Introduction; 4.2. Galactic Structure; 4.3. Galactic Coordinates; 4.4. The Motions of the Nearby Stars; 4.5. Solar Motion and Secular Parallaxes; 4.6. Systematic Motions of Stellar Groups; 4.7. Expanding Associations; 4.8. The Velocity Ellipsoid; 4.9. The Construction of Velocity Ellipsoids; 4.10. Galactic Rotation; 4.11. Functional Relationships of the Oort Constants; 4.12. Proper Motion Effects; 4.13. Actual Investigations; 4.14. Non-Circular Motions in the Galaxy; 4.15. Motions Perpendicular to the Galactic Plane; 4.16. The Dynamics of Clusters. References.

V. VARIABLE STARS   156
5.1. Introduction; 5.2. Nomenclature of Variable Stars; 5.3. Observational Methods; 5.4. The Blink Microscope; 5.5. Further Investigation; 5.6. Julian Dates; 5.7. The Cepheid Variables; 5.8. The RR Lyrae Stars; 5.9. Other Pulsating Variables; 5.10. The T Tauri and Associated Stars; 5.11. The W Virginis Stars; 5.12. Some Short Period Variables; 5.13. Magnetic Variables; 5.14. The Long-Period Variables; 5.15. The Explosive Variables; 5.16. The Novae and Supernovae; 5.17. Types of Supernovae; 5.18. Planetary Nebulae and other Gaseous Objects. References.

VI. BINARY STARS AND MULTIPLE STARS   189
6.1. The Binary Stars; 6.2. A Highly-Stylised Visual Binary; 6.3. Sirius as a Visual Binary; 6.4. Observational Methods; 6.5. The Eyepiece Interferometer; 6.6. The Analysis of Double Star Observations; 6.7. Stellar Masses and Dynamical Parallaxes; 6.8. Spectroscopic Binaries; 6.9. Mass-Ratio in a Double-Lined Binary; 6.10. Variations of Radial Velocity; 6.11. Determination of Orbital Elements; 6.12. Stellar Masses; 6.13. The Mass-Luminosity Relation; 6.14. A Highly-Stylised Eclipsing Binary; 6.15. Types of Eclipsing Binary; 6.16. Other Methods of Determining Stellar Radii; 6.17. Stars of Higher Multiplicity. References.

VII. THE GALAXY AND THE GALAXIES   222

7.1. The Galaxy; 7.2. Radio Astronomy and the Distribution of Neutral
Hydrogen; 7.3. External Galaxies; 7.4. The Classification of Galaxies;
7.5. Elliptical Nebulae; 7.6. Spiral Nebulae; 7.7. Catalogues of Galaxies;
7.8. Methods of Observation of Galaxies; 7.9. Radial Velocities of Galaxies;
7.10. The Electronic Camera; 7.11. The Distances of the Galaxies; 7.12.
The Expanding Universe; 7.13. The General Properties of Galaxies; 7.14.
The Rotation of Galaxies; 7.15. The Origin of Spiral Arms; 7.16. Clusters
and Groups of Galaxies: The Local Group; 7.17. The Local Supergalaxy;
7.18. Clusters of Galaxies in General; 7.19. Galaxies as Radio Sources;
7.20. Quasi-Stellar Radio Sources. References.

INDEX   265

Introduction

A STAR is a sphere of gas of great size, with a diameter lying in the range from that of a planet to that of the orbit of the Earth round the Sun, that is, roughly, from 10^5 to 10^8 kilometres. Its mass will lie in a range from one per cent of that of the Sun to about one hundred times that of the Sun. Most stars are composed almost exclusively of hydrogen with a small proportion of helium and an even smaller admixture of metals. They owe the major part of their luminosity to energy liberated by nuclear transformations taking place in the deep interior. For the most part these transformations result in the transmutation of hydrogen into helium, but many additional processes can occur in special circumstances. The surface emissivity of stars is determined by the temperatures of their outer layers, and these lie in the general range from 3,000°K to about 50,000°K, the upper limit referring to rather rare types of star. The average separation between stars in the neighbourhood of the Sun is of the order of 200,000 times the distance of the Earth from the Sun, or about 3×10^{13} kilometres. All stars are in motion, and those near the Sun, and the larger class of those which belong to our Galaxy, exhibit motions which are a combination of randomness and order.

Modern information on these topics has been gained by inference from observational data, using the laws of physics. A surprising proportion of these laws, including many of immediate practical application to ordinary life, have owed their initial inspiration and much of their later development to the fact that they are of importance for astronomical studies. As examples may be cited the mathematics of spherical trigonometry, the laws of mechanics, the theory of line spectra, the laws of radiation, and the first outline of a process capable of yielding nuclear energy.

Almost none of the astronomical data sketched in the first paragraph is susceptible of direct determination. Almost all of modern astrophysics is concerned with bridging the gulf between the parameters which are directly observable, and the desired objective. This is the description of the universe and its contents in terms freed from the restrictions imposed by the Earth-bound situation in which astronomers find themselves. To them, almost all stars, except the Sun, appear as luminous Euclidean points. Indeed, it seems very probable that the stars first inspired the definition of a Euclidean point, as that which has position but no parts. Observational astronomy is, effectively, restricted to the study of the position of stars, and changes in these: to the study of star brightness and star colours: and to the spectroscopic analysis of the light, or rather electromagnetic radiation in general, received from astronomical sources.

The introduction of orbiting observatories and interplanetary probes will not change this situation basically. Certain inferences will be replaced by direct observation; new ranges of wavelengths or radiation will become accessible; close-ups of planets and experiments on samples of planetary and interplanetary matter will become commonplace. All this is being achieved by the expenditure of money and effort vastly greater than at any time in the history of astronomy. A fraction of this in the past would have immensely benefited present-day conventional astronomy.

In the future, as in the past, the stars themselves will remain inaccessible, and we can expect that many of the basic techniques and ideas of observational astronomy will remain unchanged for a considerable time to come.

I
Astronomy of Position

1.1 The Celestial Sphere

ALL stars, and, with few exceptions, all astronomical bodies, are at distances so large as to be effectively infinite. To define the position of a star we need specify only the direction of the line joining the observer to the star. This is equivalent to regarding all stars as being marked by points on a sphere of large, or infinite, radius, centred at the observer. A demonstration of such a *Celestial Sphere* is provided in a planetarium, where the stars are represented by points of light projected on the interior surface of a large dome.

Imagine a celestial sphere centred at the centre of a transparent Earth. The points where the Earth's axis intersects this sphere are called the *North* and *South Celestial Poles*. A *Great Circle* on the celestial sphere is the intersection of the sphere with a plane through its centre. A *Small Circle* is the intersection with a plane not passing through the centre. The great circle defined by the plane of the Earth's equator is called the *Celestial Equator*.

Since star distances are effectively infinite, the distribution of star positions on a celestial sphere centred at any point on the surface of the Earth is the same as for a celestial sphere centred at the Earth's centre. The positions of stars relative to the horizon of an observer on the Earth's surface do, however, depend on his geographical position.

1.2 The effects of Latitude

For an observer at the north pole of the Earth, the north celestial pole will be directly overhead (in the *Zenith*); the position of the south celestial pole, cut off from view by the earth, lies in exactly the opposite direction, vertically downwards (in the *Nadir*). An observer on the equator of the Earth will have the celestial equator passing from the east to the west points of his horizon through his zenith. If the bending of light rays in the atmosphere of the Earth could be neglected, the equatorial observer would have the north and south celestial poles at the north and south points of his horizon. These are two special cases of the general rule, readily demonstrable from simple geometry, that the altitude of the celestial pole which is above the horizon is equal to the latitude of the observer if refraction is neglected. The *Altitude* of a point is the angular distance, measured on the great circle through the zenith, between the horizon and the point in question. *Zenith Distance* is the angle on the same great circle measured down from the zenith to the point. For an observer at sea with his eye at only a negligible height above the surface the sum of altitude and zenith distance is 90°. As the height of the observer increases the sum of the two quantities increases because the line from the observer's eye tangent to the surface of the Earth (i.e. the direction to the horizon) becomes progressively more and more depressed below the horizontal.

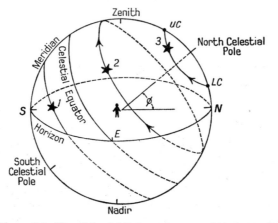

Figure I.1: The Celestial Sphere from north latitude ϕ.

Neglecting refraction, an observer at a moderate north (or south) latitude, ϕ, will have the north (or south) celestial pole due north (or south) of him, at an altitude ϕ. The celestial equator will be a great circle passing from the east to the west points of the horizon, having its highest point due south (or north) of him at an altitude of $90° - \phi$. The line joining the north and south points of the horizon, which passes through the zenith, the elevated pole, and the highest point on the celestial equator is called the *Meridian* of the observer (Figure I.1).

1.3. The Earth's Rotation

The effect of the rotation of the Earth is to produce the appearance of rotation of the celestial sphere as if it were a rigid body, with relative positions of the stars maintained, about the axis defined by the north and south celestial poles, in the direction from east to west. This rotation leaves the poles fixed, and causes the celestial equator to rotate on itself without change of position. The stars are carried along with the rotation of the sphere, and a star which is on the meridian of a northern observer, between the zenith and the south point of the horizon, is at its greatest altitude at that moment. This crossing of the meridian is known as *Meridian Passage* or *Transit* or *Culmination*. A star on the celestial equator rises due east and sets due west. For a northern observer a star south of the equator rises south of east and sets south of west: (Star No. 1, Figure I.1). A star north of the equator rises north of east and sets north of west: (Star No. 2). Stars in a restricted region of the sky near the north pole do not get down to the horizon even when at their lowest altitude on the meridian below pole to the north. These stars are known as *Circumpolar Stars* (e.g. Star No. 3), and do not rise or set. They cross the meridian above the horizon twice in each revolution of the celestial sphere, once above pole (*Upper Culmination*), (UC in figure), and once below pole (*Lower Culmination*), (LC in figure). For a northern observer there is a region of the sky centred on the south celestial pole which is always below the horizon.

For a southern observer the senses of north and south in the preceding must be interchanged. For example, for a southern observer, circumpolar stars occur in a region near the south celestial pole.

1.4 Celestial Coordinates: Declination

The two coordinates defining positions on the sky are known as *Right Ascension* and *Declination* and are closely analogous to longitude and latitude measured on the surface of the Earth. Declination is discussed first. It is defined as the angular distance of a point on the celestial sphere north or south of the celestial equator, the former being counted positive and the latter negative. The maximum numerical value of declination is 90° corresponding to the positions of the celestial poles. The computation of the meridian altitude of a star of north declination, δ, observed from north latitude, ϕ, is, apart from atmospheric refraction, a mere matter of addition and

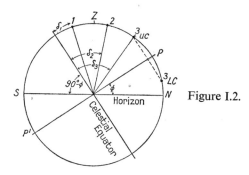

Figure I.2.

subtraction (Figure I.2). If $\delta_1 < \phi$, the star culminates south of the zenith, at an altitude of $90° - \phi + \delta_1$. If $\delta_2 > \phi$ the star will culminate north of the zenith at an altitude of $90° + \phi - \delta_2$. A star of declination δ_3 is at a polar distance of $90° - \delta_3$. If this is less than ϕ, the altitude of the pole, then the star in question will be circumpolar, i.e. we must have $\phi + \delta_3 > 90°$ for a star to be circumpolar, and its altitude at lower culmination is $\phi + \delta_3 - 90°$. It follows that, on the Earth's equator no stars are circumpolar, while at either pole all stars having declinations of the same sign as the latitude are circumpolar, the remainder being invisible. The range of declinations invisible from a given latitude is given by the rule that all stars south of declination $\phi - 90°$ (a negative value) are invisible from north latitude ϕ. The ranges of invisible declinations and circumpolar declinations refer to equal areas of sky.

1.5. Hour Angle and Sidereal Time

Since the effect of the rotation of the Earth on its axis is to cause the celestial sphere to rotate as a rigid body, a star which is on the meridian of a given place at a particular moment, will again be on the meridian of that place after an interval of time equal to the period of rotation of the Earth on its axis relative to the stars. This interval is adopted as the standard interval of time in positional astronomy, and is known as the *Sidereal Day*, and the corresponding flow of time is called *Sidereal Time*. Its passage is indicated by suitably rated clocks, with subdivisions of the sidereal day into hours, minutes, and seconds of sidereal time according to the usual scheme. If a star is on the observer's meridian at a given moment, then, after the lapse of one sidereal hour, the celestial sphere will have rotated through an angle of 15°, corresponding to a full circuit of 360° in 24 sidereal hours. When this has happened, we say that the *Hour*

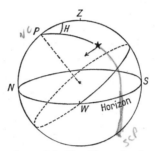

Figure I.3: The Hour Angle
of the star is H.

Angle of the star is 1 hour, or 15°. Hour angles are thought of as being measured at the north or south celestial poles, as if a pointer pivoted there, and fixed to the sky, had turned over an immovable angular scale. The hour angle of a body on the meridian is zero, and if its coordinates on the sky are fixed, its hour angle increases steadily at the rate of 15° per hour. Hour angles are reckoned as positive for bodies west of the meridian and negative for those which are east, or 360° may be added as required to make all positive and to lie between 0° and 360°. They may be expressed either in angular or time measure (Figure I.3).

1.6. The Ecliptic and Equinoxes

To complete the definition of the system of astronomical coordinates, a reference point on the celestial equator is adopted. This point, variously known as the *First Point of Aries* or the *Vernal Equinox* is designated by the symbol ♈, supposed to represent the horns of a ram (Aries = ram). It is one of the intersections of the celestial equator with the great circle marking the apparent path of the Sun round the sky in the course of a year. The apparent movement of the Sun is a reflex of the orbital motion of the Earth. As the Earth moves it causes, or would cause, if the Sun were not so bright, the Sun to be seen projected against different stellar constellations at different seasons of the year. The apparent path of the Sun among the stars is called the *Ecliptic* and is the trace on the celestial sphere of the plane of the orbit of the Earth round the Sun. This plane is inclined to the plane of the celestial equator at an angle of about 23° 27′. This is the angle between the Earth's axis and the normal to the plane of the Earth's orbit, and is known as the *Obliquity of the Ecliptic*. The coordinates of the Sun are thus continually changing. Its declination reaches its maximum positive value of about + 23° 27′ near June 21, its maximum negative value of about − 23° 27′ near December 21. The Sun crosses the equator, at zero declination on dates near March 21 and September 21 each year, the former being the crossing from south to north (negative to positive declinations). This intersection of the ecliptic and equator is the Vernal Equinox, and marks the beginning of spring in the northern hemisphere of the Earth. The other intersection is called the *Autumnal Equinox* (Figure I.4).

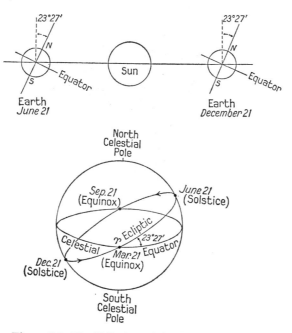

Figure I.4: The Ecliptic and the Celestial Equator.

1.7. Local Sidereal Time and Right Ascension

Local Sidereal Time at any place at any moment is the local hour angle of the vernal equinox at that moment. We especially distinguish *Greenwich Sidereal Time* as the hour angle of the vernal equinox from a point on the Greenwich meridian. The *Right Ascension* of a point is defined as the local sidereal time of meridian passage of that point. For a fixed point the right ascension is the time interval, measured on a sidereal clock, which has elapsed since the vernal equinox was on the meridian. Right ascension thus increases eastwards and is reckoned in hours, minutes, and seconds of time from zero up to 24 hours. Alternatively it may be reckoned in degrees, minutes and seconds of arc by conversion at the rate of 15° per hour. A conversion table is given in the *Astronomical Ephemeris*. For a moving body, such as the Sun, for which the right ascension continually increases, or such as a planet or comet, for which the right ascension is changing, although not always in the same sense, right ascension is determinable as the local sidereal time at the moment of meridian passage. Right ascensions at other times must be found by calculation from formulae or by interpolation.

Some simple relations are given for reference: at a place in west longitude λ, at a given moment, let the local sidereal time be *T*, and let the hour angle of a fixed object be *H*. At the same moment the Greenwich sidereal time will be *T* + λ, and the Greenwich hour angle of the same object will be *H* + λ. More generally, the local sidereal time and the local hour angle of the same object as observed at the same moment from a place in west longitude λ' will be $T + \lambda - \lambda'$ and $H + \lambda - \lambda'$ respectively. At a later time $T + \Delta T$ the corresponding times at other places will have increased by ΔT, and H will have increased to $H + \Delta T$. In these computations all quantities must be in the same measure, either time or angle (Figure I.5).

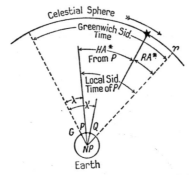

Figure I.5: Relations for Hour Angle, Local Sidereal Time, Right Ascension and Longitude.

1.8. Equatorial Mounting of Telescope

To permit pointing of a telescope at any point in the sky requires a mounting incorporating two mutually perpendicular axes. In the most usual system, called *Equatorial Mounting*, one axis, the *Polar Axis*, points to the elevated celestial pole, and is therefore inclined at an angle ϕ to the horizontal for an observatory in latitude ϕ. The axis perpendicular to this, called the *Declination Axis*, is equipped with a graduated circle which permits setting to any desired declination. The polar axis is motor driven at the diurnal rate. In many instruments one bearing of the polar axis incorporates a movable circle which can be clamped to the drive. At the beginning of an observing session this is turned so that the correct sidereal time is read off on a fixed pointer, and it is then clamped. The operation of the drive ensures that correct sidereal time continues to be read on the fixed pointer. To set to any desired right ascension, the telescope is rotated so that a pointer attached to the movable part of the mounting shows the correct right ascension on the circle. The telescope is then clamped so that it is turned by the drive and remains pointed to the chosen right ascension. The systematics are illustrated in Figures I.6(a) and (b).

In instruments with a single circle, moving with the telescope, the hour angle of the desired object (= sidereal time − RA) must be set, the time being read from a clock in each case. In instruments without circles, where the readings are shown on dials by servo mechanisms connected to the axes, the subtraction required to pass from right ascension to hour angle is performed mechanically or electronically by combining the sidereal clock reading with the servo output from the polar axis.

We discuss more fully later the change in altitude of a point produced by refraction of light rays in the Earth's atmosphere. If a telescope is adjusted so that the polar axis is inclined at the true latitude, ϕ, meridian settings near the zenith, where refraction has no effect, will be correctly shown on the declination circle. Settings near the pole will show small errors. If the polar axis is pointed to the refracted pole, settings at high declinations will be correct, but there will be small errors near the zenith. It is much easier to compensate for the latter by making the small adjustments known as *Guiding* than it is in the former case, where the errors occur at high declinations.

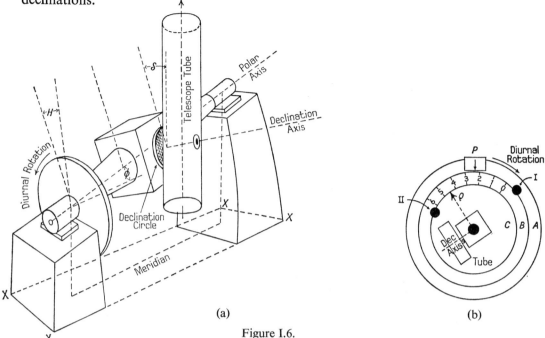

(a)   (b)

Figure I.6.

(*a*) Schematics of equatorial telescope mounting for latitude ϕ. The polar axis is in the meridian tilted at angle ϕ. The telescope is shown set to a star of declination, δ, at hour angle H. (*b*) Schematics for telescope setting in right ascension: Circle A is driven at the diurnal rate. Graduated circle B can be turned so that the fixed pointer, P, indicates correct local sidereal time, and A and B are locked by Clamp I. P continues to indicate correct sidereal time (about $2^h\ 20^m$ in the figure). Circle C is an integral part of the polar axis (the telescope tube is indicated in miniature), and this is turned until the desired right ascension is shown on pointer, Q (about $4^h\ 30^m$ in the figure). The telescope is then locked by Clamp II and continues to point to the selected star.

1.9. Other Systems of Coordinates

The simplest system for mounting a telescope consists in the provision of horizontal and vertical axes, like a piece of artillery. This permits training horizontally (in *Azimuth*) and in altitude. Both settings alter continuously as the celestial sphere rotates. This altazimuth system of mounting is mainly of importance in surveying and navigation. However, several of the largest steerable "dishes" used in radio astronomy are altazimuth mounted, because of the difficulty of constructing very large inclined tracks or bearings capable of sustaining high mechanical loads. Computers are used to convert from RA and declination to altitude and azimuth, and to provide the variable drive rates needed in both the latter coordinates.

A more important system of celestial coordinates is that of celestial latitude and longitude. These are based on the ecliptic and its pole, and find application in studies of the solar system. In these coordinates the motion of the Earth round the Sun results in a solar movement against the star background such that the latitude of the Sun is always very near zero, while its longitude increases not quite uniformly at an average rate of slightly less than a degree per day, corresponding to a complete circuit in the course of a year.

1.10. Changes in Astronomical Coordinates

Various causes produce small changes in the astronomical coordinates of stars, some of which depend on position in the sky, while others are peculiar to the individual stars concerned.

In the former category is the phenomenon of *Aberration*. In a non-relativistic treatment, with the Earth swimming round the Sun in a fixed aether, and with the light rays from the stars travelling in the same medium, it can easily be shown that the combination of orbital velocity with the velocity of light leads to apparent displacements of position of all the stars in the sky.

These take place toward the point on the sky towards which the Earth is instantaneously moving. If $\odot$ is the longitude of the Sun, then for a circular orbit the direction of motion of the Earth would be towards the point V, with coordinates in celestial longitude and latitude, $(\odot - 90°, 0°)$. The aberrational displacement of a star is towards V, and for any star is equal to $20''\cdot496 \sin V\ast$, where $V\ast$ is the angle between the directions to the star and V. The *Constant of Aberration*, $20''\cdot496$, is very close, in radian measure to the ratio of the mean orbital velocity of the Earth (29·8 km/s) to the velocity of light (299,793 km/s).† The functional form states that the aberrational displacement is proportional to the vector component of orbital motion of the Earth perpendicular to the line of sight to the star.

For an exact treatment relativity theory should be used; the ellipticity of the Earth's orbit and the variable orbital velocity must be considered, and also the rotation of the Earth on its axis. In addition the orbital motion of the Earth should be referred to the centre of mass of the solar system and not to the Sun. All these modifications are small, but not all are negligible for accurate work. They contribute to the extent that they modify the instantaneous value and direction of the observer's velocity in space.

Aberration as described produces continually changing displacements in the apparent position of a star. A star at the pole of the ecliptic describes an almost circular path in the course of a year, while one located on the ecliptic oscillates back and forth along it. In any discussion of star positions the time dependent effects of aberration must be removed so as to produce star positions as viewed from a point moving with the centre of mass of the solar system.

There is, in addition, a correction, constant for each star, and peculiar to it, which is not removed. Light from a star may take many years to reach the Earth, so that the observed star position is not the contemporary one, but an antedated one corresponding to the light time from the star to the Earth. During this time the star may have moved through a perceptible angle. Light time corrections are applied in the case of planets because of their high rates of angular motion.

1.11. Precession and Nutation

The choice of a system of coordinates based on the axis of rotation of the Earth is compulsory for the reasons of practical utility outlined above. However, the spatial direction of the axis of the Earth is not fixed because of the effects known as *Precession*

† The adopted value in the calculations of the *Astronomical Ephemeris* is $20''\cdot47$. The quoted value is a recent determination.

and *Nutation*. It is possible to define a fixed plane in the solar system known as the invariable plane, which is normal to the resultant angular momentum vector of the entire solar system. This plane is close to the plane of the orbit of the Earth (and the planets in general), about the Sun. For the moment we take the Earth's orbital plane as identical with the invariable plane. The axis of the Earth is inclined to the normal to this plane at about 23° 27'. The Earth is not spherical, but is flattened at the poles, so that its shape approximates to an ellipsoid of ellipticity $1/298 \cdot 20$. This figure is the most accurate modern value deduced from studies of changes in the orbits of artificial satellites. The Earth may thus be thought of as a sphere with a belt of additional matter round its equator. The attractions of the Sun and Moon, plus relatively small contributions from the planets, produce a couple tending to turn the axis of the Earth more nearly perpendicular to the orbital plane. The axial rotation of the Earth makes the effect gyroscopic. The action of the couple does not change the inclination of the Earth's axis, but causes it to describe a cone in space, with the normal to the orbital plane as the axis of the cone. The period of one circuit in this conical motion is 25,725 years. This is the phenomenon of *Precession* (of the Equinoxes). The north and south celestial poles are not fixed points, but, to a first order, describe circles on the sky about the poles of the ecliptic, the angular radii of these circles being about 23° 27'. Because the ecliptic is close to the invariable plane, the poles of the ecliptic are nearly fixed (Figure I.7).

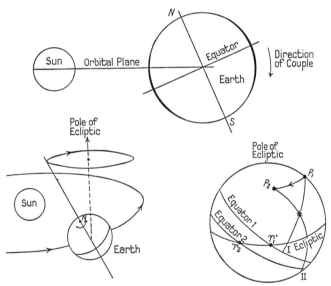

Figure I.7: Precession of the Equinoxes: The mechanical couple produced by the oblateness of the Earth, causes the axis of the Earth to describe a cone in space. When the axis moves on the celestial sphere from P_1 to P_2, the right ascension of the star increases from $\gamma_1 I$ to $\gamma_2 II$.

The phenomenon of precession has been known since its discovery in Hellenistic times by Hipparchus. The dynamical theory, starting with Newton, which explains it in terms of the mass distribution of the Earth and the dimensions and masses of other bodies in the solar system, should be thought of as being under continuous review as measuring accuracy improves. The movement of the Vernal Equinox in longitude, i.e. along the ecliptic, caused by precession is at the rate of about 50″·27 per year at the present time.

The figure would be about one part in 400 larger if only the Sun and Moon were operative: the small reduction is due to the action of the other planets. These also have the effect of causing a small progressive reduction of the obliquity of the ecliptic by about 0″·5 per annum. Precession increases the right ascension of a star on the celestial equator by about 3·07 seconds of time per annum, or about 46″·1 in angular measure. The reduction to this value from the figure first quoted is due to the obliquity of the ecliptic. For a star at right ascension α and declination δ first order formulae for the annual changes in coordinates are given by

$$\varDelta \, \alpha = 3^{\text{s}}\!\cdot\!073 + 1^{\text{s}}\!\cdot\!336 \sin \alpha \tan \delta \qquad \varDelta \, \delta = 20''\!\cdot\!04 \cos \alpha$$

More elaborate formulae are required for star positions near the celestial poles.

The word *Nutation* describes the fact that the spatial motion of the Earth's axis is a combination of the steady precessional advance with a number of smaller, oscillatory terms caused by a variety of gravitational interactions of the Earth with the Moon, Sun and planets. As an example, the fact that the Moon is now to the north and now to the south of the Earth's orbital plane introduces a series of such oscillatory effects. They can now be computed from formulae derived from the gravitational theory of the solar system, and are usually expressed functionally as the sum of many trigonometric functions, of which the arguments are functions of the time. Their relative importance can be judged from the sizes of the numerical coefficients. By far the largest term in the expression for nutation in longitude is one of lunar origin with an amplitude of 17″·2. The corresponding terms in the expression for the obliquity of the ecliptic has an amplitude of 9″·2. The terms themselves have a period of about 6,798 days (about 19 years), and are related to the fact that the orbit of the Moon, which is inclined to the ecliptic at an angle of 5° 09′, cuts the latter in two points, (the Moon's nodes), which move round the ecliptic in approximately this time. Since the most important effect on the obliquity of the ecliptic is this term in the nutation formula, the value 9″·2 is called the *Constant of Nutation*. On the other hand, the term *Constant of Precession* as used by Newcomb is the value of a certain expression derived from the dynamics of the Earth-Moon system. When combined with the planetary precession and multiplied by the cosine of the obliquity, the result approximates to the general precession in longitude.

From the foregoing discussion it will be clear that to arrive at the true astronomical coordinates of a point at any moment, the instantaneous positions of the equinox and equator as affected by precession and nutation must be used as the frame of reference. We shall later have to meet the difficulty that since we have defined local sidereal time as the hour angle of the equinox, this will, by a very small quantity, increase non-uniformly owing to the oscillatory effects of nutation. We shall, temporarily evade this difficulty by assuming that we have available a clock which indicates local sidereal time with an error not exceeding a few milliseconds, and shall consider how astronomical coordinates are determined by means of the classical meridian instrument, the Transit Circle.

1.12. The Transit Circle

If the refraction of the Earth's atmosphere is neglected, the meridian altitude of a star is simply expressed in terms of the latitude of the observatory and the declination of the star. Its right ascension is determined as the local sidereal time of meridian passage. The transit circle is an instrument for the determination of these quantities. It consists of a telescope mounted orthogonally on a single east-west axis, which is carefully levelled, so that, in principle, the telescope is constrained to move exactly in the meridian (Figure I.8(a)). If the telescope is pointed to a suitable zenith distance for the observation of a given star, then this, if above pole at meridian passage, will be seen by the observer to enter the field from the eastern side and to pass across it to the west. The apparent declination is determined from the altitude to which the telescope is elevated, and the apparent right ascension from the sidereal time at which the star crosses the centre of the field. However, no instrument is perfectly constructed or adjusted, and the major part of the theory of the transit circle and the technical refinements of its operation are concerned with the detection and correction of instrumental defects. The accuracy sought is very high. Millisecond accuracy is now readily available from quartz clocks, and in a millisecond a star on the equator moves through an angle of $0''\cdot015$, or about one fourteen-millionth of a radian. For a transit telescope of two metres focal length this corresponds to a seventh of a micron in the focal plane, and to one quarter of this on the circumference of a divided circle of diameter one metre. Accuracies of this order are certainly not obtainable for a single observation of a star. It is clearly essential to aim at the control of adjustments and errors all over the instrument within a few microns at most. Errors are broadly of two kinds: inherent errors in the construction of the instrument which change slowly and need to be reinvestigated only at long intervals: rapidly varying errors depending on, for example, meteorological conditions, which have to be redetermined frequently, sometimes as often as several times during each observing session.

The elevation of the transit telescope is read off on a divided circle fixed to the axis, of which the graduation intervals may be 5 minute of arc. In such a case it is necessary to determine the errors of the 4,320 division marks on the circle, a laborious process undertaken by well-established methods. Once done it will not usually need to be repeated for decades. Readings for observational purposes are made at six equally disposed points round the circle by interpolation between the graduations. At one time this was generally done by means of microscopes with movable micrometer wires for the determination of the position of a fiduciary mark relative to the neighbouring division marks. In modern instruments the circle is photographed and the same results obtained by measuring the films on suitable measuring machines. Six measuring stations are employed because the mean of the six values is unaffected by small displacements of the centre of the circle relative to them.

The axis bearing surfaces on which the instrument rests are ground as accurately as possible to cylindrical form. They rest on vees carried on the tops of the two piers. To minimise wear most of the weight of the instrument is carried on counterpoises leaving only a resultant load of about twenty pounds, adequate to secure proper mechanical contact between the pivots and the vees. Even so, once every few years a programme of measurements is undertaken to determine the errors of form of the pivots, and to trace how these change with wear. Corrections for pivot errors are made to right ascension observations.

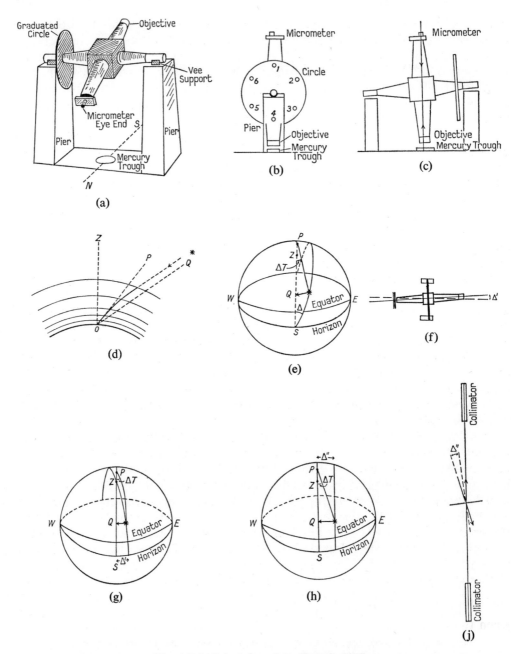

Figure I.8: Principles of the Transit Circle.

(a) Schematics of the Instrument. (b) Nadir Observations. Figures 1-6 show the six fixed positions for reading the circle. (c) Determination of Level Error. (d) Atmospheric Refraction: The true direction to the star is OQ, the observed direction, OP. (e) Effect of level error on transit times. The time correction required, ΔT, corresponds to the angle QP★. (f) Azimuth Error. (g) Effect of azimuth error. The time correction required, ΔT, corresponds to the angle QP★. (h) Effect of collimation error. Time correction required, ΔT, corresponds to angle QP★. (j) Determination of collimation error.

We may now suppose that we have the means to make an accurate reading of the circle indication corresponding to any elevation of the instrument.

1.13. The Variation of Latitude (Polar Movement)

The meridian altitude of a star is related to its declination and to the latitude of the observatory by formulae already given. The axis of the Earth is not fixed in the body of the Earth, but wanders from its mean position by a variable amount of up to about 10 metres, corresponding to about $0''\cdot3$ in angular measure. The deviations can for the most part be expressed as the sum of two periodic terms. The deviations are measured at observatories specially equipped for the task. The photographic zenith tube, described later is one such instrument. The deviations cause changes in the coordinates (both latitude and longitude) of all observatories, and the published values can be used to correct transit circle measures made at any given observatory.

1.14. Nadir Observations

To determine the apparent zenith distance of a star the circle reading corresponding to the zenith must be found. This is done by making observations of the nadir about once every two hours during observing sessions. The telescope is pointed vertically downwards towards a bath of mercury installed between the piers. The normal to this surface defines the instantaneous direction of the vertical. By means of a special eyepiece and a source of illumination the observer can see both the micrometer wires in the eye end of the instrument and their reflections in the mercury surface. He uses the wire in the east-west direction to find the micrometer reading at which the wire coincides with its own image. From the screw characteristics of the micrometer and from the circle reading can be derived the accurate circle reading corresponding to the zenith. These results are employed together with observational results on stars observed between the nadir observations to derive for them accurate values of zenith distances at their moments of transit (Figure I.8(b)).

The observer also has a micrometer wire or wires which run in the north-south direction and are movable perpendicular to themselves by a second micrometer head. The observer also determines the micrometer reading at which this wire coincides with its image. From the screw characteristics and the dimensions of the instrument can be inferred the extent to which one end of the supporting axis is higher than the other. This is known as *Level Error*. Interpolated values of level error are used in the correction of right ascension observations made between nadir settings (Figure I.8(c)).

1.15. The Determination of Declinations

When the declination of a star is to be determined the transit telescope is set to a circle reading which will cause the star to transit near the centre of the field. The observer takes up his position and waits for it to enter the field from the eastern side. Near the actual time of transit the observer will be occupied in determining the sidereal time of meridian passage, as described below, for the determination of the right ascension of the star. He makes the declination observations just before and just after transit. He does this by moving the east-west micrometer wire (the declination wire) perpendicular to itself so as to bisect the star image. Having done this he makes a mental note of the micrometer reading. This is done twice before transit and twice after transit, and the mean of the four readings gives a measure of the distance above or below the centre of the field at which the transit occurred. A star not on the equator is moving on a small circle on the celestial sphere, making its path in the eyepiece slightly curved. The micrometer measures are corrected for this, the correction being a function of declination. The micrometer measures, combined with the circle reading give the equivalent circle reading on the meridian for the moment of transit. Combination with the nadir reading interpolated to the time of observation gives the apparent zenith distance of the star at the moment of transit.

We have already seen how the division errors of the circle will be applied to declination measures. In addition two further errors must be corrected. The first is a correction for the flexure of the instrument due to its deformation under its own weight. This is determined at the same time as collimation error for which the procedure is described below, with the transit telescope in a horizontal position. It is usually assumed that the flexure correction with the instrument at zenith distance z, is given by $f \sin z$, where f is the flexure for the horizontal position. This assumption is open to some doubt for so complex a structure as a telescope, and instrumentalists have devoted considerable attention to the possibility of determining flexure corrections continuously.

1.16. Atmospheric Refraction

The correction for atmospheric refraction has already been mentioned several times. Light rays entering the atmosphere of the Earth along an inclined path do not travel in straight lines, but as they pass downwards through atmospheric layers of increasing density are refracted so as continually to diminish the inclination of the ray to the vertical. A telescope on the Earth's surface which receives the light from a star is pointed in the direction of the tangent to the path. The zenith distance of this direction is smaller than the zenith distance of the true direction to the star. The difference is the refraction (Figure I.8(d)). A first order theory, in which the atmosphere is regarded as stratified in plane parallel layers gives a formula for the refraction of $58''$ tan z, where z is the zenith distance of the star. The total angular deviation of a light ray from empty space down to an observatory depends on the refractive index of the air in the neighbourhood of the observer. More accurate refraction tables incorporate atmospheric pressure, temperature and humidity of the air, and to make use of them transit observers must make frequent observations of these meteorological parameters by means of instruments installed in and near the telescope house. Theories of refraction are being continually revised, and at high zenith distances the curvature of the atmospheric layers and anomalous effects have to be taken into account. Useful transit observations are rarely made near the horizon, but even at an altitude of 15° the first order formula and more elaborate formulae may differ in their results by as much as $5''$. Satellite observations for objects not completely clear of the atmosphere, in which the whole of the refraction is not to be applied, have been of use in recent refraction studies.

It is by no means easy for a single observatory to determine refractions experimentally. It is easy to see in a general way how the problem can be approached. Observations of upper and lower culminations of a circumpolar star can yield a good approximation to the altitude of the refracted pole. If a functional form for refraction can be adopted, the constants in it can be found from observations of stars of a variety of declinations above and below pole, and tables gradually built up. However, to observe the same star above and below pole on the same night requires a night twelve hours long, and at low latitudes the circumpolar region is small. It is no surprise that the basic work on refractions was undertaken in high latitudes, and that for example, one much used set of tables was compiled at Pulkovo near Leningrad. There are dangers in the use of tables compiled at high latitudes by other observatories since the vertical distribution of the atmosphere varies with latitude, and astronomical determinations of latitude might erroneously include some unknown fraction of the refraction. Artificial satellite observations are playing an important part, both in revealing the vertical distribution of the atmosphere, and in the production of ever more accurate geodetic positions for a limited number of widely-spaced stations on the surface of the Earth.

The assumption that the atmosphere is stratified in level layers is sometimes open to question. For example, at the Cape, there are strong seasonal winds, from the south-east in summer and from the north-west in winter. These imply a horizontal pressure gradient transverse to the meridian which is seasonal in its effects, which could introduce lateral refraction varying with right ascension. At high zenith distances lateral refraction is certainly important. Some years ago a Dutch expedition went to Kenya to make observations of stellar declinations from a point at high altitude above the sea precisely on the equator. All the stars should rise vertically at azimuths around the horizon directly indicating their declinations. The effects of refraction should have been to cause only vertical displacements, but in fact quite marked lateral refractions occurred which made the observations less valuable than they were expected to be.

1.17. Instrumental Errors and Right Ascensions

The standard theory of the transit circle shows how to allow for a variety of instrumental errors in the observation of right ascensions. Level error, already mentioned, is produced if one end of the axis is higher than the other. If this error alone is present, the true meridian is replaced by a false one which passes through the north and south points of the horizon, but not through the zenith. If the error of level is an angle, $\varDelta$, the zenith displacement of the false meridian is also $\varDelta$, and for a star of declination δ which transits at zenith distance z the angular displacement of the false meridian is $\varDelta \cos z$, corresponding to an error of hour angle (i.e. of transit time) of $\varDelta \cos z \sec \delta = \varDelta \cos (\phi - \delta) \sec \delta$. The transit occurs early, so that the correction to be applied to the observed time is positive, if the western end of the axis is the higher. (Figure I.8(e)).

Azimuth error is produced by a deviation of the axis of the instrument in the horizontal plane from the east-west direction (Figure I.8(f)). This error alone produces a false meridian which passes through the zenith, not through the north and south points of the horizon, but through two opposite points each displaced by a small angle $\varDelta'$. The displacement at zenith distance z is $\varDelta' \sin z$, and this gives an error in transit time of $\varDelta' \sin (\phi - \delta) \sec \delta$. If the eastern end of the axis is displaced to the north, transit occurs too soon for stars south of the zenith observed from a north latitude, and the correction to the observed times is positive (Figure I.8(g)).

In some books one will find a description of the determination of azimuth error from the almost simultaneous determination of transit times of two stars of known coordinates near the pole and near the equator respectively. The argument is quite correct, but it is not clear how one is to observe accurate stellar positions unless one has previously evaluated azimuth error in some transit instrument and made corrections for it. The fundamental condition which can be reproduced without reference to previous authority is that, after correcting all other errors, the azimuth is free from error if above-pole and below-pole transits of the same circumpolar star on the same night are separated by precisely twelve hours of sidereal time. One has to suppose that the instrument remains stable during the interval, and one has to keep in mind short-term effects such as changes in aberration, nutation, latitude and possibly others, depending on the accuracy which is aimed at. There is no quick fundamental method, and a fundamental investigation is a long-drawn-out matter during which the coordinates of circumpolar stars are steadily improved. When this has been achieved a continuous check can be kept on the azimuth correction by the observation of circumpolar stars above and below pole.

Alternatively use may be made of azimuth marks. In the Gill Reversible Transit Circle at the Cape such marks are provided in the meridian, north and south of the instrument, and distant some 85 yards from it. The primary marks are located at the bottoms of vertical pits dug down to unweathered rock. The transit instrument can be turned horizontal to observe secondary marks which are placed precisely over the primary ones. This is done by the method of making a cross-wire coincide with its image in a mercury bath placed at the bottom of the pit. The cross-wire is at the focus of a lens placed just above the mercury bath, so that the primary mark is the centre of the lens. These marks can be relied upon to remain stable for some weeks at a time, and observations of the marks will reveal variations in azimuth error. The deviations of the line of marks from the true meridian can be determined from observations of azimuth stars made at convenient times when observing conditions are especially favourable.

Collimation error is produced by deviation of the optical axis from exact perpendicularity to the mechanical axis of the instrument. Presence of this error causes the instrument to sweep out a false meridian which is a small circle parallel to the true meridian and displaced by an angle Δ'' from it, where Δ'' is the angular deviation from exact perpendicularity. It produces an error of timing of a transit equal to $\Delta'' \sec \delta$ (Figure I.8(h)). For a northern instrument, if displacement due to collimation error is to the east when the instrument is pointed south, the observed transit occurs early and the correction is positive.

Collimation error can be determined by the aid of two long-focus fixed horizontal telescopes set up north and south of the transit instrument. Ports are opened in the central cube of the transit instrument so that the two collimators can observe each other along a horizontal line passing through the centre of rotation of the transit telescope. Each has micrometer wires in its eyepiece which can be brought into coincidence with the images of the corresponding wires in the other collimator. When the collimators are adjusted, the transit instrument is pointed to one collimator by turning it horizontal, and the micrometer wires in its eyepiece brought into coincidence with those of the collimator. The transit instrument is then turned over to the other collimator. The wires will now not be in coincidence. The deviation left and right is twice the collimation error, while the vertical deviation is twice the horizontal flexure (Figure I.8(j)).

A further correction to the observed time of transit of a star is that due to the aberrational effect of the rotation of the earth on its axis. It is equal to $0s \cdot 021 \cos \phi \sec \delta$ for stars on the meridian.

1.18. Observational Determination of Right Ascensions

Having enumerated all these errors we can describe the method for observing a star. The eye end of the transit circle is a complex piece of mechanics. We have already noted that it incorporates a declination wire moved by a micrometer head, used not only for declination observations, but also for nadir and flexure observations. The right ascension wire is also controlled by a micrometer head and is used for observations of level and collimation errors. This wire can also be driven across the field by a motor drive with an infinitely variable gear. The object of this is to make observations of right ascension impersonal, that is, independent of the reaction time of the observer.

Before observing a star at declination δ the observer sets the variable gear to give a drive speed equal to the diurnal rate, i.e. $15'' \cos \delta$ per second of sidereal time. In addition he can advance or retard the moving wire by operating a differential control. When the star appears he first makes two declination settings as already described. He then operates his differential control so as to bisect the star image with the moving right ascension wire, and maintains this bisection as best he can throughout the time of transit. As the carriage carrying the moving wire passes over certain contacts, these record the time electrically. In some cases this is done on a two-pen chronograph, one pen showing the beats of the sidereal clock, the other, the pulses from the contacts. In other cases the time may be recorded by a printing chronograph or on a decatron display, or the result may be punched directly on to a computer card. When the transit is complete the observer will make his second pair of declination settings. Still further to eliminate personal bias, the eye end may be fitted with a reversing prism which the observer inverts between passage over the first and second symmetrical patterns of contacts. This means that he sees the second half of the transit with the star apparently moving in the reverse direction and any systematic tendency to hook to one side of the mark ought to be compensated. Bright stars are dimmed by placing wire screens over the objective since it is known that exceptionally bright stars tend to be observed systematically differently from faint ones.

This complication of equipment entails a further series of instrumental investigations to evaluate the mechanical characteristics of the positions of the contacts, the screw intervals and the properties of the timing gear.

After all the corrections are in and the records reduced, the final result is the instantaneous value of the declination of the star together with the sidereal clock time of the transit over the true meridian. In the course of the programme there may be included certain stars of which the coordinates are very exactly known which will be used to determine the error of the sidereal clock. While these may continue to be observed as a precaution, modern methods of timekeeping are so accurate as to be preferable to the values derived from the observation of clock stars. In this case the local sidereal clock as regulated by observations made with other instruments, or by time signals, may be used. If the observations are made in terms of a clock keeping mean sidereal time, the coordinates observed with the transit circle will be with respect to the mean equinox of date. Differential observations with respect to stars of known coordinates will yield positions referred to the true equinox of date and the error of the clock determined from observations of the standard stars will incorporate both the real error and the effect of polar movement on longitude.

1.19. Summary of Transit Circle Procedure

To wind up this part of the exposition we summarise the procedures involved in transit circle observations:

> Declinations: Division Errors of Circle; Nadir observation; Flexure; Refraction; Latitude variation; Curvature correction of micrometer observations.

> Right Ascensions: Level error; Azimuth error; Collimation error; Aberration due to Earth's rotation; Clock error; Pivot errors.

Further to reduce errors, the instrument is reversed on its piers once every few weeks, i.e. raised and turned so that what was the eastern end of the axis now rests on the western vee and vice versa. At long intervals the objective and eye end may be interchanged to opposite ends of the telescope tube.

One of several colleagues who read this work in manuscript objected at this point that the fundamental determination of star coordinates had not been adequately covered because the method of determination of geographical coordinates had not been described. This is a valid objection to be overcome in one way by requiring, transit observations of the Sun, so that the actual equator and equinox can be determined. Alternatively, and probably preferably because of the cumulative accuracy attainable, geographical positions will henceforth be determined by means of artificial satellites designed for geodetic purposes.

1.20. Time and Timekeeping

The notion of time is inseparable from philosophical concepts which defy definition. Time is thought of as an entity which flows uniformly, while a clock is a device which stores the contemporary indication of time and makes it available to us. We recognise that some clocks are imperfect, and we improve their performance by making corrections to their indications. These are derived by intercomparing the imperfect clock with a more perfect one. This does no more than shift the problem by one remove, and implies that our ultimate recourse is to the more perfect clock. This in its turn may have errors only demonstrable by comparisons with a yet more perfect standard. We seem never to be able to reach finality. Indeed this sequence of comparisons with time standards of greater and greater perfection epitomises the history of timekeeping. The basic principle of horology has almost always been to select some oscillatory or vibratory physical phenomenon, and to postulate that this has a standard frequency which does not change. The selected phenomenon is made to operate as a clock by some counting mechanism which keeps the score of how many oscillations have occurred in a given time. The earliest clocks were interval timers—devices which marked the passage of a given interval of time by the flow of a certain quantity of water or sand through an orifice, or by the burning of a candle of a certain length. By repetition, e.g. by inverting the sandglass immediately the sand had finished running through, a crude clock system included in the foregoing definition could be achieved. The earliest clocks of any precision relied on the synchronous property of a pendulum. In their highest development pendulum clocks achieved a remarkable precision. A good, well-mounted pendulum clock with a one second beat (two seconds for the full double swing to left and right) can be made to run with a rate of only a few tenths of a second per day, and erratic errors of about the same order. This does not, however, provide an absolute physical standard if the pendulum is exposed to the vagaries of temperature and pressure of the atmosphere. In addition the length of a seconds pendulum depends on the acceleration of gravity at the place where it is mounted, and it is not unknown for a pendulum to lengthen perceptibly over many years due to metallic creep. The highest development of the pendulum clock was the form known as the Shortt free-pendulum type. In these clocks a master pendulum was swung in a moderate vacuum and maintained at a constant temperature. The actual indications of the clock, such as driving of dials, and provision of beat signals was done by a second clock, known as the slave, which was deliberately adjusted to run slightly slow. The two clocks beat independently except that, every 30 seconds, an impulse came from the master pendulum which operated a mechanism forcing the slave pendulum into phase with the master if it had lagged significantly behind. At the same moment an impulse from the slave operated a remontoire device giving a slight push to the master pendulum, thus restoring to it the energy which it had lost during the previous half minute. Shortt clocks of this type were capable of giving rates of the order of a few hundredths of a second per day, with erratic errors of the same order. They were accurate enough to give the first indications of irregularities in the rate of rotation of the earth.

Pendulum clocks must all now be regarded as antiques, although some are so beautifully constructed as to be very valuable and desirable, and quite accurate enough for domestic timekeeping. The pendulum clock was replaced by the quartz clock, depending on vibrations of a quartz crystal maintained piezo-electrically by means of an electronic circuit. In one of the most modern forms the quartz is cut from natural crystal, with a particular orientation relative to the optic axis, in the form of a ring about 5 cm in diameter. The exciting electrodes are thin metal films deposited on the faces of the crystal. The whole is carefully temperature-controlled, and mounted, usually in a deep cellar, on a carefully designed anti-vibration mounting. The basic vibration frequency of 100,000 cycles per second is normally used, and is electronically divided to yield a continuous thousand cycle note, or seconds pips, or any desired variant. Quartz clocks give an accuracy much better than a millisecond per day, and can be used for prediction and signal control for intervals of some days or weeks ahead. This accuracy is sufficient for most astronomical purposes, and readily demonstrates seasonal variations in the rate of rotation of the Earth. The quartz clock is now an article of commerce and even portable models, used for example in geodesy, have an accuracy in the millisecond range.

Increasing accuracy has been made possible by the application of electronic techniques, and these in turn have made severe demands on horological techniques particularly in the field of the standardisation of frequencies. There are legal and economic demands for the close specification of frequencies in television and other communications systems, and in radar and electronic navigation devices. In principle, any two frequencies, no matter how high and no matter how little different, can be compared by measuring the beat frequency between them. In order to convert a frequency standard into a clock a means of counting beats must be provided, and,

B

in addition, there must be an assurance that the frequency is constant. All the devices so far mentioned rely on the perfection of their construction, and are not automatically related to the constants of physics.

1.21. The Caesium Clock

Once the field of very high frequencies became accessible through electronic developments a link was sought with atomic properties which would provide a standard of frequency defined in terms of the constants of nature. Attempts to use intrinsic oscillations of the ammonia molecule turned out less successfully than was at first hoped. A frequency standard and a system of timekeeping related to fundamental atomic properties came with the introduction of the caesium clock through the work of Dr. Louis Essen of the British National Physical Laboratory and his associates. The ground state of the caesium atom has two components separated by a small energy difference corresponding to a frequency which is low for an atomic transition, and very high for a frequency in the electronic range. The value now adopted is 9, 192, 631, 770 Hz (i.e. 10^{10} Hz to the nearest order of magnitude). It is a quantity related to the general constants of nature because it can be calculated from the known structure of the caesium atom. The transition arises from the interaction of the spin of the valency electron of the atom and that of the nucleus. The magnetic moments of the caesium atom are different in the two states and this property has been used in the construction of the caesium clock in which the atomic frequency is made to control an electronic frequency which can then be used for frequency standardisation and timekeeping. The principles used are illustrated in Figure I.9.

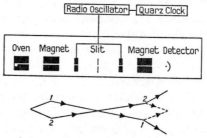

Figure I.9: Diagram of the caesium clock, showing (*above*) the arrangement of the apparatus, and (*below*) the paths followed by atoms in the beam with deflections greatly magnified. (By permission of Dr. L. Essen.)

All the components are enclosed in a highly evacuated chamber. Caesium is heated in an oven maintained at about 80°C and from this source caesium atoms stream out as a thin beam at about 200 metres per second. They then pass between the poles of a magnet designed to give a strong non-uniform magnetic field. Those in one component of the hyperfine ground state are deflected in one direction: those in the other in the opposite direction. In each case the angles are very small. A narrow slit at the centre of the apparatus allows those atoms which have emerged from the oven in particular directions and have been appropriately deflected, to pass through. Symmetrically placed at the farther end of the vacuum tube is a second magnet identical with the first. If an atom in hyperfine state No. 1 has passed through the slit, and is still in this state, then it will be deflected by the second magnet in the same sense as by the first. The same is true of atoms in hyperfine state 2. If, however, during flight down the tube, an atom has been changed from one hyperfine state to the other, the second magnet will deflect it back towards the axis of the instrument, and atoms having this property will converge again towards a point on the axis of the instrument at a position symmetrical with respect to the exit from the oven. At this last named point a detector is placed. This consists of a heated tungsten wire to which any caesium atom arriving there will give up its valency electron, leaving it as a positively charged particle. A collector plate near the tungsten wire is maintained at a negative potential, and attracts the positive ions to it. The resulting current is allowed to leak away through a high resistance, and the strength of this measures the number of caesium atoms which have reached the detector. So long as the ions in flight do not change from one hyperfine state to the other this number will be small. To cause the atoms to make this change two cavity resonators are introduced in positions symmetrical with respect to the slit. By means of a tuned circuit having a frequency close to the caesium frequency the resonators are excited through a wave guide. When the chosen frequency is very close to the caesium value the radio frequency field induces transitions from one hyperfine state to the other in the caesium atoms during flight, and an increased number reach the detector. By maximising the output from the detector the frequency of the input can be kept coincident with the caesium frequency. The object of a number of the instrumental refinements is to keep the width of the frequency maximum as narrow as possible. The original equipment gave a precision of about one cycle per second (one part in 10^{10}) but this has now been improved to one part in 10^{11} or one microsecond per day. This standard of accuracy is greatly superior to that which can be obtained by direct astronomical determination, and provides a means of calibrating quartz clocks and of standardising frequencies. The caesium clock may be regarded as providing the modern standard of frequency related to the constants of general physics, though it does have the disadvantage that it cannot, so far, be kept running indefinitely.

1.22. Astronomical Aspects of Time

It might be imagined that once the caesium clock had defined the second in terms of an atomic hyperfine transition expressible in terms of the basic constants of physics, there would no longer be any need to have an astronomical standard of time as well. This may well be correct, but it is undoubtedly the case that most of the terminology used in discussions of time is of astronomical origin. Moreover the original definition of a second is as a subdivision of the minute, hour and day, and if we can define a second to one part in 10^{11} then we need to examine the astronomical concept of the day with a correspondingly close scrutiny. Finally, astronomy frequently has reference to phenomena which occurred in the past, and even in the recent past electronic methods for the exact specification of time did not exist.

We refer first to certain elementary definitions of astronomical origin. In previous sections we have defined sidereal time at any place as the hour angle of the vernal equinox. This specifies the posture of the Earth at the given time with respect to the mean system of the stars. Ordinary civil timekeeping specifies the posture of the Earth with respect to the Sun. Now the apparent movement of the Sun is a reflex of the motion of the Earth in its orbit. The orbit of the Earth is not circular but elliptical and during the northern winter the Earth is, by chance, at a smaller distance from the sun than during the northern summer. Considerations of angular momentum, expressed as Kepler's second law (the law of equal areas) show that the rate of angular advance of the Earth in its orbit will be greater when the Earth is near the Sun (near *perihelion*) than when it is more remote (near *aphelion*). The rate of advance of the Sun round the sky will not therefore be uniform from one season of the year to another. In addition the path of the Sun against the stars is along the ecliptic and not along the equator. The remarks just made show that the rate of increase of the Sun's longitude, measured along the ecliptic, is not uniform. However, even if the advance of the Sun in longitude were uniform, the rate of change of right ascension would not be. If the Sun were to increase its longitude by an amount Δ near the equinoxes, the increases in right ascension would be approximately $\Delta \cos \epsilon$ where ϵ is the obliquity of the ecliptic. Near the solstices, an increase in longitude of Δ would correspond to an increase in right ascension of $\Delta \sec \epsilon$. The ordinary needs of civil life must be regulated with some reference to the hour angle of the Sun and it follows that, since the rate of increase of right ascension of the Sun varies by some ten per cent on either side of its mean value, then the actual Sun is not suitable as a reference body for timekeeping. In place of the real Sun a fictitious body which advances at a uniform rate round the equator is used. This body is called the *Mean Sun*: its relation to the actual Sun at any time can be computed from the characteristics of the orbit of the Earth around the Sun. As an introductory definition, requiring reconsideration in a very exact discussion, we define Greenwich Mean Time, or *Universal Time* as 12h + Greenwich Hour Angle of the Mean Sun. This gives a time reckoning system which keeps in step on the average with the real Sun and has a clock reading of 12h at the middle of the day.

The non-uniform motion of the real Sun has the consequence that it transits usually before or after mean noon, the moment of transit of the mean Sun. During the first three months of the year the Sun transits after mean noon, the difference reaching a maximum of about 14 minutes. For about seven weeks around May it transits a little before mean noon. From mid-June until the end of August it transits a little after noon, and thereafter until nearly the end of the year it transits before noon with a maximum difference of 16 minutes. The deviations of the real Sun from uniformity are thus very large. They define what is called the *Equation of Time* expressible either as equal to Apparent Solar Time *minus* Mean Time, or as R.A. Mean Sun—R.A. Sun which follows a double wave curve as described above. In certain books the opposite sign convention to that used here is employed. Since Universal Time has become available throughout the world by radio transmission the Equation of Time has become of less explicit importance even for surveying and navigational purposes and is often no more than implied in modern astronomical texts. In amateur usages, such as the construction of sun-dials, or in sun-compasses used in desert navigation during the last war, it is clearly of direct importance.

Since Universal Time is defined by means of an hour angle, the rules described above for the computation of hour angles in longitudes different from that of Greenwich will apply for the computation of local mean time at other places. By convention the local mean time appropriate to a standard meridian, almost always an integral number of hours different from the Greenwich meridian, is used in each territory of the world. Thus Britain normally keeps Greenwich Mean Time throughout, even though the local mean time may differ from this by several minutes. Again the eastern states of the U.S.A. keep a *Zone Time* which is 5 hours slow on G.M.T., while Japan keeps a Zone Time which is 9 hours fast. Legislation is often introduced to change the Zone Time by an integral number of hours during the summer. The standard times of the various territories of the world are listed in the *Air Almanac*, though it is usually not possible to keep pace with all the legislative decisions connected with the introduction of summer time. In making computations of phenomena the first step should always be to express all zone times in their G.M.T. equivalents and then to compute hour angles from the accurate geographical coordinates of the place of observation.

1.23. The Relation between Mean and Sidereal Time

The interval between successive meridian passages of a star, more specifically, of the vernal equinox, defines a sidereal day. This is divided into 24 hours, and so on, and thus defines the second, minute, hour and day of sidereal time. Since the Mean Sun advances round the equator, increasing its right ascension by 24h in a year, or approximately 3m 56s per day, the interval between successive passages of the mean sun across the meridian of any place is about 24h 3m 56s of sidereal time. This is equated to 24 hours of mean time, which is that kept by ordinary clocks for civil purposes, and by subdivision hours, minutes and seconds of mean time are defined. A sidereal clock thus gains one day of sidereal time on a mean time clock in the course of a year. An interval of $365\frac{1}{4}$ days of mean time is equal to $366\frac{1}{4}$ days of sidereal time. There is a difference of one between the number of revolutions of the Earth with respect to the Sun and with respect to the stars in the course of a year. An alternative expression of the relationship is shown in Figure I.10 where the Earth is

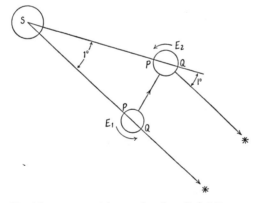

Figure I.10: The Earth's movement in a solar day. Point P comes back beneath the Sun. The Earth advances about a degree in its orbit. The originally antipodal point, Q, beneath the star at E_1 has advanced a degree past the star at E_2. The solar day is longer than the sidereal day by about $3^m 56^s$, during which the Earth rotates through nearly a degree.

pictured in the same position relative to the Sun at two positions separated by a day. Since, during this time the Earth has advanced in its orbit by about one degree, it must, as judged by the stars, turn on its axis through this angle beyond the point at which it is in the same position relative to the stars. The time required to turn through this angle is the interval of 3m 56s noted above.

Because of the extreme accuracy with which intervals of time can now be measured, it is necessary to define nomenclature with great care. Because of precession and nutation the equinox is continually changing its position among the stars. Apparent sidereal time at any place is the hour angle of the equinox of that moment. Because of the irregular movement of the equinox this is not a uniformly increasing quantity. Mean sidereal time is the hour angle of the mean equinox. This is a fictitious point analogous in conception to the Mean Sun, in which the oscillatory irregularities due to nutation are smoothed out. The difference of apparent sidereal time *minus* sidereal time is known in a similar way as the *Equation of the Equinoxes* and is tabulated in the *Astronomical Ephemeris*. During 1965 for example, the equation of the equinoxes has a mean value near − 1s with a range of ± 0·1s during the year. Apart from corrections for variation of latitude and irregularities in the Earth's rotation, which are allowed for in the determination of time, mean sidereal time is the quantity which would be shown on a sidereal dial or distributed for timing purposes within an observatory. Universal Time may now be defined as the Greenwich Hour Angle *plus* 12 hours, of a point on the equator whose right ascension from the mean equinox of date is given by

$$R = 18h\ 38m\ 45s\cdot836 + 86\ 40184s\cdot542\ T + 0s\cdot0929\ T^2$$

where T is the number of centuries, each reckoned as containing 36,525 days of universal time, which have elapsed since Greenwich mean noon on 1900 January 0. This formula is closely similar to one given by Newcomb for the right ascension of the Mean Sun, although differing from it on an important point of principle. It shows how Universal Time is constructed according to this formal definition, from mean sidereal time and from apparent sidereal time, which are determined by methods indicated below, from stellar observations.

1.24. Ephemeris Time

We are now in a position to relate astronomical timekeeping with the time of physics. The essential point about sidereal time is that it relates the position of the Earth with respect to the stellar system, and this is of great importance for many practical astronomical applications. On the other hand as we have mentioned already, the period of rotation of the Earth is not constant, so that to the accuracy now required we cannot make this the basis of a uniformly flowing time. To resolve this dilemma we postulate the existence of a uniformly flowing time, which we identify with the independent variable of physics, the variable which is called "time" in Newton's Laws of Motion and all physical applications. This may seem to introduce a tautology. The grandest verification of Newton's Laws was that they enabled astronomers to calculate the motions of the planets and to predict their positions in advance. Now it is assumed that Newton's Laws, modified as they may be in certain cases by relativity considerations, are correct, and that discrepancies between theory and prediction are not to be attributed either to defects of theory or to imperfect calculations, but, in the main, to irregularities of the Earth's rotation. This is not as unreasonable as it might seem. Methods of calculation are now so refined as to eliminate errors of manipulation. Moreover the phenomenon, at one time unexplained, that all bodies in the solar system were ahead of their ephemeris positions by amounts in proportion to their mean motions, a phenomenon naturally most pronounced in the case of the Moon, is most naturally explained by a slowing down of the Earth's rotation rate. For this there is physical justification since tidal friction in shallow seas is a known cause for the retardation of the rotation of the Earth. The physical explanation for all the features including seasonal irregularities in the rotation of the Earth does not yet appear to be perfectly clear.

Now that we have introduced Ephemeris Time, several points already mentioned require revision. The caesium frequency quoted above should now be given as cycles per second of ephemeris mean time. The expression R given above, with the time variable now given as centuries of ephemeris mean time of 36,525 days, is strictly the expression for the right ascension of the Mean Sun. The quoted expression with the argument in terms of Universal Time still defines U.T.

Determinations of the difference between ephemeris time and universal time depend essentially on observations of phenomena of the Moon because of its high angular motion. Examples are the determinations of the times of mid-eclipse for solar eclipses, and the study of the times at which the Moon passes in front of stars (*occultations*). An alternative method proposed by Markowitz was to photograph the Moon against the star background by a camera incorporating devices to dim the bright light of the Moon and to compensate its motion during exposure.

Ephemeris time is conventionally reckoned from the epoch designated as 1900 January 0 at E.T. 12h and the reduction from Universal to Ephemeris Time is tabulated in the *Astronomical Ephemeris*. During the twentieth century the difference has shown a general increase from $-$ 3s·79 in 1900·5, being $+$ 20s·48 in 1920·5, $+$ 24s·30 in 1940·5, and $+$ 33s·20 in 1960·5. The earlier values are part of a longer tabulation published by Brouwer in 1952. More recent values have become available from studies of lunar phenomena and the difference is only known with any precision usually some years in arrears. For many purposes approximate values for the future are produced by extrapolation. The modern practice of the ephemerides is to produce exact predictions in ephemeris time from which approximate predictions in Universal Time are found by using extrapolated values of the difference E.T. $-$ U.T. Comparison of prediction and observation then helps towards a definitive determination of the difference. The short-term variations of the rate of rotation of the Earth, and the secular run of the difference E.T. $-$ U.T. are illustrated in Figures I.11 and I.12.

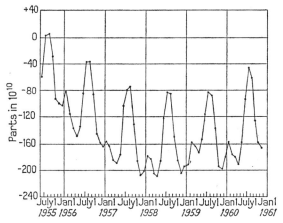

Figure I.11: Variations in the rate of rotation of the Earth (U.T. 1 $-$ Cs). (By permission of Messrs. Butterworth and Dr. L. Essen.)

It is useful to note that the Ephemeris second has an alternative astronomical definition, namely "as the fraction 1/31 556 925·9747 of the tropical year for 1900 January 0 at 12h E.T.". The *Tropical Year* is the interval during which the Sun's mean longitude referred to the mean equinox of date increases by 360° and is the scientific definition of that which is meant by the ordinary usage of the term "year" in which the seasons recur. The difficulty of such a definition of Ephemeris Time is that it does not define a standard available for new comparisons. The

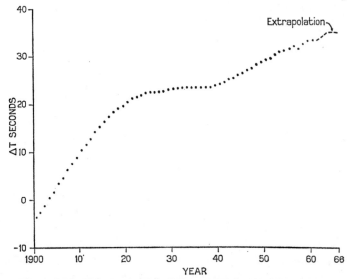

Figure I.12: Values of $\Delta T = $ E.T. $-$ U.T. in the 20th century.

definition in terms of the caesium frequency now provides such a calibration. However, astronomers often have to refer back to epochs when the only calibration available was an astronomical one, so that this definition is of astronomical importance. The only difficulty in the use of the caesium calibration is the possibility that if the constants of nature are determined by the distribution of all the material in the universe, and if the universe is expanding, then the gravitational unit of time expressed by Ephemeris Time might steadily diverge from the atomic time unit. With the accuracy of measurement now available it is possible that such a deviation might be detectable.

1.25. Universal Time

Astronomical observations as described below yield precise values of apparent sidereal time from which mean sidereal time can be derived by the application of the equation of the equinoxes. The formula quoted above shows that Universal Time is rigidly related to mean sidereal time. To produce a system judged uniform by a precision clock, the observed value of Universal Time designated as U.T. 0 must be corrected for variations in the meridian due to polar motion (yielding what is called U.T. 1) and for seasonal variations in the rotation of the Earth (yielding what is called U.T. 2). The last named is the basis of the transmission of radio time signals which are sent out from stations in about twelve countries of the world. However, since in every case a radio signal is transmitted from a precision clock of which the error has been determined from astronomical observations at some time in the recent past, the signals radiated are provisional, and their actual errors are determined and published later by the Bureau International de l'Heure. It would be inconvenient if the transmissions were corrected too frequently by small quantities, and the convention has been adopted of correcting signals only when an appreciable error has accumulated. The practice is to make changes by steps of 50 milliseconds as required, and the various time services coordinate their work so as to make these jumps at the same time. Users of precise signals thus make comparisons with the emitted signals and apply the published corrections when these appear.

1.26. The Determination of Time: The Photographic Zenith Tube

It will be clear that a great many conventions have necessarily been incorporated into the technique of timekeeping. It remains true, however, that observations of transits of stars with known right ascensions will yield instantaneous determinations of apparent sidereal time. If these depend, as in a transit circle, on a human measurer, they are not likely to be accurate enough for modern purposes. Various efforts have been made to make transit observations more accurate by the use of photoelectric devices or by moving photographic plates. At the present time, however, the most accurate means for the determination of time is provided by the photographic zenith tube. These instruments are used to observe a set of stars near our own zenith which are closely tied to the stars belonging to a certain catalogue, called the FK4 (*Fourth Fundamental Catalogue;* revision by Heidelberg, 1963). The positions of all these stars have been exhaustively discussed in the light of all the foregoing complications: they have been observed a vast number of times: the adopted positions have been discussed at great length to reconcile them with the ephemerides of the Sun and planets and with the values of the constants adopted for these computations. These 1,535 stars enshrine the practical definition of the system of stellar coordinates. Their apparent right ascensions and declinations will vary owing to the effects of precession, nutation and aberration, but the apparent positions of any of them can be computed at any time, and are published in advance. Observation of the transit times of a selection of these stars or of other stars closely tied to them will give, after application of the appropriate corrections, a determination of the error of the sidereal clock used at the transits.

If a transit circle were used, corrections for the various instrumental effects and for refraction and flexure of the tube would have to be applied. The photographic zenith tube, which is a fixed telescope pointing to the local zenith, eliminates corrections for flexure and refraction, and can be designed so as to eliminate many of the other instrumental errors. The instrument consists of an objective lens mounted in a horizontal plane above a bath of mercury which serves as a mirror (Figure I.13). Only stars close to the zenith (usually within about 15′) are imaged, by passage of the rays through the lens, reflection in the mercury surface, and convergence to the surface of a photographic plate mounted face down horizontally immediately below the lens. The system is so designed that one of the nodal points of the objective lies in the chosen focal plane, so that the positions of the star images are not affected by errors due to tilt and lateral displacement of the lens. The use of the mercury bath as a reflector automatically incorporates the direction of the local vertical in the instrument. The plateholder is not fixed but is mounted on a carriage which can be traversed in the east-west line at a rate which compensates for the rotation of the Earth. If the plate were stationary a star passing near the zenith would mark on it an east-west track with a slight curvature arising from the fact that these stars move on small circles as the celestial sphere rotates. If the plate is traversed at the correct rate, and an exposure made, the image will be a point, and much fainter stars can be photographed than would register a trail on a fixed plate. The position of the point image is displaced on the plate from the point corresponding to the zenith by a

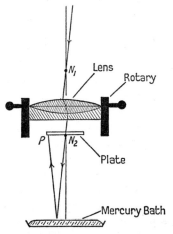

Figure I.13: The Photographic Zenith Tube: A parallel bundle of light rays arrives from a star, the central one passing through a nodal point, N_1, of the lens. The emergent pencil is centred on the other nodal point, N_2, which lies in the focal plane occupied by the plate. Some of the rays are stopped by the small central obstruction of the plate and its holder, but the remainder converge after reflection in the horizontal surface of the mercury bath to form an image at P. By definition of the nodal points, the axis of the convergent pencil at N_2 is parallel to the incident direction at N_1.

distance in the north or south direction defined by its zenith distance. The carriage and its driving mechanism, and the objective lens are mounted as a unit (the rotary) which can be turned by a motor through 180° about the axis of the lens. After rotation the plate carrying the first image of a given star has been turned through 180°, so that a second exposure will give a second image displaced from the first in the north-south direction by an amount corresponding to twice the zenith distance of the star at its meridian passage. In a complete observation each pair of exposures is repeated, so that there are four exposures of each star which have been obtained in a total interval of about two minutes. If the exposures are taken at approximately equal intervals the four images on the plate will lie at positions close to the vertices of a parallelogram; two of the parallel edges define the directions of motion corresponding to the east-west movement across the meridian. Essentially these sides define the east-west direction, while the separation perpendicular to this gives twice the zenith distance of the star at transit. If its declination is known, an instantaneous value of the latitude is found. The determination of time depends on registering the position of the plate carriage at selected times in terms of the standard clock. The methods of incorporating the time definition in the sequence of operations have varied from observatory to observatory, but if we assume that contacts are incorporated which are operated when the plate carriage is in a particular position relative to the rotary, then at these recorded instants the position of the zenith and meridian on the plate are the same for all four exposures. The positions of two of the images as they appear on the developed plate have been reflected across the plate by the rotation round this (unmarked) point. Thus the first and last exposures (one before and one after the meridian) are, say, on the right, while the middle two, also one east and one west, are on the left (Figure I.14). We follow the exposition of D.S. Perfect, and we have the following:

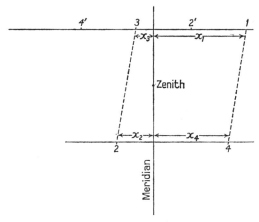

Figure I.14: Layout of PZT plate: Points 2′ and 4′ are transferred to symmetrical positions across the plate centre by reversals of the rotary, bringing the star images to positions 2 and 4.

Let the times of the four exposures in terms of the clock be t_1, t_2, t_3 and t_4. For the first two images let the star, in terms of the plate scale, be at distances x_1 and x_2 east of the meridian, and for the last two let it be at distances x_3 and x_4 west of the meridian. Let the time of meridian passage be t_m in terms of the clock, and let the speed of movement of the image, neglecting track curvature, be v. Then at time t_1, the image is x_1 east of the meridian, and

$$t_1 = t_m - x_1/v$$

and at time t_4 the image is x_4 west of the meridian, so that

$$t_4 = t_m + x_4/v$$

whence the time of meridian passage is given by

$$t_m = \tfrac{1}{2}(t_1 + t_4) - \tfrac{1}{2}(x_4 - x_1)/v$$

Now $x_4 - x_1$ is the overhang of the parallelogram at one end and is measurable provided the plate is correctly lined up in a two-coordinate measuring machine as it can be if the east-west direction is identified by two of the parallel sides of the figure. The speed v is not known, but can be found by measuring images 2 and 3 at the other side. The two sets of differences then enable v to be found and hence t_m, the time of transit. The exact method of reduction, i.e. whether t_m is found directly, or whether the offset from the meridian at the mean of the recorded times is found, varies from one observatory to another.

The very exactly performed sequence of reversals of the rotary and other operations are not done manually, but by a sequence controller, and all the operations are automatic, being initiated by pressing a button in a control house remote from the instrument. This merely provides the coarse selection, and the subsequent operations are initiated at a predetermined moment: in some cases the operations are timed to occur at a particular fraction of a second in terms of standard clock output which takes the form of a phonic motor which is never stopped, driven by a 1,000 Hz current generated by the quartz crystal clocks. Photographic zenith tubes, of which there are about a dozen in the world, most of them with focal lengths of about 4 metres have proved capable of determining time, using catalogues of zenith stars locked into the FK4 system, with an uncertainty of the order of 3 or 4 milliseconds from a whole night of observation, and of the order of about one twentieth of a second of arc for the determination of latitude. Since the restriction of observations to zenith stars is a severe limitation of choice, it is necessary for each P.Z.T. observatory to derive its own catalogue of stars for observation, many of which may be rather faint, and to tie these as closely as possible into the FK4 system by preliminary observations.

1.27. The Impersonal Astrolabe of Danjon

This is an instrument designed by André Danjon, the famous French astronomer, for the observation of stars at a constant apparent altitude in any part of the sky. The results may be used for the determination of time and latitude and for the improvement of star positions. The principle of the prismatic astrolabe has long been known, and in its original form remains valuable for survey purposes. The instrument (Figure I.15) receives two parallel beams from the same star. One is reflected in a pool of mercury, i.e. a horizontal surface. It passes into a 60° prism

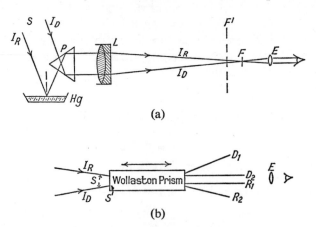

Figure I.15.

(a) The simple astrolabe. For a star at zenith distance 30°, the direct and reverse images coincide at F. However, an error in focusing, say, on to a plane F′, produces a spurious separation of the images. (b) The Wollaston prism produces two emergent beams from each incident one. D_1 and R_2 are masked off: D_2 and R_1 are parallel, and produce images of which the separation is unaffected by focus changes. Their separation depends on s, i.e. on the longitudinal position of the Wollaston prism.

mounted with its edge horizontal, passing into the glass at normal incidence, and being internally reflected at the upper face. It passes through the vertical base of the prism at normal incidence, and enters a horizontal telescope, which forms an image from this beam. The second beam strikes the upper face of the prism at normal incidence, is internally reflected at the lower face, and, leaving the glass at normal incidence, passes into the same telescope, where a second image of the star is formed close to the first. If the angle of the prism is precisely 60°, then, when the images are coincident the apparent zenith distance of the star is 30°. In practice the prism angle may be treated as an unknown to be determined, but the zenith distances of stars observed with the instrument are always very close to 30°. Danjon pointed out that in this form of the astrolabe each beam occupied half the area of the objective of the viewing telescope, so that as the rays came to a focus, the two converging pencils were inclined to each other, and that, in consequence, changes in the focal setting of the eyepiece could alter the apparent separation of the images. To overcome this he introduced, between the objective and the focal plane, a carefully designed Wollaston prism, so that each beam from the star itself produced two images. One of each is suppressed by diaphragms, while the remaining two are formed by beams parallel to the optic axis of the viewing telescope. The separation between them depends on the separation between the central rays of the two incident beams of starlight at the points where they strike the first face of the Wollaston prism. The prism is driven longitudinally by a screw with a micrometer head. If it is moved towards the objective the emergent parallel beams are separated by a larger distance. If it is moved towards the eyepiece the distance decreases to zero and further movement causes a separation in the opposite sense. Since the images are now formed by parallel beams, changes of focus have no effect on their apparent separation, but movement of the Wollaston prism does cause changes. During an observation the zenith distance of a star is changing, and this would cause a change in the vertical separation of the images but for the mode of use of the Wollaston prism. This is driven along at such a rate as to compensate the change due to changing zenith distance, and the observer operates a differential control superposed on this drive so that he always maintains the two stellar images, in principle, coincident. In fact, by tilting the leading edge of the prism slightly, the two images are formed separated by a small horizontal interval, so that the observer has to maintain them side by side between a pair of parallel cross-wires. The actual observation consists in automatically recording the position of the prism while the observer maintains this condition. Either the times when the prism passes through standard positions are recorded, or the positions of the prism at certain standard intervals of time are registered, both in terms of a precise clock. Either procedure has the advantage over the original astrolabe of permitting the observer to make the images coincide over a period of time during which several observations can be made, whereas in the original instrument coincidence occurs only at a single instant. The latter procedure has the advantage of permitting observations near the meridian where altitudes change so slowly that the moment of passage of the prism through the position corresponding to an exact zenith distance of 30° becomes ill-defined.

In its developed form the Danjon astrolabe is mounted in a rigid metal box with the optical train folded by means of plane mirrors to secure greater rigidity and compactness. The box can be rotated about a vertical axis to bring stars at all azimuths under observation, and the action of turning operates a gear box which changes the drive rate of the Wollaston prism to that appropriate to the chosen azimuth. Observations are made on stars from the FK4 in groups of 28, and an accuracy per group rather

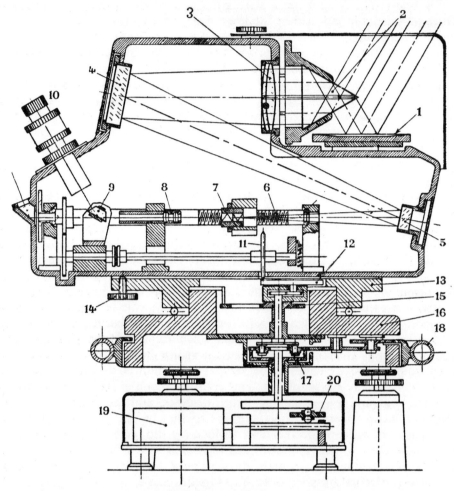

Figure I.16: Diagram of the Impersonal Astrolabe: 1, mercury bath; 2, prism; 3, objective lens; 4, plane mirror; 5, plane mirror; 6, 7, 8, Wollaston prism on its longitudinal screw; 9, inverting prism; 10, eyepiece. The structure below comprises the mount on which the instrument may be turned to different azimuths, the motor for driving the Wollaston prism, and the gearing producing a mean drive rate appropriate to the chosen azimuth. (By permission of Dr. B. Guinot and the editors of *Revue d'Optique*).

higher than that given by the P.Z.T. has been claimed for measures of time and latitude variation, though the reductions are more complicated. For the improvement of the catalogue positions of stars observed between groups the general principles are (i) that an error in declination of the star place alters the interval between rising and setting passages over the 30° zenith distance line from the expected value; (ii) that an error in right ascension moves the mean of the times of passage across this line, rising and setting, from its expected value. The instrument can only smooth out errors, but the results show that this is being achieved. Comparisons between transit circle and astrolabe observations at Herstmonceux indicate certain regions where errors of star places are considerable: these peaks are absent from comparisons between the Herstmonceux astrolabe and the Pulkovo photoelectric transit instrument. The important feature of the astrolabe is that it is an extra-meridian instrument which can link together stars widely separated in right ascension, only observable with a transit circle many hours apart. With the latter instrument the connection between stars far apart in right ascension is long enough to permit periodic errors to creep in. The astrolabe itself has its own errors, including the fact that it is not perfectly impersonal, but these errors are not likely to be the same as those affecting transit circle measures, so that it may become easier to evaluate both types.

1.28. The Mirror Transit

The P.Z.T. and the impersonal astrolabe are efforts to do some of the jobs originally undertaken by means of transit circles more expeditiously and accurately. However even the ordinary operations of the transit circle have been critically reviewed, and it has been emphasised that many of the corrections, such as, for example, collimation and flexure, are determined by separate observations, with the instrument in a position different from that to which the correction will apply. What is required is a continuous monitoring of the instrumental effects, much as the P.Z.T. and astrolabe continuously monitor the direction of the vertical. Danjon has discussed this point and has proposed a scheme whereby the transit telescope has a bi-prism mounted in front of the objective. Stars thus produce two images moving in opposite directions, and the moment of transit is determined from their coincidence. This depends on the position of the bi-prism, but this is monitored by autocollimators observing its two faces mounted along an east-west line. Another scheme abolishes the transit telescope and replaces it by a plane mirror which reflects the starlight into one or other of two horizontal fixed telescopes mounted north and south. In the form of this proposed by Atkinson, the supports for the mirror are highly sophisticated, as they must be to maintain the desired geometrical conditions, and its position is monitored by auto-collimators observing reflections in flats ground on the east and west edges of the mirror.

1.29. Mean and Apparent Places of Stars

We now see how the apparent places of stars with reference to the true or mean equinox and equator of date may be determined. The apparent coordinates include the effects of aberration and of parallax. The latter is discussed below, and, in all but a few cases produces negligible effects in the present context. If we eliminate these effects we arrive at the stellar coordinates which would have been determined had the observations been made from the Sun. We describe these as *heliocentric positions*. The term, *Mean Place*, describes the heliocentric position of a star as referred to some mean equinox and equator. The term *Epoch* is commonly used to designate the date of the observation and the mean equinox and equator of the same date. In the present sense, a transit circle programme will produce apparent places, from which mean places can be deduced by correcting for aberration and parallax, which have a variety of epochs. To facilitate inter-comparisons, these must be referred not to the mean equinox and equator of date, but to the mean equinox and equator of certain standard dates. Standard dates are almost invariably, for stellar observations, chosen at the beginning of a *Besselian year*. The beginning of the Besselian year is the moment when the right ascension of the Mean Sun, as affected by aberration (a practically constant quantity) measured from the mean equinox is 18h 40m (280°). This instant is always very close to the beginning of the calendar year, though the incidence of Leap Years causes it to vary its calendar date by about a day. The beginning of the Besselian year for 1950 is designated as 1950·0, and so on. The reduction of apparent places for an epoch such as 1963·2345 to the mean places, for 1963·0 involves the application of corrections for aberration, precession, and nutation which depend on the position of the Sun, and to a lesser extent on positions of other bodies in the solar system, at the epoch of observation. The method of carrying out reductions either from apparent to mean places or vice versa, within the same year, is given in terms of formulae set out in the *Explanation to the Astronomical Ephemeris*. They involve both the coordinates of the star and certain functions largely dependent on the position of the Sun, which vary from day to day. The latter are tabulated in the form of *Day Numbers*, and two forms, *Besselian Day Numbers* and *Independent Day Numbers* are available for use in different algebraic forms of the reduction formulae. The day numbers segregate into two groups, those concerned with aberration, and those concerned with precession and nutation. It should be noted that the definitions of the day numbers were modified in 1960. For very accurate work higher order terms and terms derived from the short period terms of nutation are to be included.

Different astronomical purposes require different levels of accuracy. The highest possible accuracy is required in the computation of apparent places of FK4 stars and a separate publication is available for each year giving the apparent places of these stars at upper transit at Greenwich at ten-day intervals for most stars, and daily for circumpolar stars.

Catalogues of star positions, which may require many years for their completion, are further reduced to the beginnings of standard Besselian years, such as 1900·0, 1950·0 or 2000·0. These reductions are carried out by the application of corrections for precession. An approximate formula for precessional corrections has already been given above, but for long intervals account must be taken of secular variations which enter owing to the changes of coordinate values produced by precession, and for high declinations more elaborate formulae must be used. The *Astronomical Ephemeris* now gives constants and formulae for exact reductions between the beginning of the Besselian year for the year of issue, and the equinox 1950·0.

If now we arrive at the situation where a difference in coordinates is found between the mean place of the same star for, say, epoch 1920, referred to the mean equinox and equator for 1950·0, and the mean place for epoch 1960 referred to the same equinox and equator, then we can infer that the difference has been caused by some real change in position of the star. These positional changes are all very small, so that scrupulous accuracy is required in the reduction of the star positions to mean places referred to the same equinox and equator.

1.30. Astronomical Causes of Positional Changes: Annual Parallax

It is still not correct to say that we have eliminated all effects due to the orbital motion of the Earth. One, always very small effect, results from the fact that the stars are not at an infinite distance. As the Earth moves in its orbit the direction of the line of sight from the Earth to the star changes, by angles which are larger for relatively nearby stars, and smaller for more remote ones. These changes in position can be measured relative to the general background of very faint, and presumably very remote, stars, for which the effect is quite negligible. If that diameter of the Earth's orbit be drawn which is perpendicular to the direction from the Sun to the star, then the maximum parallactic displacement occurs when the Earth is at the extremities of this diameter. This maximum angle of displacement on either side of the mean position is expressed in radians as r/d, where, neglecting eccentricity, r is the radius of the orbit of the Earth about the Sun (the astronomical unit = 149·600 million kilometres), and d is the distance of the star. This angle is called the (annual) *parallax* of the star and is invariably expressed in seconds of arc (Figure I.17). The standard unit for the measurement of stellar distances is the *parsec*, namely the distance of a star having a parallax of one second of arc. Since 1 radian = 206,265″, 1 parsec = 206,265 astronomical units = $3 \cdot 0857 \times 10^{13}$ km.

In the light-time measure often used in popular writings, one parsec equals 3·262 light-years, that is, the distance traversed by a photon in so many years. A useful

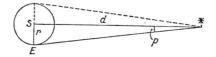

Figure I.17: Definition of the Annual Parallax of a
Star at distance d from the Sun.

approximate relation is that a body moving at 1 km/s takes 1 million years to cover a distance of one parsec. This relation is correct to about 3 per cent. The introduction of the parsec puts distances and parallaxes in a simple inverse relation, $D = 1/p$, in the appropriate units.

The path followed by a star due to parallactic motion is a conical projection of the orbit of the Earth round the Sun, the vertex of projection being the star, and the plane of projection the normal to the line of sight at a distance corresponding to that of the faint comparison stars. At the pole of the ecliptic the path is circular: on the ecliptic it degenerates into a straight line segment. For other positions the apparent path is an ellipse with the major axis parallel to the ecliptic. Maximum displacements occur when the longitude of the Sun differs by 90° from that of the star.

No star is so near that it has a parallax of one second of arc: the triple system formed by Alpha Centauri and Proxima Centauri has a parallax of about ¾ of a second of arc, which is the largest known. The number of known stars within 20 parsecs is of the order of 1,000, the majority of which are faint. Methods for the measurement of parallaxes are described in the section on Astronomical Photography below.

1.31. Proper Motions

The term *proper motion* is the somewhat archaic name used to describe the change in apparent position of a star which results from its motion in space relative to the Sun.

Only the component of motion of the star perpendicular to the line of sight has any effect on its position. If the transverse component of velocity relative to the Sun be V kilometres per second, then the proper motion μ in seconds of arc per year is given by the relation

$$V = 4 \cdot 740 \, \mu/p$$

where p is the parallax measured in seconds of arc. The total proper motion μ is often divided up into components, μ_α and μ_δ, parallel and perpendicular to the celestial equator, that is, in the directions of right ascension and declination. These are the quantities found when proper motions are determined from the changes in right ascension and declination over a long period of time, the positions at the two epochs being referred to the same equator and equinox so that apparent changes due to precession are eliminated. If the change in right ascension per annum is expressed in seconds of *time* and called μ_α, this must be multiplied by 15 cos δ to obtain the change of position in seconds of *arc* parallel to the equator. Thus with μ_α in seconds of time and μ_δ in seconds of arc we have for μ in seconds of arc

$$\mu^2 = (15 \cos \delta)^2 \mu_\alpha^2 + \mu_\delta^2$$

Occasionally proper motions are expressed in terms of centennial motion. The effects of parallax on the position of a star are oscillatory: those of proper motion are cumulative. In principle, only a lapse of time, in practice rarely less than several decades, is needed for the determination of a proper motion. The longer the temporal baseline, the greater the accuracy attainable, or the smaller the motion that may be measured, though this argument may be vitiated by a steady decrease in accuracy of the earlier positions the further back we go. The formula shows that for a cross-velocity of average size, say 20 km/s, the proper motion will be about four times the parallax, though individual cases may depart widely from this.

1.32. Orbital Motion

This is introduced here only for completeness in enumerating astronomical causes of positional displacement. It is discussed in detail later. Many stars are double or multiple, and their components orbit each other under their mutual gravitational attractions. If the angular separation between components is large enough for them to be separately observable, changes in relative position with time may be detectable, although often only in a very long time. Even if the components are not seen separated, orbital motion may produce a shift in the position of the combined image (the *photocentre*) if the two are unequal in brightness. In a few isolated cases these positional changes can be discussed from transit observations. One such case is that of the brightest star in the sky, Sirius, which moves under the attraction of a faint massive companion itself observable only with difficulty, and not at all with any transit circle.

1.33. Astronomical Photography

Many astrometric problems are investigated by means of photography: these include almost all determinations of parallax, most determinations of proper motion, and much work for the determinations of star positions in great numbers. The last-named type of programme is one where it is desired to prepare a large catalogue of star positions, comprising, let us say, all the stars in a certain declination zone of the sky down to rather faint limits. The procedure is to determine a skeleton coordinate system by observation with the transit circle of a considerable number of selected reference stars in the zone, and to use these as markers from which the coordinates of numerous faint stars can be determined.

To photograph an area of sky is simple enough: select a telescope of the necessary optical quality, check if you will the squaring on of the lens and plate, verify that the emulsion lies in the focal plane. Point the instrument at the area of the sky selected, guide the instrument by means of a guide star imaged on the cross wires of an auxiliary telescope mounted rigidly parallel to the primary instrument, and expose for however many minutes or hours may be required. If the image of the guide star is kept accurately in position on the cross-wires of the guiding telescope, and there is no differential flexure between telescope and guider, no displacement due to differential refraction, no marked change in image quality due to variations in the turbulence of the atmosphere, and nothing else goes wrong, a photograph of a small area of sky will result. Be it said that although the process sounds extremely simple, in practice the taking of astronomical photographs of superlative quality demands a level of skill and concentration possessed by relatively few observers. If the conditions approach perfection, the stars near the centre of the plate will each be imaged as small round black spots, which will be larger the brighter the star. Microscopic examination will show these images to be circularly symmetrical distributions of blackening of the emulsion with density falling off with increasing distance from the centre. Optical theory predicts that each image should be surrounded by a system of diffraction rings, but although these may be seen visually under good conditions with a high power eyepiece, the smudging effects of a long exposure will usually mask them on a photograph. Certain kinds of telescope, such as reflectors and Schmidt systems can produce images of rather strange structure, often with systems of faint rays emerging from each star image. These are purely instrumental in origin. We

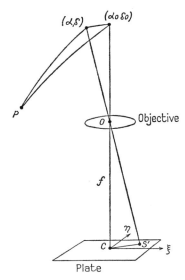

Figure I.18: Standard Coordinates on a Photographic Plate.

concern ourselves now only with rather long refracting instruments, where the images near the plate centre should be practically circular dots. According to the quality of the optics there will be a greater or less deterioration of image quality towards the edges of the plate: images near the edge may be slightly elongated in a radial direction, but these effects should be small in any instrument intended for astrometric work. The photograph is a distorted representation of the area of sky which it covers. The sky is a sphere, the photographic plate a plane. The projection relationships between points on the sky and their images on the plate are shown in Figure I.18. The axis OC of the telescope is pointed to a point on the sky having mean coordinates referred to some standard equinox and equator given by a_0, δ_0. The plate is normal to this line, and the linear scale on the plate corresponding to a certain angle on the sky is determined by the focal length, f. Since there are 206,265 seconds of arc in a radian, if $f = 2 \cdot 06$ metres, the scale is 100″/mm on the plate. For exact mapping on to the plate, axes are chosen through the plate centre parallel to the coordinate directions for the chosen equinox. The star at (a, δ) maps into the point on the plate denoted by (ξ, η) where, if we take the focal length of the objective as the unit of length, we have after some manipulation

$$\xi = \cos q \, \tan(a - a_0)/\cos(q - \delta_0)$$

$$\eta = \tan (q - \delta_0)$$

where q is an auxiliary quantity given by

$$\cot q = \cot \delta \cos (a - a_0)$$

The quantities ξ, η are called *Standard Coordinates* and, for a given plate centre their values are immediately related to right ascension and declination. If a plate of an area of sky is measured in a two-coordinate measuring machine with axes approximately in the ξ, η directions, the positions of star images will be definable by coordinates x, y which, on an appropriate scale will approximate to the standard coordinates. They will not be precisely identical because we must suppose that the plate may not be precisely perpendicular to the optic axis, that the cartesian measuring axes are not precisely perpendicular and not precisely orientated, and we must also consider the effects of differential aberration and differential atmospheric refraction. To the first order, all these errors produce linear effects and it can be shown that the standard coordinates are related to the measured x, y, when all these errors are taken into account by equations

$$\xi - x = ax + by + c$$

$$\eta - y = dx + ey + f$$

where a, b, c, d, e and f are the *Plate Constants*. If these are known, then measured values of x, y on a plate can be converted immediately into a, δ. In principle, if the right ascension and declination of any three stars on the plate are known from other means, say, by transit circle observations, the values of the plate constants can be found. In practice, more stars than this are used, and care is taken to see that they are well distributed over the plate. The determination of the plate constants is then made by the methods of least squares. In large programmes for the determination of the coordinates of all the stars in a zone down to a certain brightness limit, more elaborate formulae involving quadratic terms may be employed. The need for this arises because small differential shifts of the mean positions of star images may occur depending on brightness and colour. An off-axis blue star forms an image in a position slightly different from that which it would occupy if its light were predominantly red. All star images formed with a refractor are very low dispersion spectra, folded back on themselves if, as is usually the case, the objective is a doublet. It is impossible completely to eliminate slight residual effects of colour on image position. The range of spectrum used may be limited, either by the use of plates with a narrow range of sensitivity or by means of a filter, but in accurate work, these effects, however small, will be evaluated, and corresponding corrections introduced.

The plate scale employed in most astrometric work ranges from about $10''/mm$ to about $100''/mm$ corresponding respectively to focal lengths of the objective of about 20 metres and 2 metres. Smaller scales are employed for positional catalogues, the larger for parallax determinations.

1.34. Star Nomenclature

In ancient times the brighter stars were given individual names, of which some, of Arabic, Greek or Latin origin are still the preferred designations. Examples such as Rigel, Antares, Vega, Castor, spring readily to mind. Most of these stars have been called by many different names in successive civilisations, and there is an extensive historical literature on the subject. The sky was also divided into a number of different constellations, at first with very ill-defined boundaries, by the process of reading legendary figures and the objects of everyday life into the configurations which appeared in the sky. Some system was introduced by Bayer in 1603 when he designated the brighter stars in each constellation by Greek letters followed by the genitive form of the Latin constellation name. Usually, but not quite invariably, the Greek alphabet order is a sequence of decreasing apparent visual brightness. Still fainter stars were denoted by small Roman letters, and when these were used up, by capital letters. Capitals after Q were not needed, and Argelander employed the capitals from R onwards for variable stars, thus initiating the system of designation of variable stars described in Chapter IV. Flamsteed designated his stars by number and constellation, so that designations such as 61 Cygni are found. All these systems overlap, so that some stars will be found to have a large number of alternative designations.

However, in most professional usage, particularly when large numbers of stars are involved, the procedure is adopted of designating stars by means of the number which they have in some standard star catalogue. Even this does not completely eliminate confusion for there are many catalogues in existence, prepared for many different purposes. Without great care there is still a risk that a single star may be endowed with a multiple personality because of the numerous aliases under which it appears in the literature.

1.35. Star Catalogues

The ability to make the best use of the numerous star catalogues which exist is a specialised one, and our discussion is necessarily rather fragmentary. We may note first the *Durchmusterung* catalogues, which are, as the name indicates, lists of all the stars in given declination zones of the sky, with rough magnitudes and approximate positions. The *Bonn* and *Cordoba Durchmusterung* catalogues in the north and south respectively were observed visually. Their names are contracted to BD and CoD, and stars in them are denoted by the zone and the number of the star in the zone, e.g. BD 20° 1234. The *Cape Photographic Durchmusterung*, (CPD), produced in the closing years of the nineteenth century, contains nearly 455,000 stars, and was the first large catalogue to be based on photographic observations.

We then note catalogues based on meridian observations, in which field the leading observatories at the present time are Greenwich, Washington, Pulkovo and the Cape. These give positions with which may be associated observational errors for stars on the equator of the order of 0s·01 (0″·15) in right ascension. Probable errors in declination are of the same order of magnitude.

Elaborate comparisons between such observational catalogues are undertaken to eliminate systematic errors, and the synthesis of many such catalogues from many observatories has led to the production of a number of catalogues of precision covering the whole sky. In this class fall the *General Catalogue* (GC) of Benjamin Boss, the N30 Catalogue of the U.S. Naval Observatory, and the FK3 and FK4 Catalogues already mentioned. The G.C. contains about 33,000 stars, the N30 a total of 5,268 and the FK4 a total of 1,535.

In addition to these there are a number of catalogues giving rather specialised information about certain stars, such as spectral type, radial velocity, parallax and so forth. The *Henry Draper Catalogue* published by Harvard is strictly a catalogue of spectral types, with magnitudes and positions given approximately. It extends down to about the 10th apparent magnitude. It contains about 220,000 stars, and thus includes most stars in the sky likely to be discussed in any detail. Stars are frequently cited by their numbers (HD) in this catalogue, though brighter ones may be given their GC numbers instead, or, for fairly bright stars, HR numbers (also a Harvard designation) which are used in the *Yale Catalogue of Bright Stars* may be cited. The 1964 edition of this work contains 9,110 stars for which all the information given is as exact as possible. All these stars appear in the GC and HD.

The *Carte du Ciel* or *Astrographic Project*, an international scheme for photographing and cataloguing the whole sky using standard type telescopes was completed only after many delays. Working along different lines a number of observatories have produced photographic catalogues of precision for selected stars in certain declination zones. The observatories include Hamburg, Bonn, Yale and the Cape. In the *Cape Photographic Catalogue* for the equinox of 1950·0, which is now approaching completion after a quarter of a century of work, photographic plates on a scale of about 100″/mm were obtained, and the necessary reference star positions determined by transit circle observations made, as nearly as possible, at the same mean epoch as the photographs. As an example, the catalogue for the zone $-52°$ to $-56°$ was produced in 1955, and contains 9,213 stars with average probable errors of position of 0″·10 in R.A. and 0″·12 in declination.

1.36. Proper Motions by Photography

The determination of the place of a star at two epochs separated by some decades, with reference to the same equinox and equator should permit the deduction of the proper motion of the star by a simple process of dividing the coordinate changes by the time interval between the epochs. It will usually be necessary to pay attention to the systematic and accidental errors of the catalogues from which the star places are drawn. Except for the decrease in accuracy of positions the farther back in time we go, the accuracy of such a determination of proper motion will usually increase with the interval between the chosen epochs. If the catalogues are fundamental ones, proper motions found in this way should be absolute, and, given a sufficient time base-line, proper motions for individual stars of the order of $0''\cdot01$ per annum may be treated as quantities worthy of serious consideration, while mean values for groups of stars which are smaller than this are useful. Catalogues of star positions often also contain proper motion data, in most cases derived by comparison of the places in the catalogue with those in one or more earlier catalogues. A discussion will often be found in the introduction to such positional catalogues which shows the systematic differences between the proper motions of the catalogue and other sources.

Relative proper motions may be determined by the comparison of plates of a given area of sky, containing the selected star, which have been obtained at widely separated epochs. In this case proper motion is evaluated with respect to the reference system provided by the faint, presumably on the average very distant, stars, recorded along with the proper motion star. The two exposures should, ideally, be made with the same instrument, left undisturbed in the interim, with the proper motion star near the field centre. At one time it was proposed that the two exposures should be made on the same plate, left undeveloped for several years or decades until the second epoch exposure could be made. The risks involved are obvious, and so serious that it is now more usual to compare the first epoch plate with a separate one taken at the later epoch with the same instrument. The latter plate may be taken through the glass, with appropriate adjustment of instrumental focus, and is, therefore, a mirror image of the first. This procedure enables the observer to make more than one attempt if the new plate is not a good match for the old, which may arise, not only because of differences in observing conditions, but because modern photographic emulsions may not have precisely the same properties as those used for the first epoch plates. The two plates are now clipped securely together, film to film, with a slight relative displacement so that images of corresponding stars appear close together. The proper motion star will, in general, show a larger displacement. If the two plates were reduced separately one would evaluate the plate constants in each case through equations relating the standard coordinates to the measured x and y. The relations would be of the form

$$\xi_1 - x_1 = a_1 x_1 + b_2 y_1 + c_1 \qquad \xi_2 - x_2 = a_2 x_2 + b_2 y_2 + c_2$$

with a similar pair for η. If we subtract corresponding equations for the two epochs we have for any star

$$\xi_2 - \xi_1 = T\mu_x = M_x + ax_1 + by_1 + c$$

where T is the difference of epoch between the plates, M_x the displacement between the images in the x direction, and a, b, c are constants. We arrive at this formulation by considering that the difference between ξ_1 and x_1 is small, while x_2 is related to x_1 and y_2 to y_1 through a displacement and slight rotation of the plate, and different circumstances of aberration and refraction at the time of exposure of the second plate. As we have remarked, all these differences are expressible in linear form so that the right-hand side of the equation remains linear. The symbol μ_x stands for annual proper motion in R.A., and our hypothesis is that this is not zero for the proper motion star, but is, on the average zero for the assemblage of reference stars scattered all over the plate. The procedure is then to measure the displacements of the images in the coordinate directions for all the stars. *Excluding the proper motion star* the right-hand side of the foregoing equation can be equated to zero and the constants a, b, c found by least squares, the values being used to convert the observed $M_x = x_2 - x_1$ for the proper motion star into the proper motion in right ascension. A similar procedure yields constants d, e, f and the proper motion in declination. For large proper motions the blink microscope, described later in connection with variable stars, has sometimes been used for comparison of plates taken at widely separated epochs.

Proper motions found in this way are relative proper motions and rest on the assumption that the mean motion of the faint comparison stars is zero, or that the motion found is relative to the mean of these stars. Occasionally one of the comparison stars will be found to have a sensible proper motion, and the work will then be re-done, omitting this star. While obvious cases of this sort can easily be dealt with, it is clear that any general cooperative motion of the stars will introduce errors into the measurement of relative proper motions which will be very difficult to remove. One such, apparent, cooperative motion certainly does exist, which arises from the fact that the Sun is in motion with respect to the general field of stars in its spatial neighbourhood with a velocity of about 20 km/s towards a point (the *solar apex*) near R.A. 18h, declination + 30°. As the Sun moves through the cloud of neighbouring stars, there is thus, superposed on their own proper motions, a parallactic motion which is the reflex of this motion of the Sun. It takes the form of an apparent systematic recession from the solar apex, and convergence towards the solar antapex. In accordance with the formula for cross-velocity, the angular motion is larger for the apparently brighter, on the average nearer, stars, than it is for the apparently fainter, on the average, more distant, stars. Tables are available giving an average statistical correction for this effect, possibly very wide of the mark in individual cases. For a star of the tenth magnitude, the maximum value of the effect due to this parallactic motion lies between $0''\cdot01$ and $0''\cdot02$ per annum, depending on position in the sky.

Real cooperative proper motions may arise in regions of the sky where there are star clusters of which the members have closely similar spatial movement; if the suggestion made by Eggen is correct, namely that groups of moving stars commonly exist, the members all having the same motion, but showing no obvious spatial association as in the case of clusters, this too might give rise to difficulties. What is likely to be of more importance is the possibility that some of the adopted values of the astronomical constants are not quite correct, and that part of the residual shifts now attributed to proper motions may be due to this cause. The accuracy with which the values of the astronomical constants are known is so great that the proportional effect on larger proper motions will be negligible, but as astronomers become ambitious to study the motions of more distant and fainter stars, smaller proper motions which can be badly affected come under discussion.

The nearest approach to a fixed non-rotating reference system is provided by the remote galaxies (see Chapter V) for which not even the largest possible component of transverse velocity could produce a detectable proper motion. Work undertaken in the U.S.S.R. and at Lick Observatory has been directed towards obtaining photographs of stars relatively near the Sun on plates showing images of faint galaxies, and so linking the two together. Some practical problems are that the galaxies are faint, so that a large astrograph is required; their images are less precise than those of stars, because they are extended objects, and the position of the centre of the photographic image of a galaxy may depend on exposure. Finally, the region of the sky where the linkage is most needed is the plane of our own Galaxy, but this obscures the distant extragalactic systems. In spite of these problems the method seems to be the one most likely to put proper motion measurements eventually on a sound basis.

1.37. The Measurement of Trigonometrical Parallaxes

The first successful measurements of trigonometrical parallaxes such as those of the very near stars 61 Cygni and Alpha Centauri were based on accurate visual measurements of angles; the number of stars accessible by such methods was severely limited and many of the results were inaccurate or spurious. Photographic methods have now entirely replaced all others: the methods in use at the present time are still essentially those elaborated by Schlesinger about 1911.

The general ideas have been outlined above. The maximum displacement due to parallax alone occurs when the star to be observed and the Sun differ in longitude by 90°. Parallax observations are always made with the star as near the meridian as possible, so that for moderate latitudes optimum conditions are obtained by observing just after sunset or just before sunrise. If the observations must be made at times nearer apparent midnight, as is the case in summer in rather high latitudes, the displacement due to parallax is reduced by a simply calculated factor, less than unity, known as the *parallax factor*. Ideally, a stellar parallax could be determined from three observations of the star's position made at intervals of six months, with the star on the meridian at say, sunset, sunrise and sunset respectively. Three observations are necessary to permit the oscillatory effects of parallax to be disentangled from the progressive effects of proper motion which are usually of the same order of size. In practice because of reduced parallax factors for summer observations, and still more, because of the very small size of the effects sought, the number of observations required may be of the order of 50, and they may be spread over several years. For a star with a parallax of $0''\cdot030$ to be determined at a plate scale of $30''$/mm, the maximum value of the displacement due to parallax is about one micron, a quantity far smaller than the diameter of the star image on the plate. Understandably, extreme precautions are taken to preserve unaltered throughout a programme the adjustments of an objective to be used for parallax determinations.

The method of work is to compare the position of the parallax star with the reference system of faint stars on the same plate, exemplified by the choice of four or five comparison stars which are assumed to be much more distant than the parallax star, and hence themselves immune from displacements arising from parallax effects. If inaccuracies depending on apparent star brightness are to be eliminated, the parallax star must be of approximately the same brightness as the comparison stars. As it is usually brighter, it must be dimmed by a method which avoids the introduction of spurious displacements. A series of rotating sectors is provided, each consisting of a small disc with two opposite sectors cut away. An appropriately chosen disk is mounted in front of the parallax star, and rotated during exposure, which reduces its brightness by multiplying it by a factor equal to the proportion which the open sectors bear to 360°.

A large number of plates of the parallax star and comparison region is taken on each of which the displacement of the parallax star must be measured. The observed displacement must then be equated to the sum of the oscillatory part arising from parallax and the cumulative part arising from proper motion. Schlesinger showed that it was not necessary to go to the tedious labour of determining the plate constants for each plate. An outline of his method is as follows. Usually the plates are measured only in the coordinate parallel to right ascension, with the exception of one selected plate on which both x and y coordinates of the parallax and comparison stars are measured relatively roughly—an accuracy of one-tenth of a millimetre will suffice. These measures are to be used for the calculation of what Schlesinger called *Dependences* which represent the proportionate influence of each of the comparison stars on the accurate work which follows. The plate constants for each plate are of no interest in themselves. If they were found, and Schlesinger gives an algebraic expression for them, they would only be used to substitute in an expression giving the displacement of the parallax star, so that this becomes a linear expression in the measures of each comparison star, the coefficients being fairly complicated functions of the measured coordinates on the *standard plate only*. These coefficients are the dependences and can be computed once and for all from measures on the standard plate. This constitutes one great advantage. Another is that if the dependence on a particular comparison star turns out to be small, then it might as well not be there, and should be replaced by some other more suitable star. Detailed practice varies from observatory to observatory. At Greenwich and the Cape the work is done differentially. A blank glass plate is placed on a ruling machine and short sections of lines parallel to the coordinates are ruled with a diamond in the neighbourhood of the parallax and comparison stars. This plate is now clipped to each parallax plate in turn, and measures are made with the highest attainable accuracy, of the distance of each star image from the corresponding ruled line. If such a measure for the parallax star is X_π, and X_n for each of the n comparison stars, for which the value of the dependence is D_n, then the quantity

$$m = X_\pi - \Sigma_n D_n X_n$$

for each plate is called the solution for that plate, and is related to the parallax and proper motion, expressed in millimetres on the plate by the relation

$$m = P.p + T.\mu + c$$

where P is the parallax factor (calculated for the position of the parallax star and the time of observation), p is the parallax, T the time expressed in some suitable unit (e.g. years from some arbitrary datum), μ the proper motion in right ascension, and c is a constant. With one such equation for each plate, and a series of forty or fifty plates for each parallax star, the values of parallax and proper motion (the latter relative to the comparison stars) may be found by a least squares procedure.

The solution may be invalidated if one of the comparison stars has itself a sensible proper motion or parallax, and, in such a case if p is in reality fairly small, the physically meaningless result of a negative parallax may be deduced. In general, this means that the assumption that the fainter comparison stars are more distant than the parallax star, has broken down. Difficulties may also be introduced if any of the stars has orbital motion about an unseen companion.

Parallaxes measured by this method are subject to a small statistical correction to take account of the finite, but very small average parallactic motion of stars as faint as those chosen for comparison stars.

No star has a parallax as large as one second of arc. About one hundred are known with parallaxes over $0''\cdot1$ (i.e. are nearer than 10 parsecs), and for these the values are known with an accuracy sufficient to permit their use in simple computations of limited scope. Only a minority are exact enough to permit their use in more sophisticated calculations, e.g. as in the case of double stars, the formation of the cube of the parallax. About 1,000 stars are known with parallaxes in excess of $0''\cdot050$, and these are usually known with sufficient accuracy to permit the employment of the figures in simple computations where the parallax enters linearly, with some degree of confidence. Smaller parallaxes are of indicative value only: they may often be usefully employed pre-emptively, i.e. if the measured parallax is small, say $0''\cdot01$, it may usually be assumed that the real parallax is not large. Parallaxes have been determined for about 7,000 stars, some with several independent repetitions. The principal observatories concerned have been Allegheny, Yale, McCormick, Yerkes and Sproul observatories in the U.S.A., Greenwich and the Cape, and a number of other minor contributors. Since the number of stars within a given distance of the Sun is limited, the determination of trigonometrical parallaxes is a field of research which will eventually be worked out.

REFERENCES:

Names of some Astronomical Periodicals

The following abbreviations for the names of some of the more important astronomical periodicals are commonly used. The list is not exhaustive:

ApJ.: The *Astrophysical Journal*, published by the University of Chicago Press.
Ap.J.Supp.: The *Astrophysical Journal Supplement*, as above.
A.J.: The *Astronomical Journal*, published by the American Astronomical Society.
P.A.S.P.: *Publications* of the Astronomical Society of the Pacific.
M.N.: *Monthly Notices* of the Royal Astronomical Society, London.
Mem.R.A.S.: *Memoirs* of the Royal Astronomical Society.
Q.J.: *Quarterly Journal* of the Royal Astronomical Society.
Observatory: The *Observatory* Magazine, c/o Royal Greenwich Observatory, Herstmonceux Castle, England.
R.O.B.: *Royal Observatory Bulletins*, H.M. Stationery Office.
B.A.N.: *Bulletins* of the Astronomical Institutes of the Netherlands.
Zs.f.Ap.: *Zeitschrift für Astrophysik.*
Ast.Nacht.: *Astronomische Nachrichtung.*
Ann.Ast.: *Annales d'Astrophysique.*
J.desO.: *Journal des Observateurs.*
J.R.A.S.Can.: *Journal* of the Astronomical Society of Canada.
M.N.A.S.S.A.: *Monthly Notes* of the Astronomical Society of Southern Africa.

Observatory publications, e.g. *Lick*, *David Dunlap* (Toronto), etc., are under abbreviated versions of institution names. Where, as often happens, the same paper has been published both in a journal and reprinted in an observatory series, the journal reference is usually preferred.

General Data:
> *Astrophysical Quantities*, C. W. Allen, University of London Press, 2nd edition, 1963.

Spherical Astronomy and Related Topics:
> *Explanatory Supplement* to the Astronomical Ephemeris and American Ephemeris and Nautical Almanac, H.M.S.O., 1961. (Comprehensive and authoritative.)
> *Textbook on Spherical Astronomy*, W. M. Smart, C.U.P., 1956. (A useful introduction not including modern developments.)
> *Royal Observatory Annals*, No. 1, H.M.S.O., 1961. (Computation of Nutation.)
> *Refraction Tables* of Pulkovo Observatory, Academy of Sciences of U.S.S.R., 1956: Garfinkel, B., *A.J.*, **50**, 169, 1944. (Refraction.)
> *Report on System of Astronomical Constants*, I.A.U., Hamburg, 1964.

Time:
> *Explanatory Supplement*. (Supra).
> H. M. Smith and G. B. Wellgate, *Vistas in Astronomy*, Vol. I, Pergamon Press, 1956.
> L. Essen and J. V. L. Parry, *Phil. Trans. Roy. Soc. A.*, **250**, 45, 1957. (Caesium Clock.)
> G. M. Clemence, *A.J.*, **53**, 169, 1948. (Ephemeris Time.)
> D. H. Sadler, *Occasional Notes*, R.A.S., **3**, 103, 1954. (Ephemeris Time.)

Instruments (Transit Circle, Danjon Astrolabe, P.Z.T.):
> *Stars and Stellar Systems*, Vol. I, ed. G. P. Kuiper and B. Middlehurst, Chicago, 1960.
> D. S. Perfect, *Occasional Notes*, R.A.S., No. 21, 1959. (Herstmonceux P.Z.T.)
> J. J. Labrecque, *J.R.A.S. Can.*, **57**, No. 1, 1963. (Mirror Transit.)
> D. V. Thomas, *R.O.B.*, **81**, 1964; *R.O.B.*, **92**, 1965.

Parallax:
> Frank Schlesinger, series ending *Ap.J.*, **33**, 161, 1911.
> Also *Introduction to Yale Catalogue of Trigonometrical Parallaxes*, Yale, 1952.

Astrometry: In addition see introductions to *Zone Catalogues*, e.g. Yale and Cape.

Catalogues: The most general positional catalogue now available is the compilation, *The Smithsonian Astrophysical Observatory Star Catalog* (4 vols., Smithsonian Institution, 1966), containing positions of 258,997 stars on the FK4 system with their proper motions.

II

The Measurement and Analysis of Stellar Radiation

2.1. The Laws of Radiation: Effective Temperature

THE hot surfaces of the gaseous globes which we know as stars emit radiation of which the energy distribution is given approximately by the Planck or black-body law, with a temperature parameter near the actual gas temperature in the outer layers of the star. For a detailed discussion of the laws of radiation reference should be made to standard works on physics. There has often been a considerable variation in nomenclature and terminology between different writers on the subject, leading to a good deal of confusion. The observational astronomer is fortunately in the happy position of dealing almost exclusively with relative measures, and is rarely troubled by these difficulties.

For our present purpose we recall the more important laws of radiation. The *Stefan-Boltzmann Law* expresses the total energy emitted outwards from unit surface of a black body per unit time, as,

$$\text{Emittance} = \sigma T^4$$

where σ is the Stefan-Boltzmann constant $= 5 \cdot 669 \times 10^{-5}$ ergs cm^{-2} s^{-1} deg.$^{-4}$, and T is the absolute temperature of the surface. The formula applies in the absence of convection, and gives the energy flow to empty space or to another body at absolute zero. Thus, if a star of radius r were a black body at absolute temperature T, it would radiate into space per second a total energy given by $4\pi\sigma r^2 T^4$ ergs. If none of this is absorbed in space, the quantity of this energy received on an area of one square centimetre at distance D from the star, will be $\sigma T^4 r^2 / D^2$. If we take D to be the distance of the Earth from the star, r/D becomes the angular radius of the star's disc as seen from the Earth. For most stars this quantity is not determinable, but for the Sun at the Earth's mean distance the value is about $960'' = 0 \cdot 00465$ radians. The observationally determined value for the total energy received from the Sun just above the Earth's atmosphere is $1 \cdot 374 \times 10^6$ ergs per square centimetre per second. We can immediately determine the temperature which the Sun's surface would have if it radiated like a black body as 5,785°K. The temperature of a star determined in this way, by equating observed total energy output to the result given by using a certain temperature in the Stefan-Boltzmann law is called the *Effective Temperature* of the stellar surface.

Black-body radiation is distributed in wavelength according to the Planck formula which states that the energy radiated per unit wavelength range at wavelength λ is given by

$$F_\lambda = c_1\lambda^{-5}/(\exp.[c_2/\lambda T] - 1)$$

$$\text{where } c_1 = 3\cdot741 \times 10^{-5} \text{ erg cm}^2 \text{ s}^{-1}$$

$$c_2 = 1\cdot439 \text{ cm deg.}$$

Integration of this formula over λ gives the fourth power dependence on temperature of the Stefan-Boltzmann law. For any temperature the curve of F_λ against λ rises to a maximum at a certain wavelength, denoted by λ_{max} and then declines asymptotically towards zero at longer wavelengths (Figure II.1). The formula readily reproduces the rule (Wien's Law) that for a given temperature

$$T\lambda_{max} = \text{constant} = 0\cdot2898 \text{ cm deg.}$$

Thus, if presented with a distribution of radiation approximating to a Planck curve, we might try to assess the temperature with which it was associated by finding the wavelength or colour of light at which the energy flux was a maximum, and then apply Wien's law. The temperature so found would not coincide with the effective temperature deduced from the total radiant flux unless the distribution were exactly

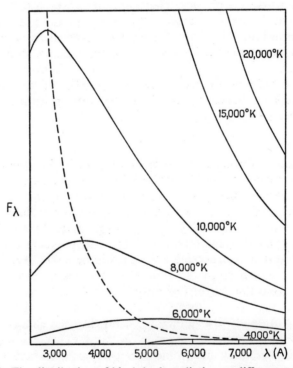

Figure II.1: The distribution of black-body radiation at different temperatures.

of the Planck type. The Planck function has been extensively tabulated, and from the tabulations the relative flux at any pair of chosen wavelengths can be read off as a function of temperature. Again, presented with a distribution which is approximately a Planck function we can choose two wavelengths and infer a temperature which, in a Planck distribution would produce the observed ratio at the chosen wavelengths. Such a temperature is called a *colour temperature* and it will not coincide with other temperature parameters unless the radiation distribution is precisely of the Planck type.

2.2. Deviations from Black-Body Radiation

The radiant energy emitted from the surface of a star originates in the deep interior and passes outwards through the gases which form the star, interacting with them and being steadily changed as it progresses towards the surface. In the deep interior the radiation is effectively enclosed by matter and the conditions for the production of black-body radiation are satisfied. When the radiation finally leaves the surface of the star it no longer has a black-body distribution. The reasons for this are manifold but some of them can be briefly sketched. The gaseous material in a star is not opaque: if it were, radiation could not flow through it. In consequence, when we look at a star, such as the Sun, we do not see a single surface. We receive radiation which has originated at a variety of depths below some rather arbitrary datum level. Since the star's radiation is flowing outwards it follows that there must be a temperature gradient within the star such that, usually, a greater depth corresponds to a greater temperature. At any given level, the composition of the gases, and the temperature at that level will determine the kind of radiation which that layer emits, and the degree of transparency of the layer to radiations of various wavelengths. The physical laws describing the interaction of matter and radiation enable equations to be written down which express the condition that at each depth there is an energy balance. The gas layer at any depth absorbs radiation from the generally outward flowing stream, because it has a certain absorptive capacity (known as its *opacity*) and radiates itself according to its temperature. The absorbed and emitted energy must balance. The energy emitted from a given depth suffers absorption as it passes outwards, but some proportion of it will arrive at the surface and be emitted into space. Thus, if we supposed that each layer absorbed radiation passing through it by a proportion independent of its wavelength we could express the total emergent radiation in the following way: the emergent radiation would be the sum of a small proportion of the radiation from a deep layer at high temperature, a larger proportion of the radiation originating from shallower layers at somewhat lower temperature, and a still higher proportion of the less abundant radiation originating in the highest layers where the temperature has its lowest value. Thus, on this hypothesis the outflowing radiation is not a simple Planck function, but an integral of a series of Planck functions with different temperature parameters weighted according to the absorption which has occurred between the originating layer and the stellar surface.

2.3. Limb Darkening

A second effect may be indicated in the following way. In the previous argument we can approximate to the total radiation flowing out normal to the surface of the star by replacing the actual complicated integral by the emission from some average depth below the surface. Alternatively we can say that when we observe a star, for example, the Sun, the radiation which we receive from the centre of the disc, where the line of sight is normal to the surface, is approximately the same as the radiation emitted from a layer at a certain depth, (D), possibly a few hundred kilometres, below the surface (Figure II.2, Ray No. 1). When we observe another part of the

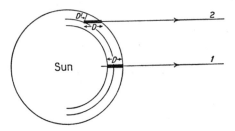

Figure II.2: Limb darkening in the Sun.

Sun's disc, nearer its apparent edge (or *Limb*) the line of sight cuts the solar surface at an angle. The depth to which we can see along this inclined line of sight will not be very different from that which applies to the centre of the disc. Now, however, this length will not penetrate so deeply into the material of the Sun, and it will, therefore, correspond to a shallower and cooler layer (Ray No. 2). This layer at depth D will emit in total less abundantly, and, since it is somewhat cooler, rather more in long wavelengths and less in shorter wavelengths. This follows because, according to the Wien Law the wavelength of maximum emission will be displaced towards longer wavelengths. The result is that the surface of the Sun falls off in brightness from the centre of the disc towards its edge. This *Limb Darkening* effect is well seen on photographs of the Sun. It is presumed that a similar effect occurs in all stars. In the Sun we can observe different parts of the disc separately: in stars we can observe only the integrated radiation from all over the stellar disc.

2.4. Stellar Spectra

A third, and very important cause of distortion of the distribution of radiation received from stars is the presence of spectrum lines. Since we now need to discuss more precisely particular wavelengths in the spectrum, we introduce the astronomical practice for the specification of wavelengths. Up to the present we can presume that wavelengths have been expressed in centimetres. The astronomical practice is to express wavelengths in *Ångström Units*, abbreviated as Å, ($1Å = 10^{-8}$ cm). In the visible range different wavelengths are sensed as different colours. The human eye is sensitive to light from about 4,000Å (violet) to about 7,700Å (deep red). Individual sensitivities vary, and much shorter wavelengths for the violet limit are sometimes quoted. The wavelength of maximum solar emission is near 4,800Å corresponding according to Wien's Law to a temperature near 6,000°K. Maximum response of the eye is near 5,030Å for illumination of low intensity and in the yellow, near 5,600Å for high intensity. There is, no doubt, a biological evolutionary explanation for the occurrence of maximum eye sensitivity near maximum solar emission.

Returning to the subject of the formation of spectrum lines in stellar atmospheres, we assume a knowledge of the general facts that incandescent chemical elements emit radiation in certain narrow bands of wavelength characteristic of the elements involved; that the observed wavelengths can be computed as due to electron transitions between energy levels in the various atoms; that these energy levels are computable from the properties of the nuclei and electron shells occurring in the various atomic species. Conversely, if light of all wavelengths passes through an atmosphere containing various elements, these can in favourable circumstances subtract radiation from the beam. This leads to the production of dark lines (*absorption lines*) within which little or no radiation is transmitted. When these absorption lines are narrow they occur at the same wavelengths as those found in emission from incandescent clouds of the same atomic species. Since, at any considerable depth below the surface of a star the radiation is enclosed, and hence of black-body type, in which absorption lines do not occur, the occurrence of absorption lines in stellar spectra is a phenomenon of the extreme outer layers, or atmosphere, of a star. For a given spectrum line of a given chemical element to occur requires not only the presence of that chemical element, but also favourable conditions of temperature and pressure. For example, the series of lines due to hydrogen, known as the Balmer series is prominent in many stars. This series of lines originates in transitions which all commence at the second energy level in the hydrogen atom. If they are to appear a considerable number of hydrogen atoms must be available which are excited to this state, as they may be if they form part of a sufficiently hot gas. On the other hand, at still higher temperatures a considerable proportion of the hydrogen atoms will become ionised, i.e. their orbital electrons will be removed from them, leaving a nucleus incapable of producing a line spectrum. Thus if we run downwards through the gamut of surface temperatures of stars we find that in very hot stars, such as those we shall later class as of type B, with surface temperatures near 20,000°K, the Balmer lines are not particularly strong, even though hydrogen is overwhelmingly the most abundant constituent of the atmospheres of these stars. At lower surface temperatures, such as among the A-type stars at about 10,000°K, the proportion of hydrogen which is ionised has fallen, but the proportion of hydrogen atoms excited into the lower state of the Balmer transitions remains high. It is in these stars that the Balmer lines have their maximum strength. The individual lines are often very broad, extending in some cases each over some tens of ångströms. The first of the series, H-alpha lies in the red part of the spectrum at 6,563Å (Figure II.3), the next, H-beta in the green at 4,861Å. Then in the blue come H-gamma and H-delta at 4,340Å and 4,101Å. In A-type stars with strong Balmer lines each of these can be seen to consist of a dark core with extensive faint wings shading off into the continuous spectrum over a great distance. The higher members of the Balmer series crowd closer and closer together towards the ultraviolet end of the spectrum, and the wings of neighbouring lines overlap so that the whole run of the spectrum is distorted by their presence. In some cases as many as twenty members of the series can be distinguished, crowding closer and closer as the head of the spectral series is approached. Finally, near the head of the series near a wavelength of 3,700Å in the near ultraviolet, there is a sharp drop in the intensity of the whole spectrum. This is the *Balmer discontinuity* which has its maximum value in stars of this temperature. For stars of lower temperature the population of the lower state from which the Balmer lines originate becomes smaller, and there are fewer and fewer hydrogen atoms available for the formation of the Balmer lines. Their strength therefore declines. The occurrence of a maximum

c

of intensity of a particular series of spectral lines at a certain temperature holds generally. At higher temperatures the lines of a given element weaken because of progressive ionisation, and the spectrum of the neutral element will usually be replaced by the spectrum of the ionised element as a series of stars of increasing temperature is reviewed. Among the hottest stars helium and ionised helium spectra are prominent. Among cooler stars the spectral lines of the metals are prominent.

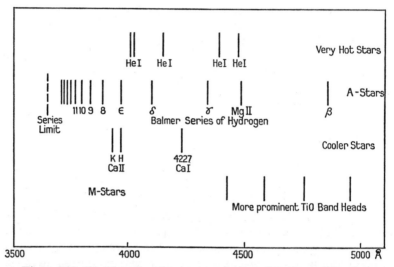

Figure II.3: Wavelengths of some prominent stellar spectral features.

Particularly striking are the H and K lines of ionised calcium at 3,968Å and 3,933Å respectively. These are just making their appearance in the A-type stars. As we pass to redder and cooler stars the line of neutral calcium at 4,227Å becomes progressively stronger along with many hundreds of lines due to other metals. At temperatures just above that of the Sun the number of metallic lines originating in practically all the metals known on earth, becomes so considerable that the general distribution of radiation is perceptibly altered. Among the coolest and reddest stars, with surface temperatures of round about 3,500°K, the 4,227Å line of neutral calcium has become by far the strongest line in the visible spectrum, the Balmer lines have become extremely faint, and the whole spectrum is crowded with metallic lines of a great diversity of strengths. Absorption bands due to molecules or radicals now become a striking feature of the spectrum. The atmospheric temperature is no longer high enough to tear these apart into their constituent atoms, and, for example, the bands of TiO in stars of the lowest temperatures (M-type) mutilate the continuum in the green region of the spectrum until the graph of intensity with wavelength is shaped like the teeth of a saw.

We shall return later to a more detailed consideration of the spectral features of stars. The foregoing sketch is intended merely to demonstrate that the radiation distribution which leaves the surface of star is much altered from the approximately Planck distribution which must prevail just below the stellar surface, and that the nature of the distortion is largely dependent on the temperature of the star.

2.5. Interstellar Effects

In its passage from the star to the Earth the radiation may suffer further changes. The space between the stars is not entirely empty of matter, but contains both gas, and what, for want of a better name is often called "dust". Both occur in irregular clouds, which have densities which by terrestrial standards are extremely low. However, over path-lengths of hundreds or thousands of parsecs, even the slightest departure from a perfect void has significant effects on radiation passing through.

The interstellar gas can imprint spectrum lines, characteristically extremely sharp, on the starlight passing through. Most prominent are the H and K lines of ionised calcium. The interstellar dust absorbs and scatters a proportion of the starlight with effects on the blue end of the spectrum which are more pronounced than in the red. After passage over a great distance in the interstellar medium, starlight is dimmed more in the blue than in the red, a situation which may be described as a dimming coupled with a reddening of the starlight.

2.6. Effects of the Earth's Atmosphere

On arrival at the upper surface of the atmosphere of the Earth, stellar radiation begins to suffer the most severe distortion of all. The atmosphere of the Earth is completely opaque to wavelengths shorter than about 3,000Å. An important consequence of this was that until the development of rocket- and satellite-borne observing devices the whole field of ultraviolet and X-ray radiation from stars was a matter of speculation rather than observation. In particular all the spectral transitions from the ground state of the hydrogen atom were unobservable. These define a spectral series, known as the Lyman series of lines, which starts at 1,216Å and has its series limit at 912Å, and is the analogue in the ultraviolet of the Balmer series in the visible range. Information on these regions of the solar spectrum is now coming in from satellite experiments at a tremendous rate.

The upper wavelength limit of atmospheric transparency is set somewhere in the near infra-red by a series of atmospheric absorption bands due to water vapour and oxygen. Practical limits are set by the availability of sensitive receivers (photocells and photographic plates), but these are being vigorously advanced further and further into the infra-red. At much longer wavelengths in the millimetre range, the atmosphere becomes transparent again. Here we enter the domain of very high frequency radio waves, with which we are not immediately concerned.

2.7. Stellar Magnitudes

The first description of the apparent brightness of the stars was given by Hipparchus in Hellenistic times. He arranged the stars in a hierarchy of brightness, calling the brightest "First Magnitude" and the faintest visible to the naked eye, "Sixth Magnitude", with four intermediate categories. In the nineteenth century, Pogson established that this was roughly a logarithmic scale, and proposed that an exact logarithmic scale be used in which a change of five magnitudes corresponded to a luminosity ratio of 100 : 1. The introduction of the telescope had made faint stars available to observation far below the original sixth magnitude. At the brighter end, exceptionally bright objects, such as the stars Sirius and Canopus, the Sun and Moon and some of the planets near maximum brightness, had to be defined by magnitudes above the old scale, that is by negative numbers.

The relation between magnitude and luminosity is defined by the equation

$$L = \text{constant} \times 10^{-0.4\text{m}}$$

The magnitudes of objects as viewed from the Earth are called *apparent magnitudes*, and the name is further qualified to define the wavelength range or colour to which the receiver is sensitive. The response of a receiver is determined not only by its intrinsic sensitivity at various wavelengths, and by the transmission of filters deliberately inserted to define a particular wavelength range, but also by other absorptions associated with a given instrument, which are determined by the transmissions of lenses, the reflectivity of the metallic coats of mirrors, and the like. All these effects come on top of those outlined earlier. Thus, although in principle the complete process from the emission of radiation by a star to the response of a given receiver could be followed through mathematically, in practice this ideal is unattainable.* In the vast majority of cases the various transmission functions are unknown, and some of them are capriciously variable with time.

The development of stellar photometry has been largely empirical, dominated until recently as much by the availability of sensitive receivers as by a knowledge of the parameters of stellar radiation which it is theoretically desirable to measure. Almost all work has been relative. Magnitudes of stars have been determined in relation to those of previously measured stars, and not in relation to the system of units of ordinary physics. The zero point of the scale has been fixed by adopting a certain star or series of stars as having a certain assigned magnitude. The reasons for this should be clear enough from the foregoing discussion.

Earliest estimates of magnitude were visual. Because the human eye has a response which, over a large range is nearly logarithmic, and because in most individuals spectral response is fairly close to a standard curve, these estimates provided a basis from which further progress could be made. Sir John Herschel attempted to improve visual estimates of magnitude by a crude measuring device which he called the astrometer. He used this during his stay in South Africa from 1834-8. A polished metal sphere mounted on a slide formed a point-image of the full Moon. The sphere was brought to such a distance from the eye that the lunar image and a star were made to match, and the star's magnitude determined from the measured distance at which the match occurred. Naturally this system could only be applied to bright naked-eye stars.

2.8. Photographic and Photovisual Magnitudes

With the introduction of the photographic plate, stellar photometry began after protracted teething troubles to be more precise. The response of the plate to a given star could be judged by the size of the image which it produced. The first experiments in stellar photography date from the middle of the nineteenth century and processes such as the Daguerrotype, and the dry and wet collodion plates were first used. By the eighties of the last century dry plates of modern type had come into use, and were employed for general charting purposes of the sky, notably by Gill of the Cape Observatory, working in collaboration with Kapteyn of Leiden, and by the brothers Henry at Paris. These early plates were blue-sensitive with a maximum response

---

* Ažusienis and Straižys of Vilnius, who did the computations in 1966, concluded that the effective wavelength of Johnson's U (para. 2.11), ought to be increased.

near 4,300Å, and when employed at the telescope gave a record of the incident intensity centred near this wavelength with a range of some 600Å on either side of the mean. Magnitudes so determined are photographic magnitudes, designated as m_{pg}. When photographic plates sensitive in the yellow became available it was possible to specify a particular combination of plate and filter which recorded the intensity of starlight in the yellow region of the spectrum. The system of photovisual magnitudes, m_{pv}, thus defined corresponded to a mean response near 5,400Å, with a total band-width of about 600Å. The figures given should be treated with some reserve, since, with various telescopes, and even with the same instrument under different conditions (e.g. the age of the reflecting coat on the mirror of a reflector), variations can occur.

As we have seen, the temperatures and hence the mean colours of stars differ from one to another so that stars having the same m_{pg} will usually not also have the same m_{pv}. We can define a parameter, a *colour-index* of the form

$$C = m_{pg} - m_{pv}$$

which will indicate the colour of any star for which measures on both magnitude systems are available. The zero points are customarily chosen so as to make the colour indices of A-type stars near zero. Hot blue stars then have negative colour indices, and cooler redder stars have positive ones.

The Pogson scale of magnitudes is logarithmic with a scale constant of 0·4. A basic problem in setting up a magnitude system on this scale by photographic means has always been the establishment on the plate of a calibrated intensity ratio. The properties of a star image on a photographic plate depend not only on the star itself, the telescope, filters and plate sensitivity, but also on meteorological conditions, and on the times of exposure and development. It is therefore essential to produce the standard ratio on a photograph of a star field in such a way as to eliminate these variable factors. The variety of methods tried has been legion. A star field may be exposed on one half of the plate with full aperture, and the same field on the other half with the aperture of the objective reduced by a known factor. Again, half of the plate may be exposed through a neutral filter of known transmission or through a rotating sector with a known opening. In so far as each method produced on the same plate an image of the same source, once undimmed and once dimmed by a known ratio, the photographic conditions being otherwise the same, the desired result was achieved. All kinds of difficulties were encountered, such as deviations of neutral filters from neutrality and uniformity, variation of transparency of the objective, and the effects of intermittent exposure produced by the rotating sector. These methods are now only of historical interest, for the modern method is to determine the magnitudes of a number of stars on the plate by photoelectric photo-metry, in which the response of the recorder is very closely linear. One photographic method, that of the coarse objective grating, retains usefulness.

2.9. The Objective Grating

If a grating consisting of a series of parallel wires or bars of equal thickness, with equal spacing be placed immediately in front of the objective or entrance pupil of a telescope, the stellar images will be found to be replaced each by an undisplaced central image, flanked on either side by a series of symmetrically disposed side images. These are produced by the diffraction effects of the objective grating, and lie along a line perpendicular to its wires. In general the brightness of the side images falls off with increasing order in the series. Each side image is actually a very low dispersion spectrum, but by control of the conditions of use, for example by limiting the effective spectral range by means of filters, and by slightly softening the focus, the side images can be made indistinguishable in appearance from ordinary star images. If d is the thickness of the wires, l the space between them, λ the wavelength of light, and f the focal length of the telescope, the theory shows that the spacing on the plate between the central image and the first order side image is given by $D = \lambda.f/(l + d)$. The intensity ratio between the image of order n and the central image is given by $(np\pi)^2\, I_n/I_0 = \sin^2 np\pi$ where $p = l/(l + d)$. The quantity p is the proportion of the objective free from obscuration by the wires. If $p = \frac{1}{2}$, wires and spaces are equal, and then all images of odd order have zero intensity, giving an exception to the general rule that side images decrease in intensity with increasing order. The constants of a grating can be chosen so that the separation and magnitude difference of close binary stars can be well matched, thus enabling the magnitude differences to be rather closely estimated. For the general establishment of an intensity ratio on a photographic plate the use of gratings has been superseded by photoelectric photometry, but as Wesselink has pointed out, they can be used to curtail the photoelectric calibration needed in a given region. He takes as an example a grating giving a 5 magnitude difference between the central image and the image of order unity. Let a star field be photographed with the grating in position with an exposure reaching a limiting magnitude of 20. Then side images will be seen for stars down to the 15th magnitude, and it will only be necessary to calibrate the field photoelectrically down to the 15th magnitude to have a calibration on the plate using the recorded secondary images, down to the 20th magnitude. This facility can represent an immense saving in labour.

2.10. Magnitude Sequences

The calibration of the magnitudes in a particular area of sky is normally done by the establishment of a *Sequence* in or near the area. A sequence is a series of stars covering a range of apparent magnitude of which the magnitudes, and usually the colours have been very carefully determined. The magnitudes and colours of other stars in the region are then determined by interpolation, using methods described below. In the most convenient case the stars to be observed can be photographed on the same plate as the sequence stars. In other cases the sequence may be transferred, for example by making a double exposure with sequence area and the investigation area photographed in succession on the same plate. To permit ready identification of stars, and to smooth out errors, quadruple exposures are often employed, care being taken that the sequence and investigation areas are photographed at the same zenith distance so that the absorption effects of the atmosphere are the same for both. If A denotes an exposure on the sequence area, and B on the investigation area, the exposures are made according to the scheme ABBA, the two A exposures being slightly displaced in right ascension relative to each other, and the two B exposures in declination. Star pairs on the plate displaced in R.A. thus belong to the sequence area, and pairs displaced in declination to the investigation area.

Sequences have been established in many areas of the sky, for example, conveniently adjacent to star clusters or variable star fields. The most famous sequence of general utility is the "North Polar Sequence" intended to provide a series of stars near the pole which would be available at all times to any northern observatory. This has now fallen out of favour, partly because of criticisms of its accuracy but also because it did not provide a sufficient colour check. It is, of course, not at any time available to southern observers.

A valid international system of photometry must enable different observers to produce essentially the same results. However, even if equipment at different observatories is constructed as nearly as possible to a standard pattern, differences will occur, and at any individual observatory atmospheric conditions and the transmission of lenses and the reflectivity of telescope mirrors will change with time. Individual instruments tend to have natural systems of colour and magnitude of their own, and the results have to be converted by numerical transformations to the international system. In many cases these transformations are linear functions of magnitude and colour in which the constants have to be determined from observations of standard stars. To determine these constants accurately a large colour range in the standard stars is required. A defect of the North Polar Sequence was that it did not contain any very blue stars which made the establishment of colour conversion difficult. Readers of photometric literature will continually encounter conversions of various kinds. As an example, we choose at random the conversion proposed in 1958 from the Cape photographic photometric data, with photovisual magnitudes denoted by SPv, and colour indices denoted by $S'CI$, to the photoelectric system, denoted by B, V described below. These were

$$V = SPv + 0.082 \ S'CI + 0.008 \ (S'CI)^2 - 0.06$$

$$B - V = 0.87 \ S'CI + 0.28$$

The differences between the two systems are not small, but conversions of this kind enable them to be precisely expressed.

Since World War II, the photomultiplier tube has become the sensitive receiver of almost universal use. Photoelectric measures made with ordinary photocells date back to before World War I, but the multiplier tube and linear amplifier have transformed photometry and produced a spate of new results. Two properties are especially important: one is the linearity of response which removes all doubt concerning the actual value of the steps in the logarithmic scale: the other is the vast range of brightness accessible to observation with few, if any, of the uncertainties which plague photographic methods when applied to faint stars. Prominently associated with the development of photoelectric systems of stellar magnitudes have been Stebbins and his numerous pupils at Madison, Wisconsin. The systematic introduction of photomultiplier tubes into photometry dates from an investigation by G. E. Kron in 1946, though there had been isolated experiments several years earlier.

2.11. The Photometric System of W. W. Morgan and H. L. Johnson

This was originally proposed as a rationalisation of the international system based on the North Polar Sequence with the addition of the third colour, the ultraviolet. It is the natural system of a reflecting telescope with aluminised mirrors using a 1 P 21 photomultiplier tube and a certain selection of filters.

The system was introduced in 1951 and uses three colour ranges now designated as U, B, V. The ultraviolet measure, U, is made through Corning filter No. 9863, and gives an overall response which peaks near 3,550Å. The mean is near 3,450Å, that is, at a wavelength definitely shorter than that of the Balmer discontinuity, and the band-width between 50 per cent points is about 500Å. The B-response is close to the photographic system, with a peak near 4,100Å, a mean near 4,350Å and a band-width of about 650Å. This is produced by Corning filter No. 5030 together with the minus ultraviolet glass GG 13 which prevents any contamination by short wavelength radiation. In the yellow, Corning filter No. 3384 is used giving a peak near 5,300Å, a mean at 5,500Å and a band-width of 600Å; it corresponds fairly closely to the response of the photovisual system. In 1953 Johnson and Morgan listed photoelectric measures of 340 stars together with their spectral classifications, and two years later Johnson published an even longer list with a greater variety of stellar types. This system of photometry has come to be widely used and may at the present time be regarded as standard, though it is not without its critics, and in more recent work observations have been made in a greater variety of colours. The lists which have been mentioned may be regarded as defining the system for a wide variety of individual stars and for a number of special sky areas and star clusters. It incorporates the convention that the colour indices B − V, and U − B are made zero for stars which we shall later classify as of spectral type A0V where the U, B, V measures have been corrected to eliminate the absorption of the atmosphere of the Earth. The zero-point of the visual magnitude scale was made to coincide with that of the North Polar Sequence, but this is not a point of any great importance. In the northern hemisphere the photometrist would use the best available photometric data for stars in the Johnson lists or in observations tied to them, and would not normally refer to the North Polar Sequence.

2.12. Developments in the Southern Hemisphere

In the southern hemisphere stellar photometry by photographic methods dates from the introduction of the Fabry method (described below) by R. O. Redman and E. G. Williams during the early part of World War II at the then uncompleted Radcliffe Observatory at Pretoria. The method was taken up by A. W. J. Cousins who later joined the Cape Observatory and made long series of observations. Photoelectric photometry was started there on a small scale in 1948 under the influence of R. H. Stoy, and, during his directorate photoelectric programmes at the Cape have undergone a great development. The Cape has been, up to the present, the major, though by no means the only, southern hemisphere producer. The original intention was to reproduce the international magnitude system in the southern sky, but lack of opportunities for comparison with northern results led in the first instance to the establishment of an independent southern system. To provide a widely distributed system of accurate colours and magnitudes a large programme on the E-regions was undertaken. These are a set of nine sky areas at declination − 45° designated by Harvard as areas for special study. Many hundreds of stars were observed in these areas, at first only in blue and yellow, but later in three colours. The programmes have broadened to include many other stars, and there have been, not only meticulous tie-ins with the Johnson stars, but also joint observational programmes from the two hemispheres of the equatorial zone of the sky. There is thus little uncertainty about the conversion from the natural systems of the Cape instruments to the U, B, V system. Results are now published on this system and in 1963 Cousins and Stoy published photometric data for some 6,000 southern stars. At the time this represented a better coverage by accurate photometry of, in general, the brighter stars, in the southern than in the northern sky. Details of the various filters and multiplier tubes employed on the various instruments with which these observations were made are listed in the introduction to the catalogue. These differ somewhat from those used by Johnson and transformations have been applied to the actual observations.

The range from the equivalent wavelength of B to the equivalent wavelength of V may be regarded as a base-line. If, for one reason or another, an observatory adopts a somewhat shorter or longer base-line, the measures of colour difference will be correspondingly smaller or larger, and will require multiplication by an appropriate factor to convert them to the standard system. The use of a physically thicker filter for a given colour will reduce all the instrumental responses in that colour, and will necessitate a change of zero point. Effects will also flow from the use of filters which have a smaller or larger band-width of transmission than the standard. For the most part the transformations required will be linear, although, occasionally, as in the example already cited, small high order terms may be introduced. After the application of transformations, first quality observations of the same star by different observatories on the same photometric system ought not to show discrepancies of more than one or two hundredths of a magnitude. However, even with good equipment and good climatic conditions not all published photometric results are of first quality.

A somewhat different situation arises in connection with the Cape practice, adopted in the first place because the observatory then had no reflector, of determining ultraviolet magnitudes with refractors. Here the glass of the objective imposes a cut-off in the near ultraviolet and moves the middle of the band to a point quite close to the Balmer discontinuity. Because of the roughly step formation of the stellar spectrum, the transformation from $(U - B)_c$, the notation used for a refractor ultraviolet colour index, to the Johnson U-B, is rather complicated, and involves B-V as well. Because the refractor measures of the ultraviolet did not reach such short wavelengths as those made with reflectors, they were at one time less highly regarded. The Lithuanian work already noted shows that the difference is smaller than previously thought: moreover, the refractor measures have a smaller band-width and greater stability than the reflector, and often have advantages for diagnostic purposes. Both systems are now in wide use at the Cape.

At the present time the U, B, V system is the one which has been most widely discussed in connection with other properties of stars, and is the most generally adopted by observers. It is, however, by no means the only one. The photometric work of Stebbins and Whitford employed six colours: the work initiated at the Leiden Southern Observatory in South Africa by Walraven used five colours, two of which were in the ultraviolet. The most recent work of Johnson uses eight, while Kron has pioneered photometry in the red and infra-red. The last named is of importance for redder stars where the radiation flux at short wavelengths is so small as to be but a poor indication of the star's emission of radiation. These developments have resulted from the improvement of receiver sensitivity and wavelength range, and presage still further developments in stellar photometry.

2.13. **Photoelectric Equipment**

Although the design of photoelectric equipment varies widely it is possible to sketch the essential features of apparatus suitable for routine work on stars of moderate brightness. By this is meant stars bright enough to be seen and identified with little trouble. The practical limit for a 24-inch telescope is probably round about the 14th magnitude. It is possible to observe invisible stars by a technique of off-setting from visible objects, but doing this immediately makes the work of a new order of difficulty.

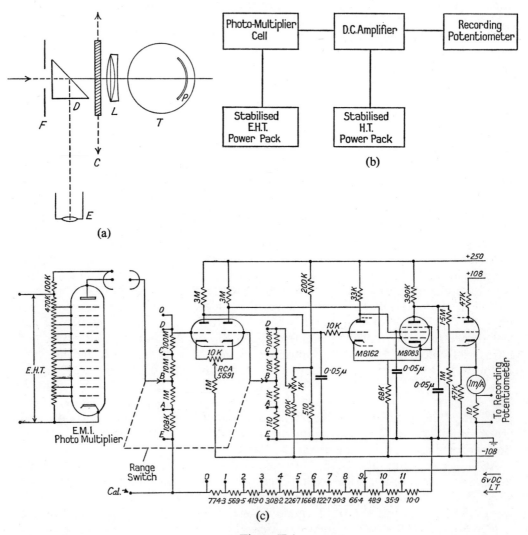

Figure II.4.

(a) Basic optics of a photoelectric photometer: The star is imaged at the focal plane, F, where one of a series of interchangeable diaphragms limits the field. For collimation check this can be viewed by the eyepiece, E, and the movable prism, withdrawn during observations; C is one of several filters, mounted on a slide for rapid interchange. The Fabry lens, L, images the entrance pupil of the telescope on the photocathode, P, of the multiplier tube, T. (b) Block diagram for a simple photometer. (c) A simple D.C. photometer.

The photometer mounted on the telescope receives light through a focal plane diaphragm of suitable size (Figure II.4(a, b, c). Diaphragms in the range from 10 to 60 seconds of arc are fairly commonly used, the choice being determined by the optical characteristics of the telescope, among the most important being image scale, and by seeing conditions. Filters or filter combinations are inserted to limit the incoming light to chosen wavelength ranges. The incoming light passes through a Fabry lens which images the objective of the telescope on the cathode of the photo-multiplier tube. This has the consequence that the same patch of cathode surface is used for all stars, and eliminates effects of variable sensitivity of this surface. It also reduces fluctuations due to scintillation. The photocurrent produced by the incoming light is fed to a very accurately linear amplifier. This is provided with a series of amplification settings changing in coarse and fine steps. In most of the Cape amplifiers coarse settings correspond to ratios of 10:1 (2·5 magnitudes) and fine settings to steps of one third of a magnitude. The setting chosen for each star is aimed at producing roughly the same recorder response for all stars. This avoids very large responses for bright stars and very small ones for faint stars. The output from the amplifier is carried to a self-balancing potentiometer recorder, giving an effectively constant deflection for a constant incident intensity on the photometer. Scintillation and shot effect superpose random noise of greater or less importance on the constant deflections. When a star image is in the diaphragm the deflection corresponds to the starlight together with the sky light from the diaphragm area, for the filter and amplifier gain employed. To determine the deflection corresponding to starlight only, a determination of sky light is made by moving the telescope slightly so that the star no longer falls in the diaphragm. If the star is in a dense field such as a cluster with many faint stars, there may be difficulty in measuring their contribution which is included with the sky. If three-colour photometry is being undertaken, each complete star observation will consist of three measures of star plus sky, one in each colour, and three corresponding measures of sky light. While these observations are being made, a reading is made of a clinometer attached to the telescope which shows the instantaneous value of zenith distance (or its secant) at the moment of observation.

Basic equipment is more or less the same at most observatories but there are widely varying elaborations. These include cooling of the multiplier tube with solid carbon dioxide to minimise dark current, which is a fairly common practice. In other cases readings of deflections and of zenith distance are digitised and appear as printed numbers, or are even presented in a form ready for feeding into a computer.

2.14. Observations and Reductions

The observational programme is usually presented in the form of a list of unknown, or programme, stars, together with a list of standard stars of known magnitude and colour occupying the same general area of sky. Observations of the two groups of stars are intermingled. A standard at every third star is usual at the Cape. The results of an observing session are in groups of six, one group to each star, each being accompanied by a measure of zenith distance and a record of the amplifier gain employed. Subtraction of the sky readings from those of star plus sky gives a group of three numbers corresponding to measures of starlight alone in the three colours. These are first corrected for the known values of amplifier gain to give apparent magnitudes of each star at the moment of observation, each with reference to some arbitrary zero point. The values of the amplifier steps are re-calibrated several times a year but are usually very stable. In each colour the starlight has suffered some extinction in its passage through the atmosphere of the Earth. In magnitudes this is proportional to sec z, as long as z is not very large, the factor of proportionality being different for each colour and being found in separate investigations. At the Cape, the values for the filters corresponding to U, B, V are, on the average, 0·60, 0·35 and 0·20 magnitudes respectively. The factors for correction of *colours*, U − B, and B − V, are differences between these, namely 0·25 and 0·15 magnitudes respectively. To minimise the effects of these corrections, many programmes have been carried out at nearly constant zenith distance, so that any uncertainty in the values of these constants had only a very small effect. Cape practice is to correct the observed values to the zenith by applying corrections proportional to (sec z − 1), and then to examine values of extinction at the zenith by comparing observations of the standard stars with their adopted magnitudes and colours. The size and variation of these corrections indicate the quality of the night. From them running corrections are derived in visual magnitude and colour which are applied to the programme star results to yield final values of their observed magnitudes and colours.

2.15. A Technical Miscellany

The foregoing discussion by no means exhausts either the variety of practical methods or of theoretical concepts. We note briefly a few of the more important investigations. Between the wars, Greaves, Davidson and Martin of Greenwich, in a pioneer observational study of the continuum in stars of various kinds, introduced the concept of *Photometric Gradient*. This depends on the remark that if F_λ is the Planck function quoted earlier, then the differential of $\log_e F_\lambda$ with respect to $(1/\lambda)$ equals

$$5\lambda - (c_2/T)/(1 - \exp[-c_2/\lambda T])$$

If now we have two stars associated with temperatures T_1 and T_2 and we consider the ratio of their fluxes, and form

$$-\frac{d}{d(1/\lambda)} \log_e (F_1/F_2) = \phi_1 - \phi_2$$

$$\text{where } \phi = (c_2/T)/(1 - \exp(-c_2/\lambda T)$$

we call ϕ the photometric gradient of the star concerned. For a wavelength of, say, 4,000Å $= 4 \times 10^{-5}$ cm, and T, say, equal to 5,000°K, the quantity $c_2/\lambda T$ has a value of about 7, so that very nearly $\phi = c_2/T$. For higher temperatures this simple approximation ceases to be valid. Within its range the differential constructed above is independent of wavelength and depends only on the temperatures of the stars. To determine observationally the relative gradient of two stars thus requires only a determination of the relative emission of two stars at two different wavelengths, i.e. the measurement of F_1/F_2 at two wavelengths. If this is done with the same instrument at the same zenith distance or if atmospheric absorption is otherwise taken into account, instrumental and atmospheric effects can be got rid of. Most of the Greenwich work was done using wavelengths of 4,100 and 6,500Å. The results give differences of reciprocal colour temperatures, and require comparisons with a source of known temperature to enable actual temperatures to be evaluated. The standardisation of the Greenwich system led to the definition of a Greenwich gradient, G_G such that $\phi = G_G + 1 \cdot 11$ magnitudes and $G_G = 0$ for A0 stars. The terminology is still sometimes used but has fallen from prominence in recent years.

The description of the methods of photoelectric photometry given above has been in terms of static deflections of a suitable recorder. As an alternative a variety of integration methods can be used. Soon after the war, Yates, at Cambridge, introduced equipment which operated by counting the pulses due to the arrival of individual photons at the photocathode. Pulse counting methods are of special utility in the observation of extremely faint sources. A leader in this field is Baum at Mount Palomar who has used this technique on faint extragalactic nebulae employing integration times of very great length. The technique of integration can also be employed in a somewhat different way in ordinary routine photometry. In this application the cell output is measured as a current and not as a series of pulses, and is allowed to charge a capacitor for a certain standard integration time. The potential so built up is then recorded either on a digital voltmeter or in the form of a numerical print-out. The method has advantages in smoothing out current variations due to circuit noise and twinkling of the stars, and is, for example, now in routine use at the Cape where an integration time of 30 seconds is normally employed.

The U, B, V system of photometry is sometimes called a broad-band system because of the considerable band-widths of the filters. In recent years a considerable development has taken place in narrow-band photometry, either using interference filters which pass only a few ångströms of spectrum or by selecting a short range from a high dispersion spectrum. The techniques, associated first with the names of Strömgren and Gyldenkerne, and later, especially with the Cambridge workers under Redman, have been concerned with the photoelectric evaluation of particular spectral features. The total strength of a strong line, such as a Balmer line, can, for example, be related empirically to the results of three narrow-band measures, one on each side of the line and one at the position of the line itself. Strengths of band-heads can be expressed numerically by comparing responses from two narrow-band filters placed on either side of the band-head. The difference indicates the extent of the discontinuity associated with the band-head, just as, in a rather rough way, the ordinary U and B measures give some indication of the size of the Balmer discontinuity. Since narrow-band filters transmit so much less energy than broad-band ones, the magnitude limit for narrow-band studies applies to much brighter stars than in the latter case. In certain observatories equipment is available which can scan along a spectrum and produce photoelectrically the same kind of scan which we encounter later in dealing with photographic spectrophotometry.

One of the few investigations which has resulted in the photometry of stars in the ordinary energy units of physics was that undertaken some years ago by Willstrop at the Cape. Any such investigation demands the use of a terrestrial source with a calibrated output. The standard difficulty has always been the enormous disparity in colour between the low temperature terrestrial source and even the coolest of stars. This difficulty was, for example, encountered by Greaves and his associates in the calibration of photometric gradients. In Willstrop's work this difficulty was surmounted by the use of carefully designed filters such that, when they were combined with the terrestial source, a much better colour match with the stars was produced.

The determination of the transmission of the filters at various wavelengths was then a laboratory investigation which could be carried out with high precision.

The group of French workers headed by Chalonge have made an approach to the study of stellar continua which differs considerably from that of the normal U, B, V photometry. The radiation distribution received is characterised by the following three parameters: (i) The height of the Balmer discontinuity expressed as the common logarithm of the ratio of the intensities of the continua to the long and short wave sides of the discontinuity, i.e. if $D = 0.3$ the intensity drops rapidly to 50 per cent of its value on crossing to the short wave side; (ii) the wavelength of the mid-point of the sudden decrease. This is called λ_1 and runs from a minimum value of about 3,703Å for the brightest A stars with the strongest Balmer lines to near 3,760Å for the hottest B stars and for cooler stars in which metallic lines are prominent. It never reaches the Balmer series band-head wavelength because only a limited number of Balmer lines is ever seen, and indeed, the number of the last visible line is used as a criterion of atmospheric electron pressure; (iii) the blue spectrophotometric gradient, ϕ_b, determined for the range 3,800-4,800Å. This is ϕ as defined above, not the Greenwich system, G_G.

These parameters have been correlated with spectral classes and luminosities (see below), but the amount of photometry done in this system is much less than the vast mass using U, B, V.

2.16. Photographic Photometry

From the earliest introduction of the photographic plate into astronomy it has been obvious that a brighter star makes more of an impression than a fainter one, but the choice of feature to express this with precision has varied. Image diameter for an exposure under standard conditions was once used, but has now been superseded. A method giving results of fairly high precision has been mentioned: this is the Fabry method, utilising the fact that it is possible to measure the density of a uniform patch on a photographic plate with considerable accuracy. In this method the objective was imaged on to the plate by a Fabry lens, so that all stars, no matter how bright were imaged as a uniform patch of the same size. The density of the patch under carefully controlled conditions of exposure and processing could be used as an index of the brightness of the star responsible. The method is equivalent to measuring the brightness of the illumination produced by the star on the objective of the telescope. Calibration was usually achieved by impressing on part of the plate not used for the astronomical exposure a series of spots produced by light sources of known intensity ratio with an exposure time as nearly equal to the stellar exposure times as possible. A common means of doing this was by means of a tube sensitometer.

The tube sensitometer is an extremely simple instrument, illustrated in Figure II.5. The intensity of illumination at the exit ends of the tubes is proportional to the area of the hole at the entrance end, if the tube assembly is pointed towards a uniformly illuminated source area. The source area can be an unglazed tile or a magnesium carbonate block, and uniform illumination can be secured by illuminating it from a source at a considerable distance. The tubes themselves should have liners in them to stop extraneous light entering by reflection at grazing incidence along the walls of the tube. If these are omitted each exit patch will be seen to have a zone of higher intensity at its outer edge. The liners should not, of course, encroach on any direct ray from the entrance area to the exit area of any tube. The entrance areas are chosen to give a good range of densities of the exit patches, and calibration is by measurement of the entrance areas, which are normally circular. When exposed patches are placed on an unused part of a photographic plate, of which another part carries Fabry patches produced by stellar exposures, it is possible to determine the relative intensities produced by the stars. This topic is discussed in more detail below.

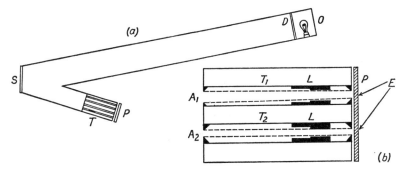

Figure II.5: A Tube Sensitometer.

(a) Shows the general arrangement: O is a light source, D an opal glass diffuser, S the source area, T the tubes, and P the photographic plate. (b) Shows detail of tubes, T_1 and T_2, with entrance areas, A_1 and A_2, producing patches, E, on the plate. LL are suitable liners to stop internal reflections. All the structures are internally blackened.

Another method for replacing star images by uniform patches is that of the schraffierkassette or "jiggle camera" in which the photographic plate is oscillated during exposure by means of uniform motion cams, so that each image is replaced by a uniform rectangular exposed patch. This technique has been used for the determination of the magnitudes of distant galaxies. It is sometimes rather difficult to secure proper conditions of operation, but the method has the advantage over the Fabry method of allowing a number of objects scattered over the plate to be observed simultaneously. Attention must then usually be paid to systematic variations with distance from the centre of the field.

Modern methods of photographic photometry depend on the measurement of the total blackening in a star image by means of one of several available kinds of instrument. We recall that, even with perfect guiding during exposure, the image of a star on a photographic plate is not a geometrical point. Turbulence in the atmosphere of the Earth causes rapid and erratic wandering, to which must be added diffraction effects due to the finite size of the entrance pupil of the telescope, and the effects of image spread and graininess in the emulsion. Even for faint stars the centre of a stellar image is usually saturated, that is, all the grains in the emulsion capable of being developed are actually developed there. All the effects mentioned above produce a spreading of the image so that, on microscopic examination every star image is seen to be at best, a circularly symmetrical distribution of density which rises to a maximum at the centre. A graph of density along any radius gives a bell-shaped curve which falls to a minimum value defined by the level of sky fog plus fog due to chemical effects. We have so far used the term *Density* in a general sense. It also has a strict definition: If a parallel beam of light of intensity I_0 falls normally on an area of a developed photographic plate and a beam of intensity, I_t, is transmitted, then the density of the exposed area is

$$D = \log_{10} I_0/I_t$$

Thus a density of unity transmits ten per cent of the incident light. This is the straightforward way of measuring photographic densities, and gives the numerical basis for the measurement of photographic densities whether produced by Fabry or jiggle camera methods, or by a tube sensitometer.

A light source is mounted so that it illuminates uniformly a slit or diaphragm, which is then imaged on to the surface of the photographic plate by a suitable lens

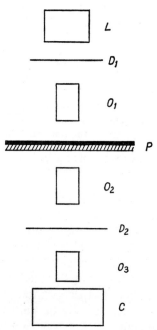

Figure II.6: Schematics of devices for measuring photographic density. L: Light source. D_1: Plane of first diaphragm. O_1: Optics imaging diaphragm on to the plate, P, which can be moved in its own plane, manually or mechanically. O_2: Optics receiving transmitted light, and imaging on to D_2 (second diaphragm, if present). O_3: optics feeding light to photocell, C.

system. The light passing through the area of plate so defined is then imaged by further optics on to a suitable photocell, or in older instruments a thermocouple, which is then connected to a suitable recorder. In some cases a second diaphragm is inserted in the later part of the train so that this, rather than the first, limits the area of plate analysed. The response of the recorder can then be used to measure density in the strict sense of the foregoing definition (Figure II.6). The practical approach can be more empirical. If the recorder reading is r_d when the incident light is cut off altogether, and is r_c for a part of the plate which has not been exposed to light, we can form a quantity $(r - r_c)/(r_d - r_c)$, which is zero for unexposed areas of the plate, and unity for very heavily exposed areas. It measures the blackening of the plate produced by the light intensity incident on it during exposure. If the recorder is linear in its response, the quantity is closely related to $(1 - T)$, where T is the transmission of the exposed area of plate $= I_t/I_0$.

For a given calibrated plate we can use the sensitometer spots to draw a characteristic curve relating blackening to exposure, usually in the form of log (intensity). Whatever photographic parameter is plotted the characteristic curve has a similar form. For low intensities response is at first zero and then increases slowly, to form a "toe". The mid-section of the curve is an inclined straight line (the straight-line portion), while the upper part, corresponding to strong exposure bends over (the "shoulder" of the curve) as saturation sets in due to all available photographic grains being developed. The general style is illustrated in Figure II.7. The same kind of curve is obtained for exposure at constant intensity for different lengths of time.

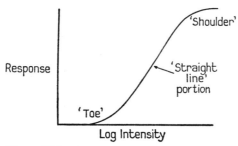

Figure II.7: Photographic calibration curve.

If the photometric device is modified so as to measure the total blackening in a stellar image a similar kind of characteristic curve is obtained. In this kind of instrument a circular area of illumination is formed on a photograph of a star field by means of a diaphragm. Total obstruction produced by a star image is then measured by comparing the readings when there is no star in the field, and when the plate is moved so as to bring a required star image into the diaphragm. Calibration is effected by having a sequence of stars of known magnitude on the plate in the way already described, and distance corrections depending on the distance of a star from the centre of the field may have to be applied. The calibration curve will resemble the one illustrated if a constant diaphragm size is used. For faint stars, i.e. ones of which the images are very small compared with the area of the diaphragm, the reading will be insensitive to magnitude. Then will come a range within which response is more or less linear, and above this a range within which the star image blocks out most of the light passing through the diaphragm. Choice of diaphragm size, associated with plates of a certain exposure time, thus limits measures to a certain range of magnitude. The fixed diaphragm size also imposes limitations on the closest distance at which two images can be measured separately, and in dense star fields may make it hard to find an area in which to get a "no star" reading. The instrument with a fixed diaphragm size is associated with the name of Schilt. More recently newer versions, associated with the names of Eichner, Haffner (Sartorius), and Becker have been produced. These are iris diaphragm instruments in which the diaphragm is variable and a reading is made by finding the diaphragm diameter for a certain constant reading. The diaphragm is closed down for fainter stars and thus some of the difficulties associated with dense fields are avoided. In these instruments the operator can see the star field and choose the image to be measured by means of various kinds of optical projection scheme. The cartesian coordinates of the images can either be read or set so as to facilitate identification. Different astronomers have personal preferences for machines of different types. At best very high rates of measuring have been achieved.

As in the case of photoelectric photometry, attention will have to be paid to conversion of observed magnitudes to standard systems. A blue sensitive plate such as Kodak IIa-O or 103a-O plus a minus ultraviolet filter such as GG13 will produce blue magnitudes fairly close to the B system, while a panchromatic plate, such as 103a-D plus a yellow filter such as Omag 301 will give an approximation to the V magnitude system. In many observatories twin telescopes or cameras on the same mounting are used to make the photographs in the two colours simultaneously, thus eliminating some of the effects of atmospheric variation. In reflecting telescopes of conventional Newtonian design off-axis aberrations such as coma come in very rapidly with increasing distance from the centre of the field. Coma spreads the same total intensity of light over a larger area, and because of the saturation characteristics of the photographic plate a given total illumination produces more blackening in a comatic image than in an aberration-free one. The larger the distance corrections the less accurate they become, and reflectors are often diaphragmed to reduce the aperture, thus extending the useful angular field on the plate. In instruments with more sophisticated optics which produce good images over a very large angular area, e.g. several degrees across, difficulties are sometimes encountered with variable vignetting of the field produced by the rather complicated systems of stops which these instruments sometimes contain.

Photographic photometry is not usually as accurate as photoelectric photometry, though it is often very much faster because the actual measures are done in bulk in the laboratory. The photographic density produced by the star-free night sky can often be considerable. What is more insidious is the presence of faint stars, possibly in the form of fairly dense clouds, too weak to be registered individually. Owing to the non-linear properties of the photographic plate a faint star which is not itself recorded may perceptibly alter the reading for a brighter star with which its light may be combined. The photoelectric observer who actually examines the sky often has a better chance of noting the presence of these near companions than the operator who only sees a photograph.

2.17. Direct Photography

So much has already been said by implication that little further is required. Direct photography of an area of sky would seem to be the simplest of operations. Correct focus must, of course, be assured. With refracting telescopes having iron tubes there are usually only slight difficulties, since the effects of variation of temperature on the glass and metal happen practically to compensate each other. Reflecting telescopes require a focus test at the beginning of the night, and once or twice later depending on the rate at which the temperature falls. Once the temperature has become stable the observer using a Newtonian instrument operating at, say, f/5, need usually only make rather infrequent focus tests. These are done by means of the Foucault test. A knife edge is moved in at the focal plane with the telescope pointed at a moderately bright star. The observer looks at the main mirror directly. As the knife edge cuts into the cone of starlight he will see a shadow cross the mirror, in one direction if the knife edge is outside focus, in the opposite direction if it is inside focus. When the knife edge is precisely at focus the knife edge is cutting into a star image slightly spread by seeing and diffraction. If it were a true point the mirror would darken all over simultaneously. As it is not he usually sees a general shadow pattern, rendered unstable by seeing fluctuations, which covers the mirror nearly simultaneously and coming in in a direction perpendicular to the movement of the knife edge. It is usual to knife-edge in two perpendicular directions since stellar images are slightly elongated perpendicular to the horizon by differential atmospheric refraction which is more pronounced for blue light than for red. The compromise position usually produces the smallest and roundest star images.

In some telescopes, such as those of the Schmidt pattern, where the focus is extremely critical, special compensating devices are sometimes fitted to remove changes of focus caused by variations of temperature. In any instrument the observer can always determine the best focus by taking a series of short exposures of a fairly bright star, slightly displaced from each other, at different focal settings, and choosing the focal setting corresponding to the best of the series.

For anything but the shortest exposures it is usually necessary to guide so as to compensate for a variety of effects. These include errors in drive rate, misadjustment of the polar axis inclination (it cannot be correct for all accessible declinations except at the poles of the Earth), and variation of refraction. Occasionally, as in photography of fast-moving objects such as comets or minor planets, the telescope has to have small changes of setting during the exposure so as to follow the moving object. In such a case the star images come out as short trails. In the normal case guiding is either done by means of cross-wires in the eyepiece of a telescope on the same mounting carefully collimated with the main instrument, or by moving the plate holder by means of screws provided. In the former case the cross-wires are set on a suitable guide star. In the latter the guide star is picked out from the edge of the field being photographed by means of an optical train involving one or more prisms and an eyepiece. This is adjusted so as to bring a suitable guide star on to the eyepiece cross-wires after the telescope has been set and before the exposure commences. In a reflector the star image used in the latter case may be markedly comatic. The guide setting should be made on the centre of light of the comatic image, since this will not change if the quality of the seeing alters during the exposure. Some modern telescopes are fitted with automatic photoelectric guiders.

Direct photography, that is, making a picture of an area of sky, is the maid of all work of astronomy, and takes many different forms. We have noted the cases of parallax and proper motion plates and of astrometric charting earlier. In addition it can be used for records of planets and comets, star clusters, emission nebulae, and deep sky objects such as extragalactic nebulae. All kinds of filters can be used, some passing a wide range of wavelength, others only a few ångströms. In the former class we have noted filters to exclude the ultraviolet, to restrict registration to the yellow region, and a whole gamut of plate and filter combinations is available for registering other broad spectral regions. Narrow pass filters such as interference filters passing only a few ångströms are now available. A red-sensitive emulsion behind a filter tailored to the wavelength of the H-alpha Balmer line will show up the distribution of hydrogen in an object.

Sometimes more than one filter may be used with the same plate. Repeat exposures on the same area, one with an ultraviolet pass, and one with a red pass, slightly displaced from each other, will show objects especially strong in the ultraviolet. With a refractor, in which the foci for different colours are slightly different, super-posed exposures in blue and red will produce a sharp blue image surrounded by a ring due to red light. The appearance of the combination will change according to the type of star producing the image, and this may be used for picking out stars of different kinds. There is almost no end to the variety of techniques which can be devised.

The subject is too wide for adequate discussion here, but mention must be made of the possibilities of increasing the effective speed of photographic emulsions by various treatments. At one time chemical methods, such as placing a plate in a box along with a globule of mercury, were much in favour, but this is exceedingly dangerous, since other plates in the same dark room can be affected. The methods most used at present are baking of plates in a suitable oven at a controlled tempera-ture for a number of hours, and pre or post exposure of the emulsion to a controlled light source. This topic has been discussed at length by William C. Miller of Mount Palomar Observatory. The essential point is that the treatment must be fitted to the type of emulsion and to the use intended to be made of it. An unintelligent or un-discriminating use of these techniques will do more harm than good.

2.18. The Effects of Focal Ratio

If photographs of the same star field are taken with two different telescopes, there will, naturally be some resemblance between them, but there will also be important differences. Stars and other point sources will be imaged more strongly in a given time with the larger telescope. This follows because the total intensity of incident light packed into a given image is, other things being equal, proportional to the area of the objective. If we neglect losses due to absorption in lenses, reflection losses, and losses due to obscuration by secondary mirrors, this area can often be roughly represented by the square of the aperture of the telescope. The scale of the picture is proportional to the focal length, that is, quite apart from any considerations of aperture, the image distance between two stars will be proportional to the focal length of the telescope. Even if we put the photographs taken with different instruments into an enlarger and blow them to the same scale, there will be differences in the representation of areas of continuous brightness.

Consider for example a circular area of constant brightness. On the photographic plate this will be imaged as a circle of which the diameter is proportional to the focal length, f. The total light energy which goes to form this image will be proportional to the square of the aperture, D. Thus the intensity of the image of a certain extended source on the photographic plate will be proportional to D^2/f^2, that is, inversely as the square of the f-number or focal ratio. This is the commonplace rule of the amateur photographer, and applies equally to astronomical instruments. A refracting tele-scope working at f/15 will thus image extended areas of brightness only one-ninth as brightly as a Newtonian instrument of the same aperture working at f/5. A relatively short exposure on the latter instrument may thus show areas of luminosity which are so faint that their images never get off the toe of the responsive curve even with a long exposure on the former instrument.

Photographs taken with still smaller f-numbers would still further enhance the relative prominence of the continuous luminosity on the final product. A series of different instrument designs is available nowadays which are variants on the original design of Bernard Schmidt of Hamburg. Compare these with the classic Newtonian reflector with a parabolic main mirror. This has a definite axis and as we have seen, off-axis images deteriorate rapidly with increasing distance, becoming noticeably aberrant only a few minutes of arc off axis. If the parabolic mirror were replaced by a spherical one, the images everywhere would be subject to sensible aberrations, but they would be the same everywhere, since a spherical mirror has no preferred axis of symmetry. In the Schmidt camera the main mirror is spherical, and the image is formed on a curved surface concentric with this. Aberrations of image formation are

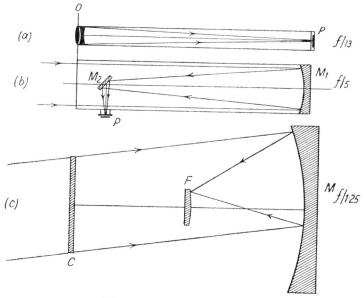

Figure II.8: Types of telescope.
(a) Refractor with doublet objective O, and photographic plate, P. (b) Newtonian reflector, with parabolic main mirror, M_1, plane secondary mirror, M_2, and photographic plate, P. (c) Formation of an off-axis image in a Schmidt camera: C is the corrector plate, M, the spherical main mirror, and F is the curved focal surface to which a film or plate must be bent.

removed by means of a correcting plate in the plane of the centre of curvature of the primary mirror. This correcting plate is a large thin lens of low power figured to a carefully computed aspheric form. Characteristics of the Schmidt system are: The field of good image formation is very large—a diameter of 5 degrees may be taken as typical; the f-number is normally small so that the representation of continuous luminosity is very good. Reference to Figure II.8 will show that the diameter of the correcting plate has to be smaller than that of the main mirror to permit the use of a large field, and that different parts of the main mirror are used in imaging different parts of the field. A very high standard of uniformity of reflectivity of the main mirror is therefore required. The curvature of the focal surface necessitates the use of films or the bending of thin glass plates with a risk of breakages. The telescope tube is twice as long as that for a Newtonian reflector of the same aperture and focal length. The Palomar Schmidt, used to make the National Geographic Survey of the whole of the northern and part of the southern sky, has a correcting plate aperture of 48 inches, a main mirror of 72 inches diameter, an f-number of 2·5 and a scale of 67"·5/mm. The linear scale of many Schmidt photographs is small, but the high resolution allows them to be enlarged many times.

Schmidt-type systems are used in television cameras, as spectrograph cameras and for many other purposes. The limiting f-number attainable with glass-in-air optics is 0·5, and in practice this cannot be reached. To attain values of this sort or even smaller, oil immersion optics are sometimes used, or Schmidt cameras are constructed out of a single block of glass with all the optical surfaces figured on suitable faces fixed rigidly in their proper relationship. These highly-bred optics are all small in size and are mainly applied in spectrographs.

Full-sized telescopes used for celestial photography which derive from the Schmidt system and share its characteristics of large field and high speed are the Baker-Schmidt, the Baker-Nunn (used in satellite tracking), the Maksutov system, and the reflector-corrector system. The last named has a parabolic mirror, an annular corrector plate in the focal plane of the mirror (so that the telescope tube is no longer than that of a Newtonian instrument) and a further field flattening lens some distance in front of the photographic plate, to allow flat plates to be used.

2.19. The Measurement of Radial Velocities

The radial velocity of an astronomical object is its component of motion towards or away from the observer in the line of sight. Radial velocities are one of the few astronomical parameters which are measurable directly in ordinary physical units, in this case, kilometres per second. The method depends on the Doppler-Fizeau principle which may be stated as follows. Given a wavelength λ of electromagnetic radiation emitted from a luminous source which has a radial velocity relative to the observer of v, then the wavelength measured by the observer will differ from that emitted by a quantity $\Delta\lambda$ given by

$$\Delta\lambda/\lambda = v/c$$

where c is the velocity of light, and velocities of recession are counted positive. Relativity theory predicts a small effect due to transverse motion, but this has, so far, only been taken into account in very accurate radar observations of the planets.

If stellar spectra consisted of emission lines of known origin, radial velocities might be measured by direct comparison of the same spectrum line emitted from an astronomical and a terrestrial source. Most stellar spectra consist mainly of absorption lines, which are not simple, but blends, but extensive studies of stellar spectra from the point of view of the measurement of radial velocities have been made, especially in recent years by R. M. Petrie and his colleagues in Canada, and we may assume that good values of wavelength are available for a selection of absorption lines in stellar spectra from most kinds of star. One of the most useful terrestrial sources of spectrum lines is the iron arc which produces large numbers of spectrum lines in emission of which the wavelengths are accurately known. The basic principle of the method is then to obtain spectra of a star and of a terrestrial source, such as an iron arc, on the same plate at the same time with the same spectrograph, and to determine the displacement of the stellar source using the lines of the comparison spectrum to provide a wavelength scale all along the spectrum by a process of interpolation.

Most determinations of stellar radial velocities are made with blue sensitive plates, and all the spectrum lines measured lie in the range from 3,800Å to 4,900Å. At 4,000Å a radial velocity of 1 km/s produces a wavelength shift of a little over 0·01Å. Most spectrographs used for radial velocity determinations have dispersions in the range from 10Å/mm to 100Å/mm, so that a radial velocity of 1 km/s produces a line shift of about 1 micron at the high dispersion end of the instrumental range and one-tenth of this for the lowest dispersions commonly used. Among relatively bright stars radial velocities with numerical values up to some 30km/s are common, values in excess of 100km/s are unusual, and values over 200km/s are rare. In all cases the Doppler displacements are small and must be measured with great care. Accuracy of results depends on the dispersion and resolution of the spectrograph, the care taken

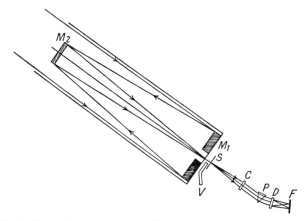

Figure II.9: Schematic arrangement of Cassegrain spectrograph. M_1: Main mirror. M_2: Hyperbolic secondary mirror. S: Plane of slit. V: Viewing device for seeing star image on the slit. C: Collimator producing a parallel beam. P: Prism. D: Camera lens. F: Plate at focal plane of the camera.

by the observer and the character of the lines in the stellar spectrum. The real probable error of a stellar radial velocity determined from four measures made on separate occasions is rarely better than 0·3km/s and may go up to 5 or 10km/s in the most unfavourable cases.

A great proportion of radial velocity measures has been made using spectrographs mounted at the Cassegrain foci of large reflectors. This arrangement is illustrated in Figure II.9. Incoming starlight is reflected at the main mirror, returned down the tube by a convex hyperboloid secondary mirror mounted near the top of the tube, and comes to a focus in a plane just behind the mirror cell having passed through a hole in the main mirror. Focus is adjusted by moving the secondary mirror up and down the tube. The spectrograph is mounted on the back of the mirror cell where it can be fixed very rigidly with its centre of gravity fairly close to the declination axis of the telescope. This arrangement facilitates balancing of the instrument. The focal length of the Cassegrain form is large, usually giving an f-number of about 18, with a good scale at the slit of the spectrograph. The star image is focused on the plane of the slit, the starlight which passes through it enters the collimator where it becomes a parallel beam, and then enters the dispersing system of the spectrograph, which may consist of one or more prisms or a diffraction grating. So that no starlight is wasted the f-number of the collimator is made equal to that of the Cassegrain form of the telescope. To ensure accurate measurement of radial velocities the collimator must be exactly aligned so that the incoming cone of star light just fills it. After dispersion the light is brought to a focus either by a camera lens or, usually, when high speed and low dispersion are required, by a Schmidt camera system. Since the star image on the slit of the spectrograph is a point or a small blob, this produces a thin streak of spectrum on the plate. To make its details measurable this must be broadened. This is achieved either by having the observer guide the telescope so as to run the star image back and forth along the slit, which he can do because he has a viewing system which enables him to see the blob of light bisected by the dark line of the slit, or there is a rotating, square-sectioned, prism just behind the slit which broadens the spectrum while the star is kept fixed on the slit. Opinions differ as to which method is preferable. The overall speed of the equipment depends on a number of factors each of which plays a part in determining the brightness of the spectrum on the plate. The length of trail along the slit is one such factor. The slit width can be adjusted so as to let in more light up to the limit at which slit width becomes comparable with image diameter. The price of this gain is a loss of resolution of image detail on the plate. Since the f-number of the collimator has to match that of the telescope, and the diameter of the camera lens is equal to, or only slightly larger than that of the collimator, the scale on the plate in the direction of the slit is reduced as compared with that of the telescope in the ratio of their f-numbers. This is equivalent to saying that, along the slit, the scale is that of a telescope having the same diameter as the actual one, and an f-number equal to that of the camera.

In the direction of the dispersion the spectrum scale is proportional to the dispersive power of the spectrograph and to the camera focal length, and the projected slit width for a given slit opening in the focal plane of the telescope, is also proportional to the latter. Effective resolution also depends on the relation between image size and photographic grain. There are thus a considerable number of disposable parameters in the optimum operation of a stellar spectrograph, and only experience will produce the best compromise between such competing factors as loss of light due to the use of a narrow slit, and gain of resolution and measuring accuracy. To fix the ideas, we quote the example of the Cassegrain spectrograph of the Radcliffe observatory 74-inch reflector at Pretoria. This has a Cassegrain focus of f/18, giving a scale of 6"/mm on the slit. Data for three camera lenses are tabulated below:

Camera lens	Dispersion (A/mm)	Slit width (mm)	Limiting Magnitude 1 hour, II-aO
f/6	29	0·050	8·6
f/3·7	49	·075	9·8
f/2	84	·100	11·2

The limiting magnitude is much affected by seeing conditions and by variations in reflectivity of the telescope mirrors with age.

2.20. Observational Procedure

On the photographic plate each stellar spectrum appears flanked on either side by a comparison spectrum, often that of an iron arc. This is imposed using the ends of the slit, through a prism system, immediately before and immediately after the stellar exposure. The star is then centred on the slit and the image trailed up and down by one of the methods already mentioned. With a long focal length, images at a considerable zenith distance show pronounced elongation due to atmospheric refraction. The star images are themselves tiny spectra when they arrive at the telescope. This can make guiding difficult and introduce errors, because the wavelength region recorded on the plate is distinctly bluer than that to which the eye is most sensitive. If the atmospheric spectrum is at an angle to the slit, the star may be guided on the wrong part of it, so that the collimator is filled asymmetrically with the light which will affect the photographic plate. A way of getting over this is to mount the spectrograph on the telescope through a rotatable ring. The whole spectrograph can then be turned so as to place the slit in the direction of atmospheric dispersion rather than in its normal east-west position. Use of this facility demands that the axis of the spectrograph collimator should coincide very closely with the mechanical axis about which the rotation takes place. The same facility can be used to obtain separate spectra of components of a double star. In this case the spectrograph is turned so that the slit is roughly perpendicular to the line joining the two stars. It is usually found that to obtain accurate results exposure times of at least ten minutes must be used so as to smooth out guiding errors. These arise partly because of image movement produced by seeing in the Earth's atmosphere, independently of the perfection of the drive mechanism of the telescope. If a bright star is to be observed on a low dispersion a neutral filter is used to reduce the starlight and to bring the exposure time above ten minutes. The reason for doing this is to provide a check on systematic errors of measured radial velocities by having a set of standard stars some of which are observed each night with whatever spectrograph camera is in use. In good climates exposure times can usually be judged from experience, but in bad conditions exposure meters may be useful. These take a variety of forms but usually depend on funneling a small proportion of the incident light to a photocell connected to circuitry which integrates the total intensity and signals when a certain total has been reached.

An important source of error in the measurement of radial velocities is flexure. It is a difficult matter to maintain the optical components of a precise instrument exactly in their designed relative positions while this instrument is turned into all kinds of postures with the movements of the telescope. Careful design can overcome the worst effects, but slight flexures must occur, and it is for this reason that the iron arc comparison spectra are imprinted in two or more partial exposures, with the spectrograph inclined as it is for the corresponding stellar exposure.

2.21. Measurement and Reduction of Spectra

The appearance of an exposed plate is indicated in Figure II.10. The light from the star has produced the stellar spectrum in the form of a blackened strip in the centre. This is crossed by two absorption lines which appear as white streaks. Above and below are lines of the comparison spectrum, which being in emission have produced narrow black lines on the negative. If the comparison spectrum is that of an iron arc, and if the stellar lines are due to iron in the stellar atmosphere, as a first approximation the displacement of the stellar lines as compared with the comparison lines, which is seen to be towards the right (longer wavelength) can be measured and attributed to a velocity of recession of the star, which can then be calculated. The practical method is an elaboration of this. For the determination of radial velocity a number of spectrum lines, perhaps as many as thirty per plate, if available, are measured. Star lines are often blends of lines due to several different elements. The

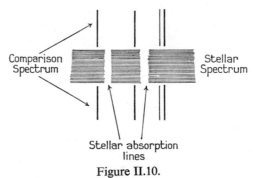

Figure II.10.

wavelengths found from laboratory studies on pure substances cannot be used. Empirical values of wavelength are then adopted from experience, and special attention is given to lines of which the wavelengths show little variation with stellar properties. Because of the variation in character of stellar spectra with temperature and other features, discussed in more detail below, the selection of spectrum lines suitable for hot stars is quite different from the selection used for cooler stars. The Canadian workers under the leadership of R. M. Petrie have made extensive studies of this problem and have produced recommended sets of standard lines and their wavelengths which are widely used. Much work has also been done on selecting the best lines in comparison spectra, especially those of iron and neon. To minimise certain kinds of measuring error it is usual to measure spectrum plates in both directions, e.g. from blue to red, and then from red to blue, and to work all calculations in terms of the difference quantities, "Direct *minus* Reverse".

Standard procedure is to provide for each camera of each spectrograph, tables of measures in millimetres, correct to the nearest micron, of the positions of all the comparison and star lines to be used. These will be computed by means of a Hartmann formula of the type, $\lambda - \lambda_0 = \text{constant}/(n_0 - n)$ where n is the measure, for a prism spectrograph, or by means of a linear formula for a grating spectrograph. These tables will be arranged so that a certain selected line near the middle of the spectrum, e.g. the Fe line in the comparison spectrum at 4,202Å, comes at a certain standard reading, e.g. 60·000 mm. The plate is set up on the stage of the measuring machine and the selected star and comparison lines measured as they are encountered, starting at the blue end of the range. The plate is then reversed and the measures repeated. Differences "Direct *minus* Reverse" are then formed and compared with the tabulated values. Differences will occur in the values for the comparison spectrum, partly because the plate may not have been perfectly positioned, partly because the formulae are not perfect, and partly because of slight variations of conditions of exposure. For example, all large prism spectrographs are kept in temperature-regulated enclosures, since dispersion varies with temperature, but the thermostat setting will usually be varied between hot and cold weather. A graph of the differences between the observed and tabular values for the comparison lines shows what corrections must be applied to these and to the star line measures to bring them on to the system represented by the formula. In the latter case there will still be residual differences, and these we attribute to the Doppler displacement of the stellar lines. For each line we have previously computed tables showing the radial velocity in kilometres per second corresponding to a difference of one micron in the "Direct *minus* Reverse" measures. Each stellar line yields a radial velocity measure: in the best cases they are closely accordant. The result for the plate is given by the mean, and is associated with the probable error determined from the scatter in the results.

This mean value requires further correction resulting from the fact that the telescope with which the spectrum was obtained had the motion of the Earth in its orbit and the motion of the Earth on its axis. The latter is zero for objects observed on the meridian, and its maximum possible value is only about 0·4 km/s (the equatorial velocity of the Earth) which could only be attained for objects observed just at rising or setting on the celestial equator. Corrections are applied, although except for spectra at fairly high dispersion it is doubtful whether the velocity measures are accurate enough to warrant this.

The orbital motion of the Earth varies from 29·3 km/s to 30·3 km/s according to the season of the year, and its direction is in the plane of the ecliptic and always within a degree of perpendicularity to the line joining Earth and Sun. An exact formula giving the component of this motion along the line from Earth to star is used. This has to be added to the observed radial velocity to give the heliocentric radial velocity of the star. The correction is zero for a star observed on the meridian at local midnight, is negative for stars observed on the meridian during the evening, and the positive for stars observed on the meridian during the morning hours.

Certain technical improvements may be noted. Measuring machines are now often digitised and measures are produced in the form of punched cards ready for feeding into a computer. Measurement by visual estimation of the correct position of the cross wire in the eyepiece of a measuring machine with respect to a very broad spectrum line, such as a Balmer line in an A-type star, is often very inaccurate. Cathode ray displays have been developed to identify the line centre with improved accuracy. Cathode ray display methods have also been used to show the relative positions of the comparison and stellar spectra simultaneously and the velocity measure is made by determining as a single measure the shift between the two which produces best overall coincidence.

The method known by the name of Hartmann involved a comparison of a standard plate with a known apparent velocity with a plate of a closely similar spectrum for which the radial velocity was required. The instrument used brought into the same field of view sections of the two comparison spectra and stellar spectra. The comparison lines were first made to coincide. Then the offset necessary to make the star lines coincide was measured, usually in several spectral regions along the plate. This used to be thought a very accurate method, but it does necessitate having very similar spectra and very nearly identical dispersion, and it later fell out of favour. Attempts have recently been made to revive this technique in the form in which the spectrum of a star is imaged on to a plate of a very similar star. The position of coincidence is determined by determining a micrometer reading at which the amount of star light passing through the plate dips to a minimum, i.e. the point when the absorption lines of the unknown star coincide with those of the standard star. A photoelectric method of this type has now been successfully used by Griffin.

The measured heliocentric radial velocity of a star gives an averaged value of the heliocentric radial velocity of the stellar surface. In many cases this may be identified with the radial velocity of the centre of gravity of the star. In a later chapter we shall meet the pulsating stars in which the velocity of the surface is variable. Velocity variations also occur when one star is in orbital motion round another. We can also encounter variations of radial velocity within a spectrum due to systematic motions of particular atomic species. An inconsistency which is easy to deal with by recording a separate result, is the case of the ionised calcium lines, H and K, produced in distant stars by the gas clouds in interstellar space through which the light has passed. They will normally have a velocity different from that of the star in which they appear.

The errors of radial velocity measures are composed both of the internal error expressing the consistency of the separate line measures and of an external error, possibly variable from night to night or even from hour to hour. The real errors of radial velocity measures depending on, say, four spectra per star are always distinctly greater than the value inferred from the internal errors alone. It is often a matter of considerable difficulty to decide whether a star has a variable velocity for one of the reasons mentioned above, though an objective test has been proposed by the Canadian workers.

Spectra are also obtained at other foci of large reflectors for a variety of purposes. Spectroscopy of faint sources, such as extragalactic nebulae, is undertaken usually with spectrographs of small dimensions and high speeds mounted at the Newtonian or prime focus. This topic is considered further in the chapter on Galaxies. The coudé arrangement available on most large reflectors incorporates several mirrors according to the scheme illustrated in Figure II.11. The final beam emerges in a

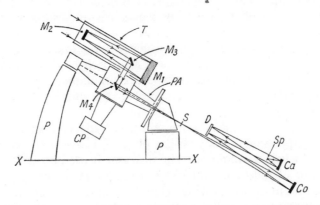

Figure II.11: Arrangement of a coudé spectrograph. PP: Telescope piers. T: Telescope tube. CP: Counterpoise. M_1: Main mirror. M_2: Hyperbolic secondary. M_3, M_4: Inclined flats. S: Coudé focus at slit of spectrograph. Co: Collimator mirror of spectrograph, paraboloid, slightly tilted. D: Diffraction grating. Ca: Schmidt camera mirror. Sp: Spectrum focused on curved plate or film. *Note*—The whole spectrograph assembly is in a controlled temperature housing.

fixed direction parallel to the polar axis of the telescope, and the coudé focus is fixed, though the field rotates as the telescope moves. Spectrographs using this focus are fixed instruments which can have very large dispersing elements, usually diffraction gratings. To give the necessary beam diameter the collimator, usually a concave mirror, must be large, and since the f-number of the instrument in this form is very large (f/28 in the case of the Radcliffe instrument), the focal length of the collimator is considerable. On the other hand, by the use of Schmidt optics cameras of quite short focal length can be used. Thus the resolution of the dispersing element is high, the projected slit width on the plate is small because of the large reduction factor between slit and plate, and the scale of the image on the slit is large. In spite of the fact that all the components are in fixed positions and can be mounted on massive steel beams so as to maintain their relative positions very accurately, it is not always easy to achieve a satisfactory level of stability in this type of spectrograph.

The standard source of radial velocity data in the literature is the *Mount Wilson General Catalogue of Radial Velocities* compiled by R. E. Wilson, published in 1953. It contains some 15,000 entries. Recent work has been by the staffs of the Radcliffe and Cape Observatories, using the reflector at the former institution, by the Stromlo observatory at Canberra, by the Canadians at Victoria and Toronto, and by a number of other observatories in the U.S.A. and Britain. The French observatories have produced a large volume of results by the objective prism method described below. Results are probably available for about 5,000 stars not previously observed, and these are now being incorporated in a supplement to the *General Catalogue*.

2.22. Radial Velocities from Objective Prism Spectra

The foregoing description covers only one aspect of spectroscopic work. Several other types are practised. Slitless spectroscopy is used, particularly for extended objects such as planetary nebulae which have spectra consisting only of bright lines, to produce a series of monochromatic images of the object, each originating in a different atomic transition. In objective prism spectroscopy a large prism with an angle of only a few degrees is mounted in front of the objective, and every star in the field which is bright enough produces a low dispersion spectrum. In the past this has been mainly used for classification of stellar spectra according to type.

The proposal to use an objective prism for the determination of radial velocities is due to Fehrenbach. Under conditions of very good seeing the star images approximate to point sources and can produce low dispersion spectra of fair quality. The Fehrenbach method depends on the construction of a normal field objective prism of exquisite quality. The prism is mounted on a ring and can be rotated through 180°. If two exposures are made in succession, the first with prism base left, the second with prism base right, the telescope being given a slight displacement in declination between the exposures, then the resulting plate will be found to contain pairs of spectra of all the stars in the field down to a certain magnitude, each pair consisting of adjacent spectra of the same star with the dispersions running in opposite directions. The normal property of the prism implies that it itself introduces no shift on reversal, and the observed shifts are then interpeted as due to radial velocity. For proper control each field must contain a number of stars for which the radial velocity is already known, to serve as a calibration. After several years of development work the Fehrenbach method has now begun to produce results of fair accuracy in important quantities. It is of particular value in the case where there may be many stars in the field, a proportion of which are moving with a rather high common velocity. In such a case the method permits ready identification of members of the latter group. A case in point is provided by the Magellanic Clouds, and it is not surprising that although the method was developed in France and is being applied at the Haute Provence Observatory, some of the most important observations have been made on the Magellanic Clouds from a station established at Zeekoegat in South Africa. This point is mentioned again in a later section.

2.23. The Diversity of Stellar Spectra

At numerous points in the foregoing pages it has been implied that the spectra of stars show a wide variety. Without attempting to discuss in detail the mechanisms which are responsible for the production of these diverse spectra, we hope now to make it plausible that this variety should exist. The majority of stars are known to consist of an overwhelming proportion of hydrogen, a moderate or considerable proportion of helium, and small amounts of most of the metallic and other elements found on the Earth. Under suitable conditions lines of all these elements may be excited, often far more strongly or far more weakly than might be expected *a priori* from their proportionate abundance. All the lines which are observed in stellar spectra are produced in the outer layers of the star, and are the result of a flow of radiant energy in a general outward direction through atmospheric layers associated with certain conditions of temperature, pressure, numbers of free electrons, and chemical composition. Each spectrum line is associated with a transition between two quantum states in an atom, and relies for its production on the interaction of that atom with quanta of radiation having a frequency very close to that corresponding to the energy difference between the states in question. If an atom in the lower state is present, and if the radiation field contains an appropriate quantum, there is a definite probability that the atom will absorb the quantum and will undergo a transition to the upper level. This will subtract the quantum from the generally outward going radiation flow. At a later stage, the excited atom may make a downward transition, possibly to the original level, and will return the quantum to the radiation field. However, the direction in which the re-emitted quantum will go is random, so that on balance there will be a reduction in intensity from the outward flow. The statistical superposition of vast numbers of similar transitions associated with the same pair of levels will produce the reduction of intensity over a small range of frequency about a certain mean value which we recognise as an absorption line in the spectrum.

Thus one of several important factors is availability of atoms in the appropriate state. This is determined by the statistical law known as Boltzmann's distribution which may be written in the form that if the total number of atoms of a given species be N, then the number N_m in a given energy level E_m is given by

$$N_m/N = (g_m/B(T)).10^{-5040\,E_m/T}$$

where g_m is what is called the statistical weight of the state and $B(T)$ the partition function, E_m is in volts and T in degrees Kelvin. The dominating factor in this expression is the last one, from which it will be seen that as the temperature of the assemblage (i.e. the stellar atmosphere) is increased the population of a given level as a proportion of the whole may be expected to rise. Thus for example at a very low temperature nearly all the atoms in an assemblage of atomic hydrogen would be in the ground state, and there would be few atoms in the second quantum level from which all the Balmer lines originate. For the comparison of the populations of the first and second levels in the hydrogen atom, the formulation can be put much more simply, and the function $B(T)$, which really ensures that all atoms must be in some energy state, need not be mentioned explicitly. For the hydrogen atom $g_m = 2m^2$, so that $\log (N_2/N_1) = -51,160/T + 0.60$, from which it is clear that as T goes from 5,000°K to 10,000°K, the proportion of atoms in the second level, ready to absorb the Balmer lines from whatever suitable quanta come along, goes up by about 10^5 times. This follows because the two energy levels are 10·15 volts apart.

As the temperature rises the phenomenon of ionisation becomes of greater and greater importance its incidence being described by an equation originally due to Saha. This runs:

$$\log (N^+P_e/N) = -5040I/T + 2.5 \log T - 0.48 + \log (2B^+(T)/B(T))$$

where we are considering a particular chemical element of which there are N neutral atoms, N^+ ionised atoms, the ionisation potential is I volts, and the partition functions of the ionised and neutral atoms are $B^+(T)$ and $B(T)$ respectively at absolute temperature T. A similar equation applies to each higher level of ionisation. Thus in the case of hydrogen the population in the second quantum level, at 10·1 volts rises with increasing temperature and, other things being equal, the intensity of the Balmer lines of hydrogen increases, until stars with a surface temperature of about 10,000°K are reached; thereafter ionisation becomes important in the range of electron pressures, P_e, encountered in stellar atmospheres, and the proportion of available atoms falls as they are converted into ions. The primary feature which causes one spectrum to differ from another is temperature of the stellar atmosphere in question and if the spectrum of a star is classified on its appearance, that is on the relative strengths of various lines which appear in it, this corresponds to a first, and very rough approximation to a statement about the temperature of the atmosphere of the star.

A second important feature of a stellar atmosphere which causes differences in spectral characteristics is provided by the density of the atmosphere in which the lines are formed. As we shall see, stars even of the same temperature are far from being built to a pattern. Some stars are what is known as giant or supergiant stars, which have enormous radii, and low surface gravity, in which the atmosphere is extremely tenuous and deep. These are contrasted with dwarf stars in which the surface gravity is high, the atmospheric density high, and the total number of atoms producing a spectrum line, which is comparable with that in the giant or supergiant, is concentrated in a relatively short line of sight in a dense medium, rather than being spread along a great length in a rarefied medium. The increased density manifests itself through a variety of physical effects which are dominating at different spectral types. We have so far concerned ourselves only with the availability of suitable species of atoms, that is with the total number of a given element, the proportion in the desired state of ionisation, and the population of the particular energy level of the desired atom or ion. If we revert to the Balmer series as formed in a star with a surface temperature near 10,000°K, where these lines are strong, one could easily imagine that so many hydrogen atoms would be available in a suitable state as to abstract all the outflowing radiation at a particular wavelength and give a line which was completely black. It is in general true that this does not happen, partly because there is a certain intrinsic width in atomic energy levels, i.e. each level is not an exact one but a small spread about a certain mean value, and because the atoms in the hot stellar atmosphere are in motion, resulting in a Doppler-Fizeau effect due to temperature movement, and hence a spread in the value of absorbed wavelength. This is what occurs in a tenuous supergiant, where the lines are seen to have a certain width, although this is small. If all the absorptions were exactly superposed, the total absorption in the spectrum line would be much less than it is observed to be in the case where there is a statistical spread; in the former case the line would show what is called saturation, whereas in the actual case far more of the outgoing radiation is stopped by the line when the absorption of an individual atom may effect a subtraction from a part of the spectrum not already affected by a previous one. With increasing pressure much more powerful effects make themselves felt: now the atoms are crowded close together, and, at near encounters, ions passing by produce electrical disturbances of the energy levels in the absorbing atoms. This is the phenomenon of intermolecular Stark effect and it causes an immense reinforcement of the absorbing capacities of the hydrogen atoms concerned in the production of the Balmer series by producing a large statistical spread around the mean value of the energy levels. It has the consequence of producing spectrum lines many ångströms wide, and it enables the spectroscopist to say whether the Balmer lines have been produced in the rarefied conditions of the giant, or the crowded conditions of the dwarf.

Now consider stars of lower surface temperature. A great many elements, particularly the metals, have first ionisation potentials between 5 and 10 volts, decidedly lower than the 13·5 for hydrogen. Calcium is particularly instructive, for it has three strong lines in the photographic part of the spectrum, a strong pair in the spectrum of ionised calcium at wavelengths 3,968Å and 3,934Å (the H and K lines) due to the ionised element, and a strong line of the neutral element at 4,227Å. Successive ionisation potentials are 6·1 volts, 11·9 volts and 51·2 volts. The last named is so high that we need not concern ourselves with the triply ionised state. The second value is quite moderate, so that for stars at temperatures distinctly above 10,000°K the calcium is mostly doubly ionised, and the lines of the singly ionised element, still more the neutral element, are not found. With falling temperature we find the H and K lines of the ionised element becoming strong for stars with surface temperatures below about 8,000°K. However, as the temperature drops still further the strength of the neutral line increases, until in very cool stars, with surface temperatures of the order of three to four thousand degrees, the 4,227Å line is the strongest in the whole spectrum. By this stage the hydrogen lines have almost disappeared and the spectra are crowded with lines due to metals and even to so called molecules, that is chemically-bonded groups which can exist at these low temperatures. All this is a question simply of variation of temperature: the discrimination of the effects of a second variable, such as pressure, specifically electron pressure, demands criteria which vary with spectral type. We have already mentioned one which applies over a fair range of temperatures near 10,000°K. Another of an even wider range of applicability has been well expounded by Thackeray in his book on astronomical

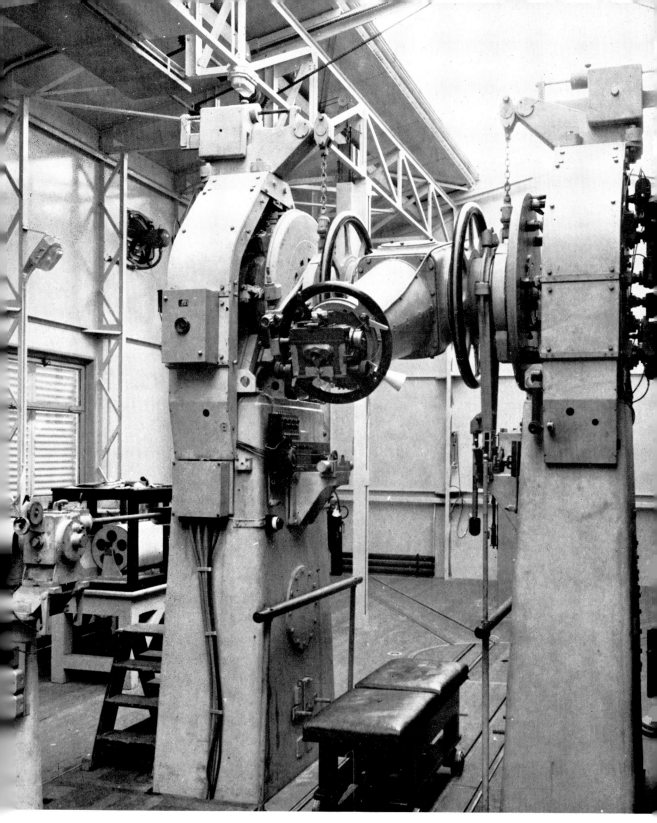

Plate 1. The Transit Circle of the Royal Greenwich Observatory. (By permission of the Astronomer Royal.)

Plate 2. The original National Physical Laboratory Caesium clock. The coils round the beam chamber compensate for the Earth's magnetic field. (Crown Copyright: *N.P.L.* photograph.)

Plate 3. The Photographic Zenith Tube of the Royal Greenwich Observatory.
(By permission of the Astronomer Royal.)

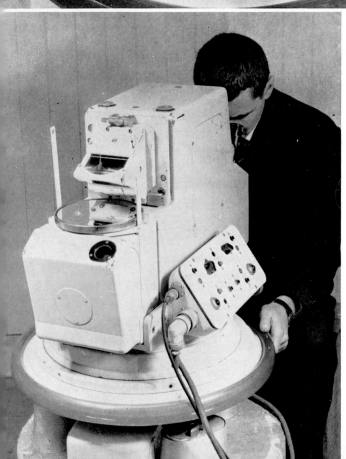

Plate 4. The Impersonal Astralobe of Danjon: (a) Drive mechanism of Wollaston prism. (b) General view. (By permission of Dr. A. Danjon.)

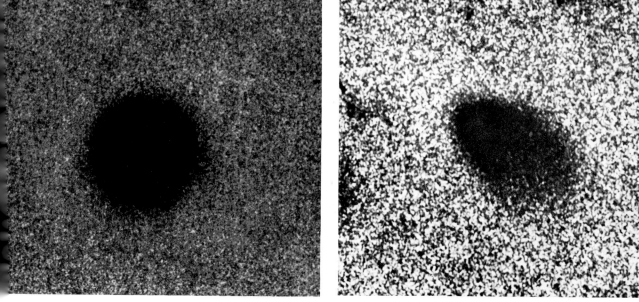

Plate 5. Enlarged photographs of star images: (a) Near the centre of a refractor plate. (b) Comatic image near the edge of a reflector plate. (c) Near centre of a Newtonian reflector plate; the diffraction rays are an artefact produced by the supports of the secondary mirror. (By permission of H.M. Astronomer at the Cape.)

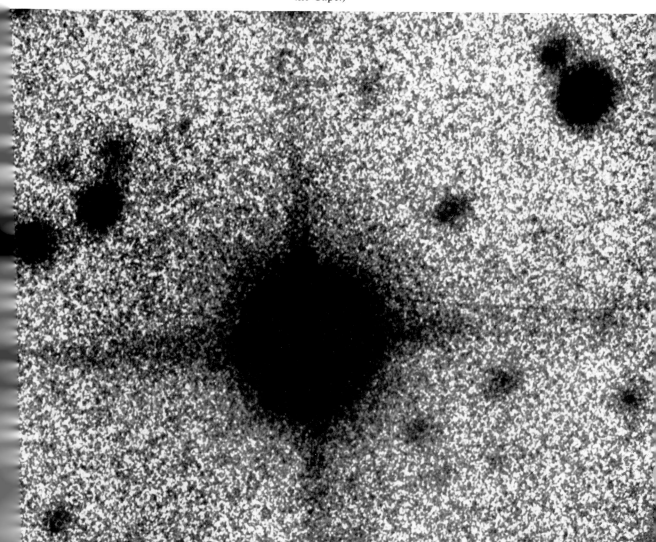

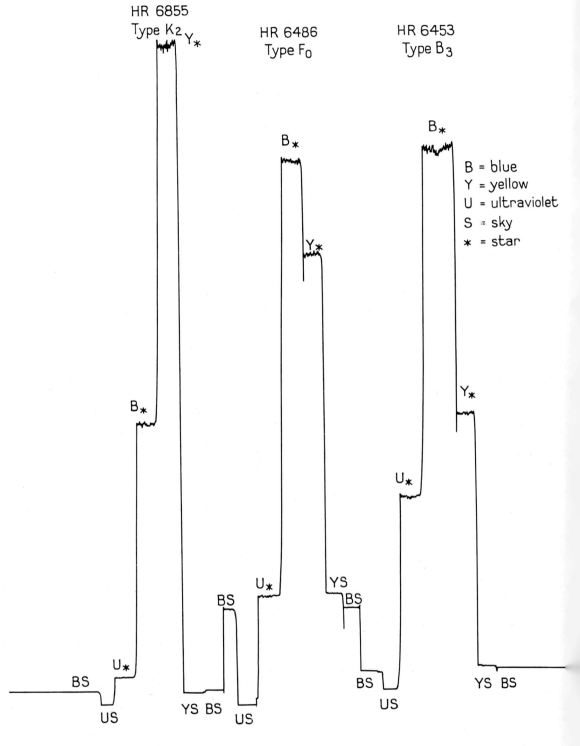

Plate 6. Typical photoelectric traces. (By permission of H.M. Astronomer at the Cape.)

Plate 7. An iris-diaphragm photometer. The plate under study is on the horizontal staging: a magnified image shows on the screen. The indicator showing when correct diaphragm size has been found, is immediately above the screen. (By permission of H.M. Astronomer at the Cape.)

Plate 8. The 40-cm. aperture objective prism instrument at Haute Provence Observatory used for measuring radial velocities. (By permission of Professor Ch. Fehrenbach.)

Plate 9. Objective prism plate of a star field (single exposure). The prominent spectrum lines are almost all those of the Balmer series of hydrogen in blue stars. (By permission of Professor Ch. Fehrenbach.)

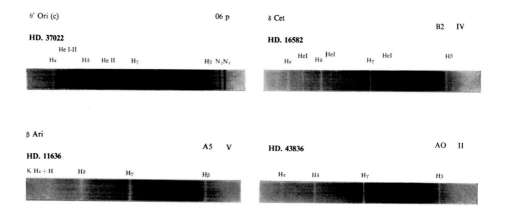

Plate 10. Spectra of early type stars. HD 37022, in the Orion nebula, is of type O6 p, with emission lines of forbidden oxygen and hydrogen. The absorption lines are due to hydrogen and helium. HD 16582, a B2 IV star, shows lines due to neutral helium and hydrogen. In HD 43836, (A 0 II), the strong lines are due to hydrogen, but these are narrower than in the dwarf, HD 11636 (A 5 V), which, at a later type, also shows some metallic lines. (By permission of H.M. Astronomer at the Cape.)

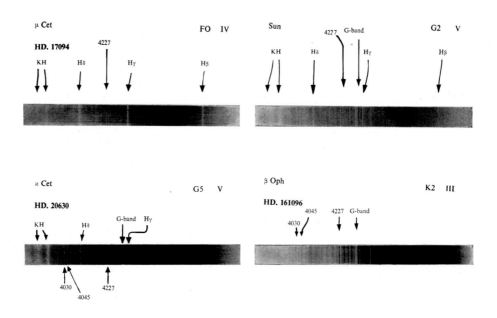

Plate 11. Spectra of later type stars. The temperature falls along the series from HD 17094, (F 0 IV), where the K and H lines of ionised calcium are prominent at the short-wave end of the spectrum, through the Sun (G2 V) where these have strengthened, and the G-band is prominent near the middle of the spectrum. Still later, in HD 20630 (G5 V), the metallic lines have strengthened, and in the red giant, HD 161096 (K2 III), the blue end of the spectrum is very weak and the metallic lines have completely eclipsed those of hydrogen. (By permission of H.M. Astronomer at the Cape.)

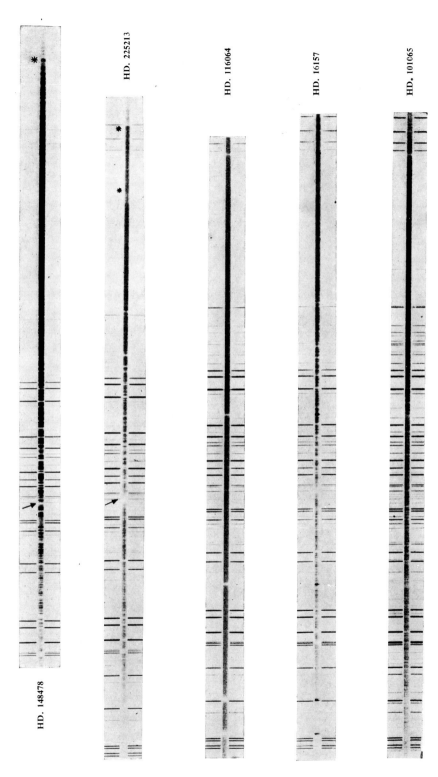

HD. 148478

HD. 225213

HD. 116064

HD. 16157

HD. 101065

Plate 12. Some unusual spectra. HD 148478, M1 Ib is the supergiant, Antares. HD 225213, M 4 V, is a red dwarf. Arrows mark the line 4227, which is stronger in the dwarf, and asterisks some of the TiO band heads, which are more prominent in the later type. HD 116064 is a high velocity subdwarf with a velocity of about 140 km/s, shown by displacement of the faint metal lines to the red. HD 16157 is a red dwarf with hydrogen emission lines. It is also a spectroscopic binary and a light variable. HD 101065 is the freak star, unclassifiable in the MK system, discovered by Przybylski.

Plate 13. The young double cluster, h and χ Persei. (By permission of the Director, Mount Wilson and Palomar Observatories.)

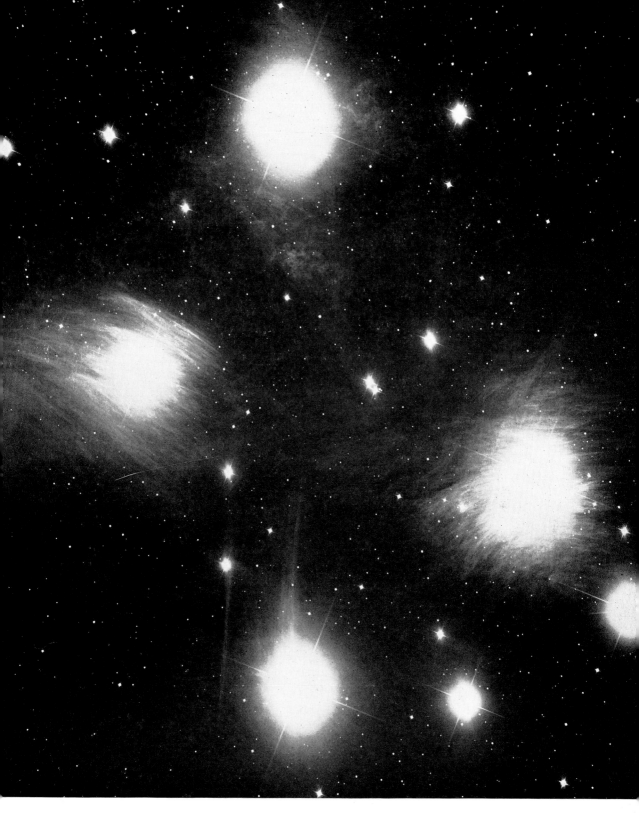

Plate 14. The brightest stars in the Pleiades are of rather later types and illuminate neighbouring gas clouds. (By permission of the Director, Mount Wilson and Palomar Observatories.)

Plate 15. Kappa Crucis, (Herschel's Jewel Box), a southern galactic cluster with stars of various colours. (By permission of the Director, Radcliffe Observatory.)

Plate 16. The southern globular cluster, 47 Tucanae. (By permission of the Director, Radcliffe Observatory.)

Plate 17. Gas and dust clouds in Centaurus: the black patches are "globules", dense dust clouds which may play a rôle in star formation. (By permission of the Director, Radcliffe Observatory.)

spectroscopy. This is the phenomenon of the increase in strength of certain lines, of which the line of ionised strontium at 4,078Å has the widest validity, with passage from the dwarf to the giant stars. The range of applicability of this criterion includes the cooler stars, and Thackeray's example refers to what is called a K-type star with a surface temperature round about 4,000°K. The spectroscopist seeking to classify such a spectrum on appearance only relies on the relative strengths of lines due to neutral and ionised metals, among which iron is very prominent, which has a first ionisation potential of 7·9 volts. A spectrum will be classified the same if the proportionate ionisation of iron is the same, and the example chosen shows that for a giant star, where the electron pressure is only a fraction of a dyne per square centimetre, the ratio Fe^+/Fe will be the same as in a dwarf with $P_e = 10$ dynes/cm² for a lower temperature in the giant than in the dwarf. We meet this phenomenon again when we come to consider differentiation by colour. This has the effect of making the ratio Sr^+/Sr, the ionisation potential of strontium being 5·7 volts, about three times as great in the giant as in the dwarf. In other words, for similar chemical composition, spectra of general similar appearance can be discriminated by the appearance of the ionised strontium lines, of which 4,078Å is the most persistent. In other classes of spectra, of stars both hotter and cooler than the two examples cited, criteria for estimating a second parameter have been developed.

In conclusion it is important to mention that there are other causes of broadening of spectrum lines, of which rotation of the star is one important example. Since the spectrum is produced by integration all over the disk of a star, then if the star is in rapid rotation, the differential Doppler-Fizeau effect from various parts, notably the opposite ends of the equator if the axis of rotation is perpendicular to the line of sight, produces a broadening of all lines in the spectrum, and not, as in the case of the intermolecular Stark effect, only the especially susceptible hydrogen lines.

2.24. The Definition of Spectral Types

When the differences in spectra between one star and another were first recognised, the various types were designated more or less arbitrarily by Roman numerals or by letters of the alphabet. With increasing knowledge it has become clear that the original designations did not represent a rational sequence (e.g. of temperature or general excitation), and the original Roman number designations due to Secchi were rearranged in the Harvard alphabetic designations. They were redefined with the addition of luminosity designations by Morgan, Keenan and Kellman, who produced an Atlas of spectral types, thereafter known as MKK types, in 1943. In 1953 Johnson and Morgan revised the system to a minor extent, defining it by the method of stating that certain stars which were also photometric standards, were stars which defined the standard spectral types. This system, now known as the MK system, requires the observer to match an unknown spectrum with the spectrum of one of the standards, and this gets over the difficulty of the distinctly different appearance which spectra of the same star can present when photographed with different instruments. Since many of the standards are in the north, this method can present a problem to southern observers. However, in recent years sufficient work has been done to make it reasonably certain that there is no serious systematic difference between north and south.

The meaning of a spectral type is not always properly understood even by some

D

astronomers who make use of them. A perfect description of a stellar spectrum would consist of a graph showing the incident radiation received from a star outside the atmosphere of the Earth at all wavelengths. This statement would contain so much information that it would be unmanageable, and what would strike the observer most forcibly would be the fact that all stars differ from one another in detail. Spectral types are useful because they focus attention on similarities, and a spectral type is a brief summary of the broad general features of a stellar spectrum. Photometrists abstract from the mass of information conveyed by the incoming radiation in one way: the spectroscopist in another, and it is not surprising that there are useful correlations between the two ways of looking at the same original material. Spectral types also have the defects of their virtues: they are determined by rather empirical methods and it is inevitable that experts will differ in minor respects when faced with the same material.

Spectral types are denoted by the letters O, B, A, F, G, K, M, forming a sequence of decreasing surface temperature. In addition the letters R, N, S distinguish different types of very low temperature stars in which different types of molecule or compound radicle are prominent. At the high temperature end of the sequence there is a class of very high temperature stars, known as Wolf-Rayet stars, designated by W, which have broad bright emission bands of helium, oxygen and silicon and either nitrogen or carbon, but not both conspicuous in the same star, and hydrogen rather weak.

It was originally intended that each of the spectral classes denoted by letters should be subdivided into ten steps, designated 0 to 9, but in practice the sub-division of types is usually not as fine as this.

O-type stars, show absorption lines of ionised helium and multiply ionised elements, together with the Balmer lines of hydrogen. Designations start at O 5 and continue to O 9·5, with the lines of hydrogen and neutral helium increasing in strength.

B-type stars show neutral helium and hydrogen lines, the former fading out at B 9, and some rather high excitation metallic and other lines.

A-type stars have the Balmer series at maximum at A0 with some metallic lines, especially the H and K lines of ionised calcium, the last named lines increasing in strength through the class. The metallic-lined A stars belong a little uneasily here: these are of various kinds including stars which show lines of chromium, europium, strontium or silicon. Some of these peculiar stars show evidence of strong magnetic fields.

F-type stars show both strong hydrogen and fairly strong metallic lines, with the H and K lines of ionised calcium strong, and neutral calcium beginning to be prominent. At F 5 a feature known as the G-band at 4,290-4,300Å first shows.

G-type stars, of which the Sun (type G 2) is a typical example, have metallic lines still stronger and the hydrogen lines weaker. The Hδ line falls below the Fe line at 4,045Å at about G 2, and the G band increases in strength.

K-type stars see the end of the hydrogen lines on low dispersion spectra. The H and K lines remain strong but the neutral calcium line at 4,227Å begins to outstrip them. The spectra are crowded with metallic lines and near K 3 the G-band begins to break up into several distinct blends.

M-type stars are distinguished by the great strength of the neutral calcium line at 4,227Å, and by the appearance of bands due to titanium oxide mainly in the longer photographic wavelengths. A good idea of spectral class can be gained simply by counting the band-heads, which, in the later classifications mutilate the spectral distribution in this part of the spectrum.

The luminosity classes represent a second parameter defining, as we shall see, the intrinsic brightness of the stars at each spectral class. We can define the following scheme:

Supergiants: Luminosity classes I, Ia, Ib, II.
Normal Giants: Class III.
Subgiants: Class IV.
Normal dwarfs, or "Main Sequence Stars": Class V.
Subdwarfs: Class VI.

Not all luminosity classes occur at all types, and we have already said enough to indicate that the rules for assessment of classes form a kind of complicated "Act of Parliament" of which a few of the clauses are: At early A, the fainter classes have broader hydrogen lines: from about mid-F to early K, strong 4,077Å is an indication that the star is intrinsically bright: strong hydrogen lines in later types indicate giantism, but strong 4,227Å at M indicates dwarfishness: near 4,215Å in the range from about G3 to early K a stronger continuum to the blue of this line than to the red, often indicates high luminosity, while absence of this and a weak line at 4,215Å indicates that the star is faint. The list of rules is too extensive to be set out in full. On the whole they work well, but there are stars which cannot be fitted in. If slightly peculiar, they can usually be assigned a spectral type and the letter "p". A designation "p" alone means that the spectrum cannot be classified at all. An extremely useful compilation of spectral types is that by Jaschek, Conde and Conde de Sierra, which lists all MK classifications published up to a certain date. The only difficulty is that there is no distinction in this catalogue between classifications made from spectra, and classifications repeated from previous authors. The number of references quoting a given estimate of spectral type where more than one is given, is not necessarily an indication of the merit of this estimate.

2.25. Spectrophotometry and Spectral Types

Most estimates of spectral type are based on visual comparison of spectra with spectra of similar standard stars, and this is in general an adequate procedure. The MK criteria originally evolved for dispersions round about 100Å/mm, tend to be difficult to apply both for very high and very low dispersion spectra. Workers using low dispersion objective prism plates have tended to develop their own criteria, which are modifications of the MK system adapted to lower dispersions, usually with some loss of discrimination. Nothing can replace an experienced human eye as a means of picking out the odder members of the stellar family as revealed by their spectra, but there is, undoubtedly, a tendency to move away from qualitative assessment of normal spectra towards the establishment of numerical criteria. The narrow band photometry of Strömgren and Gyldenkerne has already been mentioned, while photoelectric techniques for the determination of total line strengths are used on the

Balmer lines in B and A stars to fix luminosity classes. We also see an increasing use of techniques of photoelectric scanning of spectra. The determination of the total strengths of spectrum lines by photographic methods is thus likely to be superseded eventually, for it is demanding and laborious. On the other hand it can be done with relatively simple means and may remain an established technique for a considerable time. The notation used is common to all measuring techniques.

Many causes, some already mentioned, give a spectrum line a certain width. On a graph of intensity against wavelength, each line is a steep-sided, often nearly symmetrical, valley. The decrease is at first slow, in the so-called *"line wings"*, and then follows a sharp drop to the line centre or *"core"*. The graph is called the *"line profile"* or *"line contour"*. If we are dealing with an isolated line we can readily imagine that there is some continuous intensity which would apply if the line were not there, and we can estimate what this should be by going sufficiently far from the line centre to escape all interference by the line wings. In practice, with many lines which overlap, and no certainty as to how far one must go to get clear of the wings of a wide line, this can be far from easy. The intensity of this hypothetical continuum is taken as 100 per cent, and at each point within the actual line we define a *"residual*

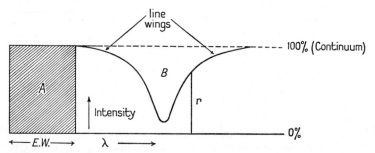

Figure II.12: Spectrophotometric concepts. Residual intensity, r, is expressed as a proportion of the continuum: area A = area B and defines the equivalent width of the line profile, B.

intensity", often denoted by *r*, which expresses the actual intensity as a percentage or fraction of the continuum at that point. The total blackening or amount of continuum blocked off by the presence of the line is the integral of $(1 - r)$ across the line. If the result is expressed in wavelength units, we find the *equivalent width* of the line, expressed as the number of ångströms of complete darkness which would produce the same total obscuration as the actual line. The term *"half-width"* is used to denote the interval in ångströms between the points symmetrical with respect to the centre which enclose half of the equivalent width. These concepts are illustrated in Figure II.12.

Spectrum plates to be used for spectrophotometry have to be processed with meticulous care, should be free from chemical fog and not too densely exposed. Reference back to Figures II.5, 6 and 7 will make the methods of measurement clear. The plates may be calibrated by several methods. Use of a tube sensitometer with the wavelength range limited by a filter to that near the spectral region under study is one possibility. Strictly the calibration exposure is a continuous one, whereas trailing makes the spectroscopic exposure intermittent, but in many cases the errors so introduced are small. If the calibration varies with wavelength, the plate to be used can be cut in half. One part is used for the stellar spectrum: the other portion is put in a calibration spectrograph which has a slit cut stepwise to give spectra in known ratios of intensity. Calibration curves at various wavelengths can be drawn by making density measures across the strips at selected wavelengths.

The measurement of density, or rather plate blackening in the sense described earlier is done with equipment (a microphotometer) of the type illustrated in Figure II.6. The light source is limited by a narrow slit perpendicular to the dispersion short enough not to spill over the sides of the stellar spectrum strip. The plate is driven through by a motor at a speed slow enough to obtain a true registration and the recorder shows the variation of intensity transmitted through the plate. Light cut-off and clear plate readings are also shown. The function given on page 66 is then computed for each point on the trace and values of blackening listed in terms of wavelength. Wavelengths are fixed by identifying the traces of spectrum lines on the recorder output. The calibration curve derived from similar measures of densitometer spots or calibration spectra is drawn and values of intensity in terms of blackening derived for each point on the stellar spectrum trace. The specification of line profile depends only on the ratio between spectrum line and continuum, so that the logarithm of the residual intensity can be plotted against wavelength and the equivalent width or other parameters found. This requires point by point measurement of the microphotometer trace and is very laborious. The work can be reduced if a direct-registration instrument is available. The calibration curve is previously determined in the ordinary way and is then introduced into the instrument, according to its type, either in the form of a cut-out curve, or as a curve to be followed by a curve-follower. Conversion to residual intensity then follows immediately and is registered as the output. The results in either form are affected by photographic grain, which is prominent if the analysing slit is narrow. If grain is smoothed by making this wider, there is a loss of resolution. In any case the overall combination of spectroscope and microphotometer necessarily produces a loss of resolution. An infinitely narrow line is recorded as a line of finite width having a standard shape known as the instrumental profile. If a true line profile is required this instrumental profile has to be determined and an integral equation solved to eliminate its effects. This can be done by feeding in a line of known contour such as an emission line of an inert gas, or an absorption line produced, for example, in sodium vapour at a known temperature. Refinements of this sort are usually reserved for very high dispersions. For lower dispersions the result of interest is usually the equivalent width of certain lines in the spectrum. The values for this are not affected by instrumental contour, though they are reduced as compared with the true values if there is any perceptible degree of scattered light within the spectrograph. Blooming of optics helps to get rid of this.

A full description of the various uses to which data on equivalent widths and line profiles can be put would carry us too far afield. Some are immediate: if all the lines in the spectrum of a star have similar dish-shaped profiles of the same width, this can be attributed to axial rotation of the star and the component in the line of sight evaluated. This arises because the observed spectrum is an integral over all the stellar disc, and if some parts are receding at high velocity and some approaching the line profiles can be shown to have a characteristic form.

Another immediate application has been made by Petrie and his colleagues. The negative correlation between the intensity of the Balmer lines and luminosity in the A stars has already been mentioned. Petrie has given this quantitative expression by providing a calibration of the absolute magnitude—Balmer line equivalent width relation for B and A stars.

It may be convenient to mention at this point the work of O. C. Wilson and M. K. Vainu Bappu on the correlation between the overall width of the CaII emission lines, especially the K-line, and absolute magnitude in stars later than G. An empirical allowance for instrumental line broadening has to be made, but apart from this, the measure of the emission width on very heavily exposed spectra gives absolute magnitudes with uncertainties of the order of only 0·2 magnitudes. The rationale of the measure is the correlation between turbulence in the high atmosphere (the chromosphere) and absolute magnitude.

The equivalent width of a spectrum line depends on many physical factors. First, there is the abundance of the element responsible. Secondly, the temperature of the atmosphere determines the relative populations in the various energy levels, and affects the line strength by determining the population of the lower level concerned in the transition. If we consider a number of transitions all starting from the same energy level, but going to different upper levels, we have a spectral series or multiplet, and the relative numbers of transitions are in part determined by certain constants determinable from the structure of the atom concerned. The total width of the line is dependent on the both atomic constants and on parameters of the stellar atmosphere. The latter include the particular atmospheric model adopted, together with two others connected with the velocities of atoms in the atmosphere. One is temperature. The higher the temperature the more rapidly the atoms are moving. The transitions from individual atoms are shifted in the spectrum by the Doppler effects of their temperature motions, and tend to spread the line in wavelength. This makes the equivalent width larger than it would be at a lower temperature by enlarging the core of the line where absorption is high. Stellar atmospheres also exhibit turbulent motions in which larger packets of gas have a velocity distribution and this effect also can enlarge a spectrum line. The theory of the *Curve of Growth* relating equivalent width of a line to the number of atoms available for its formation has been well developed. Actual cases can be studied by drawing curves of growth for lines of the same element in a given star, and shifting them along their logarithmic coordinate scales until they coincide with a standard curve or with the curves for a rather similar star which has been previously analysed.

A full-scale analysis will yield among other things, the relative abundances of elements in the observed star and the standard star chosen for comparison, and the excitation temperature, which means that temperature which best represents the population distribution among the various energy levels. If the lines of a neutral element can be compared with those of its ions, or if two different stages of ionisation can be compared, then, provided some estimate of electron pressure can be made, the proportions in these states can be determined. A corresponding ionisation temperature can be derived, which best represents these ratios.

Neither excitation temperature nor ionisation temperature are strictly temperatures in the sense of the thermodynamicist and because of departures from thermodynamic equilibrium in the stellar atmosphere, neither is usually equal to colour temperature or effective temperature.

Analyses of this kind have been undertaken for many stars often based on high dispersion coudé spectra, and they are usually very lengthy and complicated.

The result which we need for later developments is that in the vast majority of stars, excepting the small number of hydrogen-poor stars which have been found, overwhelmingly the most abundant constituent is hydrogen, while the proportion of metallic elements is very small. Even so, the actual abundance of metallic elements can vary by a large factor, and this feature is of great significance for our understanding of the evolutionary history of stars.

REFERENCES:

General Properties of Stellar Atmospheres:
A. Unsöld, *Physik der Sternatmosphären*, Springer, 1955.

Stellar Photometry:
Reports of I.A.U. Commission No. 25, *Transactions of I.A.U.*, Vol. 8, 1952 et seq.
Stars and Stellar Systems, Vol. 2, "Astronomical Techniques", ed. Hiltner, Chicago, 1962.
"Photoelectric Magnitudes and Colours of Southern Stars", R.O.B., No. 64, A. W. J. Cousins and R. H. Stoy, 1963.

Objective Gratings:
A. J. Wesselink, "Astronomical Objective Gratings", *Applied Optics*, Vol. 3, 889, 1964.

Photometry and Spectroscopic Standards:
H. L. Johnson and W. W. Morgan, *Ap.J.*, **114**, 522, 1951: *Ap.J.*, **117**, 313, 1953.
H. L. Johnson, *Ann.Ast.*, **18**, 292, 1955.

Photographic Photometry:
Review Article, Harold Weaver, *Encyclopaedia of Physics*, Vol. 54, Astrophysics V, Springer, 1962.
See also papers by W. Becker *et al* in *Zs.f.Ap.*

History of Astronomical Photography:
Astronomical Photography, G. de Vaucouleurs, Faber & Faber, 1961.

Spectral Types:
An Atlas of Stellar Spectra, W. W. Morgan, P. C. Kennan, and E. Kellman, Chicago, 1942. (Also Johnson & Morgan *supra*.)
Catalogue of Stellar Spectra Classified in the Morgan-Keenan System, C. Jaschek, H. Conde and A. C. de Sierra, La Plata, Vol. 28(2), 1964.
B. Strömgren & K. Gyldenkerne, *Ap.J.*, **121**, 43, 1955 (and later papers): Narrow band photometry for spectral typing.

Radial Velocities:
Stellar Motions, W. W. Campbell, 1913.
"La Mesure des Vitesses Radiales au Prisme Objectif", Ch. Fehrenbach, *J.des.O.*, Vol. 38, 165, 1955 (and numerous subsequent articles).
Astronomical Spectroscopy, A. D. Thackeray, Eyre and Spottiswoode, 1961.

Spectrophotometry and Interpretation:

L. H. Aller, *The Atmospheres of the Sun and Stars*, Ronald Press Company, New York, 1953.

The Abundance of the Elements, Interscience Publishers, New York and London, 1961.

Standard Wavelengths:

See papers by staff members of the Dominion Astrophysical Observatory, Victoria, B.C., in their own publications and in the *Journal* of the Royal Astronomical Society of Canada.

III
Interrelations Between Observed Quantities

3.1. Introduction

IN the previous chapter we outlined the observational methods which enable astronomers to measure a number of physical properties of stars. The theory of the internal structure of stars, as well as general physical ideas, make it seem probable that the different data for a star will not be independent of each other, but will show various types of interrelation. Nowadays we think this is reasonable because we can refer to ideas of gas and radiation and electron pressure, and processes for the generation of nuclear energy; it should be remembered that many of these ideas originated with astronomers, and that correlations of the kind about to be discussed had been found empirically long before there was any possibility of matching stellar conditions by experiment.

3.2. Absolute Magnitudes

We now need parameters describing the intrinsic properties of stars, and the most important of these is some measure of the intrinsic luminosity. This is expressed by the magnitude which would apply to a star if it were placed at a standard distance from us in space. Let L be the apparent luminosity of a star, that is, a measure of the energy in some band of the spectrum which it sends to the Earth from its actual distance in space; this we suppose to be d parsecs $= 1/p$, where p is the parallax in seconds of arc. Suppose L_0 is the apparent luminosity which would apply if the star were moved to a standard distance of 10 parsecs, in space which is perfectly transparent. The observed magnitude at the actual distance is denoted by m, and is called the *apparent magnitude* of the star. The magnitude corresponding to a distance of 10 parsecs is called the *absolute magnitude*, M, of the star. Then by the inverse square law and the definition of the magnitude scale

$$L/L_0 = 100/d^2 = 100 \, p^2 = 10^{-0.4(m-M)}$$

or by taking logarithms to base 10,

$$M = m + 5 + 5 \log p$$

This is the inverse square law in disguise. The relation may be applied to any kind of magnitude, e.g. U, B, V or any other, and the difference $(m - M)$ is called the *distance modulus* of the star or other object considered, which is the same whatever type of magnitude we may be considering.

3.3. Extinction and Reddening

If the space between a star and the Earth is not empty, the discussion requires modification. If the intervening material produces a general absorption with an exponential law, this may be described as a dimming of transmitted light by, say, k magnitudes per parsec, or k/p altogether and we have

$$M = m - k/p + 5 + 5\log p$$

If the value of k is dependent on the wavelength region considered then in addition to absorption there will be a change of colour. This can easily be seen if we write the last equation twice, for two different colours with small letters for apparent values and capitals for absolute.

Then we have, for example,

$$B = b - k_b/p + 5 + 5\log p$$

$$V = v - k_v/p + 5 + 5\log p$$

so that

$$B - V = b - v - (k_b - k_v)/p$$

If k_b is greater than k_v the observed value of b $-$ v will be greater than the intrinsic B-V and the *colour excess*, $(k_b - k_v)/p$, will bear a constant ratio, independent of p, to the extinction produced in either colour.

Reasonably accurate values of absolute magnitude can be derived from trigonometrical parallaxes if these are large enough, say, $0''\cdot040$ or greater, that is, for stars lying within about 25 parsecs of the Sun. Parallaxes as large as this are usually known with sufficient accuracy to make the calculation itself reliable, and at such distances absorption is negligible. The volume of space concerned is, however, extremely small, and contains very few stars, and none at all of certain types. Their number is, however, sufficient to permit them to be studied as a group, providing a sample stellar population from which conclusions can be drawn and applied to similar stars too remote for their parallaxes to be trigonometrically measurable.

3.4. The Hertzsprung-Russell Diagram

A Hertzsprung-Russell diagram for a collection of stars is a plot of absolute magnitude against colour. Almost any kind of absolute magnitude may be chosen, such as photographic or visual magnitude, though the absolute magnitude, often denoted M_V corresponding to V in the Johnson photometry is often chosen nowadays. The colour parameter offers a wide choice, such as spectral type, or colour index on any of several systems, of which the Johnson B-V is among the most favoured. These are directly measurable parameters, but for many theoretical discussions the inferred parameters *absolute bolometric magnitude* and *effective temperature* are preferred.

The latter was defined in the case of the Sun in Chapter II. The effective temperature, T_e, is defined by making a forced fit of the total energy flux from the solar surface with the formula of Stefan's law. Bolometric magnitude is the corresponding parameter, and means a magnitude defined in terms of the total energy output in all wavelengths emitted by a star. These quantities are determinable without much uncertainty in the case of the Sun. The angular diameter, which enters into the definition of effective temperature is directly measurable. The total energy flux is measurable with a fair degree of accuracy even from the surface of the Earth, and with rocket and satellite borne receivers is now certainly known with all the accuracy needed for this purpose. Discussions of stellar radiation often emphasise the extent of deviations from black-body distributions. For many purposes one can equally stress how good a first approximation the assumption of this type of distribution can be. Even before the era of high altitude experiments, a fair estimate of the probable energy losses of solar radiation due to atmospheric absorption could be made. This remains true of the cooler stars, so that correction of data obtained in accessible parts of the spectrum so as to arrive at estimates of bolometric magnitude are not very uncertain. In the case of hot blue stars the losses are very considerable, and recourse must be made to theoretical calculations based on stellar models. The determination of angular diameters of stars incidental to the specification of effective temperatures, has, until recently, been almost always done indirectly from studies of binary stars. Although direct methods are now coming into use, the subject is discussed in the chapter on variable and multiple stars. The classic paper on the effective temperature scale was written by G. P. Kuiper in 1938 using binary star data, and a limited number of direct measures made with the stellar interferometer. This remains the standard calibration, though in the near future a new calibration based on direct measurements is likely.

In the specification of bolometric magnitudes the early work of Pettit and Nicholson played an important part. They used the 100-inch telescope with a vacuum thermopile to measure the total radiation from bright stars. The results are expressible in ordinary physical units if there is a calibration by means of a standard source. A water cell was used to take out the infra-red contribution when required, and, by a series of rather involved calculations they were able to assess the visible and infra-red contributions from stars of various colours. These radiometric magnitudes are a better approximation to bolometric magnitudes than the results of ordinary photometry, but still require some corrections which have only a theoretical basis.

The six-colour photometry of Stebbins and Whitford, mentioned in the previous chapter also helped very much in defining the radiation distribution received from stars.

3.5. The Main Sequence

If we construct a Hertzsprung-Russell diagram, plotting, say, the visual absolute magnitude, M_V, against colour, B-V, for stars having trigonometrical parallaxes large enough to give reasonably accurate values of the former, we find that the distribution of points on the diagram exhibits a number of areas of concentration. The most striking is a concentration towards an inclined line running down and across the diagram (Figure III.1). It begins with the intrinsically bright, blue stars at the upper left and descends to intrinsically faint, red, stars on the right. The scatter of the points about the median line is due in part to uncertainties in the trigonometrical parallaxes used, so that the stars belonging to this group, usually known as the

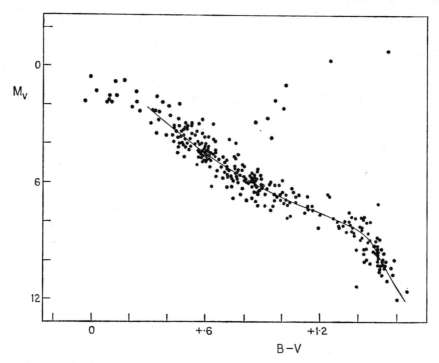

Figure III.1: The Hertzsprung-Russell diagram for the nearby stars. (Reproduced from Lowell Observatory Bulletin, No. 91, by permission of the Director.)

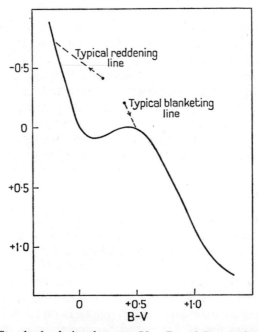

Figure III.2: Standard relation between U − B and B − V for normal stars. For details of the reddening and blanketing lines, see text.

Main Sequence seem to be built fairly closely to a pattern. There is thus a close correlation between colour, or spectral type, and absolute magnitude. Other names for these stars are, in the MK spectral classification system, Class V stars, or, at any rate for the redder members, the term *"dwarf stars"*. The location of the Main Sequence has been studied by numerous authors, and, amalgamating the work of several, we may tabulate a mean line as follows:

B-V	M_V	U-B	Type	T_e
− 0·25	− 2·10	− 0·89	B2 V	20,300
− 0·20	− 1·10	− 0·70	B3 V	18,000
− 0·15	− 0·30	− 0·52	B5 V	15,000
− 0·10	+ 0·50	− 0·33	B8 V	12,800
− 0·05	+ 1·10	− 0·16	B9 V	11,800
0·00	+ 1·50	0·00	A0 V	11,000
+ 0·05	+ 1·74	+ 0·05	A2 V	9,700
+ 0·10	+ 2·00	+ 0·08	A3 V	9,100
+ 0·20	+ 2·45	+ 0·07	A7 V	8,100
+ 0·30	+ 2·95	+ 0·02	F0 V	7,000
+ 0·40	+ 3·56	− 0·01	F3 V	6,800
+ 0·50	+ 4·23	0·00	F7 V	6,300
+ 0·60	+ 4·79	+ 0·08	G0 V	6,000
+ 0·70	+ 5·38	+ 0·24	G8 V	5,320
+ 0·80	+ 5·88	+ 0·43	K0 V	5,120
+ 0·90	+ 6·32	+ 0·63	K2 V	4,760
+ 1·00	+ 6·78	+ 0·87	K3 V	4,610
+ 1·10	+ 7·20	+ 1·03	K4 V	4,500
+ 1·20	+ 7·66	+ 1·13	K5 V	4,400
+ 1·30	+ 8·11	+ 1·21	K6 V	4,000

Different authorities differ slightly on the values to be adopted, and the spectral types quoted, some of which are intermediate between classifications most commonly used, exhibit minor irregularities because they form a discontinuous scale. The values of B-V for a given value of U-B are not single over a small range. The curve defining the relation between these two parameters contains an S-bend in the region of the A and F stars arising from the effects of the size of the discontinuity at the head of the Balmer series, the lines of which are near their maximum strength in this region. The Sun is a fairly typical G2 V star, with an absolute magnitude of about + 4·8, so that the range of stars listed in the table is from some 500 times as bright as the Sun to about one-twentieth of the solar brightness. However, this by no means exhausts the range of star luminosities which will be encountered.

Beyond the end of the table lie redder and fainter stars of very late K and M types. On a plot of M_V against B-V there ceases to be a well-defined relationship between colour and magnitude for these very red dwarfs. At any given B-V colour in the range from about B-V = + 1·3 to about + 1·55 there may be a range in M_V of about two magnitudes. This must indicate some degree of variation in intrinsic properties of the stars concerned since otherwise the same results would be obtained for them. On the other hand, because at these colour indices, V and still more B, are quantities describing only a minute proportion of the radiation, a better description of the properties of such stars is given by measuring a red-infra-red colour where the chosen bands lie much nearer the wavelength of maximum intensity of the radiation.

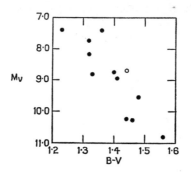

Figure III.3: The absolute magnitudes of M-type dwarfs show a considerable scatter. The open circle is an emission-lined star. (By permission of the Editors of *Observatory*.)

It is understood that this may much reduce the scatter on the corresponding diagram. At all events, the mean line for red dwarfs continues on down rather steeply to an absolute visual magnitude of about + 15 for the reddest of known dwarfs.

3.6. Observational Selection

A colour-magnitude diagram can only plot what is available. The selection of stars having large parallaxes is a selection from a given volume of space: stars which are rare in space will occur sparsely: stars which are abundant will occur frequently or to the extent to which they have been discovered. The distribution in space bears little resemblance to the distribution of stars seen in the sky with the naked eye. Even though the table of the Main Sequence given above does not extend quite so high there certainly are stars with absolute magnitudes at least as high as − 5, that is, ten magnitudes, or 10,000 times as bright as the Sun. At the other end of the scale, there are stars as faint as ten magnitudes below the Sun. Now, when we look at the sky with the naked eye or any other instrument we set a limit for detection of stars at a certain apparent magnitude. Suppose for the naked eye this is $m = + 6$; then we shall see all the stars with absolute magnitudes of + 6 which lie within ten parsecs of us. Stars of absolute magnitude − 4 will lie above the threshold of visibility if they have a distance modulus less than 10 magnitudes, that is up to a distance of 1,000 parsecs. A star of magnitude + 16 would be visible to the naked eye only if it lay within 0·1 parsec of the Sun, and so far as is known, no stars lie within this range. The volume of a sphere of radius 1,000 parsecs is one million times as great as the volume of a sphere with a radius of ten parsecs, and this is again a million times as great as the volume of a sphere with a radius of 0·1 parsecs. Thus in the night sky we shall see all stars with an absolute magnitude of − 4 which lie in a volume a million times as great as that which contains all the visible stars with an absolute magnitude of + 6. The dice are loaded a million times in favour of the bright stars and a million times against the very faint dwarfs. The naked-eye sky is full of what we shall learn are rarities such as hot blue stars; the roster of local space contains none; we see no faint dwarf stars, but they are probably the commonest of all in space, and only the very nearest of them are known to us. Contrariwise we can demonstrate the rarity of intrinsically very bright stars in neighbouring space by noting the absence of apparently very bright stars. The brightest star in the sky is Sirius (actually as an A1 V star not intrinsically very bright) but since for Sirius $m = -1 \cdot 4$ there can be no star with an absolute magnitude of -5 within about 50 parsecs of us. The nearest star of this brightness is the second star in the sky, Canopus, for which $m = -0 \cdot 8$, $M = -5$, so that its distance is about 70 parsecs. It will now be noted that the tabulated Main Sequence data go somewhat beyond the limits defined by the nearby stars at the brighter end. Absolute magnitudes for intrinsically brighter stars require the search for suitable objects to be continued into greater depths of space where trigonometrical parallaxes cease to be of any great accuracy. We shall discuss later some of the methods used to establish absolute magnitudes of intrinsically bright stars, but for the time being we can remark that trigonometrical parallaxes remain of some value out to distances, possibly as great as some hundreds of parsecs, not for individual objects, but for the establishment of mean values for a number of stars.

3.7. The Giant Stars

From stellar data suitably selected from a wider field of inquiry than the nearby stars, further occupied regions of the Hertzsprung-Russell diagram can be defined. One is a not very well defined band starting to the right of the diagram among the M-type stars at an absolute magnitude of zero or a little brighter. It runs to the left across the diagram, inclining downwards so that at G0 the absolute magnitude is about $+1$. These are the stars which have been called giants, a name bestowed soon

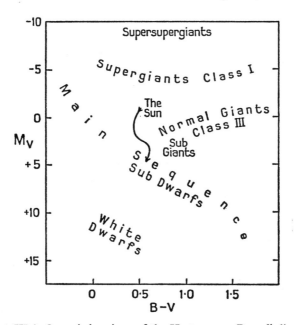

Figure III.4: Occupied regions of the Hertzsprung-Russell diagram.

after the Hertzsprung-Russell diagram was first drawn to emphasise the fact that at the later spectral types among stars of the kind found in a rather large solar neighbourhood, two distinct sorts seemed to occur. For example, at type K5, Nature seemed willing to provide either a dwarf star with a visual absolute magnitude near + 7·5, or a giant, some thousand times as bright, which as we shall see had other features of giantism too, such as large mass and large radius. Perhaps, in early days, selection of data had something to do with the stress on two branches, giant and dwarf, with no stars in between, and as will become clearer later, this is still the situation at types as late as K5. However, at somewhat earlier types, such as G5, where the giant-dwarf luminosity ratio has fallen to something like 100 to one, the space between giants and dwarfs on the diagram is no longer quite empty, but two sequences are distinguishable even with the most complete modern data. When giants were first so called, their sequence stopped at round about the early G stars, but in the MK classification system, where the old style giants are called stars of luminosity Class III, the mean for this luminosity class continues on up into the early type stars, being there about two magnitudes above the Main Sequence. It is a little misleading to equate exactly the terms, "Class III" and "Giants", for there are probably very significant differences between early type Class III stars and late type ones. It will be remarked that we have described the giants in terms of spectral type rather than B-V colour, a circumstance which arises because for the later type Class III stars there is not the same close approximation to a standard pattern as was found for the Main Sequence. We learned in the discussion of spectral types that if stars are judged by the appearance of lines of predominant elements, such as iron, then the differences of electron pressure between a giant and a dwarf produce the same general spectral appearance, apart from certain indicator lines such as the Sr^+ line at 4,077Å, at a lower temperature in the giant than in the dwarf. Spectral type is an expression of spectral appearance, so that for the G and early K stars, the giants have a lower temperature, and a redder colour, by about 0·2 magnitudes in B-V, than do the dwarfs. In terms of colour the giant branch extends from a colour of about + 1·5 for an early M-type star to about + 0·80 for an early G-type giant.

An abridged table of effective temperatures for the giant stars runs as follows:

Type	T_e	Type	T_e
F5	6,470°	K0	4,200°
F8	5,620°	K5	3,550°
G5	4,650°		

As far as numbers in the various magnitude ranges are concerned we may profitably refer to a recent compilation by Gliese who summarised all known data about the stars, numbering about 1,000 altogether, so far found within about 20 parsecs of the Sun. Of this number only 8 were giants, a number insufficient to define their branch on data for nearby stars alone. All the giants within this distance must already be known. He then listed 44 main sequence stars brighter than $M_V = 10$ within a distance of 7 parsecs, which would correspond to a total of about 1,000 stars on the Main Sequence, known and unknown, within 20 parsecs. For the range of M_V from 10 to 13 he noted 18 stars within 5 parsecs, corresponding to possibly another 1,100 stars, known and unknown within the 20-parsec limit. To complete the Main Sequence he listed 7 stars fainter than $M_V = 13$ within 3 parsecs, and these might correspond to a total of 2,500 such stars within the 20-parsec limit, most of them being too faint either for many kinds of observation or for easy identification. Although the process of multiplying small numbers by large factors is admittedly uncertain, there seems little doubt that the real number of stars within 20 parsecs might be several times as great as the thousand identified so far. Probably most of the nearby stars down to $M_V = 8$ have already been discovered, so that the unknown ones will almost all be faint. As we shall see, they will add only a rather small fraction to the total mass of all the stars, but it is nevertheless an intriguing thought that even the immediate spatial neighbourhood of the Sun has so far been explored only inadequately so that only a fraction of the stellar population in it has been identified.

3.8. The Supergiant Stars

These are stars of very great intrinsic brightness, of all spectral types from O to M, with luminosity classes on the MK system denoted by II, Ib and Ia in order of increasing brightness. The magnitude range is from about -2 for the later Class II supergiants, up to about -7 for the Class Ia supergiants. Discriminants are very varied, but a general property of bright supergiants is the possession of very narrow spectrum lines (the so-called "c characteristic"), indicating formation in an extremely low pressure atmosphere. Recent studies in the Magellanic Clouds by the Pretoria observers, with confirmation by the French observers also working in South Africa, have defined a class of super-supergiants, with absolute magnitudes of -9 or -10, for which the designation Ia-0 has been proposed. This case illustrates how, in a group of stars all at the same distance, the very brightest intrinsically will be the most prominent, even though, by numbers in space, they may be extremely rare. In Gliese's list there is only one star above Class III, and that only a Class II. It follows that the only way to study supergiants as a class is to observe them in remote regions of space, casting the net wide enough to collect a goodly number, preferably in regions where there are groups of such bright stars all at a common distance. The Magellanic Clouds offer such an opportunity, but for ordinary supergiants and intrinsically bright stars in general, much nearer and more convenient opportunities are available.

3.9. The Subgiants

In the original formulation of the Hertzsprung-Russell diagram the area between the giant branch and the Main Sequence for the later type stars seemed to be practically unoccupied. During the last few decades however, a class of stars known as subgiants, and designated as luminosity Class IV, has been identified, the members of which lie in this gap. The early versions of the diagram were severely affected by observational selection: many nearby dwarfs were shown because they had large parallaxes and these had been measured: many giants were shown because of the selection effects already mentioned. Nearly all their measured parallaxes were too small to be of much significance; although the mean line for the giants lay in approximately the right position, the observational scatter arising from errors of measured parallax smudged out some of the more significant features which can be seen on accurate modern diagrams. Although spatially less numerous than the dwarfs, subgiants are more common than giants. Gliese lists 22 within a distance of 20 parsecs from the Sun, and this is probably a full score since a subgiant nearer than this limit is a moderately bright star. There has been some controversy over the specification of subgiants and some measured criteria only permit the definition of Classes III and V, but the spectroscopists find no difficulty in defining intermediate classes, either described as Class IV stars, or even subdivided by such terminology as III-IV, IV and IV-V. The subgiants scatter over an area on the Hertzsprung-Russell diagram between the giant and dwarf sequences. The area is definitely bounded on the right (red) side, so that no subgiants are found with spectral types later than early K. In the MK terminology the Class IV stars of early type are those definable as lying between the mean lines drawn for Classes III and V, which, in the range from B to F are separated by about two magnitudes in M_V.

3.10. The Subdwarfs

These stars have come into prominence only relatively recently and are usually assigned to luminosity class VI. On the M_V, B-V diagram for the later types, say from early F to late K, they lie below the Main Sequence, possibly by less than a magnitude in the early part of this range, and by up to about two magnitudes in the later part. Among A stars there are also fairly numerous examples which are subluminous by possibly as much as two magnitudes, but there are reasons for thinking that these should be differentiated from subdwarfs of later type. One difficulty concerning statements about absolute magnitudes of subdwarfs is the paucity of cases with good parallaxes measured trigonometrically. The few nearby examples among F stars may not be in fact markedly subluminous, and their kinship with the later subdwarfs which certainly are so, is based on spectroscopic and photometric data. The subdwarfs from early F to middle G have marked spectroscopic peculiarities which are attributable to a very much lower metallic content than the stars on the normal main sequence. Subdwarfs in this spectral range have spectra with a characteristically washed out appearance. The metallic lines are all extremely weak and luminosity criteria indicate a dwarf classification. The weakness of the lines makes the application of classification criteria very difficult in the case of extreme subdwarfs. In the past many of them have been wrongly classified, especially if this was done on low dispersion spectra. Quite startling reclassifications, for example from A5 to G5 are occasionally encountered. The specification of luminosity class is often difficult, since this depends on the estimation of line ratios, a task which becomes almost impossible when both spectral lines involved are very weak. We encounter not only dwarf stars which have very low metallic content, but also occasionally subgiants. The former ought to go into Class VI, the latter into Class IV, and it is sometimes hard to make a decision from spectral appearance alone. This seems a very large uncertainty in luminosity class, but it can be claimed that this is not so. The metal-weak stars of Class VI and Class IV occupy contiguous areas of the diagram, and, as we shall see, belong to a different kind of population which is superposed on the more common type of population in the neighbourhood of the Sun.

The absence of strong metallic lines in the spectrum of a star in the spectrum range under discussion leads to a redistribution of energy in the spectrum, resulting in an ultraviolet brightness which is higher than that of a star of similar spectral type and colour with normal metal content. It is expressible as an ultraviolet excess defined by comparing the U-B colour of a subdwarf with that of a normal dwarf at the same B-V colour. As an example take the star γ Pavonis, one of the very few subdwarfs with a large parallax. This has V = 4·21, B-V = 0·48, U-B = − 0·15, and parallax = 0″ ·111. Authorities disagree slightly, but the normal U-B for this colour is between − 0·02 and 0·00. Thus γ Pavonis has an ultraviolet excess of about 0·14 magnitudes. Spectrum classifiers can usually put a qualifying remark to their classifications which turns out to be well correlated with ultraviolet excess. γ Pavonis is a fairly well marked, though not extreme specimen, and the ultraviolet excess is considerable, though not very high. As compared with a normal star γ Pavonis is about 0·2 magnitudes subluminous. Only the large parallax enables us to be sure of this. With a more distant star such a small degree of subluminosity would be swamped by uncertainties in derived absolute magnitude. At later types the degree of sub-luminosity seems to become more marked. At later types too, the effects of metal deficiency on spectral appearance become less pronounced, since atmospheric conditions then favour the production of strong metallic lines. Thus in stars of K-type we lose the useful criterion of ultraviolet excess. Only a careful abundance analysis can reveal metallic deficiency. Most known dwarfs and subdwarfs in this spectral range have large parallaxes, so that the latter can be picked out from the fact of their subluminosity. However, our knowledge of these stars is so incomplete because so many faint, nearby stars remain to be discovered, that statistical argu-ments are dangerous. Finally, for very red stars, we encounter the confusing situation, possibly due for resolution by infra-red photometry, of the scatter in absolute magnitude which seems to affect the lower end of the normal main sequence. (Figure III.3.)

The spatial density of subdwarfs is not yet clearly defined. Possibly a fairly high proportion of those which do exist in the solar neighbourhood are known. In many cases the clue to identification has come from ultraviolet excesses established photo-metrically. This applies to only a limited range of spectral type, and is, by itself, not conclusive, since excesses can occur for other reasons than metal deficiency in a dwarf star. Subdwarfs are also distinguished by high spatial velocities relative to the Sun, and possible candidates can readily be picked out from parallax catalogues. These are stars with high proper motions, in excess, say, of 0″·2 per annum, which on measurement are found to have small parallaxes, say, of the order of 0″·010. Such stars usually get into parallax programmes because the high proper motion is thought to be due to a moderate spatial motion and a large parallax. In the subdwarf case the explanation is a very high spatial velocity and a small parallax. Again, this provides no more than a hint. Moreover if this is the sole way in which subdwarfs are found there is a very serious risk of collecting a very biased and misleading sample, unless it should be proved that the vast majority of subdwarfs which exist do in fact have very high spatial velocities.

3.11. Line Blanketing

The significance of metallic content of stars especially in relation to their velocity characteristics will be pursued later. Computations have shown that in a Hertz-sprung-Russell diagram in which the coordinates are bolometric absolute magnitude (M_{bol}) and effective temperature (T_e) there is no real distinction between the main sequences for stars of normal and reduced metallic content. In stars of high metallic content the spectrum lines blanket the outgoing radiation. The effects of this blanket-ing have been computed. A low-metals star with a certain observed ultraviolet excess δ (U-B) would be moved to a new position on an M_V, B-V diagram by increase of its metal content to a new position found by applying corrections Δ (B-V), Δ (U-B) and Δ V which would bring it on to the normal (U-B), (B-V) line and on to the normal, high metal content main sequence. The latter is sometimes called the Hyades main sequence. The so-called *blanketing line* on the (U-B), (B-V) diagram is given by Δ (U-B)/ Δ(B-V) = 2·70(B-V)$_H$ + 0·62 and the magnitude correction is given by Δ V/ Δ (B-V) = 0·75(B-V)$_H$ − 0·97. Metal weak stars occur above the normal (U-B), B-V) line (Figure III.2) and application of blanketing corrections moves them down so as to remove their ultraviolet excesses. The effect is readily observed near the central part of the curve. At the right-hand end changes of position corresponding to changes in metallicity occur practically parallel to the curve.

3.12. The White Dwarfs

These are intrinsically very faint stars which lie in a compact group at the bottom left-hand corner of the M_V, B-V diagram. Absolute magnitudes are mostly fainter than about +10. Colours are such as to place most of them in spectral classes A and F, which led to the use of the name "White Dwarf", but by convention the name is still applied even to a few members which have colour indices as high as +1·0 and are far from white. Several spectral varieties have been distinguished, mostly with very broad hydrogen lines. In some cases there are spectral features of unknown origin. The general blue colour of the class indicates a high effective temperature, and high surface brightness. The low luminosity shows that the total emitting surface of one of these stars must be very small indeed, and that their dimensions can be hardly greater than those of the largest planets. Indications of mass, discussed in the chapter on multiple stars, are that masses are comparable with that of the Sun. It follows that their mass densities are extremely high, in the range of thousands of times that of water. The main body of material in these stars is in what is known as a degenerate state, completely ionised by the effects of pressure. Extensive theoretical studies of the state of matter in white dwarfs have been undertaken by Schatzman, while Greenstein, Luyten, Kuiper and Eggen and Greenstein have been active in the discovery and observational study of these objects.

It is obviously a matter of considerable difficulty to pick out objects which are intrinsically so inconspicuous as white dwarfs. Most of those known have large trigonometrical parallaxes. Several owe their discovery to the fact that they are components of double stars, of which the primary component is a normal star. The companion of Sirius is the classic case. Gliese lists 5 white dwarfs, all within 5 parsecs. This figure might correspond to a total of something like 300 white dwarfs within twenty parsecs. The computation is so uncertain that the actual figure might be much less or much more, but there is no conflict with observation in supposing that white dwarfs are stars which are very common in space.

The foregoing sketch lists some of the commonest categories of stars to be found on the Hertzsprung-Russell diagram. It by no means exhausts the variety of stars found in space. In particular nothing has been said concerning variable stars, which will be discussed in a later chapter. Neither has the significance of the distribution of points on the diagram been discussed. The general distribution is indicated schematically in Figure III.4.

3.13. **Magnitudes and Colours in Clusters**

So far discussion has been confined to stars in the solar neighbourhood, but we know that, in the case of intrinsically bright stars, the sample so provided is inadequate. Nearby stars have meaningful trigonometrical parallaxes which permit a Hertzsprung-Russell diagram to be plotted. This is also possible in the case of a group of stars all at the same distance, even though we cannot immediately say what this distance is. For such a group of stars their apparent magnitudes can be used as a measure of relative intrinsic brightness. A Hertzsprung-Russell diagram of apparent magnitude against colour can be plotted, and we leave to a later analysis the question of what distance modulus to apply to arrive at absolute magnitudes, knowing that the value will be the same for all the stars plotted.

This case arises when all the stars belong to a *star cluster* of which several types are known. It is curiously difficult to give a satisfactory logical definition of a cluster though in practice it is not usually difficult to recognise one. Any kind of observation of the sky, whether visual or photographic, will show that the distribution of stars on the sky is not smooth, and that here and there relatively large numbers of stars are found in relatively small areas. These concentrated groups which stand out from the background are the clusters, and although there are a few spurious cases arising from accidental apparent concentrations of stars at widely different distances, in most cases the apparent concentration is produced by the presence of a large number of stars in a small volume of space. For all except the nearest clusters the spatial extent is only a small fraction of the mean distance, so that all the members may be treated as being at the same distance from us. Of course, what may be loosely described as the general apparent density of stars produced by random scattering of stars of all intrinsic brightness at all sorts of distances—sometimes called *field stars*— continues through the area of the cluster. Thus in its direction there may be a few stars which are either nearer or more remote than the cluster, but these can usually be differentiated and removed from the statistics of the cluster itself. In addition, if a cluster is remote from us, the light from its stars may have been subjected to interstellar absorption and reddening on the way. This means that an allowance must be made to the distance moduli of all the stars to take account of this, and that the observed colours must be corrected to get rid of the effects of reddening before we can compare one cluster with another. Characteristic features of clusters which enable them to be classified according to form and content, include the dimensions, the density of stars and the way in which this varies from the centre to the outer parts, and the general shape of the cluster, usually expressed by means of an ellipse of greater or lesser eccentricity, For studies of the content of clusters, ideally, one requires data for magnitudes, colours, spectral types, radial velocities, and sometimes proper motions, for a representative sample of stars. This ideal, which would make exclusion of foreground stars relatively easy, represents such a massive work for each cluster that it has only rather rarely been attained.

The principal kinds of cluster are usually known as galactic and globular clusters.

3.14. **Galactic Clusters**

Several important galactic clusters including the Pleiades and Hyades, are recognisable with the naked eye, while others, for example, Praesepe, and the double cluster h and χ Persei, are recognisable with only slight telescopic aid. Clusters of this kind have the following general properties: they are regions of relatively high star density where the brightest stars are of about the same magnitude and are well resolved from one another; the total number of stars in a galactic cluster is fairly small, and rarely exceeds two or three hundred; the brighter stars may be so few that they can hardly be said to define a shape for the cluster and for anything like a continuous distribution function recourse must be had to the fainter stars, though these are never so numerous as to provide, as they do in the case of the globular clusters, a continuous background of unresolved stars which are cluster members. The star distribution may be of almost any kind, ranging from the very loose to a well-defined concentration. Most of these clusters tend to occur in the sky fairly near the plane marked by the Milky Way which gives them their name of Galactic Clusters, but the term *Open Clusters* is used as a frequent alternative.

The unsatisfactory nature of this description of the galactic clusters has to be admitted, and it will be obvious that some of the properties mentioned will change with distance for otherwise identical clusters: some quite prominent clusters would be lost against the general background of Milky Way luminosity if their distances were increased by ten or a hundred times, and some stellar groups have been identified as clusters when the reality of any special concentration is doubtful. Large numbers of clusters are recognised and are the object of intensive research at the present time.

In 1958, Alter, Ruprecht and Vanýsek produced a card catalogue of star clusters of various kinds which included 576 open or galactic clusters; to this must be added various supplements (also published by the Publishing House of the Czechoslovak Academy of Sciences, Prague), including data from a number of new sources, of which the richest was the Sky Survey made by the Palomar Schmidt telescope, which have since increased the total number of galactic clusters known to 867. Some of the better known clusters have been the object of very intensive study indeed: for example, the original catalogue listed some 300 papers on the Pleiades, and the supplements contain some dozens more. The volume of published work on the Hyades is almost as great.

Observations of colours and apparent magnitudes of stars in many clusters, of which the Hyades, Pleiades, and Praescepe may be taken as examples, yield results which are in many respects closely parallel to those found for stars in the solar neighbourhood. In each case there is a main sequence which may be even narrower than that found for stars in the solar neighbourhood. Part of the observed width in the latter case is attributed to the fact that the stars near the Sun are a mixture of stars with different metal content, and this element of diversity will not be present in a cluster if all its stars have originated from material having a particular chemical composition. There are usually stars of luminosity Classes other than V, but for a fair proportion of its length, the main sequence in a cluster will closely resemble that found for the stars in the solar neighbourhood. Subject to corrections for reddening and absorption, which will be small if the cluster is not too remote, the distance modulus may be determinable by imposing the condition that the two main sequences should be superposable. At the same time, since the apparent magnitudes of the giants, and other bright stars in the cluster will have been determined with an accuracy at least as good as that which applies to the dwarfs, the absolute magnitudes of the bright stars in the cluster can be determined. In this way information about bright stars not occurring in the solar neighbourhood can be obtained from clusters. This is a very powerful method: we now consider some applications of it, and some of its possibilities and limitations.

3.15. The Hyades

A colour-magnitude diagram for the Hyades was determined by H. L. Johnson and C. F. Knuckles in 1955. (Because of the vast bulk of available observational results some injustice is done by the selection of a particular investigation for discussion, but this is unavoidable.) For most clusters the linear dimensions are so small compared with distance from the Sun that all the members may be considered to be at the same distance, but in the case of the Hyades the extension in depth is a significant fraction of the mean distance, and the observed points on the main sequence show a scattering because of this. The observational results were reviewed by Heckmann and Johnson in 1956 making use of another feature of clusters which is of great importance. This is the feature that for the continued existence of a cluster its members must have spatial velocity components which do not differ too widely. There must be some reservations about this statement, since obviously, if a cluster is very massive it could provide a relatively concentrated aggregate mass which would cause individual cluster members to orbit round it. However, if the gravitational binding is not strong it may be assumed that individual members will have motions which will not change appreciably with time, and if this is so, all the motions must be nearly identical. This argument is often used in deciding cluster membership by considering whether the radial velocity of a possible member is close to the average for the known members. The closeness of equality of velocity which is required to preserve a cluster in existence can easily be estimated. If two stars, now near together, had total velocities differing by 10 k/ms, then after the lapse of a million years they would be separated by 10 parsecs, a distance comparable with the dimensions of most clusters. Since we have reason to believe that the ages of a great majority of clusters are many orders of magnitude greater than a million years, the identity of motion must be very close. Lengthy studies using accurate proper motions and radial velocities have demonstrated that the Hyades stars are all moving together in space relative to the Sun with a velocity close to 45 km/s in the direction of the point at R.A. 6h 16m, Declination + 8°. This brings out an important point of which much will be made later that the identity of motion makes it overwhelmingly probable that all the stars in the cluster originated together, in a small volume of space and in a brief period of time. For the Hyades the proper motion data are excellent: all the proper motion vectors converge to a point which is the perspective point of the parallel vectors in space. (Figure III.5.) The radial velocity measured for each star will be the projection of the common vector along the line of sight, while the proper motion of each star in angular terms will be given by the component perpendicular to the line of sight divided by the distance to the star in question. If V is the cluster velocity relative to the Sun, taken by Heckmann and Johnson to be 45·3 km/s, and if λ is the angle between the direction to the convergent point and to the star, the proportion contributing to the proper motion will be $V \sin \lambda$, and the proper motion due to this cause will be given by

$$V \sin \lambda = 4 \cdot 74 \ \mu/p$$

where μ is the annual proper motion in seconds of arc, and p is the parallax of the star concerned. The fact that the observed radial velocity must be $V \cos \lambda$ enables the value of V used in this formula to be found. In this specialised case the parallax of each star in the cluster is found by a method quite independent of the usual trigonometric one. Heckmann and Johnson found distance moduli for individual stars which showed a range from 2·56 to 3·43 magnitudes, with a mean of 3·03 in good agreement with the mean found by van Bueren. Use of these moduli eliminates most of the scatter from a narrow main sequence except for a few cases attributed to the fact that although the observed stars all look single, some of them may

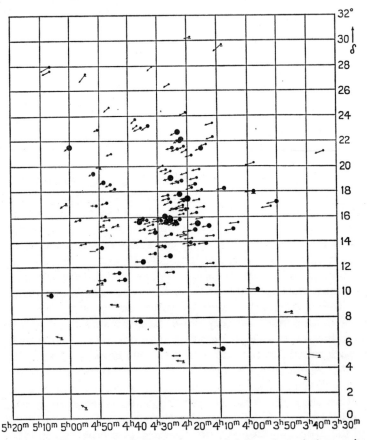

Figure III.5: Map of the Hyades, showing stars brighter than ninth magnitude, and their proper motions. (After H. G. van Bueren, by permission of the Director, Leiden Observatory.)

actually be doubles of such small separation that they cannot be resolved. If there are such stars with equal components, and the same colour, then their total light will be twice as great as that of a single star of the same colour, and the corresponding point on the diagram will appear 0·75 magnitudes above the position expected for that colour. If the components are unequal the deviation from the point appropriate to the brighter one will be smaller. Possible effects of unresolved double stars must always be kept in mind when discussing Hertzsprung-Russell diagrams. (Figure III.6.)

The parallax of the Hyades is thus determinable in several different ways, which yield consistent results: from their motions; from superposing the mean observed main sequence on the mean main sequence for solar neighbourhood stars, or, an improvement, first making differential corrections using motion data; finally, since the modulus is only 3 magnitudes, direct trigonometric measurement. However, the

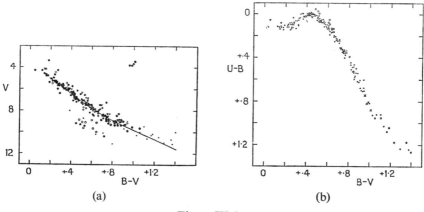

(a)   (b)

Figure III.6.

(a) Colour-magnitude diagram for the Hyades, after Johnson and Knuckles. Among the fainter stars, cluster members are picked out over a large area of sky from among much more numerous background stars. Membership is judged from proper motion and radial velocity. Open circles and small spots indicate doubtful membership, and latest opinion would exclude the stars below the main sequence, once called "Hyades sub-dwarfs". (b) Colour-colour relation for Hyades stars (compare Figure III.2), also after Johnson and Knuckles. (By permission of the Editors of the *Astrophysical Journal*.)

last named is not very accurate since the value found is small, namely $0''{\cdot}025$ (corresponding to 40 parsecs or to the stated modulus of 3 magnitudes), and for the individual stars the results from the motion are far superior. Extension in depth affects the discussion of the cluster known as the Ursa Major Group at 24 parsecs, and the only other cluster nearer than 100 parsecs is the Coma cluster at 75 parsecs from the Sun.

3.16. Interstellar Absorption and Reddening in more Distant Clusters

For more distant clusters the assumption of equality of distance of all the members, judged in proportion to the mean cluster distance, is so nearly true that differential effects may be neglected. However, for distant clusters we encounter a new phenomenon, namely the fact that space is not empty. The density of interstellar material is very low, but its effects become appreciable when distances of the order of hundreds or thousands of parsecs are concerned. The material shows a concentration towards the plane of the Milky Way and is therefore of special importance in connection with distant galactic clusters. The material includes gas clouds of various dimensions distributed in a random way. Over long light-paths these can impress on the spectra of distant stars absorption lines of the elements in the clouds, the most important being the H and K lines of ionised calcium, but many others have been detected. Since interstellar material is at a low temperature the lines are narrow, and the velocity they show is the average of the various clouds producing the lines and not of the stars providing the light. In some cases multiple lines produced in clouds with significantly different velocities have been observed.

For the present purpose we are more concerned with another component of inter-stellar material which is usually termed "dust". This material reduces the intensity of transmitted light differentially, the reduction being greater in the blue than in the red, so that, as we have remarked, B-V colours of distant stars are greater than those of similar less distant ones. Studies of the polarisation effects produced by inter-stellar "dust" showed up some peculiar properties which could barely be accounted for even on the hypothesis that the "dust" consisted of thin iron needles, very much longer than their thickness, which, in certain circumstances had to be assumed to be practically perfectly aligned. However, in 1955, Platt, proposing an astronomical application of certain physical chemical results, suggested that particles of dimensions less than 10 ångströms, involving free radicals and unsaturated organic compounds, some of which might develop at the low temperatures and extremely low densities of interstellar space, could show the quasi-metallic, paramagnetic and optical properties required. The uncertain, and, necessarily, unusual nature of the inter-stellar material demands the inverted commas when it is called "dust". Platt's is by no means the only theory: others postulate graphite needles, or a combination of ice crystals and graphite ("dirty ice").

In approaching the problem of the intrinsic colours and magnitudes of bright stars the expositor has a choice between answering the questions: "How was this problem solved?" or "What would be the best way of solving this problem now?" The choice is important: to answer the former leads through a tortuous labyrinth of successive approximations by a trail of inordinate length, exploring many side turnings on the way. The second question is unreal, for we not only know that we know the answer, we know which ancillary topics are important and which are not. However, unrealistic though it may be, the second is our choice, and we put a false gloss of simplicity on the account by presenting it as a simple logical development from hypotheses to conclusion.

We collect, in imagination, the data for the nearby stars: from this we establish the lower part of the main sequence, and gain an approximate idea concerning the magnitudes and colours of giants. By pushing out a little further, to less reliable parallaxes, we can get some rough notions of the positions of intrinsically brighter stars on the colour-luminosity diagram. Now we can take data for a number of nearby clusters which appear to have distributions similar to the nearby stars, but which also contain a number of intrinsically bright stars. This is, in fact, the pro-cedure adopted by Johnson and Morgan, who used the Pleiades, Praesepe, and N.G.C. 2362. To fit these moderate distance clusters into position an estimate of the small amounts of reddening involved must be made. This can be done by comparing colours of stars with identical spectra, for there is a good overlap, in the clusters and in the solar neighbourhood stars. The Pleiades show a reddening by 0·04 magnitudes in B-V, and N.G.C. 2362 by 0·11 magnitudes, while Praesepe is un-reddened. Correction for this effect requires the distribution for the corresponding cluster to be shifted towards the blue by the corresponding amount. Next, the lower parts of the main sequences in the Pleiades and Praesepe are fitted to the main sequence for the nearby stars, thus obtaining apparent distance moduli for these clusters, and providing a main sequence of unreddened stars which continues up into the fairly bright blue stars much farther than does the diagram for the nearby stars. The fitting on of the main sequence of N.G.C. 2362, adjusted for reddening, carries this process on, because most of the stars observed are bright blue stars, going as bright as $M_v = -3.7$ and the fit must be made in the upper parts of the joint sequence established by the other groups. This feature illustrates an important point connected with later use of composite diagrams of this sort, namely that in a distant cluster only the brighter members may be observable with accuracy, and the fainter members may be difficult or impossible to observe, particularly spectro-scopically, though this depends very much on the equipment available. In other words, study may be limited to the bright blue stars and the upper part of the main sequence which are not represented in the stars near the Sun. The stepwise extension of the data fills this gap.

Johnson and Morgan then made a plot for the unreddened main sequence stars relating U-B to B-V and found the S-shaped curve which has been mentioned previously. Then, for stars which are not so near, but for which accurate spectral types and colours are established, it is possible to compare the colours as affected by interstellar absorption and reddening with the same colours for stars not so affected. In each case the colour index is increased by an amount called a colour excess, and this is denoted by E_u for the U-B colour and E_y for the B-V colour. As a first approximation Johnson and Morgan arrived at the result from the nearer stars that E_u/E_y was constant and equal to 0.72. If this is so, then a quantity can be constructed for a star, no matter if strongly reddened, which is independent of the reddening. This was called Q and expressed analytically as (U-B) $- (E_u/E_y)$(B-V), so that, if the ratio of colour excesses has the value first estimated, Q is a number which can be calculated from observed quantities for any type of star, independently of reddening. This should also enable spectral types to be determined, with certain limitations, from observed values of Q, for, in their initial formulation Johnson and Morgan assigned a value of about -0.92 for all types from O9 to about B0, after which Q changed linearly with type to A0. Observation of a series of stars with identical spectra occurring at a variety of distances can verify whether Q is a proper indicator of spectral type. If it is, then all such stars can be assumed to have the intrinsic colours found for stars of this kind in nearby clusters where reddening will be small or zero. This procedure will not carry us to the determination of intrinsic colours for bright blue stars, but, if a cluster can be found which contains both the stars already studied, and bright blue stars, then, provided it can be assumed that the reddening is the same for all members of the cluster, intrinsic colours and values of Q can be established for the bright stars.

The critical reader may think that the formulation of the previous paragraph is a little reserved in style; if so, he is quite correct. In a later discusion in *Lowell Bulletin* No. 90, Johnson modified some of his original statements. The ratio of colour excesses is not constant, but varies slightly with spectral type. As modified, $E_u/E_y = X + 0.05 E_y$, where, for luminosity Class V stars X is 0.72 at the beginning and end of the range from O5–O9 to A3, and falls to 0.62 at the middle of the range. The intrinsic B-V colour is given as $0.332 Q$. Johnson gave a nomogram enabling an observer to deduce the intrinsic colours from his two-colour observations. As originally formulated, once intrinsic colours had been established, they defined an S-shaped curve on the U-B, B-V plane, and the effect of reddening was to transport the point corresponding to a star along lines of constant slope. To get back to in-trinsic colours the observer merely had to move his observed point along such a reddening line until he arrived at the standard relation, and in this way he found the intrinsic position of the star. (Figure III.2.) This process only failed if the colour anomaly was due to some other cause than reddening, such as undetected duplicity, or if the point fell in such a region that the reddening line through it cut the S-shaped curve at more than one point. In the revised version some variation of slope and some curvature has been introduced into the reddening line so that there is now not a single line, but several, but the principle is not much affected. Removal of the effect of reddening by the evaluation of E_v permits the point for a given star to be plotted on the Hertzsprung-Russell diagram with the correct value of B-V. It has already been suggested that, for transmission of light through material of given physical properties the extinction in any colour will be numerically proportional to the colour excess. We have shown that the extinction in V is proportional to the colour excess in (B-V), and it is customary to adopt a factor of 3·0 by which the latter is to be multiplied to obtain the former. It is curiously difficult to justify the choice of this constant value. One can well imagine that different physical conditions along the line of sight might easily produce different values of the ratio in different parts of the sky. There is positive evidence of variations in certain cases. Most of the information on this point has been obtained indirectly from computations based on hypotheses of the physical properties of the interstellar medium, or from photo-metric observations of stars subject to extinction. For a direct observational deter-mination we should require to know the distance of a star subject to perceptible extinction by a method equivalent to the trigonometrical determination of parallax. However, if the parallax is large, extinction will be negligible: if it is small, it will be of no use. If we use a method which depends on the identification of stellar species and the assignation of an absolute magnitude we cannot tell how to apportion the observed modulus between the effects of distance and the effects of extinction. To a first order, extinction is independent of spectral type, so both effects produce a vertical displacement of a Hertzsprung-Russell diagram. Absolute magnitudes of most types of star can be established from investigations of clusters where extinction is small. Absolute magnitudes of very bright stars, usually determined from distant clusters, may be uncertain by some tenths of a magnitude because of unknown extinc-tion corrections. If such types of star are then used for still greater distances, where extinction may be even more severe, the uncertainties will be still further multiplied.

For the nearer clusters, with small extinction corrections introduced, distance moduli can be estimated by securing the best superposition of main sequences to that given by the nearby stars. For the Pleiades the modulus is 5·8 magnitudes (144 parsecs), for Praesepe 6·2 magnitudes (174 parsecs) and, for the rather distant cluster, N.G.C. 2362, showing a reddening of 0·11 magnitudes, Johnson and Morgan find a modulus of 11·6 magnitudes, corresponding to a distance of 2,090 parsecs.

If the Hertzsprung-Russell diagrams of all clusters were the same, then their distance moduli could be found by adopting that value which produced exact superposition of all parts of an observed diagram on a standard one. This is now known not to be the case: for the purpose of distance determination the lower part of the main sequence must be superposed on the standard main sequence. The reasons for the differences between one cluster and another will be discussed below, beginning with those systems, the globular clusters, which show the sharpest contrast with the galactic clusters.

3.17. The Globular Clusters

The name is a very apt one for, in appearance these objects are of a globular form, their shapes ranging from circular to distinctly elliptical. The notion of shape is readily definable, for in all globular clusters the apparent density of stars decreases outwards from a maximum at the centre, and the shape of a cluster can be defined from the form of the closed curves marking regions of equal density. Alter, Ruprecht and Vanýsek listed 117 globular clusters in their original catalogue, and it has been estimated that there may be some 200 associated with the Galaxy. In very many respects globular and galactic clusters are in contrast. Galactic clusters lie near the Milky Way. Globular clusters are found anywhere in the sky, and, if they seem to avoid the Milky Way this is because nearer clouds of dust and gas obscure them from view. For a fuller discussion of the relation between the globular clusters and the Galaxy, the reader is referred to Chapter IV. The galactic clusters as we know them are all rather near to us in space because the more distant ones become lost in the star clouds of the Milky Way, and most of the best known ones are at distances less than 2,000 parsecs. All the globular clusters happen to be at distances greater than 2,000 parsecs, Most galactic clusters are well resolved and there is no continuous background of unresolved stars, a natural consequence of the fact that they mainly have diameters less than 10 parsecs and rarely as many as 300 members. By contrast globular clusters have diameters which, in individual cases can be traced out to between 20 and 100 parsecs, and the membership of each is probably of the order of 100,000 to 1 million stars. Actual star counts do not go as high as this, but in most globular clusters the faintest members are not resolved and appear as a continuous background of illumination, so that their numbers are somewhat conjectural. It was pointed out many years ago by Shapley that the colour-magnitude diagrams of globular clusters were different from those of galactic clusters or of the stars in the solar neighbourhood, for in the globular clusters the brightest stars are red, whereas in many galactic clusters the brightest stars are blue. This can be seen instantly in, for example, the most prominent of all the globular clusters, the southern one, Omega Centauri, when it is viewed with a reflecting telescope, that is, an instrument giving a good colour rendering, of quite moderate size. There seems no particular reason why the implications of this fact should not have been realised a good many years ago, but its significance has been brought out only rather recently following accurate photometric studies of some of the northern globular clusters by workers such as Arp, Baum, Sandage and Johnson.

Towards the end of the eighteenth century Messier produced a catalogue of about 100 prominent non-stellar objects in the skies visible from the northern hemisphere —galactic clusters, globular clusters and galaxies. Items in this catalogue are denoted by the letter M followed by a number, and many of the more prominent northern globular clusters have designations of this type. The two apparently brightest clusters of all are not so designated, for they are both in the southern skies. These are Omega Centauri and 47 Tucanae, both roughly a degree in diameter to their outermost parts, both visible to the naked eye, and both at distances approximating 5,000 parsecs. Although these clusters have not been studied so extensively as some of the northern ones, one feature of contrast is well established, namely that Omega Centauri contains some hundreds of variable stars, whereas 47 Tucanae contains only a handful. In the north there are some half-dozen globular clusters with diameters over one-third of a degree: these are the ones in which it is profitable to undertake photometric studies with the object of establishing Hertzsprung-Russell diagrams, for these are the nearer objects in which resolution of individual stars, say as faint as the Sun, may be possible. The high star density introduces considerable difficulties, and such studies are usually confined to the outer parts of the larger globular clusters. The larger northern globular clusters include M 3, M 4, M 5, and M 13, the last named being the celebrated cluster in Hercules. A number of the northern clusters have now been investigated photometrically, and with them must be associated other clusters such as the galactic cluster M 67 and the cluster N.G.C. 6397, the latter so near in space (2,400 parsecs) and so relatively loose in structure, that its affinities with the globular clusters were for some time not realised.

   The globular clusters form a spatial system symmetrical about the galactic centre, and since this lies in the southern sky a majority, including many faint ones rather near the centre of the Galaxy, lie in the southern skies.

3.18. The Hertzsprung-Russell Diagrams of Globular Clusters

Beginning some ten years ago, accurate colour magnitude diagrams began to be determined for a number of northern globular clusters at the Mount Wilson and Palomar Observatories by a number of workers including Arp, Baum and Sandage.

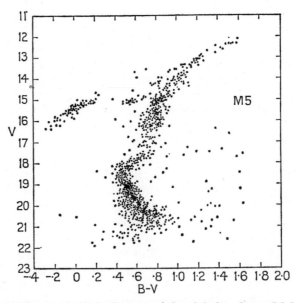

Figure III.7 Colour-magnitude diagram of the globular cluster M 5, after Arp.
(By permission of the Editors of the *Astrophysical Journal*.)

This involved photoelectric photometry of very faint stars past the 20th magnitude. All the diagrams showed the same general character. (Figure III.7.) Beginning with the faintest stars there is a main sequence closely resembling that found in a galactic cluster or for the stars in the solar neighbourhood. However, as this continues upwards to the left, towards brighter and bluer stars, a novel feature is found. The sequence quite suddenly leaves the line for the galactic cluster main sequence and turns off sharply upwards and to the right, at a point, different for each cluster, which has come to be known as the "break-off" or "turn-off" point. The globular cluster sequence then follows a zigzag path leading almost vertically upwards, before swinging smoothly up and to the right to give a giant sequence lying somewhat above the giant sequence for the galactic clusters which we have met in previous discussion. This giant sequence comes to an end, but there remains one further sequence on the diagram: this is the *"horizontal branch"* which may be thought of as originating near the terminal point of the giant branch and extending at first downwards and to the left forming a cusp with the giant branch. It then turns horizontal, continues to the left and turns downward to peter out at a colour of about B-V $= -0 \cdot 3$ and at an absolute magnitude around $M_V = +1$. The final feature to be remarked is that the horizontal branch is not quite continuous but has a clean-cut gap in its centre near B-V $= +0 \cdot 35$ and about two-tenths of a magnitude in extent in B-V. The colour corresponds roughly to that of an early F-type star and it is within this gap that the variable stars specially characteristic of globular clusters occur. Some globular clusters also contain other types of variable not found in this gap.

Diagrams of this general character describe a type of stellar population known as Population II to distinguish them from the kind of diagram associated with galactic clusters or with the solar neighbourhood, which in recent years have come to be called Population I. These terms originate in a most important paper written during World War II by the late Walter Baade, who reported the first resolution into stars of the objects known as elliptical nebulae (see the chapter on "Galaxies"). Using the 100-inch reflector at Mount Wilson Observatory, and aided by the Pacific Coast war-time black-out of nearby Los Angeles, Baade was able to make extremely long exposures on nights of superb seeing, and to produce photographs of the elliptical nebulae companion systems to the Andromeda nebula, which showed that they actually consisted of vast numbers of individual stars. The smaller effective resolution available up to that time had only shown clouds of continuous luminosity. Baade was also able to show that the brightest stars in these systems were red, in contrast to the accurate Hertzsprung-Russell diagrams current up to that time, which all applied to Population I objects.

The realisation of the significance of these facts came rather slowly. To anticipate, we may say that the differences are connected with the processes of stellar evolution, a fact explicitly brought out for the first time in an important paper by Sandage in 1954. It is presumed that the chief difference between Population I and Population II is one of age, the latter being the older. With efflux of time the diagrams of galactic clusters will come to resemble those of globular clusters, except for the important difference that Population II objects were formed at times when the material available for formation of stars was much simpler, and in particular, contained little or none of the metallic material, which had become available by the time the younger clusters were created.

To give even a cursory sketch of the background ideas involves a considerable digression, which at best can amount to no more than a partial recapitulation of some of the more important points.

3.19. Stellar Structure

The beginnings of ideas about stellar structure date back to the first years of this century, a most important landmark being the publication by Emden in 1907 of a book entitled *Gaskugeln*, dealing with the configurations of self-gravitating spheres of gas. These ideas were taken up by a number of workers, most prominent among whom was Eddington, who used these configurations as models for stars. The basic idea was that at each point in such a spherical model the gravitational field due to the whole distribution determined the rate of decrease of pressure with increasing distance from the centre. The temperature distribution was determined from the equation of state postulated for the stellar material. This was complicated because the material consisted of a mixture of atoms, ions, electrons and radiation. The pressure of the last named became important in very bright and massive stars. If one considers that in Eddington's day there was no more than a suspicion of the mechanism of the generation of nuclear energy, and no knowledge of its dependence on physical and chemical properties of the medium, and that for many years he had no idea of the overwhelming preponderance of hydrogen in the material of stars, it is amazing with what skill he contrived to make his stellar models begin to represent the observed properties of stars. It is four decades since the publication of his book, *The Internal Constitution of the Stars* but, even in a field which has seen revolutionary changes, this work can be read with profit. Although he was driven to make a number of arbitrary assumptions in order to integrate the differential equations, he produced a number of results which have survived to the present day. One of the most important was the demonstration that there must exist a relation between the mass of a star and its total luminosity, or bolometric absolute magnitude.

Eddington was the most outstanding of a number of outstanding research workers who, in the twenties and thirties laid the foundations of the modern theory of stellar structure. For further progress a number of important steps had to be taken. The first attempts to elaborate a cycle of nuclear interactions capable of producing energy at high temperatures and pressures were made by Atkinson, but knowledge of nuclear processes was at that time insufficient. In 1932, Bengt Strömgren pointed out that values for the opacity of stellar material consistent with observation required that stars should contain a very high proportion of hydrogen. In 1936, Cowling, for reasons connected with stability considerations introduced a series of stellar models with a convective region near the centre. Abundance analyses of stellar atmospheres by H. N. Russell showed that stellar atmospheres, contrary to appearances in many cases, must contain the extremely high proportion of hydrogen demanded by analyses of stellar interiors.

3.20. The Generation of Stellar Energy

The stage was now set for rapid progress. It had become certain that the key process in the generation of energy in normal stars must be the conversion of the overwhelmingly abundant hydrogen fuel into helium. The atomic weight of hydrogen is 1·0080 units: that of helium is 4·0028. The conversion of four hydrogen nuclei into a helium nucleus thus involved a small mass loss, which, if converted into energy was quite adequate to provide the enormous emission rates required to explain stellar radiation. A conviction that this must be the basic process was one thing. To devise an actual sequence of reactions capable of carrying it out, when knowledge of what nuclear actions were possible was so defective, and commercial nuclear energy generation lay in the far future, was quite another.

Just before World War II, von Weizsäcker and Bethe proposed a catalytic sequence of nuclear reactions, now known from the names of the catalysts involved as the Carbon-Nitrogen-Oxygen cycle, capable of converting hydrogen into helium under the conditions obtaining in stellar interiors. At first this was thought to be the only process of importance, but, more recently, with the vast increase of experimental information on nuclear properties resulting from commercial and military applications of nuclear transformations, prominence has been given to another and more direct sequence of reactions known as the proton-proton chain. These two processes have been summarised by William A. Fowler in his contribution to the 1959 Liège Symposium. When these processes were first mooted they were known only in rudimentary form; now detailed data on reaction rates, not only for the main processes, but for all side reactions likely to occur under stellar conditions are well known. Listing only the main reactions we have, according to Fowler the following:

The Proton-Proton Chain:

$$H^1 + H^1 \rightarrow D^2 + \beta^+ + \nu$$

$$D^2 + H^1 \rightarrow He^3 + \gamma$$

$$He^3 + He^3 \rightarrow He^4 + 2 H^1$$

or

$$He^3 + He^4 \rightarrow Be^7 + \gamma$$

$$Be^7 + e^- \rightarrow Li^7 + \nu + \gamma$$

$$Li^7 + H^1 \rightarrow 2 He^4$$

or

$$Be^7 + H^1 \rightarrow B^8 + \gamma$$

$$B^8 \rightarrow Be^{8*} + \beta^+ + \nu$$

$$Be^{8*} \rightarrow 2 He^4$$

Here β^+ denotes a positive electron, ν a neutrino, γ a quantum of gamma radiation, and the asterisk an excited nuclear state. The alternatives refer to the final stage of the cycle and denote processes which are proceeding simultaneously. Crudely expressed, this process is equivalent to the direct synthesis of helium from hydrogen by successive adhesions of hydrogen nuclei.

The Carbon-Nitrogen-Oxygen Cycle:

$$C^{12} + H^1 \rightarrow N^{13} + \gamma$$

$$N^{13} \rightarrow C^{13} + \beta^+ + \nu$$

$$C^{13} + H^1 \rightarrow N^{14} + \gamma$$

$$N^{14} + H^1 \rightarrow O^{15} + \gamma$$

$$O^{15} \rightarrow N^{15} + \beta^+ + \nu$$

$$N^{15} + H^1 \rightarrow C^{12} + He^4$$

E

or

$$N^{15} + H^1 \rightarrow O^{16} + \gamma$$

$$O^{16} + H^1 \rightarrow F^{17} + \gamma$$

$$F^{17} \rightarrow O^{17} + \beta^+ + \nu$$

$$O^{17} + H^1 \rightarrow N^{14} + He^4$$

In this cycle, whichever alternative route is followed in the last stage, the process is catalytic: successive hydrogen nuclei adhere to a carbon nucleus, which, with its intermediate transformation products, isotopes of nitrogen and oxygen, emerges from the cycle unchanged, as do catalysts in chemical reactions. In the Carbon-Nitrogen-Oxygen cycle the alternative last stage proceeds at a rate which is only a small fraction of the rate of the former alternative.

It must be realised that even these rather complex sequences of interactions represent severe simplifications of the actual conditions, and that many more side reactions might be listed. For any of these nuclear actions to take place at all requires that the energy of the interacting particles be high, and that the bombardment of one nucleus by another should take place with relative velocities corresponding to the thermal velocities attained at very high temperatures, of the order of millions of degrees. Both the energy generation processes listed may be expected to be temperature dependent, and the dependence for the two processes is different. Both processes will play a part in most stars but their relative importance will depend on the maximum temperature in the star, and on the availability of the hydrogen fuel and the nuclear catalysts. The dominance of one process or the other will profoundly affect the structure of the star, and lead to the establishment of convection either in a central or relatively peripheral zone, and these physical conditions will, in turn determine the relative rates and the degree of completeness of the two chains mentioned. A vast intellectual effort has been expended on the calculation of models of various kinds, and the situation is now clear enough to be summarised in the following distinctly crude form. For low central temperatures, below 21 million degrees (such stars include the Sun), the proton-proton chain is the dominant process. For stars with a high metal content the C-N-O cycle predominates for central temperatures above this value: for stars of lower metallic content the dominance of the C-N-O cycle is delayed until higher central temperatures, possibly as high as 27 million degrees. It seems well established that the star models associated with different types of energy generation are different: massive bright stars in which the C-N-O cycle is dominant have convective cores and radiative envelopes, while fainter stars in which the proton-proton chain is the more important do not have convective cores, but do have a convection zone removed from the centre.

3.21. Stellar Evolution

Whatever the detailed mechanism of conversion, the majority of stars produce their energy by the conversion of hydrogen into helium. Clearly in an intrinsically bright star this conversion is proceeding much faster than in a faint one. For an absolute magnitude range of 15 magnitudes, approximating the range in which the majority of stars is observed to lie, this corresponds to a range of a million to one. On the other hand, as we shall see later, the range of masses exhibited by stars is far smaller than this, probably of the order of only a thousand to one between extremes. It follows that the rate of dissipation of hydrogen fuel by the intrinsically brightest, albeit the most massive stars, is not only absolutely greater than for fainter stars, but greater in relation to the available stocks. If changes are to result from the consumption of fuel stocks, the intrinsically brighter stars will feel the pinch sooner than the fainter.

This theoretical problem was attacked by Chandrasekhar and Schönberg, (with results later somewhat modified by Roy), for the case of a Cowling model star, that is, one with a convective core, within which conversion of hydrogen is taking place. Eventually the supply of fuel within this core will become exhausted, and the core will be replaced by an isothermal one, within which there are no energy sources, and comprising about 12 per cent of the mass of the star. Arrival at this configuration means that there is no longer any fuel available at the centre of the star, but it does not imply that the star will cease radiating. It does imply that from this point onwards there must be a change in the structure of the star which will permit it to draw on fuel resources in other parts of its mass, or to utilise other energy cycles. The point is thus one at which a completely new model must be used to describe later stages in the evolution of the star.

The importance of Chandrasekhar and Schönberg's work is that it described the changes taking place during this evolutionary stage, and the length of time necessary to cover it, for stars of various kinds. It predicted that in the evolution to the limit a star would increase its brightness by one magnitude, increase its radius by a factor of 1·7, and that, to take an example used by Sandage, a star initially at bolometric absolute magnitude of + 4·5 would evolve to the critical stage in about 5,000 million years. This was not the first time temporal parameters had been introduced into ideas of stellar evolution, but this was the first occasion on which a long-term temporal parameter had been introduced based on reasonably complete ideas of stellar structure and reasonably accurately known values of physical constants. This step has had the most profound effect on astronomy and has guided numerous later researches in estimates of the time-scale of stellar evolution.

3.22. Stellar Evolution and Globular Clusters

These ideas were applied to the interpretation of globular cluster colour-magnitude diagrams in a most important paper communicated to the 1953 Liège Symposium by A. R. Sandage. In this paper it was supposed that the colour magnitude diagram of a globular cluster arises as the result of the processes of stellar evolution, caused by the consumption of the hydrogen fuel, and acting much more rapidly on intrinsically brighter stars than on fainter ones, operating on a group of stars originally lying on a line in the Hertzsprung-Russell diagram effectively coincident with the Population I Main Sequence. All the stars will move on the diagram on lines which lead along upward-going curves from their starting points, but the brighter stars will be displaced far more rapidly. The first effect of evolution will be to replace the original Main Sequence by another, practically coincident with the original in its lower parts, but curving smoothly away from the original, upwards and to the right, for the brighter stars. This situation is illustrated by the Main Sequences of various galactic clusters, and has been made use of in discussing the intrinsic luminosities of bright stars. The Main Sequences of these clusters proved to be superposable in their lower parts, but the upper part of each sequence turns away from the mean, leaving it at a certain point which we have already noted as being called the "break-off point". These points can now be given an interpretation in terms of age of the clusters, for the greater the span of time since the formation of the coeval stars of a cluster, the farther down the main sequence this break-off point will fall. Thus the Hertzsprung-Russell diagrams of the general run of galactic clusters, composed of relatively young stars can be arranged in order of age, and even roughly dated from a consideration of the evolutionary displacement of the upper part of the sequence according to the Chandrasekhar-Schönberg theory, so long as the evolutionary development does not go beyond their limit.

Sandage now attempted to go beyond this limit and, in a semi-empirical way to discover how stars must evolve after the limit is passed. There was no theory to guide him, but there were the colour-magnitude diagrams of some globular clusters which had to represent the end-product of the same evolutionary processes acting for a much longer time. Sandage addressed himself to the photometric results published for the globular cluster, M 3, where the break-off point occurs near $M_V = 4$. From absolute bolometric magnitude 7·0 (the faintest stars observed) up to 4·4, the character of its Main Sequence merely reflects the initial stellar evolution according to the Chandrasekhar-Schönberg theory. Sandage's estimate of the age of M 3 was based on the idea that the break-off point occurred at the end of this range, and that according to the formulae of Chandrasekhar and Schönberg, evolution to the limit would have occurred in about 5×10^9 years. For stars above the break-off point evolution in this time must have caused the original main sequence to be mapped into the observed dog-leg sequence characteristic of the globular clusters. Considerations of what is called the *luminosity function*, namely the observed numbers of stars in each interval of magnitude, enabled him to draw a number of semi-empirical evolution tracks on the Hertzsprung-Russell diagram showing the expected later history, beyond the Chandrasekhar-Schönberg limit, for stars originally on the main sequence and now on the globular cluster sequence. Although the conversion of hydrogen into helium involves some loss of mass, which reappears as radiation, the proportion is very small, so that Sandage's original scheme was one for evolution of stars at effectively constant mass. The mass-luminosity relation has already been mentioned, although the discussion of practical methods for the determination of star masses is deferred until later. If this law applies to main sequence stars, then their ordering along this sequence in a progression of luminosity is also an ordering by mass. However, in course of time, as evolution carries stars off the main sequence with a change in absolute magnitude but only a relatively insignificant change of mass, stars will be found which do not satisfy this relation.

The general interpretation of globular cluster colour magnitude diagrams given above permits estimates of distance moduli to be made from superposition of the lower parts of their main sequences, and estimates of age to be made from the observed positions of the break-off points of their main sequences (Figure III.8). The ages of globular clusters are all very great, and we should note for a more ready comprehension of discussions which follow that membership of Population II, deficiency in metal content (a property which globular cluster stars share with subdwarfs and high velocity stars), great age, and spherical distribution in the Galaxy, all go together.

We shall return to estimates of some of the parameters mentioned above after brief reference to the difficult and contentious topic of stellar origins, and to more detailed researches on stellar evolution which have had the effect of modifying Sandage's original work.

3.23. The Origin and Evolution of Individual Stars

Recent discussions of these topics have led to a fairly generally agreed picture of which a crude summary is now given. It has to be assumed that stars are formed from the interstellar gas available in the Galaxy. This consists mainly of hydrogen but it also contains metals in much the same proportions as are found to occur in the Sun and other stars of which the composition has been analysed in detail. The fact that the very old stars of the globular clusters are found to have metal content only of the order of one per cent or less of that found in relatively young stars, such as those of the Hyades cluster, suggests that in the distant past the metal content of interstellar material was much lower than it is now, and that some mechanism involving nuclear interactions must exist for the manufacture of heavy nuclei out of lighter ones. The spherical distribution of the old low-metal stars, contrasted with the present situation where the galactic clusters and the interstellar gas are closely confined to the central plane of the Galaxy, goes to suggest that the globular clusters were formed at a time when the Galaxy had not acquired its present flattened form. These topics will be discussed again at a later stage.

The problem now is to consider the early stages of the history of a star which must begin as a self-gravitating mass of gas, vastly more distended than a star. Once the stage has been reached where the self-gravitation of the mass is dominant, the general course of subsequent development is clear enough. The proto-star will be spherical; the gas of which it is formed will be relatively cool; there will be no radiation pressure to keep it distended, and it will steadily collapse on itself. As this process proceeds, internal pressures and temperatures increase, and a distribution will develop such that both these parameters decrease outwards from the centre of the configuration. As the temperature rises the mass will begin to radiate and will become self-luminous. During this phase, which is called the Kelvin-Helmholtz contraction phase after the two authors who discussed this mechanism as a possible source of stellar energy long before the discovery of nuclear energy, the proto-star is drawing the energy which it radiates from its own store of gravitational energy. During this time the object does not satisfy the mass-luminosity law, and the point corresponding to it on the Hertzsprung-Russell diagram moves on an almost horizontal track from right to left, that is, there is only a slight increase in luminosity, but the surface temperature is steadily increasing. Finally the proto-star will arrive on the Main Sequence, the internal temperatures will have risen sufficiently to light up nuclear reactions, and the proto-star will have become a star and satisfy the mass-luminosity relation. Numerical estimates of the length of time needed for this contraction phase have been made by Herbig. For a star of 20 solar masses, the contraction time is about 30,000 years: at 3 solar masses it is 2 million years, 50 million years for the Sun, rising to 200 million years for two-thirds of the solar mass, and to about 10^9 years for a dwarf star of one-fifth of the solar mass. These contraction times become so long for stars of very low mass that it may be possible to discover many which have not yet reached the main sequence, and it is tempting to think that the observed breakdown of a close relationship between spectral type and absolute magnitude for very late type dwarfs may be in some way connected with this.

Once arrived on the main sequence the stars begin to evolve at different rates which can be judged by the time needed to arrive at the Chandrasekhar-Schönberg limit. In addition to the value already mentioned as used by Sandage, we have the following approximate values which may be useful in fixing the ideas. For a B0 star, with a mass of roughly 20 solar masses, the time to the limit is about 10^7 years: for an early G-dwarf like the Sun (having of course a mass of unity), the limit is about 10^{10} years, while for a late type dwarf of type M, and a mass of one-fifth, the time may run up to 10^{12} years. The very low masses cited for faint dwarfs are the bases of the assertion made earlier that the unknown dwarfs near the Sun do not seriously affect the total estimated mass of the stars in the solar neighbourhood.

Problems still remain in connection both with the very earliest stages of star formation, and with the later stages of stellar evolution. With regard to the first there is one problem of a most elementary kind which proves almost impossible of solution. Comparison of the densities of interstellar matter, even in its densest parts, with the densities found in stars, show that the processes of star formation involve compression of matter by an enormous ratio. All interstellar clouds exhibit random or turbulent motions as well as taking part in the rotary motion of the Galaxy of which more will be heard later. Almost inevitably a section of interstellar cloud of stellar mass will have a certain resultant angular momentum which is not zero. If this is conserved during contraction the corresponding equatorial velocity computed on the assumption that the extreme differential velocity in the cloud is only of the order of 1 km/s works out at many times the velocity of light, a value so far into the range of physical impossibility as to be quite derisory. Among the early type stars high rotational velocities, even of the order of some hundreds of kilometres per second at the equator, have been encountered, but vastly greater velocities would destroy stars by centripetal force or inhibit their original formation. For general discussion of the problems of the origin of stars the reader is referred to a volume of prize essays by G. R. Burbidge, F. D. Kahn, and by Ebert, von Hoerner and Temesváry collected in a volume entitled *The Formation of Stars by the Condensation of Diffuse Matter*. With regard specifically to the angular momentum difficulty, McCrea has proposed a mechanism which rests on the hypothesis that any individual star will be formed by the aggregation of a number of floccules, of which those which combine together will necessarily be selected as happening to have low velocity relative to each other. In this way, so the argument runs, the star itself will have only a low angular momentum although its bodily motion relative to other incipient stars may be quite perceptible. Yet another basic difficulty is connected with the size of condensations which can arise in gas of a given density and temperature. The solution to the problem of the minimum size of condensation, determined by the fact it must contain enough mass to produce a gravitational field at its surface high enough to make the escape velocity greater than the kinetic velocity of the molecules, was solved many years ago by Jeans. The critical mass turns out to be far greater than the mass of a single star, and even of an order of magnitude greater than that of a globular cluster, if the density and temperature assumed are typical for interstellar matter. While such condensations might be invoked in a theory of the origin of globular clusters, they seem to have no relevance to the formation of individual stars or small groups.

However, stars obviously are created in spite of the heavy theoretical objections, and most modern work on the theory of star formation has been directed towards the provision of plausible physical mechanisms for the production of condensations having masses of no more than a few hundred times that of the Sun. To do this involves a search for a force other than gravitation alone: one set of ideas has exploited the possibility that in regions of space occupied by dust and gas—and it is practically certain that stars are formed in such regions—the radiation pressure from existing stars and the shadowing effect of dust grains might play a part in causing compression of material. The existence of dark masses of dust and gas, known as globules, which occur in such regions has been pointed to as evidence for a mechanism of this kind.

Other mechanisms proposed have postulated the action of magnetic fields: this is a very plausible idea, for, as we have seen, there is evidence of the existence of preferred directions in interstellar space, based on observations of polarisation; in certain extragalactic nebulae there are jets reminiscent of the trajectories of ions under the action of magnetic fields; and the entire approach to the existence of sources of radio waves in astronomical objects, mentioned again in a later section, assumes the presence of magnetic fields.

In spite of all this, the essential key does not yet seem to have been found. We can only say that stars are formed, and that there is little doubt that in the past stars have been formed almost simultaneously in the same region of space, so that a cluster has been formed which can survive many aeons of vicissitudes. The oldest clusters are the most massive and populous, possibly because when they were formed, only such large clusters could be created, possibly because clusters of all sizes were created, but only the largest have survived assaults on their identity. Of the younger clusters none seem so populous as the old globulars, and many give evidence of what should be reckoned as a strange paradox: young they are, but the term is relative, and their members have kept together over many millions of years. Their identity of velocity proves that they were formed together under conditions of the closest association, but although they have moved together through all this time, they have done so independently for no mutual interaction has caused any change in their velocities.

3.24. Stellar Associations

The tendency for stars to be formed in groups, whether of many thousands, or scores, or merely as double or multiple stars, has permitted some progress to be made: for example, the luminosity functions of clusters have been used by Limber and others to derive the distribution of masses among newly-formed stars.

That the seat of star formation lies most probably in regions of dust and gas is common cause at present. Two kinds of object have come into prominence in this connection. The T Tauri stars, called after the prototype of the class, are irregular variable stars associated with nebulosity. Their spectra show emission lines together with absorption spectra lying in the range from F 8 to M 2. These stars often occur in groups known as *T associations*, and give signs of being very young stars, lying to the right or above the normal main sequence. They are presumed still to be in the contraction phase of stellar evolution, and Herbig and Haro have produced photographs of a region in the Orion nebulosity showing stars present on later photographs which were earlier absent.

The very bright blue O-type stars also occur in associations and give evidence of being very young. Claims have been made (and contested), that some of these associations are expanding, and a backward extrapolation in time to the epoch of closest concentration yields a figure describing the age of the association. Values of the order of a few hundred thousand to a few million years have been obtained in this way.

Geoffrey Burbidge has summed up the present situation in the words, "The postulate can be made that the O- and T-associations are the seats of all star formation in the Galaxy at the present time". Reference should be made to the discussion in his prize essay for further details. Numerous problems remain. O-Associations and T-Associations sometimes occur together, so that the possibility of a diversity of mechanisms of stellar origin exists. Another problem is that occasionally young blue stars are found remote from the galactic plane in such positions that they could not apparently, even in their whole lifetime, have travelled to their present positions from any region now occupied by relatively dense clouds of interstellar matter. To mention a third: a limited number of hot stars is known which have no hydrogen lines of any kind. These cannot be fitted into the theoretical scheme outlined above, and serve to remind us that although current theories of stellar evolution have proved far more fruitful than those of the past, they too may require modification in the future.

3.25. Age Parameters in Astronomy

Sandage's original discussion of stellar evolution was largely empirical and used ideas based only on initial evolution away from the Main Sequence according to the Chandrasekhar-Schönberg computations. His work stimulated attempts to follow theoretically the later progress of evolution of a star, and Hoyle and Schwarzschild were able to compute a dog-leg path on the Hertzsprung-Russell diagram, closely resembling the observed globular cluster sequence, which might be followed by a star during these later stages. A great many complications were encountered, involving drastic changes in the constitution of a star during this process, the development of a series of zones of different chemical composition, and the possibility at later stages of the occurrence of instability of a dramatic kind leading to a stellar explosion. It also became evident that these processes could lead to the formation of heavy elements which could be redispersed into the interstellar medium, so becoming available for the formation of later generations of stars. Hoyle has given an account of these ideas in his book, *Frontiers of Astronomy*, while in a far more technical review, he, working together with Fowler and the Burbidges, has recapitulated all the known processes likely to be operative in the formation of heavy nuclei from light ones. The basic idea will be clear enough: heavy nuclei can be formed only in physical conditions such as obtain in the deeper interiors of highly evolved stars. To make these available so as to account for their presence in stars not themselves capable of producing such nuclei, requires the hypothesis that they be returned to the interstellar cloud by a mechanism which can disperse a sensible proportion of the mass of a star. The very old stars which we see now as members of globular clusters or very old galactic clusters, were formed from interstellar material of low metallic content.

The old stars, such as subdwarfs, which do not belong to clusters can possibly be supposed to have belonged to clusters which have failed to survive as separate entities, so that their members are now dispersed in space. Young stars will have been formed from material already containing metals and heavy nuclei.

In 1959 Hoyle and Haselgrove undertook calculations of the evolutionary history of stars of various compositions, taking as models two types of star: the first with a high metallic content was denoted by $X = 0.75$, $Y = 0.24$ and $Z = 0.01$, where X was the initial proportion by mass of hydrogen, Y that of helium and Z that of the metals. It will be noted that even so small a value of Z is reckoned as a high metal content, and all the previous instances of the use of the terms describing metallic content of stars can be interpreted according to the numerical values now being given. This first type of star serves as a model for galactic clusters. After the passage of a very long time the Main Sequence turns to form a dog-leg even more pronounced

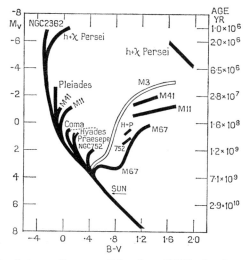

Figure III.8: The famous diagram of Sandage (1957) showing superposition of colour-magnitude diagrams for various clusters, and the original age-calibration of their break-off points. (By permission of the Editors of the *Astrophysical Journal*.)

than that found in globular clusters, the break-off point then occurring for stars practically as faint as the Sun. The shape involves the corollary that there are no very late-type subgiant stars, a feature already remarked in our first discussion of the spectral sequences. Sequences of this kind are found in two very old galactic clusters, M 67, for long thought to be the oldest known, and for N.G.C. 188, which on the basis of recent observations by Sandage must now be regarded as the senior. The age estimates based on this work gave an age near 10^{10} years for M 67 and about half as much again for N.G.C. 188. These enormous figures must be contrasted with the estimates by various workers (understandably showing a wide range), of about 5 million years for the age of the double galactic cluster, h and χ Persei, and for N.G.C. 2362: the age of the Pleiades is estimated at about 60 million years, with about 600 million years for Praesepe, the Coma Cluster and the Hyades.

The low-metal model for globular cluster stars was defined by $X = 0\cdot99$, $Y = 0\cdot009$, and $Z = 0\cdot001$. For clusters such as M 3, M 13 and M 5, for the last-named of which Arp has recently published augmented data, ages of the order of $2\cdot5 \times 10^{10}$ years are derived. The assumed helium content is critical and should this be as much as 25 per cent instead of the $0\cdot9$ per cent assumed, the ages given will be reduced by about one-third.

There is no particular difficulty in arranging clusters in order of increasing age from the position of their break-off points, but the actual values quoted have tended to increase rapidly in recent years. In a field where results are being published at a phenomenal rate, new observational data, or new interpretations may render conclusions obsolete almost as soon as they are reached. It is of interest that it has recently been suggested by Woolf that some of the great ages quoted imply a lifetime for a star longer than is warranted by its available fuel capacity, and that ages near $2\cdot5 \times 10^{10}$ years are too great by a factor of about two. This may mark a reversal of recent trends in thinking.

REFERENCES:

Radiometric Magnitudes:
  E. Pettit and S. B. Nicholson, *Ap.J.*, **68,** 279, 1928.
Effective Temperatures:
  G. P. Kuiper, *Ap.J.*, **88,** 429, 1938.
Interstellar Material:
  J. R. Platt, *Ap.J.*, **123,** 486, 1956.
  H. C. van de Hulst, *Light Scattering by Small Particles*, John Wiley, 1957.
  Interstellar Matter in Galaxies, ed. L. Woltjer, W. A. Benjamin, 1962.
The Hertzsprung-Russell Diagram:
  H. C. Arp, *Encyclopaedia of Physics*, Vol. 51, "Astrophysics", p. 75, Springer, 1958.
  Bengt Strömgren, *Q.J.*, Vol. 4, March 1963.
  O. C. Wilson, *Ap.J.*, **136,** 793, 1962.
Intrinsic Colours and Magnitudes:
  H. L. Johnson, *Lowell Bulletin*, No. 90.
  H. L. Johnson and B. Iriarte, *Lowell Bulletin*, No. 91.
  A. Blaauw, *Stars and Stellar Systems*, Vol. 3, p. 383, 1963.
Nearby Stars:
  W. Gliese, Mitt. A. No. 8, 1957, Astronomisches Rechen-Institut, Heidelberg:
    Zs.f.Ap., **39,** 3, 1956.
Super-supergiants:
  A. D. Thackeray, M. W. Feast and A. Wesselink, *M.N.*, **121,** 337, 1960.
  Ch. Fehrenbach and M. Duflot, *Comptes Rendus de l'Académie des Sciences de France*, **254,** 1380, 1962.
Subdwarfs:
  O. J. Eggen and A. R. Sandage, *M.N.*, **119,** 255, 1959; *Ap.J.*, **136,** 735, 1965.

White Dwarfs:
E. Schatzman, *White Dwarfs*, Amsterdam, 1958.
O. J. Eggen and J. L. Greenstein, *Ap.J.*, **141,** 83, 1965.
W. J. Luyten, *Minnesota Pub.*, **3,** No. 15, 1965.
Line Blanketing:
O. J. Eggen and A. R. Sandage, loc. cit.
R. L. Wildey, E. M. Burbidge, A. R. Sandage and G. R. Burbidge, *Ap.J.*, **135,** 94, 1962.
Hyades:
H. G. van Bueren, *B.A.N.*, Vol. 11, 385, 1952.
H. L. Johnson and C. E. Knuckles, *Ap.J.*, **122,** 209, 1955.
O. Heckmann and H. L. Johnson, *Ap.J.*, **124,** 477, 1956.
Cluster Diagrams:
H. L. Johnson and W. W. Morgan, *Ap.J.*, **117,** 313, 1953.
H. L. Johnson and A. R. Sandage, *Ap.J.*, **121,** 616, 1955.
A. R. Sandage, *Ap.J.*, **135,** 333, 1962.
Globular Clusters:
H. C. Arp and H. L. Johnson, *Ap.J.*, **122,** 171, 1955.
H. L. Johnson and A. R. Sandage, *Ap.J.*, **124,** 379, 1956.
H. C. Arp, *Ap.J.*, **135,** 311, 1962.
Sir Richard v. d. R. Woolley, *Observatory*, **81,** 161, 1961.
Population Types:
W. Baade, *Ap.J.*, **100,** 137, 1944.
Symposium, Pontifical Academy of Sciences, Vatican, 1958.
Nuclear Processes:
Contributions by A. G. W. Cameron and W. A. Fowler in *Symposium, Memoires*, Société Royale des Sciences de Liège, 5th Series, Vol. 3, 1959.
G. R. Burbidge, M. Burbidge, W. A. Fowler and F. Hoyle, *Review of Modern Physics*, 29, 547, 1957.
Stellar Evolution:
M. Schönberg and S. Chandrasekhar, *Ap.J.*, **96,** 161, 1942.
A. R. Sandage, *Liège Memoires*, 4th Series, Vol. **14,** 254, 1954.
A. R. Sandage, *Ap.J.*, **135,** 349, 1962.
N. Woolf, ibid., p. 644.
Star Formation:
Prize Essays, *Die Entstehung der Sterne*, Springer.
W. H. McCrea, *Liège Symposium*, 1959, loc. cit.

IV
The Motions of the Stars

4.1. Introduction

AMONG the measurements described in Chapters I and II are those which enable the motions of stars with respect to the Sun to be determined. The radial velocity gives the motion of a star in the line of sight, and, with proper control of systematic and accidental errors, measurements of this quantity may be treated, for all stars except possibly those near the faintest attainable, as sensibly free from uncertainty.

The formula, $V = 4\cdot74\mu/p$, for the transverse velocity in kilometres per second, of a star of parallax p, having a proper motion of μ seconds of arc per year, has been quoted several times. If both proper motion and parallax are large an accurate value of V usually follows. For more distant stars, uncertainty in V is produced more by lack of precision in p than in the measured components of proper motion. If trigonometric parallaxes can be replaced in this range by parallaxes determined by spectroscopic, photometric or other methods, quite small proper motions of fairly distant stars can be put to good use. Thus, for example, if a star can be recognised as lying on the ordinary Main Sequence, either from a study of its spectrum, or from its spectrum and its colour, then a distance modulus can be found which is superior to a direct trigonometric parallax measurement for all except the very nearest stars. For more distant stars, say, beyond 100 parsecs, where only indirect determinations of parallax are of any value, the uncertainties in proper motion data for individual stars begin to assume importance. Statistical studies of groups of stars can however be made to yield useful results even when the proper motions are of the order of $0''\cdot010$ or even smaller per year.

If the observational data can be assumed free from error, then it is possible to compute the motion of a star relative to the Sun in a coordinate system natural to that star, and peculiar to it. This is the system in which the radial velocity, the proper motion in right ascension, and the proper motion in declination are used to specify motions relative to the Sun in kilometres per second parallel to three mutually perpendicular axes defined in this way. For the comparison of spatial motions of stars in different parts of the sky, transformation from these individual axes to a system of axes of more general validity and significance is required.

4.2. Galactic Structure

Significant coordinate systems are related to the structure of the Galaxy or Milky Way. Anticipating a fuller description to be given later, we may say that the Sun and all the stars in its neighbourhood, and all the individual stars visible to the naked eye, are but a few members among many millions, of a star system known as the Galaxy or Milky Way. It is roughly circular in outline and has a diameter of the order of 30,000 parsecs. The Sun lies at about 10,000 parsecs from its centre, not far, by sheer accident, from its median plane. The Galaxy is strongly flattened so that in profile or section it would appear as a system in which the lines of equal star density would be very elongated curves, approximately ovals or ellipses, with their longer axes coinciding with the trace of this median plane. If an analogy for the shapes can be found, the nearest to the form of the surfaces of equal star density, save for those near the very centre, is that of the discus used by athletes. The star density decreases outwards so that there is the same indefiniteness about dimensions as there is in the case of star clusters. Since the Sun is near the median plane and fairly remote from the centre, our view of this system is an interior one. As seen by the naked eye there is no particular concentration of the brighter stars, for, although some of them are at considerable distances, few are at distances comparable with the dimensions of the Galaxy. The more remote stars however do reveal their large-scale distribution, and although they are so far away as to be individually invisible, the total effect of hundreds of millions of faint stars produces a general distribution of faint luminosity. This luminosity increases in intensity towards the plane of the Galaxy, and, because the Sun is near this plane, it reaches its maximum intensity along a line which forms a great circle round the celestial sphere. If the Sun were markedly displaced from the galactic plane this zone of greatest luminosity would be eccentric and lie on a small circle of the sphere. We have, hitherto, used the terms "Milky Way" and "Galaxy" alternatively, but the most common usage reserves the former for the band of luminosity spanning the sky, that is, for the terrestrial appearance, while the latter is used to mean the actual system which is responsible for this appearance. Since the Milky Way is a very large-scale phenomenon, and since the Sun is placed very eccentrically in the Galaxy, the Milky Way does show by enhanced intensity and greater elaboration of structure, the direction in which the centre of the Galaxy lies; this point is on the borders of the constellations Scorpio and Sagittarius. Possibly with the naked eye, and certainly with the slight optical aid afforded by binoculars, it is easy to see the concentration of star clusters towards the plane of the Milky Way. The concentration of the gas and dust clouds towards the same plane is less easily demonstrated, but the dark rift in the system towards the centre, and the black patch, known as the Coal Sack, alongside the Southern Cross, are two easily recognisable examples of dust clouds near the plane.

The median plane of the Galaxy as marked by the centre line of the Milky Way is a great circle which defines on the celestial sphere the line known as the *Galactic Equator*: normal to this is an axis, marking the line through the Sun perpendicular to the galactic plane, intersecting our celestial sphere in points called the *North* and *South Galactic Poles*. Because the Galaxy is strongly flattened, the distance to which its star clouds extend from the solar neighbourhood in the direction of the galactic poles is small. The vast majority of the member stars lie within 250 parsecs of the central plane of the Galaxy at the Sun's distance from the galactic centre. The general illumination of the Milky Way is due to bright stars, such as giants and supergiants seen at great distances. Since a distance of 250 parsecs corresponds to a distance modulus of 7 magnitudes we can easily see why the visual appearance of the sky down to apparent magnitude 6, say, differs in the direction of the galactic poles from that seen in the direction of the centre. Supergiants with absolute magnitudes between -5 and -2 must appear as bright stars between apparent magnitudes $+2$ and $+5$, but not fainter because the supply runs out at 250 parsecs. We tend to see more of these as apparently bright stars in the Milky Way than towards the poles because these are young stars which favour the galactic plane, where the young galactic clusters are found. Ordinary giants are seen at 250 parsecs at the limit of visibility at apparent magnitude 6: our unaided sight range does not now extend beyond the limits of the system and we are not particularly conscious of any anisotropy in their distribution on the sky. Since they outnumber the supergiants in a given volume of space they make a considerable contribution to the number of apparently bright stars and smooth out the tendency to concentration towards the plane and centre of the Milky Way which would be noticeable if we confined attention to the supergiants. Dwarfs, as we have seen are visible only if they happen to be very near, and the scale of which we are conscious in their case is so small that the volume of space reflects no internal change related to the grand structure of the Galaxy.

4.3. Galactic Coordinates

The system of galactic coordinates has recently been reformed by changes principally in zero point. Both old and new systems defined galactic latitude as the angular distance of a point north or south of an adopted galactic equator, while galactic longitude is an angular measure starting from some zero point and increasing from $0°$ to $360°$ along the galactic equator. The effect of the reformation has been, except in high galactic latitudes, to change all galactic longitudes by a nearly constant amount and to leave galactic latitudes practically unchanged. Galactic longitudes and latitudes are denoted by l and b, and the old, or Ohlsson system, is now distinguished as l^I, b^I. In this system the coordinates of the centre of the Galaxy were near $l^I = 327°\cdot9$, $b^I = -1°\cdot3$. In the new system, introduced in 1959, the direction to the galactic centre is intended to define the zero point, so that for it, in the new notation, we have $l^{II} = 0$, $b^{II} = 0$. The formal definition is that the north galactic pole lies at R.A. 12h 49m, Dec. $+27°\cdot4$ (equinox 1950·0), while the zero of latitude and longitude (i.e. the direction to the centre) lies at 17h 42m·4, $-28°$ 55′, and the sense of measurement is such that on the galactic equator increasing galactic longitude and increasing right ascension correspond.

It is now customary to compute the velocity components of stars relative to the Sun, in terms of axes valid for all stars. These axes define three velocity components, u, v, w, which are specified as follows: u is the velocity in the direction opposite to the galactic centre, w is in the direction of the north galactic pole, while v forms a *left-handed* triad with the other two, in the order u, v, w. Coordinate axes, x, y, z, corresponding to these have their origin at the Sun.

For a star at (α, δ) with proper motion components in the R.A. and declination directions amounting to μ_α, μ_δ in seconds of arc per annum, and with a radial velocity V_r expressed in km/s, the velocity components in the plane of the sky and radially are given by

$$V_\alpha = 4\cdot74 \; \mu_\alpha/p, \quad V_\delta = 4\cdot74 \; \mu_\delta/p, \quad V_r$$

If we take an intermediate set of right handed axes in equatorial coordinates defined by $X = (0^h, 0°)$, $Y = (6^h, 0°)$, $Z = (-, 90°)$ we have the transformations (Figure IV.1):

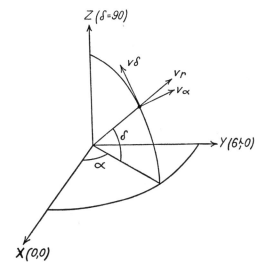

Figure IV.1: Space motions in X, Y, Z coordinates.

$$V_X = - V_a \sin \alpha - V_\delta \cos\alpha \sin \delta + V_r \cos\alpha \cos \delta$$
$$V_Y = + V_a \cos \alpha - V_\delta \sin \alpha \sin \delta + V_r \sin \alpha \cos \delta$$
$$V_Z = \qquad\qquad + V_\delta \cos \delta \qquad + V_r \sin \delta$$

The direction cosines of a point (α_0, δ_0) with respect to the (XYZ) system are

$$l_0 = \cos \delta_0 \cos \alpha_0 \qquad m_0 = \sin \alpha_0 \cos \delta_0 \qquad n_0 = \sin \delta_0$$

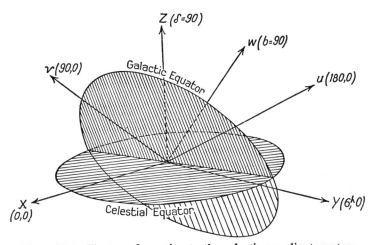

Figure IV.2: The transformation to the galactic coordinate system.

so that the resolved velocity of the star in the direction (a_0, δ_0) is $l_0 V_X + m_0 V_Y + n_0 V_Z$. To obtain velocities in the (u, v, w) system take the values of a_0, δ_0 corresponding to the appropriate galactic coordinates, thus (Figure IV.2):

	l^{II}	b^{II}	a_0	δ_0	l_0	m_0	n_0
u	180°	0°	85° 37′	$+28°$ 55′	$+\cdot0669$	$+\cdot8729$	$+\cdot4836$
v	90°	0°	317 34	$+48$ 07	$+\cdot4928$	$-\cdot4504$	$+\cdot7445$
w	—	90	192 15	$+27$ 24	$-\cdot8676$	$-\cdot1884$	$+\cdot4602$

4.4. The Motions of the Nearby Stars

Gliese has computed the (u, v, w) velocity components of all the stars in his catalogue for which data on motions were available. Many of the gaps in his list have been filled, and some additions made to the roster of stars within 20 parsecs, by observations made since he wrote, to a large extent by the Cape observers using the Radcliffe telescope. Gliese's discussion of his own results will serve our present purpose. Each of the stars considered may be regarded as having an individual or "peculiar" motion, superposed on systematic motions of various kinds. The Sun is no exception to this rule, and since all the measured velocity components are relative to the Sun, any peculiar motion which the Sun may have with respect to the mean of the neighbouring stars, will introduce a systematic effect into their measured velocity components with respect to the Sun. In general the mean velocity of any class of object with respect to the Sun is not zero. This mean value is often called the *Solar Motion* though it represents the velocity of the Sun with respect to the average of the group, with sign reversed. Another concept is that of the *local standard of rest* which is defined by the mean of all the neighbouring stars. The peculiar motion of the Sun relative to the nearby stars is often quoted as $u = -10$, $v = +15$, $w = +7$ km/s, corresponding to a total velocity of about 20 km/s directed towards R.A. 18h, Dec $+30°$, a point in the constellation Hercules. The nearest bright star is Vega. However, considerable caution must be exercised in discussing values of solar motion. There are the purely arithmetical troubles over the signs used, depending on whether the velocity of the Sun relative to the star system or vice versa, is meant, and whether a left-handed coordinate system, such as the one we have chosen, or a right-handed one with the sign of u reversed, is being employed. These ought not to cause confusion, but in fact they do. More sophisticated difficulties are introduced by the fact that different values of solar motion are found for different types of star. The most important distinction is between low velocity stars, and stars with larger velocities, the limit being taken at a total motion of somewhere between 60 and 70 km/s. This is easily demonstrated. Gliese deals with the topic, or we may take data from Cape publications giving velocity components of nearby stars. In Figure IV.3 data for dwarfs in the range G0V to G3V are shown, that is, for stars closely similar to the Sun. The systematic offset of the distribution of points is well shown. Gliese's mean point for this type of star lies more or less in the centre of a clutch of stars. Segregated to one side are a group of high velocity points for which the mean offset from the origin is much larger. It is not a tautology to say that the mean motion with respect to the high velocity stars is greater than that with respect to the low velocity stars. The high velocity points could, conceivably, have been distributed symmetrically about the origin, but they are not.

Computed values of solar motion, even for low velocity stars, probably show some increase with later spectral types but a word of caution is necessary. The increase is correlated with the incompleteness of our information about dwarf stars of the types in question, and observational selection is important. As we have seen all dwarfs of types A, F, and almost all dwarfs of type G, within Gliese's 20-parsec limit have been identified. Dwarf stars of type K, and still more, of type M, have such faint absolute magnitudes, that they cease to be conspicuous. There has been a marked tendency, of the kind mentioned in the previous chapter in connection with subdwarfs, to pick out those distinguished by high proper motions. The roster of the fainter dwarfs has thus been biased in favour of high velocity stars, and, because of the asymmetrical distribution of points in a (u, v, w) diagram this has led to inflated values for computed solar motions.

Vyssotsky and Lindblad independently developed a criterion for picking out dwarf M-type stars on objective prism plates, namely that these stars showed a

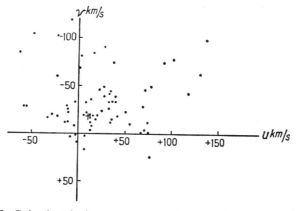

Figure IV.3: Galactic velocity components relative to the Sun for nearby dwarf stars of solar type (G0V-G3V). Note the systematic displacement due to solar motion. The cross marks the mean point for G stars of low velocity according to Gliese. Note also the asymmetrical segregation of a number of high velocity stars. (Data for southern stars from the Cape Observatory.)

general depression in spectrum brightness starting near the calcium line at 4,227Å and extending to the red. Considerable numbers of such stars have been picked out by Vyssotsky and his associates at the Leander McCormick observatory. Gliese demonstrates that these stars, which are not subject to the same observational selection as those chosen by proper motion criteria, do not show a solar motion increased as compared with the earlier spectral types.

4.5. Solar Motion and Secular Parallaxes

The solar motion with respect to a homogeneous group of stars can often be used to estimate their absolute magnitudes and parallaxes. Suppose that there is a definite solar motion causing a distortion of the apparent random motions of the stars, and, in kilometres per second let this have components X, Y, Z in equatorial coordinates. In an ideal case we need to know the radial velocities and the proper motions of all the stars under discussion. However, we may begin with the radial velocities only.

We argue that these are the combination of the systematic motion of the group plus radial motions peculiar to each star. We write an equation for each star which endeavours to represent the observed radial velocity as due to this systematic motion

$$lX + mY + nZ = V_r$$

for the star at (a, δ) where $l = \cos a \cos \delta$, etc. If there are n stars the n corresponding equations cannot all be exactly satisfied so XYZ are found by a least squares procedure as the solution of

$$X \, \Sigma \, l^2 \; + Y \, \Sigma \, lm \; + Z \, \Sigma \, ln \; = \Sigma \, l \, V_r$$

$$X \, \Sigma \, lm + Y \, \Sigma \, m^2 \; + Z \, \Sigma \, mn = \Sigma \, m \, V_r$$

$$X \, \Sigma \, ln \; + Y \, \Sigma \, mn + Z \, \Sigma \, n^2 \; = \Sigma \, n \, V_r$$

The velocities $X \, Y Z$ so found can be converted to galactic coordinates afterwards. These equations give the mean motion of the group. If it is thought that the group is expanding an additional term, known as a K-term can be included. Such terms have been introduced in many analyses, but their status is often equivocal, and the values found have often been no larger than the systematic uncertainties affecting radial velocity measures. The efficacy of such a group analysis is the greater the more homogeneous the character of the stars concerned. In the thirties much work was done simply by collecting all available data. The more discriminating analyses now in vogue may be based on a careful selection of stars of a given spectral type, luminosity class and apparent magnitude—to take a possible example—and the results will have the greater physical significance because of the care taken in selection.

Parallel discussions using only proper motion data can be undertaken, most profitably if all the stars are at about the same distance. For this situation, the assumption of some definite solar motion vector has the consequence that the proper motions of the chosen stars all include a systematic component which is a reflex of the solar motion. The stars will appear to be opening out from the point in the sky towards which the solar motion is directed (the solar apex), and closing in towards the antipodal point (the solar antapex). The effect is precisely that seen, say, from the deck of a moving ship and can be vividly demonstrated on a moving picture representation of the actual proper motion data. The viewer has the sensation of movement through a cloud of stars, each, it is true, with its own random motion, superposed on the systematic effect, but it is the latter which makes the strong impression. If V is the solar velocity, then for a star lying at an angular distance λ from the solar apex, the systematic proper motion due to the parallactic effect is $Vp \sin \lambda/4 \cdot 74$ seconds of arc per annum, directed towards the antapex, where, in this formula, p is the parallax of the star concerned. For a star at a distance of 100 parsecs, assuming $V = 20$ km/s, the maximum value of this parallactic motion is $0'' \cdot 04$ per annum, and is attained for stars in directions perpendicular to the solar apex. Much smaller values, corresponding to greater distances, can be handled with some confidence, provided that the assumption is satisfied that the motions for the stars in question are random apart from the systematic effect produced by the solar motion. If both radial velocity and proper motion data are available, parallaxes can be obtained from such studies which are well reconciled with those obtained by other methods. They are known as statistical parallaxes. A closely associated concept is that of *secular parallax* which may be defined as the proper motion resulting from the movement of the Sun through space in the course of a year. We have so far used the term "parallax" without qualification to refer to the positional shift produced by the orbital motion of the earth round the Sun. Strictly these are *annual parallaxes* for the base-line is provided by the annual motion of the earth: secular parallaxes are those in which the base-line is the length traversed by the Sun in its secular motion during a year. If n is the number of seconds in a year, the secular motion of the Sun is $20n$ kilometres, approximately, while, since the orbital speed of the Earth is near 30 km/s, the distance of the Earth from the Sun is near $30n/2\pi$ kilometres. The ratio between these two lengths is thus near $4\pi/3$—more accurately, $4\cdot1$—and this is the ratio between secular parallax and annual parallax. For given apparent magnitudes the following are samples of secular parallaxes which have been determined:

m_v	6	9	12
$b = 0$	$0''\cdot045$	$0''\cdot017$	$0''\cdot007$
$b = 90$	$0''\cdot070$	$0''\cdot027$	$0''\cdot010$

The dependence on galactic latitude is explained by the fact that towards the galactic plane a star of a given apparent magnitude has a higher probability of being an intrinsically bright, and therefore more distant, star, than in the regions near the galactic poles. For a given apparent magnitude the secular parallaxes are therefore larger in the latter regions. This point illustrates the importance of selecting groups of stars as homogeneous as possible for the application of the method. An example of a recent investigation is the determination of the secular parallaxes of the Mira variables by Osvalds and Risley.

4.6. Systematic Motions of Stellar Groups

In the previous chapter a discussion was given of clusters of various kinds, mainly from the photometric standpoint. In addition in the case of the Hyades the feature of community of motion was mentioned. Here we have an extremely homogeneous group of stars, recognisable not only by spatial association, but also by an identity of velocity so close that a striking perspective diagram of proper motions can be constructed. All the members of the Hyades cluster have velocities exceedingly close to $(u, v, w) = (+40, -17, -3)$ and what is known as the *velocity dispersion* among the stars is very small indeed. In this case a far more restrictive analysis than that sketched above can be applied, by requiring all member stars to have essentially the same velocity. Van Bueren concluded that the Hyades contain about 350 stars and that about half the mass of the cluster was contained within a sphere of radius about six parsecs centred at $40\cdot4$ parsecs from the Sun. As we saw, in the case of the Hyades, parallaxes of individual stars are determinable, and the figures given show that these have a considerable range. The possibility then arises, with so near a cluster, that there may be members of the cluster, even in totally different parts of the sky, which belong to the Hyades group of stars. This is a very difficult question. There are bound to be stars which, by chance, possess the correct velocity components within the uncertainties of measurement. They are not difficult to find. Star HD 205067 has $(+41, -19, -3)$, HD 217877 $(+35, -15, -2)$ and HD 200968, depending on assumptions about parallax has values between $(+37, -16, -1)$ and $(+44, -16,$

—9). The differences from the Hyades values could easily be reconciled by making slight changes in the adopted parameters. All these stars lie at right ascensions between about 21 and 23 hours and in the southern sky, and they have no obvious spatial association with the Hyades. It is not impossible that they are members, but this conclusion would imply that the Hyades group had a very large, though not impossibly large spatial extent. The assignment of a star to a group such as the Hyades provides an extremely powerful method of investigation but its very power demands caution in its application.

Several other moving groups and clusters are known, having been identified by community of motion and spatial association. The Ursa Major Cluster has been studied by various authors including Nancy Roman in 1949, and Petrie and Moyls in 1953, with somewhat varied results. Miss Roman obtained a space motion corresponding to $(u, v, w) = (-14, +1, -11)$, and confirmed the idea that the cluster showed a characteristic, claimed also for others, that it consisted of a small number of stars which precisely defined the motion, together with a much larger peripheral group having approximately the same velocity. The distance of the nucleus stars is of the order of 25–30 parsecs, and there are a number of stars quite near the Sun which have approximately the systematic motion of the cluster. The presence of numbers of stars having the ordered motion associated with these two systems exercises a distorting effect on the distribution of stellar motions in the solar neighbourhood.

Besides these, the Pleiades, Praesepe, the Coma group and the Scorpio-Centaurus cluster all at somewhat greater distances, have been extensively studied. Velocities relative to the Sun may be cited as 29 km/s for the Pleiades, 41 km/s for Praesepe, 8 km/s for the Coma group, and 24 km/s for the Scorpio-Centaurus cluster. If the motion of the Sun relative to the local standard of rest is removed, these figures become 12, 27, 14 and 10 km/s respectively.

In all these cases, membership was originally judged not only by the fact that a star possessed the correct velocity, but also by obvious spatial association through situation in the sky near to the group to which it was assigned. Many years ago, however, tentative assignments to membership of various groups had been made on the grounds that they possessed the correct spatial velocity, of stars having no obvious spatial association with the group to which they were assigned. There is no denying that this is a reasonable notion. If the Sun were in the middle of the Hyades, the criterion of spatial association would be lost, the group would still exist, and its members would be found in all parts of the sky. Eggen has been particularly active in attempting to identify co-moving groups of stars in which there is no obvious spatial association, using his unrivalled command of the literature of photometry and proper motions. He has identified a number of stellar groups, usually by finding a number of stars, often not very numerous, which have the same spatial motion as some prominent or relatively bright star which gives its name to the group. In this way he has named such groups as the Beta Hydri, Z Herculis, 61 Cygni, Epsilon Indi, Eta Cephei and Groombridge 1830 groups. The sceptic might claim, with some support, that it is clear that, given any star whatever, it must be possible, by casting the net sufficiently widely, to discover any number of other stars, physically unrelated, which, by coincidence, have the same components of space velocity. The creation of spurious groups becomes even easier when one considers that, in his later thinking, for reasons of undoubted validity, Eggen has removed the requirement that the w-components of motion should be identical among members of a group. When a group has been identified it is presumably an inference that all its members must share a common origin, composition and age. At least the u and v components of motion must be so nearly identical that improved values of stellar parameters can be inferred from the conditions which make them precisely identical. The proven existence of considerable numbers of discrete groups of stars would be a matter of such great importance for the understanding of the origin of the stars in the solar neighbourhood, that it is legitimate to examine the proposition very closely. If the proposition were correct, it could legitimately be expected that on plots of all well-established values of u- and v-components of stellar motions, marked areas of abnormal concentrations of points should occur, blurred no doubt by the effects of observational error, but recognisable none the less. This does not appear to be the case.* Identity of two or three components of velocity is, in general, only a necessary, not a sufficient condition. An exception should probably be made in the case of abnormally high velocity stars, where there is some evidence of clumping of points. Thus, the velocity of Groombridge 1830, with components $(-263, -151, -22)$ does seem to be significantly close to that of several other stars including the variable star, RR Lyrae, discussed at length in a later chapter. In this case there is an additional feature beyond the more or less forced coincidence of values of velocity components which strengthens conviction. Possibly the same may be said of a group of five stars with values of v all near -330 and values of u rather widely scattered between -150 and -184. In the case of the 61 Cygni group, with $v = -53$ and u near $+90$, and the Eta Cephei group, with $v = -97$ and u near $+40$ attention has been paid to ultraviolet excesses which strengthen conviction by providing an extra condition that the stars in question are of similar composition. If it is true that all stars have originally been formed in clusters each characterised by a certain age and composition, then relics of this situation should be detectable by the dissection of the present smooth distribution of stars into individual lots of cluster debris. That examples of this can be found there is no doubt. Whether so many cases can be legitimately identified is possibly a matter still to be proved.

4.7. Expanding Associations

A different type of group cooperative motion was suggested some years ago by Blaauw. In a previous chapter we met the idea, originally proposed by Ambartsumian, of stellar associations, including those comprised of O-type stars, known as O-associations. These occur in regions of space rich in gas and dust, and, as we now know, are composed of very young stars. Blaauw and Morgan studied the proper motions of member stars of an association near the star 10 Lacertae, and detected a general expansion by arguing backwards to a time when all the members of the association must have been concentrated into a small volume, they put an age to the association of only a few million years, at that time a surprisingly small figure. The same order of magnitude is now indicated by evolutionary theory. The conclusion was, however, contested by Woolley and Eggen, who pointed out the importance of systematic errors in the determination of proper motions and showed that these could produce

* Clumping near points corresponding to well-known groups is illustrated in "Luminosities and Motions of A-type Stars", O. J. Eggen, *A.J.* **68**, 1963, Figure 5, p. 710.

spurious effects, both of expansion of stellar groups, which seems reasonable, and contraction, which does not. Subsequent work has confirmed the reality of expansion in a number of the nearer associations, in which the concentration of mass is inadequate to bind the members into a cluster, and where the proper motions are large compared with their uncertainties. Ages deduced from kinematic arguments are comparable with those deduced from Hertzsprung-Russell diagrams. A good example is the estimate by J. Delhaye and A. Blaauw of an age of $1 \cdot 5 \times 10^6$ years for the association, II Persei (in the region of ζ Persei), (*B.A.N.*, **12**, 72, 1953). Naming of the better-known associations follows the list at page 348 of Vol. XIIB, *Transactions of the I.A.U.*, 1964.

4.8. The Velocity Ellipsoid

Leaving now the cases of cooperative motions of groups of stars we turn to properties of motions of the field stars in the neighbourhood of the Sun which were already known in the second decade of the century. A device often adopted to summarise the proper motions of the stars in any relatively small area of sky was the construction of a certain polar curve from the available data. In this curve, the length of the radius vector in any position angle was drawn proportional to the number of stars found to have proper motions in that direction. Obviously, in practice, the stars selected for study would be chosen according to some criterion of homogeneity, and stars so distant that their proper motions would be too small to be significant would be excluded. Subject to these provisos, it is clear that, if all directions of motion were equally likely, and if enough stars were available to rule out the worst statistical fluctuations, the observed diagram would approximate to a circle. In fact, however, in most areas of the sky the diagrams were found to be bilobar affairs, such as might be produced by the superposition of two oval curves with their axes at an angle to each other. (Figure IV.4.) The angle between the two lobes varied with the position of the test area on the sky and the axes of the ovals defined directions which were concurrent, within observational uncertainty, at two distant points on the sky. The idea was then propounded that all the stars concerned belonged to one of two intermingled systems, each of which was called a "Stream" or "Drift". The concept of a drift, an idea recognisably indebted to the kinetic theory of gases, was that of a group of stars having random motions the statistical distribution being isotropic and governed by the law that $N(u, v, w)\, du\, dv\, dw$—the number of stars with component velocities in the range from (u, v, w) to $(u + du, v + dv, w + dw)$ was given by $N = \text{const} \times \exp(-k^2 V^2)$, where k is a constant expressing the velocity dispersion, and V is the total velocity ($V^2 = u^2 + v^2 + w^2$). Like a cloud of midges hovering in the summer air, the drift in itself had no systematic motion, but unlike the cloud of midges whose members turn back and preserve the spatial identity of the cloud, a drift would in time disperse in space. Only the velocities of the member stars were under consideration, and the possibility of velocity change did not come within the scope of the theory. Clearly, a diagram of proper motions of drift members as observed from a point at rest relative to the mean of the drift, would yield a circular plot. A plot of proper motions observed from a point in motion relative to the mean of a drift becomes an oval of which the form varies according to the location of the test area on the sky with respect to the relative motion vector. Thus if all the stars in the sky were assumed to belong to a single drift, and the Sun were supposed to be in motion relative to it, then the proper motion plots in the directions of the apex and antapex would be circles, while those for regions of the sky at right angles to the solar motion would be ovals in which the majority of stars would reflect the motion of the Sun through the drift. The observed facts are not capable of so simple a representation: for the stars relatively near the Sun for which considerable proper motions are available, the observational situation can be described by the hypothesis that there are not one, but two drifts moving independently. One, comprising about 55 per cent of the stars has a motion of 31 km/s towards a point at R.A. 6h, Dec. —11°: the other at 16 km/s moved towards 18h 40m, —67°.

Descriptively the hypothesis is satisfactory enough: from a more general point of view it leaves much to be desired. Every star with which we are now concerned is a member of the Galaxy and is pursuing an orbit under the gravitational attraction of

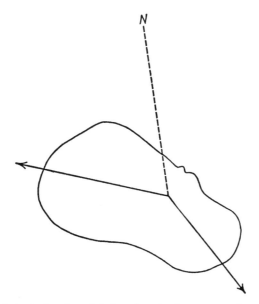

Figure IV.4: A typical polar plot showing the frequency of proper motions in each direction for a particular sky area. On the "Two Drift" Theory, this would be represented as the combination of two oval curves. (Data after W. M. Smart, *Stellar Dynamics*, C.U.P. 1938, p. 106.)

the system as a whole. Members now near the Sun, itself no more than an undistinguished member of the Galaxy, will, in time to come have moved elsewhere to be counted in the statistics of other space volumes. The two drifts which describe the motion of stars relatively near the Sun are both considered to be in motion relative to the Sun. More generally, we can leave the Sun out of the picture and say that the drifts are receding from each other, and this line of mutual recession defines a direction along which there is greater mobility than in perpendicular directions.

The elder Schwarzschild expressed this in an elegant mathematical form in 1907 when he propounded the notion of the "*velocity ellipsoid*". In a given part of the Galaxy the number of stars having velocities near U, V, W is given as proportional to $\exp\left(-k^2U^2 - h^2V^2 - h^2W^2\right) dU.\,dV.\,dW$. If the constant k is less than h there will be a larger spread of velocities in the direction called U than in perpendicular directions. Observed from a point at rest relative to this distribution, the function will produce a polar curve of proper motions which is an ellipse for all regions of the sky. Observed from a point in motion relative to the distribution the law will produce more complicated curves approximating to those previously represented by the two-drift theory. The restriction to equality of the coefficients of V and W need not be retained. The exponential can then take the form $-u^2/k_1^2 - v^2/k_2^2 - w^2/k_3^2$ and we can then call k_1, k_2, k_3 the semiaxes of the velocity ellipsoid. We also introduce the term "*velocity dispersion*" denoted by σ and defined for n stars by the equation $n\sigma^2 = \Sigma(u - \bar{u})^2$ for the velocities in a particular direction, of which $\bar{u}$ is the mean value. If the velocity dispersion is ellipsoidal, the exponent having the generalised value given above, the velocity dispersion in the u direction is given by $2\sigma^2 = k_1^2$. Some authors draw this distinction between velocity dispersion and the semiaxis of the velocity ellipsoid. Trumpler and Weaver, however, write the exponent of the exponential as $-\frac{1}{2}(u^2/k_1^2 + v^2/k_2^2 + w^2/k_3^3)$ and call k_1, k_2, k_3 the semiaxes of the velocity ellipsoid. This makes them identical with the dispersions along the principal axes, and is a simplification because dispersions can be calculated immediately from a list of velocities. The variations of usage by different authors are, however, often a source of considerable confusion.

4.9. The Construction of Velocity Ellipsoids

Numerous examples exist in the literature. Several cases can be distinguished. For nearby stars for which large and accurate values of trigonometrical parallax are available, the space velocities are computed according to the precepts given above, and means taken to define the centre of the ellipsoid. If the distribution is ellipsoidal and enough stars have been plotted, the distributions in the various coordinate planes will often have palpably elliptical lines of equal density which can assist the fitting of the best ellipses. A full dress investigation for the determination of the constants of the quadric of best fit can be rather tedious. It is, of course, essential to verify that any given distribution of points is legitimately represented within the observational errors by an ellipsoidal distribution. This is usually done as a check after the ellipsoid of best fit has been found. In the case just described the stars discussed need have no special distribution on the sky.

A velocity ellipsoid can be constructed for a homogeneous group of stars using radial velocities only, but this normally requires a knowledge of stellar data all over the sky. The systematic motion of the Sun with respect to all the stars in the group is determined first by methods outlined above. Then the residuals from the radial component of group motion are considered for the stars in each area of sky. If the velocity distribution is ellipsoidal the distribution of residuals will be Gaussian and the velocity dispersions will be related to the constants of the ellipsoid. In these circumstances the constants of the ellipsoid will be found in units of kilometres per second. No additional information on absolute magnitudes of the members of the group can be derived from the radial velocity analysis alone. For example, the stars selected might be all the Class III stars with types between G 5 and K 5 and apparent visual magnitudes between 8·0 and 8·5. A selection of this type would give a good body of data well distributed over the sky. All the member stars would be fairly similar to each other, and the result would show how this sort of star was moving.

From the radial velocity data only we should not be able to derive any information about the absolute magnitudes of these stars.

A velocity ellipsoid can be constructed from a homogeneously selected group of stars using proper motion data only. A great deal of proper motion data is available although of varied quality. Specialists in the field have expended much effort on intercomparisons of proper motion data from various sources and in most cases tables of systematic corrections from one system to another are available. Except for very large proper motions it is essential to examine and correct proper motion data according to these precepts before subjecting them to analysis. In this case the constants of the ellipsoid can be derived from the polar curve of frequency of proper motion in a given sky area against direction, though the use of several areas is better. Alternatively, if the distribution on the sky of the stars considered does not lend itself to analysis area by area, the distribution of proper motions for stars more or less uniformly distributed over the whole sky can be considered. In this case the constants of the ellipsoid are not found in absolute units but in terms of the secular parallax of the average star corresponding to the systematic motion of the Sun with respect to the group in the course of a year. No information on absolute magnitudes of the group members can be obtained by the discussion of proper motions alone.

The limitations in the various cases above can be removed in a variety of ways. If radial velocities and proper motions are available, absolute magnitudes can be determined. There is now more than enough information for the solution of the problem and it may be somewhat difficult to reconcile it all. The same is true if the solar motion can be assumed (in km/s), in an analysis of proper motion data, though now the problem is only just determinate.

In any discussion of this kind it is necessary to ensure that the distribution of motions can be ellipsoidal. Stars exhibiting other kinds of systematic motion, such as members of the Hyades or Ursa Major groups, must be omitted. For reasons which will be clear later, it is usual to exclude high velocity stars from the statistics, for example, of nearby stars in general.

The number of investigations in the literature is considerable. In 1946 Strömberg analysed the motions of 444 stars within 20 parsecs of the Sun for which data were then available. He divided these into groups according to spectral class, and treated all together. He found a systematic motion of the Sun with respect to all the groups, and for all stars together a velocity of 26 km/s in the direction near 18h, $+ 30°$ already quoted. All the velocity ellipsoids showed a velocity dispersion along the major axis between one and a half and twice as great as in the two perpendicular directions, which were roughly equal. The direction of the axis of greatest mobility lay roughly towards the centre of the Galaxy. The dimensions of the ellipsoids increased with lateness of spectral type, from about 17 km/s for the longest axis in the A stars to about 48 km/s for the M stars. Gliese carried out a similar analysis for the larger number of stars for which data had become available ten years later with very similar results. In his case there are reservations connected with selection effects among the dwarf M stars and attention is also called to the differentiation in velocity dispersion in the w-direction between dwarf M-type stars with and without emission lines. This is connected with the age of the stars concerned. In 1958 J. Alexander analysed the motions of 475 A-type stars for which radial velocity and proper motion data were available. If supergiants and peculiar stars are omitted a very homogeneous group results, for which Alexander was able to obtain an average absolute magnitude of $+0 \cdot 14$ by the methods indicated above. Another investigation of a rather homogeneous group is that by M. W. Feast on the long-period variable stars in 1963. These are intrinsically rather bright stars and have been observed out to great distances where the effects of galactic rotation, discussed below, must be taken into account.

If the stars were molecules of a gas they would all have the same kinetic energy on the average. The parallel, though tempting, is not a particularly good one. As we shall see later bolometric magnitudes can be used to estimate masses of stars of various kinds and the corresponding velocity dispersions, specifically those in the w-direction, combined with these to evaluate the mean kinetic energy of stars in the various groups. There is an order of magnitude similarity for a wide range of dwarf types, but giant stars are decidedly more energetic.

The results for different classes of star found by various investigators have varied a good deal. We can hardly do better than quote from C. W. Allen's *Astrophysical Quantities* at page 243 to give a general impression of current views:

	Direction of longest axis:	Dispersion (km/s) Axis No.		
	l^{II}	1	2	3
BO-stars	350°	12	9	4
AO-stars	22	17	9	7
FO-stars	16	23	13	12
GO-dwarfs	10	32	21	18
GO-giants	10	22	15	15
MO-dwarfs	10	45	27	18
MO-giants	10	27	18	19
Nearby stars	13	38	24	18

4.10. Galactic Rotation

A rough description of the Galaxy has already been given. It is a vast flattened assemblage of stars having a nucleus where star density is high, the density generally decreasing outwards in all directions. The mode of decrease is such that in its outer parts the form of the system approximates, so far as the Population I stars are concerned, to a relatively thin disk. The plane of the disk marks the galactic equator, and in it are found the clouds of gas and dust from which the Population I stars are formed. The Sun is a fairly old member of this population and lies near the median plane at a point remote from the nucleus.

This is a static description of the system as we see it. The Galaxy is, in fact, a dynamic structure in which the motion of each star is determined by the gravitational distribution due to all the members, each of which contributes its mite to the total. Only the possession by each star of sufficient kinetic energy assures the system of some degree of permanence against collapse under the mutual gravitation of them all. The system has a store of angular momentum corresponding to a general rotation about an axis through the nucleus normal to the galactic plane. At each distance from the centre there is a certain value of circular velocity, such that a star having this velocity normal to the radial direction can move in a circular orbit whose centre is the centre of the Galaxy and whose plane is the median plane of the Galaxy. The value of the circular velocity at the distance of the Sun is now taken to be 250 km/s and the distance of the Sun from the centre to be 10 kiloparsecs. Both these figures were revised upwards in 1964 from somewhat smaller values quoted with distinctly greater precision, which had held the field for many years. The mean velocity of the stars in the solar neighbourhood relative to the Galactic centre can be taken as closely identical with this circular velocity, and the direction is the positive direction of v in the coordinate system already described, i.e. towards the point with co-ordinates $l = 90°$, $b = 0°$. The situation is illustrated in Figure IV.5. The value of the circular velocity at the Sun's distance from the centre depends on the total mass interior to the corresponding circle. The circular velocity decreases outwards in the

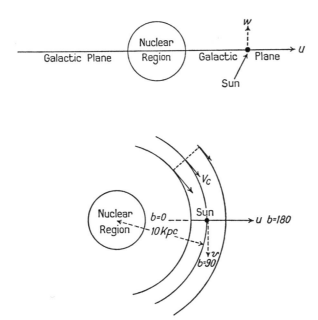

Figure IV.5: Schematic structure of the Galaxy: *above*, section perpendicular to the plane; *below* section in the plane, showing variation of circular velocity with central distance.

general way indicated by the vectors V_c in Figure IV.5. The values of velocity disper-sion quoted in the previous section are all quite small fractions of the circular velocity. Hence, if we neglect the high velocity stars we can make quite a good approximation to the state of motion of the Galaxy at distances comparable with that of the Sun from the centre, by regarding the stars as moving in circular orbits in each of which the circular velocity is maintained. This is the model of Galactic Rotation proposed by Lindblad and Oort in the twenties. The effect on the large scale motion of stars can now be considered. In Figure IV.6(a) let a small part of three concentric rings of stars be represented as moving with velocities corresponding to the lengths of the vectors. Those interior to the Sun are moving faster: those exterior, slower. In Figure IV.6(b) we have subtracted the circular velocity at the Sun so as to give relative motions. Stars on the interior track are now, on the average, gaining on the

Sun: those on the exterior track are being overtaken by the Sun. Those on the same track as the Sun have zero velocity relative to it. Now consider the radial velocity relative to the Sun of stars seen in the eight marked directions, resulting from this effect. Those towards the galactic centre have a transverse motion, so stars seen in Direction 1, will show no effect. Neither will stars in Direction 5, for the same reason Stars seen in Directions 3 and 7 will show no effect because these have the same circular velocity as the Sun and neither gain nor lose on it. In Directions 2, and 6, however, the arrows show that there will be a component of recession in radial velocity while in Directions 4 and 8 there will be a component in the radial direction giving a velocity of approach. Several features of the situation are immediately clear. The occurrence of an effect due to Galactic Rotation depends on the variation of circular velocity with distance from the Galactic Centre. As drawn in the diagram the magnitude of the effect corresponds, so to speak, to a comparison between the solar track and the immediately adjacent tracks on either side. If more remote tracks

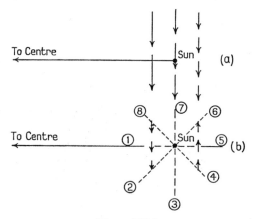

Figure IV.6.
(a) Smoothed motions in galactic rotation. (b) Motions relative to the Sun produced by differential galactic rotation.

were considered, reaching to those where the difference of circular velocity was larger, then the size of the effect would increase. The effect is thus more pronounced for more distant stars. The variation with galactic longitude is such that there are zeros in four directions, giving a double wave form.

There is now no difficulty in understanding the mathematical formulation. The radial velocity ρ produced by differential galactic rotation in a region of the sky denoted (in the revised coordinate system in which the origin is the centre of the Galaxy) by l, b for stars at distance r is given by

$$\rho = r A \sin 2l \cos^2 b$$

where A is called the first Oort constant, and the term in cos b takes account of regions not in the galactic plane. From the foregoing discussion it will be clear that the value of A refers only to the solar neighbourhood, and that a different value would be found for regions at other distances from the galactic centre. The foregoing formula is a first approximation which applies to values of r which are a fairly small fraction of the dimensions of the Galaxy. More elaborate formulae to be applied to distant regions have been developed, for example by Camm and by Titus.

The value of A adjudged as best in 1964 by the I.A.U. Commission on Galactic Structure is 15 km/sec/kiloparsec, replacing the previously adopted value of 19·5 km/sec/kiloparsec. If r is 1,000 parsecs a series of observations round the galactic plane should give a double wave curve with an amplitude of about 15 km/s. This corresponds to a modulus of 10 magnitudes. If we wish to have reasonably accurate radial velocities we must avoid stars of too faint an apparent magnitude which could only be observed on low dispersion. If we set the limit at apparent magnitude 8, say, then to demonstrate the effect we must observe stars with absolute magnitudes near -2. This means that B stars, which occur abundantly in the galactic plane must be observed, and these have provided a large proportion of the information from stellar sources on the phenomenon of galactic rotation. They have a low velocity dispersion, because they are young stars only recently formed from inter-stellar gas and reflect fairly closely the generally circular motion of the latter. The magnitude of the first order effect to be demonstrated is increased if more distant, apparently fainter, B stars are observed and it is among these stars that evidence for higher order terms must be sought. The observational problem is that measuring errors of radial velocities increase when the observed stars are fainter, so that an increased bulk of material is required. To derive a value for the quantity A information on the distances of the stars observed is necessary. Since the B stars lie close to the galactic plane they are particularly subject to extinction and reddening. Photometric data must be determined for the stars and estimates of these effects made according to the methods described in Chapter III, using spectral classifications of the stars. All the uncertainties associated with the absolute magnitude calibration of intrinsically bright stars, and of the ratio of general extinction to reddening have to be met, and make the problem one of considerable difficulty. The extent of the difficulty can be judged by the fact that after many years during which astronomers were willing to quote the value of A to an accuracy of a few per cent, the adopted value was changed in 1964 by a quarter and the number of decimal places reduced by one.

Programmes for the study of galactic rotation from radial velocities of B stars have been carried on for many years. In the north the Canadian observers have been particularly active and analyses date from the pioneer work of J. S. Plaskett and Pearce in the thirties. Velocities of B stars in the southern sky were lacking until the establishment of the Radcliffe Observatory at Pretoria. Observational material has been provided, particularly by Thackeray, Wesselink and Feast since the fifties, and an analysis of both northerly and southerly B star radial velocities was under-taken by Feast and Thackeray in 1958. Another class of star of high intrinsic luminosity belonging to Population I which has been of value in studies of galactic rotation has been the type of variable star known as a Cepheid, discussed at greater length below. Modern studies based on the Cepheids have been undertaken by Joy, by Stibbs, by Gascoigne and Eggen, by Walraven, and others.

4.12. Proper Motion Effects

Differential galactic rotation produces systematic effects on the proper motions of stars moving in approximately circular orbits round the galactic centre. The first

order formula corresponding to that quoted for radial velocities is for a star in
the galactic plane,

$$\mu_G = A \cos 2l + B$$

where A has the same meaning as before, and B is known as the second Oort constant.
The characteristics of this formula are that differential galactic rotation produces a
proper motion effect which is the sum of a constant part, together with a variable
portion, which, like the radial velocity effect is a double wave, but which has zeros
in the directions for which the radial velocity effect is a maximum. Subject to the
condition that the distances of the stars concerned must not be so large that the
first order formula ceases to be valid, the effect is shown to be independent of distance.
The value of A, 15 km/s/kiloparsec already quoted may be converted into a proper
motion measure through the relations that 1 km/s is nearly equal to 1 parsec in a
million years, and that 1 radian $= 206,265$ seconds of arc. The constant A then
becomes $0''\cdot003$ per annum. B, for which the presently adopted value is -10 km/s/
kiloparsec converts to $0''\cdot002$ per annum. The function given above ranges between
between $+ 0''\cdot005$ and $- 0''\cdot001$ per annum. Quantities so small as this are difficult
to determine, in particular because in the mean the effect is one of a small rotation of
whole stellar system, which is particularly difficult to detect unless a non-rotating
reference system is available. The constant, B, only determinable from proper
motions, is directly affected by errors in the precession constants: hence the importance of the use of the galaxies as a reference system. (See 1.36.)

4.11. Functional Relationships of the Oort Constants

It is clear that the constants A and B are functions of position and the general
dynamical behaviour of the Galaxy. If V, a function of R, is the circular velocity in
the Galaxy at distance R from the centre, then $K(R) = V^2/R$ is, in appropriate units
the acceleration at distance R produced by all the material in the Galaxy. It can be
shown that, at distance R the values of the Oort constants will be given by

$$A = (V/4R) \left(1 - \frac{R}{K} \frac{dK}{dR} \right)$$

$$B = A - V/R$$

The term V/R is the angular velocity at the solar distance and is equal to $A - B$,
which, with the values quoted gives $0''\cdot005$ per annum, corresponding to a circuit
time of 250 million years. Young stars are still in the same general position in which
they were created, while a star such as the Sun, with an age near 5,000 million years
has made about 20 revolutions. Stars which are neighbours in space and with similar
velocities describe epicyclic ellipses relative to each other, so that to a first order
there is a tendency for neighbours to remain so. The motions discussed in connection
with the velocity ellipsoids have this character, and a good deal of attention has been
paid to the problem of the relation between galactic rotation and the constants of the
velocity ellipsoids. It has been shown that if the dispersions along the axes of the
ellipsoids are taken as h, k, k, with the two shorter axes equal and $h > k$, then
$k^2/h^2 = - B/(A - B)$. With the values adopted this leads to k/h approximately
equal to 2/3 not far from the general run of values found. In this formulation the long
axis always points precisely to the galactic centre, and much argumentation has been

directed towards the problem presented by the fact that for most kinds of stars near the Sun the long axis deviates from this direction by some 10 degrees.

4.13. Actual Investigations

In spite of the fiat of the Galactic Structure Commission of the I.A.U. it is not to be supposed that every investigation of galactic rotation no matter how meticulously carried out, will yield values of the Oort and other constants identical with those adopted. The virtue of the adopted values is that they represent a considered opinion by a number of experts whose task it was to reconcile as best they could the whole corpus of modern data derived from a variety of sources, of which the analyses of stellar radial velocities and proper motions are but two. The decision is far from being a final word, and the extent of the changes from previously adopted values ought to inspire proper feelings of caution and humility.

It is instructive to recapitulate the steps of an actual investigation, and that of Feast and Thackeray of 1958, already mentioned, is chosen. Data for 314 stars were available, in the form of radial velocities, photoelectric photometry and MK spectral types. They naturally come from a variety of sources and some attention has to be paid to the systematic consistency of, for example, radial velocities derived from different observatories. The radial velocity data give, for most stars, two items of information. One is the radial velocity of the star itself. The other is a measure of the interstellar calcium lines already mentioned. These are formed along the line of sight by the interstellar gases and it is usual to assume that the velocity which they indicate is the velocity of the interstellar gas at the mid-point of the path. Since the motion of early type stars differs but little from that of the interstellar clouds, the interstellar calcium line measures can be regarded as providing a completely independent approach to the solution of the problem.

Some attention must then be paid to the corrections which must be applied because the Sun is not moving with the circular velocity. The term *basic solar motion* was introduced by Emma Williams and Vyssotsky to describe this difference, and it has been the subject of extensive investigations and of rather variable opinions. After correction of the measured velocities for this effect the data are in a form when they can be matched to theoretical predictions. The photometric data came next to attention. Data on reddening gave the total extinction, with the customary factor of 3·0 mentioned in a previous chapter. Absolute magnitudes were taken from calibrations of the various spectral types, and distance moduli deduced. The stars could then be divided into groups with the distance ranges between one and two kiloparsecs, between two and three kiloparsecs, and over three kiloparsecs. These were denoted by A, B, C and there was also a group drawn from the same data, denoted by AB, formed of stars with distances between 1·5 and 2·5 kiloparsecs. Corresponding groups for the interstellar lines were formed. Plots of velocity against galactic longitude gave double wave curves which were matched both to the Oort-type formulae and to a formula containing higher terms due to Camm. These resulted in determinations of Ar for each group and for the longitudes of the directions in which the effects were zero. Attention is also paid at this point to the K-term mentioned previously. A positive K-term would indicate a general expansion, a negative one a general contraction of the group under discussion. Some evidence was found for a negative K-term, but this could be accounted for by systematic errors in radial velocities.

Discussions of galactic structure which appear in a later chapter indicate that in certain parts of the galaxy there may be marked deviations of gas flow from purely circular motion, and this could produce positive values of K-terms in some parts of the galaxy, negative values in others, for stars derived from this gas. The conclusion of Feast and Thackeray seems to be one of some doubt as to the reality of this term. Velocity residuals enable ellipsoids to be constructed and a velocity dispersion of about 15 km/s is found in the radial direction, with transverse values near one-half of this. In the case of the most distant stars, those for which r is in excess of three kiloparsecs, the ratio r/R_0, where R_0 is the distance of the Sun from the galactic centre, is no longer negligible. Formulae due to Titus express the effects of galactic rotation on radial velocities for such distant stars and involve the ratio as a coefficient. It is therefore possible to determine this, possibly not very accurately, from the data for distant stars. Finally when the best values of constants have been decided upon it is possible to determine the distance of each star from its measured radial velocity, in much the same way as it is possible to determine the distance of a cloud of interstellar hydrogen from the measure of its velocity using adopted values of the constants. This latter topic is discussed in the chapter on Galaxies. The results found for stars of various luminosity classes show a good accordance with previous calibrations. Although this gives the appearance of a somewhat circular argument, this is not the case, for it at least establishes the relative absolute magnitudes of early

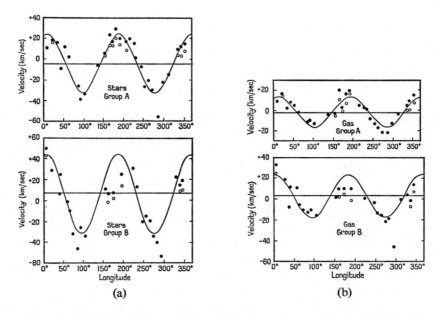

Figure IV.7: Radial velocities of distant B-type stars show evidence of differential galactic rotation.

(a) Stars of Group A are at average distance 1·5 kiloparsecs, Group B at 2·3. The amplitude of the double-wave curve is enhanced for the latter. The horizontal dotted line shows the level of the K-term. (b) The interstellar calcium lines in the same stars, produced by intervening gas, show an effect corresponding to half the stellar distance, i.e. 0·75 and 1·15 kiloparsecs in the two cases. (After Thackeray and Feast, *M.N.R.A.S.* **118**, 125, 1958, by permission of the authors and the Royal Astronomical Society.)

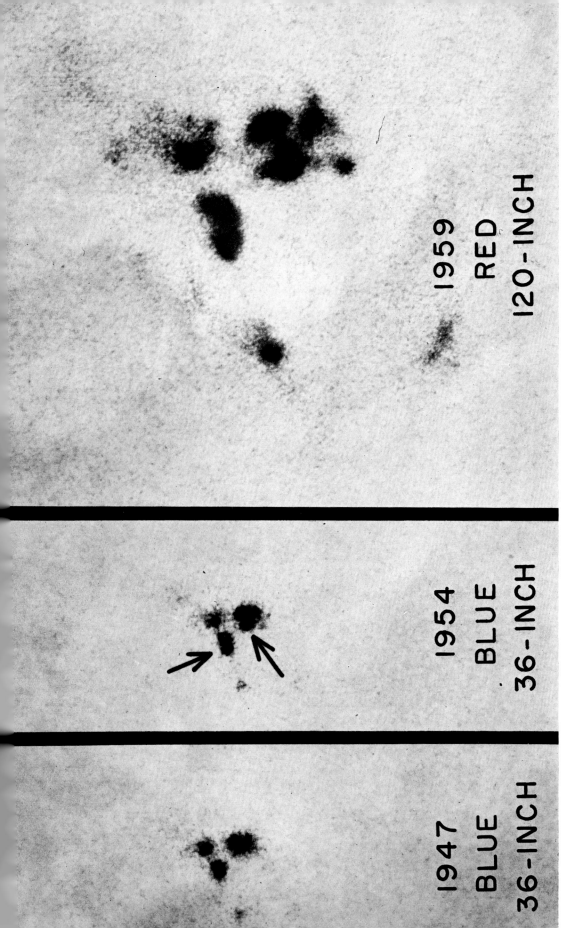

Plate 18. New stars appear from interstellar material in the region of the Orion Nebula, on this series of photographs by Dr. G. H. Herbig. (By permission of the Director, Lick Observatory.)

Plate 19. Photograph on a red-sensitive plate of the Galactic Centre. Note the enormous numbers of stars and the concentration of dust and gas clouds to the Galactic Plane. (From the National Geographic-Palomar Sky Survey, by permission.)

Plate 20. The spiral nebula, NGC 5236 (= M 83), showing a well-marked nucleus, dust and gas lanes, spiral arms and stellar associations. The Galaxy may resemble this, with the Sun located near the outer edge. (By permission of H.M. Astronomer at the Cape.)

Plate 21. The edge-on spiral NGC 4565, showing the nucleus and obscuring matter in the central plane. The Galaxy seen edge-on would resemble this. (By permission of Mount Wilson and Palomar Observatories.)

Plate 22. Spectrum variation in the 5-day Cepheid HR 5527. (a) Near maximum light, (b) near minimum light. Strength of metallic lines relative to hydrogen is greater in (b), indicating later type. (By permission of H.M. Astronomer at the Cape.)

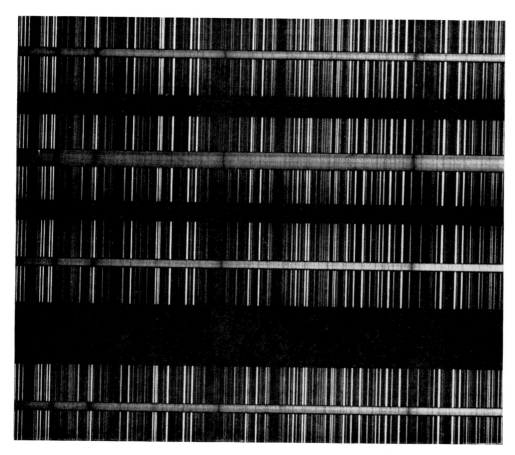

Plate 23. These spectra of V 703 Sco, a Type c RR Lyrae star with a period of 2·77 hours, cover one hour, starting near maximum light. Metallic lines, except H and K at left, are always weak compared with hydrogen. Hydrogen has much weakened by the fourth exposure. (By permission of H.M. Astronomer at the Cape)

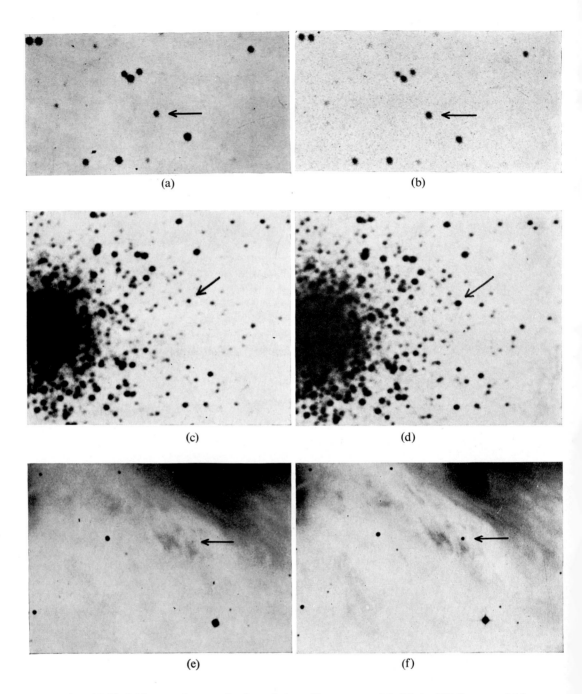

Plate 24. Variable star photographs from Asiago Observatory. (a), (b) An RR Lyrae variable in M 53. (c), (d) A Cepheid in M 15. (e), (f) A flare star in the Orion nebula. (By permission of Professor L. Rosino.)

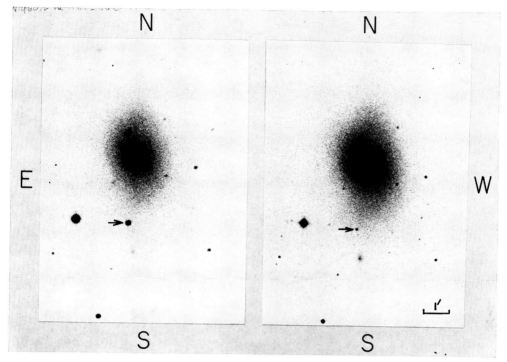

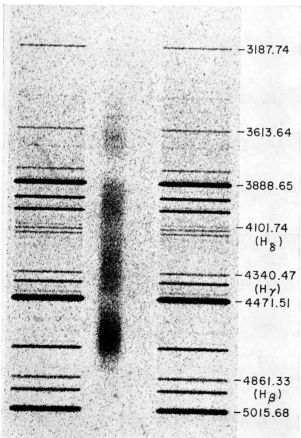

Plate 25. (a) The 1960 supernova in M 85 (= NGC 4382) is seen during its decline on January 15 and June 6, 1961. (b) A spectrum of this supernova obtained in April 1961 with the 200-inch telescope. All spectral features consist of broad bands. (By permission of Dr. F. Zwicky.)

Spectrum wavelength labels:
- 3187.74
- 3613.64
- 3888.65
- 4101.74 (H$_\delta$)
- 4340.47 (H$_\gamma$)
- 4471.51
- 4861.33 (H$_\beta$)
- 5015.68

Plate 26. The Crab Nebula, NGC 1952, remains of the supernova of A.D. 1054, photographed in red light. (By permission of Mount Wilson and Palomar Observatories.)

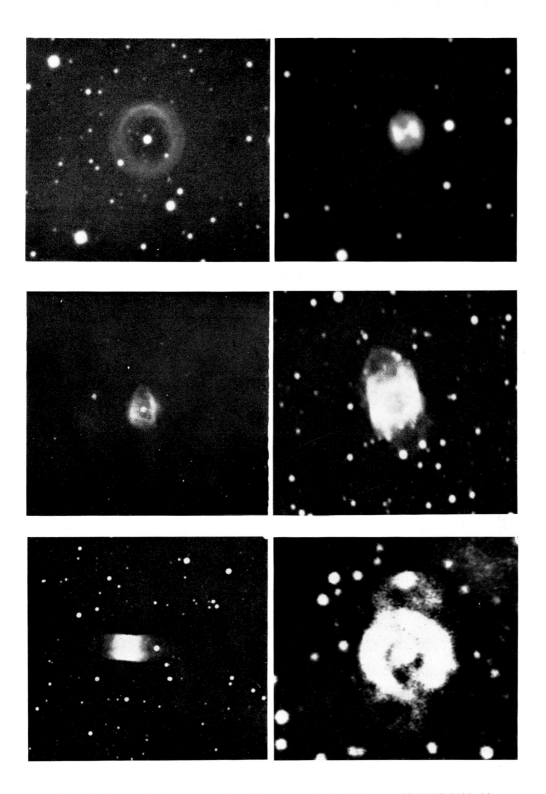

Plate 27. Types of planetary nebulae. (a) A ring nebula in Norma. (b) NGC 3195. (c) NGC 6153. (d) Also in Norma, near the galactic plane, this structure may be a kind of helical tube. (e) The remarkable structure, IC 4406, has a central star hidden in the bar of gas. (f) A third planetary nebula in Norma has a breached gas ring twisting into faint helices. (By permission of the Radcliffe Observer)

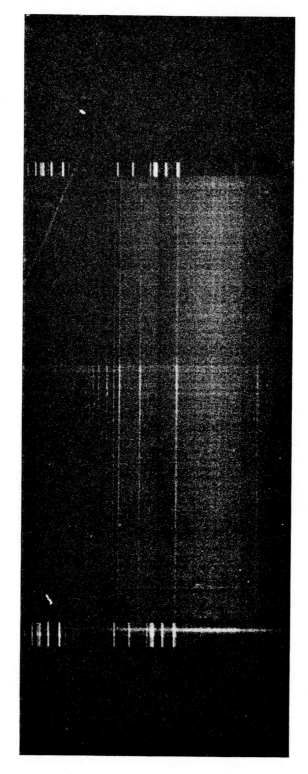

Plate 28. Spectrogram of a flare in the flare star, EV Lacertae. This unique observation was obtained by W. Kunkel at McDonald Observatory in December 1965. The plate is driven along perpendicular to the spectrographic dispersion for about $3\frac{1}{2}$ hours. Time increases towards the left: in mid-exposure the star flared, the emission lines suddenly brightened, and then slowly died away. (By permission of Department of Astronomy, University of Texas.)

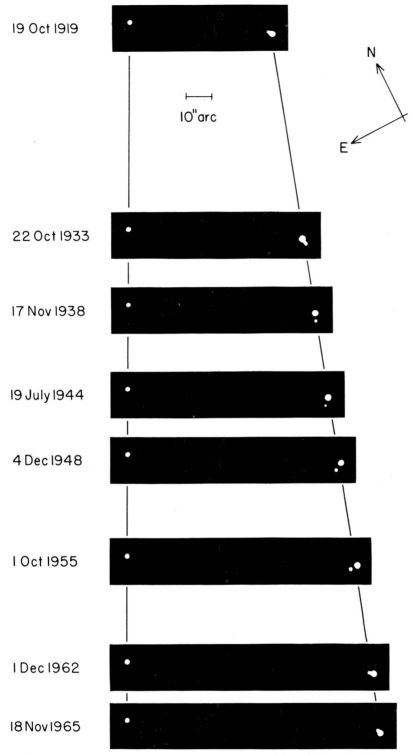

Plate 29(a) These photographs, made with the McCormick and Sproul refractors show the orbital motion of the components, A and B, of the binary star, Krüger 60 (*at right*), and the proper motion of this pair, at $0''\cdot90$ per annum with respect to the optical companion, C (*at left*). Vertical spacing proportional to time gives linear motion of the mass centre of A, B with deviations due to parallactic displacements. Parallax of Krüger 60 is $0''\cdot25$, and the morning exposure of summer 1944 is visibly displaced by $0''\cdot4$ with respect to the other, winter, exposures, made in the evening.

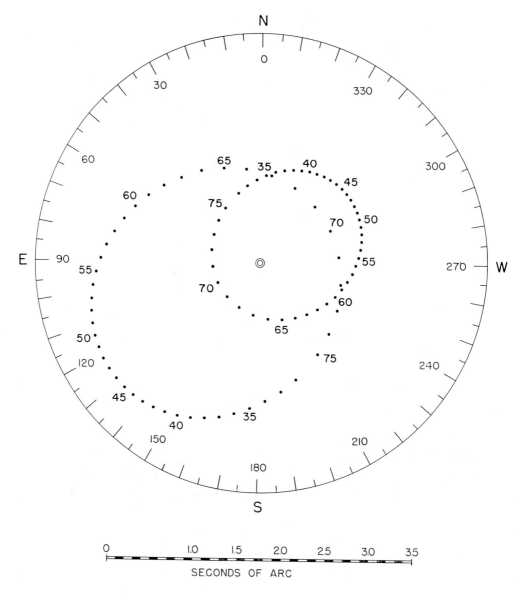

Plate 29 (b) Orbital motion of components A (small orbit) and B (large orbit) relative to
their mass centre at dates in the 20th century. Position angles are of B relative to A.
(By permission of Dr. van de Kamp.)

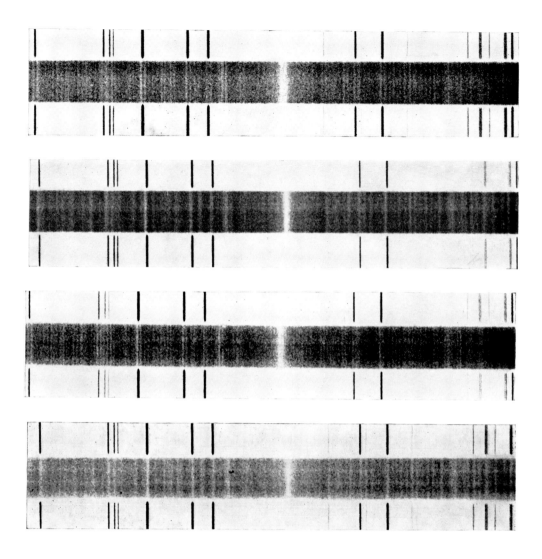

Plate 30. The spectroscopic binary HD 153890 shows variation of line-splitting at different phases. The period is 34·8 days, eccentricity 0·42, the components not quite equal with velocity ranges of 101 and 107 km/s. The strong line is Hδ (4101 Å) and the comparison line at extreme left is 4005 Å. (By permission of H.M. Astronomer at the Cape.)

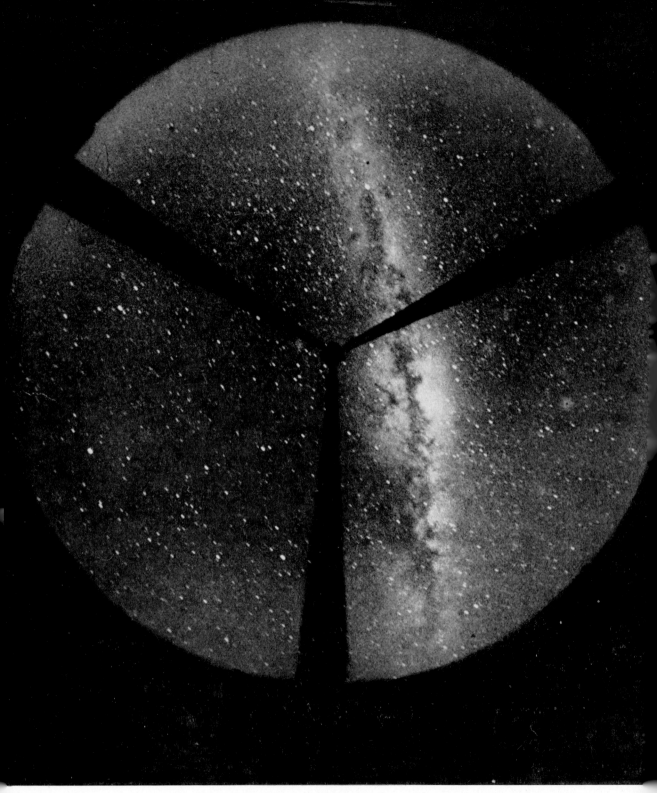

Plate 31. This famous all-sky photograph shows our Galaxy as it might be seen from intergalactic space. (By permission of Drs. A. D. Code and T. E. Houck.)

Plate 32. The Andromeda nebula, M 31, photographed with the Palomar Schmidt. When Hubble classified this as Sb he was emphasising the absence of a bar, and the moderately open spiral structure. (By permission of Mount Wilson and Palomar Observatories.)

Plate 33. NGC 205, the more distant of the two elliptical companion galaxies to M 31, resolved into stars on a red exposure with the 200-inch telescope. (By permission of Mount Wilson and Palomar Observatories.)

type stars in different luminosity classes by a method which has some equivalence with a purely geometrical one. The final adopted values are $A = + 17\cdot5 \pm 1\cdot5$ km/s, $R_0 = 8\cdot9$ kiloparsecs. If one considers that results for previous analyses have ranged from $A = 10\cdot8 \pm 1\cdot8$ km/s to $A = 18\cdot6 \pm 18\cdot6 \pm 2\cdot0$ km/s (all errors are standard errors), the differences between the results of this investigation and the adopted I.A.U. values are not large. Correspondence between observed and computed results is shown in Figure IV.7(a) and (b).

4.14. Non-Circular Motions in the Galaxy

All the stars so far discussed are in motion round the centre of the Galaxy in orbits which differ little from circles in the galactic plane. This follows because the solar motion with respect to the various groups is small, the Sun itself is moving in a very nearly circular orbit, and the velocity dispersions in the ellipsoids for various types of star are all rather small fractions of the circular velocity. We now come to the rather varied classes of star included in the general designation of "high-velocity stars". In Figure IV.8 we compare two stars, one moving in a circular orbit, the other in a highly-elongated orbit. In general this will not be a closed curve because of the complexity of the distribution of matter in the Galaxy, but, if the latter can, temporarily, be represented as a point mass at the galactic centre, these elongated orbits will be ellipses. The stars of the solar region are moving with very nearly the circular

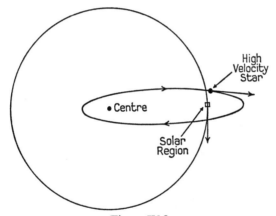

Figure IV.8.

velocity, which we have taken as near 250 km/s, in the direction of the arrow, which is that of the v-velocity component. The motion of the typical high-velocity star is more nearly radial than tangential, and it therefore has a v-component relative to the Sun, in the case illustrated, which is not far short of $- 250$ km/s. Its high velocity relative to the Sun, is produced by the fact that it is lagging behind the Sun in galactic rotation. Moreover, we see that in such a case far more time is spent on the inward and outward journeys than on the high-curvature sections of the orbit near what are called *apogalacticon* and *perigalacticon*, the parts of the orbit most remote from and nearest to the galactic centre. The stars of this kind will thus exhibit the enhanced mobility in the radial direction characteristic of velocity ellipsoids. Moreover since one may expect as many of them to be on the outward leg as on the inward leg, the

F

mean motion of these stars will have only a small systematic value in the u direction. Since the stars as a group are lagging behind the Sun they will have a systematic motion in the v-direction which is negative relative to the Sun. This is the explanation of the asymmetrical distribution of high-velocity star velocity vectors which can be seen in Figure IV.3. The orbital planes of high-velocity stars are not restricted to the galactic plane. Their spatial distribution is much more nearly spherical than the flattened system associated with the younger stars of Population I. The distribution of eccentricities, orbital planes and semiaxes majores of the orbits is such as to produce a much more nearly spherical system, in which the number density falls off from the galactic centre outwards. These stars form a kind of halo about the galactic system and are often given the name of halo stars. Eggen has beautifully demonstrated the identity of the high-velocity stars with Population II, such as we have found in globular clusters by selecting from the nearby stars groups which have galactic orbits of different eccentricities. He showed that the Hertzsprung-Russell diagrams of groups of increasing eccentricity show a graduation from the type of diagram associated with Population I to the type associated with the Population II stars of globular clusters. The distribution of the latter is more or less spherical, and these clusters must be pursuing very elongated orbits which bring them briefly to regions near the galactic centre. The spatial distribution of these clusters resembles that of the Population II stars, and their velocity characteristics are similar. The high-velocity stars show similar evidences of great age, for in general they show ultraviolet excesses and weakness of metallic lines, and would be classed, so far as their dwarf members are concerned, as subdwarfs. It may well be that these stars were originally formed in globular clusters which have since dispersed.

If the Galaxy could be replaced by a point mass then a star with a velocity equal to $\sqrt{2}$ times the circular velocity could escape completely from the Galaxy from a point near the Sun. A star in the solar neighbourhood with a v-velocity equal to $+ 100$ km/s would have the necessary velocity of 350 km/s and it is to be presumed that any star which possessed such a velocity would already have departed from the Galaxy. The fact that the Galaxy is not a point mass will change this figure somewhat. Estimates have been made by a variety of authors many of whom favour a value somewhere near 380 km/s. A figure even as high as 350 km/s brings a difficulty in its train. Before the change in adopted values of the galactic constants already mentioned the adopted value of the circular velocity was about 215 km/s and the usually accepted value of the escape velocity was 63 km/s higher than this. This particular number had been arrived at from the consideration that the uppermost limit of the value of the v-component of velocity relative to the local standard of rest corresponded to that figure, and this was taken as indicating the velocity of escape. If the higher value indicated above is adopted, it is something of a problem to explain why somewhat higher velocities are not observed in the direction of rotation. The orbital characteristics of a star with a given set of velocity components can be demonstrated graphically by means of the type of diagram introduced by Bottlinger in 1933. The axes are u, and v velocity components. A value of circular velocity must be assumed and is plotted along the v-axis. For a point-source model the limiting area corresponding to an infinite semiaxis major is a circle with radius equal to $\sqrt{2} \, V_c$. For other models a somewhat different radius would be used. The circle of radius V_c is the locus of points moving on circles in space equal to the solar distance from the centre of the

Galaxy. Curves of equal eccentricity are ovals centred on the point $v = V_c$. (See Figure IV.9.) Points outside the outer circle denote stars with enough energy to escape from the system. Are there any such stars known? This is difficult to say. Star $- 29° 2277$ has a radial velocity measured as $+ 543$ km/s relative to the Sun, to say nothing of a proper motion of $0''\cdot4$ per annum. If the circular velocity were 215 km/s and the escape velocity about 63 km/s higher, then this star which is in a retrograde orbit would be bound to have more than the escape velocity on grounds of its radial velocity alone. The higher value of escape velocity quoted above would just leave it a member of the Galaxy. One would expect a search for very high velocity stars to show a cut-off near the limit, but equally, there may be a number of stars still within the confines of the Galaxy which have amassed the necessary

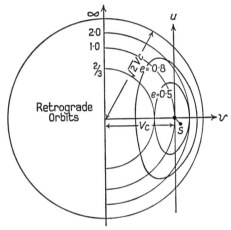

Figure IV.9: Bottlinger diagram for a point model galaxy with the Sun at a distance R_0 from the centre at which the circular velocity is V_c. Velocity values are plotted with axes (u, v) with the origin at the mean point for stars near the Sun. The Sun itself falls at a point S. For motions in the plane the semi-axes majores and eccentricities in galactic orbits can be read off from the two sets of curves: circles give the former in units of R_0. The ovals give eccentricities. (Adapted, by permission of the authors and editors of the Astronomical Journal from Emma T. R. Williams and A. N. Vyssotsky, *A.J.*, **53**, 96, 1947.)

energy and are on their way into outer space. The difficulty is that this is not an instantaneous process: even at 500 km/s an escaping star would take 10 million years to pass from the solar distance to the limits of the system.

The systematic velocity of high-velocity stars with respect to the Sun depends on the eccentricity of their orbits and this is correlated with other features. Values are uncertain. For the RR Lyrae variables, to be discussed later, which are metal-poor stars, the systematic velocity lies in the range from 150 km/s to 200 km/s. For globular clusters the value is near 170 km/s. For subdwarfs there is a variation with ultraviolet excess, or metal deficiency, with values in the range from about 130 km/s for the mildest subdwarfs up to about 200 km/s for extreme cases. Eggen, Lynden-Bell and Sandage, in a recent study have used the observed correlation between eccentricity of galactic orbit and metal weakness, interpretable also as age, as the basis of the hypothesis that very old stars were formed during a period when the Galaxy was collapsing inwards. The epoch is put at some 10^{10} years ago, and the scale of collapse to the present dimensions is by a factor of about 10 in the radial direction, and by about 25 times in the direction normal to the present galactic plane, thus transforming the original nearly spherical protogalaxy into the present highly flattened system.

4.15. Motions Perpendicular to the Galactic Plane

The motion of member stars of the Galaxy in the galactic plane invites a parallel with the motion of the planets about the Sun, with the more distant ones having not only longer orbital times but smaller space velocities. The parallel is not, however, a just one. Superposed on the general orbital motion which, at the solar distance occupies a time of some 250 million years, is an oscillation normal to the plane of the Galaxy which may occupy a much shorter time, say, sixty million years. The distribution of matter in the Galaxy shows the concentration towards the plane already remarked. The attraction of this sheet of material causes stars to move towards it, to pass through the plane, and so back again in the oscillatory mode envisaged. The period of this oscillation is so much shorter than the orbital times concerned for a large portion of the Galaxy that the identity of the stars in a cylinder of defined area normal to the plane can be thought of as unchanged during the time required for several oscillations. The attractive force which causes the oscillations is provided by none other than the member stars themselves. Solutions of the problem can be made in which the distribution in velocity of the stellar motions normal to the plane follows an exponential law of the type $dN = \exp(-k^2 w^2)\, dw$ where w is the velocity normal to the plane. More sophisticated analyses may replace the single exponential by the sum of a number of similar terms, in each of which the number typified by k is a constant. The distribution in velocity must satisfy the condition that the space density of numbers remains unchanged with time. Bell-shaped curves of the type which result do give a good description of the observed stellar density variation with the coordinate z normal to the plane. Finally, by integrating the number density it is possible to estimate the total mass of material which is related to velocity dispersions of a given type and magnitude normal to the plane. The observational data are rather easily accessible. Data on the radial velocities of stars in the regions of the galactic poles, i.e. the sky areas near $b^{II} = +90°$ and $-90°$ yield values, which, with little or no adjustment for the fact that the stars are not precisely at the poles, represent the required w-velocities. Attention is then paid to photometric data and spectral classification for the same stars. Again there is relatively little difficulty. Extinction of star light in directions near the plane may be large, but near the poles it is slight, and the more distant stars are certainly clear of the absorbing material of the plane. Analyses of the K-giant stars have been made by Woolley: for the A-type stars near the south galactic pole, similar results have been obtained by Wayman from his observations and analysis of the A-type stars. The conclusions depend as usual, to some extent on the style of treatment, but, with rather little uncertainty it has been concluded that the spatial density of matter in the solar neighbourhood must be about 10^{-23} grammes per cc, corresponding to about 0·15 solar masses per cubic parsec, or roughly 5,000 stars like the Sun within the 20-parsec range of the Gliese catalogue. As we have seen the actual catalogue only contains some 1,000 stars, and even making allowances for undiscovered stars only brings the total mass of stars to about 40 per cent of the required value. This must be increased by about one-half to take account of matter in gaseous form, but there is still a large, and at present, unsolved discrepancy. Attribution of the missing mass to undetected interstellar material would involve multiplying this contribution by a factor which would be generally regarded as unacceptably large.

4.16. The Dynamics of Clusters

Arguments based on photometry and stellar evolution have led to estimates of the ages of clusters which, in the case of some galactic clusters, and most globular clusters, are very large indeed. There are many dynamical effects at work which tend to cause clusters to disintegrate and it is instructive to consider briefly the problems involved. Stars in the Galaxy which are close together and have nearly the same velocity components are expected to describe epicyclic orbits relative to one another. Their relative positions and velocities will change in an oscillatory way, though in a time far too long for the process to be followed observationally, and though, at some epoch, they may have a certain relative velocity, it will not usually be correct to make the extrapolation that they would continue to separate with this velocity. Although in this case their common membership of the galaxy preserves a relation between the stars, differential galactic rotation also helps to disperse stars. The members of a group which extended over some range in distance from the centre would have their outmost members lagging behind the inner, so that the group would tend to be sheared out of existence. Woolley concluded from a consideration of a group of stars ejected from the same point with a range of velocities, that, in later life they would be strung out according to their initial velocity of projection, so that their common provenance might be detectable. Because oscillations perpendicular to the galactic plane occur with such a relatively short period it would not be expected that their values of w-velocity would retain a common value, but would show a scattering over a range. This is the basis of a remark made earlier in connection with co-moving groups, that identity of the w-velocity component cannot be insisted upon.

It is a fact of observation that certain star clusters exist in which the velocity components of all members are closely similar and there is an obvious spatial association between the members. In these cases the cluster has a gravitational field which plays a part in binding the members together. The stronger the binding, the higher is the velocity dispersion observed among the members. The existence of a certain value of velocity dispersion does not express the extent to which the cluster is dissipating because the velocities of individual stars are different. It expresses the extent to which the gravitational field of the cluster is capable of changing the velocity of an individual member. The velocity dispersion in many galactic clusters is low, probably of the order of a few tenths of a kilometre per second. This is so small a quantity that in no case does it seem to have been measured with certainty. A consequence is that should the velocity of a star change even slightly, possibly by so little as a quantity of the order of 1 km/s, the star in question would then begin to separate from the cluster and eventually lose any obvious association with it. A series of repetitions of this occurrence would lead to the dispersal and eventual loss of identity of the cluster. For small changes in velocity the process would be a slow one, and one might expect to find, as is indeed the case with certain galactic clusters, that there was a true cluster with a small velocity dispersion and a small spatial range, forming the core of a more dispersed system within which a much larger range of stellar velocities was to be observed.

The event which can cause a change in the velocity of a star is that of a stellar encounter. This means the relatively close passage of two stars, which while near each other, move under their mutual attraction in curved paths. In general each star will have a velocity relative to their common centre of gravity which is greater than the escape velocity. The orbits will then be hyperbolae, and, after the encounter the stars will recede from each other with the directions of their velocities changed. The way in which the velocities are changed has been discussed in detail by various authors. In any given case the final circumstances are precisely determined by the initial hypotheses adopted. A general discussion must be made from the statistical standpoint. The stellar encounter is the analogue of a collision between molecules in the elementary kinetic theory of gases. In the stellar case there is no theoretical obstacle to the occurrence of actual physical collisions between stars. In practice such collisions would be almost infinitely improbable, and even encounters close enough to produce sensible changes in stellar velocities are extremely rare. The degree of rarity can be readily demonstrated by such a simple example as the case of a cubic lattice of stars spaced at a density of, say, two or three stars per cubic parsec, to correspond roughly to the stellar density near the Sun. We can fire off a test body with some plausible velocity say roughly 20 km/s in a random direction and inquire the chances of a passage sufficiently close to one of the stars to affect its velocity. A figure of the order of 100 million kilometres might be taken as suitable. The test body will take some 10^4 or 10^5 years to cross the lattice space and will have a probability of the order of 10^{-10} of having an encounter with one of the bounding stars of the lattice cell from which it is emerging. Even if this is multiplied by the number of stars in the system, and even if the figures adopted are varied within wide limits the conclusion remains that encounters are very rare.

Chandrasekhar has given a formula of general validity for the relaxation time in various conditions, that is, the average time needed to produce a significant change in the energy of a star. This depends on the star mass, the velocity dispersion the number of stars per cubic parsec, and the total number of stars in the system. For ordinary stars in the solar neighbourhood the figure of 5×10^{13} years has been given for the relaxation time. This is so long that it may be concluded that encounters in the stellar field as it now is are quite ineffective in modifying the velocity distribution. In this respect there is a marked difference between the behaviour of stars and the behaviour of molecules in a gas.

For a cluster such as the Pleiades with about 350 solar masses in a volume of radius about 1·7 parsecs, and a low velocity dispersion, a relaxation time of only some 20 million years is found, or about one-third of the estimated age of the cluster.

Globular clusters have a total membership of some hundreds of thousands of stars, and central densities of some hundreds of solar masses per cubic parsec. O. C. Wilson and Mary Coffeen found a velocity dispersion determined from radial velocities of about 4·5 km/s for the globular cluster M 92 (= N.G.C. 6341). Figures in this range are comparable with the scatter due to observational errors of measurement of the radial velocities of individual faint stars in these clusters. The true velocity dispersion is derived by subtracting from the square of the dispersion of the observed velocities, the square of the dispersion to be expected from observational errors. This can often be a very tricky procedure. Feast and Thackeray found dispersions ranging downwards from about 5 km/s for the globular cluster 47 Tucanae (N.G.C. 104). The results depended rather sensitively on the statistical treatment, and in one case produced the impossible result that the observed velocity dispersion was less than that to be attributed to observational error alone. It can probably be expected that the velocity dispersions of globular clusters are in the range from 0 to 5 km/s and probably nearer the upper limit. Schwarzschild and Bernstein have given a formula relating the mass of a cluster to the velocity dispersion through a general theorem known as the Virial Theorem. The formula is $V^2 = GM/\bar{r}$ where V is the total velocity of a member star, and $\bar{r}$ is a mean radius deduced from star counts. If the dispersion in radial velocities is σ, then $V^2 = 3\sigma^2$. A mass of about $1\cdot4 \times 10^5$ solar masses was inferred for M 92. Feast and Thackeray gave limiting masses on various hypotheses for 47 Tucanae indicating the same order of magnitude. Their studies also led them to assign a distance of 4·4 kiloparsecs to 47 Tucanae and an integrated photographic absolute magnitude of − 8·7. Velocity dispersions of the order thought probable give relaxation times of the order of 10^9 years. It thus appears that except for very young clusters, relaxation times are only a fraction of ages. Velocity distributions can therefore be expected to be Maxwellian, and mean free paths much greater than cluster dimensions.

The structure of globular clusters was discussed by Woolley in his Halley lecture for 1961. The observations of Kron and Mayall on the distribution of surface brightness in globular clusters are discussed in relation to the finding that the conditions of motion must be those of quasi-equilibrium. In these circumstances the analogy with a gaseous structure becomes valid. There is a parallel between the isothermal gas sphere studied in connection with stellar structure, and the structure of globular clusters. The changes in form, from a strictly globular shape, to an elongated one characteristic of a rotating system have also been studied.

When cluster members have their velocities changed by encounters, some of them will acquire enough energy to permit them to escape from the cluster. Their departure will leave the rump less able to restrain the escape of the next high energy star. The process thus accelerates. Disintegration does not proceed uniformly rapidly throughout a cluster, for its outer regions are more vulnerable to interactions with the environment, namely, parts of the stellar structure of the galaxy or gas clouds, than are the inner: the relaxation time through the cluster is different for different regions and different masses of stars: less massive stars will have, through equipartition of energy, higher mean velocities, carrying greater risk of passing the velocity of escape, than more massive ones. These problems have been the subject of study by Spitzer, and on this work we can only make the general comments that, proportionately, large clusters are much more resistant to the forces of disintegration than small ones, and that once disintegration has begun it is a process which accelerates rapidly. Estimates have been made that the lifetime of a galactic cluster can be only of the order of 10^8 to 10^9 years, whereas the much more populous globular clusters will have much longer lives. In his Halley lecture Woolley quotes an estimate, based, of course, on a particular model for a globular cluster and a certain velocity of escape, that a large cluster might lose 3,600 stars in 10^{10} years through an escape mechanism, but this is not serious if there were 10^5 or more stars to start with. We thus see that arguments along these lines yield figures, admittedly uncertain, which are reasonably consistent with the life estimates made in an earlier section which were based on studies of the Hertzsprung-Russell diagram.

REFERENCES:

Galactic Coordinates:
  Report of Sub-Commission; A. Blaauw, C. Gum, J. L. Pawsey and G. Westerhout, *M.N.*, **121**, 123, 1960. Printed in most standard journals.
  Conversion Tables: *Lund Annals*, Nos. 15, 16, 17, 1961.
Standard Data Compilations:
  Mount Wilson General Catalogue of Radial Velocities, 1953 (supplement in preparation).
  Yale General Catalogue of Trigonometrical Parallaxes, 1952 (supplement 1963).
  Yale Bright Star Catalogue, new edition, 1965.
  For proper motions see the *Boss General Catalogue*, the *Washington N 30*, and *Zone Catalogues* of various observatories.
  A Catalogue of 9,867 Stars in the Southern Hemisphere with proper motions exceeding 0″·2 annually, W. J. Luyten, Minnesota, 1957.
  A Catalogue of 7,127 stars in the Northern Hemisphere with proper motions exceeding 0″·2 annually, W. J. Luyten, Minnesota, 1961.
  A Catalogue of High-Velocity Stars, O. J. Eggen, *R.O.B.*, No. 84, 1964.
  Space Velocity Vectors for 3,483 stars, O. J. Eggen, *R.O.B.*, No. 51, 1962.
  Eigenbewegungs Lexikon, Bergedorf, 1936.
  Geschichte der Fixsternhimmels, Berlin Academy of Sciences (many volumes).
Nearby Stars:
  G. Strömberg, *Ap.J.*, **104**, 12, 1946.
  W. Gliese, *Zs.f.Ap.*, **39**, 1, 1955.
  R. v.d. R. Woolley, *M.N.*, **118**, 45, 1957.
  The series on dwarf M stars by A. N. Vyssotsky and colleagues begins with *Ap.J.*, **97**, 381, 1943.
Ursa Major Group:
  Nancy G. Roman, *Ap.J.*, **110**, 205, 1949.
  R. M. Petrie and B. N. Moyls, *M.N.*, **113**, 239, 1953.
Secular Parallaxes (among many others):
  V. Osvalds and A. M. Risley, Leander McCormick Publications, Vol. XI, Part XXI.
  M. W. Feast, *M.N.*, **125**, 367, 1963.
Mathematical Methods:
  W. M. Smart, *Stellar Dynamics*, Cambridge University Press, 1938.
  R. Trumpler and H. Weaver, *Statistical Astronomy*, University of California, 1953.
Applications (among others):
  Helge Nordström, Lund Publications, Series II, No. 79, 1936.
  J. Alexander, *M.N.*, **118**, 161, 1958.
Expanding Associations:
  R. v.d. R. Woolley and O. J. Eggen, *Observatory*, **78**, 149, 1958.

Galactic Rotation:

   M. W. Feast and A. D. Thackeray, *M.N.*, **118,** 124, 1958.

   D. W. N. Stibbs, *M.N.*, **116,** 253, 1956.

   G. L. Camm, *M.N.*, **99,** 71, 1938; **104,** 163, 1944.

   J. Titus, *A.J.*, **49,** 1, 1940.

   F. K. Edmondson (Basic Solar Motion), *A.J.*, **61,** 175, 1956.

   J. H. Oort (H. N. Russell Lecture), *Ap.J.*, **116,** 233, 1952.

Various topics:

   O. J. Eggen, *Vistas in Astronomy*, III, 258, 1960. (HR diagrams for stars in different velocity groups).

   T. J. Deeming, *M.N.*, **123,** 272, 1961 (subdwarfs).

   T. D. Kinman, R.O., *B. No.* 37, 1961 (RR Lyrae stars).

   N.U. Mayall, *Ap.J.*, **104,** 290, 1946, and T. D. Kinman, *M.N.*, **119,** 157, 538 and 559, 1959 (globular cluster motions).

   O. J. Eggen, D. Lynden-Bell, and A. R. Sandage, *Ap.J.*, **136,** 748, 1962.

Motions Perpendicular to Plane:

   E. R. Hill, *B.A.N.*, **15,** 1, 1960.

   J. H. Oort, *B.A.N.*, **15,** 45, 1960.

   R. v.d. R. Woolley, *M.N.*, **117,** 198, 1957.

   P. A. Wayman, *R.O.B.*, No. 36, 1961.

Stellar Encounters and Relaxation Times:

   S. Chandrasekhar, *Stellar Dynamics*, Chicago, 1942.

Globular Clusters:

   R. v.d. R. Woolley, Halley Lecture, *Observatory*, **81,** 924, 1961. (References to Kron and Mayall and others.)

   M. W. Feast and A. D. Thackeray, *M.N.*, **120,** 463, 1959.

   M. Schwarzschild and S. Bernstein, *Ap.J.*, **122,** 200, 1955.

V
Variable Stars

5.1. Introduction

A VARIABLE star is one whose light varies for one reason or another. The two most important causes of variation are, first, intrinsic variability; second, variability due to eclipses of a binary star having an orbital plane which passes through the earth or near it.

Intrinsic variability may take a wide variety of forms, and space permits reference only to a selection of topics. All intrinsic variability is due to a temporary imbalance between the expansive forces of radiation and gas pressure, and the contractive forces of the mutual gravitation of the parts of a star. If the star is intrinsically stable a slight deviation from equilibrium conditions will cause an oscillation. The radius of the star will vary, and hence so will the measured radial velocity, which refers to an average over the stellar surface. As the star contracts, effects of compression and change of opacity of the stellar material will produce increases in radiation and gas pressure, and possibly, also, in the rate of production of nuclear energy. These will eventually cause the star to expand again, and to overshoot the equilibrium configuration. The next contraction will begin from the slightly distended configuration reached at the end of the expansion in which the pressures are no longer quite adequate to maintain the increased radius of the star. In most cases there is a definite period of oscillation, but there may be higher harmonics or beat periods, and in some cases, slow secular changes of period. The subject of the theoretical calculation of the period and nature of oscillations of various star models about their stable configurations has been brought to a high degree of elaboration. The early developments are associated with the names of Jeans, Eddington and Rosseland: among the most prominent of contemporary workers are Ledoux and his associates.

Oscillatory phenomena in stars are closely linked with the storage of energy, especially in their outer layers, and its re-emission after a time delay. In this respect the processes of ionisation and recombination of hydrogen, present in enormous abundance and having a high ionisation potential, and the second ionisation of the very abundant helium, may be specially important. Certainly, many types of variable star occur in those regions of the Hertzsprung-Russell diagram where the ionisation of the hydrogen in the stellar atmospheres is partial, so that to produce a slight increase in surface temperature would require the absorption of large quantities of energy to complete the hydrogen ionisation, while a slight drop would be accompanied by the release of large amounts of energy set free by the recombination process.

However this may be, intrinsic variability will be accompanied in principle by cyclic changes of stellar radius, radial velocity, temperature, and spectral characteristics. Among the many varieties of intrinsic variable which exist, these different expressions of variability assume a great or lesser importance. In the case of late-type, low surface temperature variables, in which by far the major proportion of emitted energy comes in the red or infra-red spectral regions, a comparatively slight fall in surface temperature, leading to only a small change in bolometric magnitude, may lead to a large change in blue or visual magnitude, because the slight shift towards the red of the curve of spectral emission leads to a very large relative change in the small proportion of the energy emitted in the blue or visual ranges.

The various kinds of variable star are frequently given the name of the first star of the kind to be discovered. Such prototype stars are Delta Cephei, RR Lyrae, Beta Canis Majoris, W Virginis, Mira (Ceti) and so on. The members of the various groups are distinguished by their absolute magnitudes and spectral types, and by the forms of their light curves, together with such features as the magnitude range of variability, the occurrence of overtone oscillations and the occurrence of additional irregular variations of period and magnitude.

The importance of intrinsic variable stars to the observer lies to a great extent in the fact that they are recognisable as belonging to one or other class, permitting estimates, some more accurate than others, of their mean absolute magnitudes to be made. The identification of a variable of a given type in a particular situation, whether in isolation, or as a member of a cluster or galaxy, permits the astronomer to make an estimate of its distance modulus, and hence also of that of the structure in which it has been found. Since this can be done solely from measures of magnitude and colour, which are in general possible for stars too faint for spectroscopic observation, even very faint variable stars may have a great importance. Since most of the intrinsic variables are bright stars, giants or supergiants, they can be used to make distance estimates even of very remote objects.

In certain cases the star undergoing variation is not stable because the processes of stellar evolution have established within it a special kind of internal structure. In such a case the star does not oscillate about an equilibrium configuration but undergoes a sudden explosive increase in brightness, becoming a *nova* or a *supernova* according to the type of star involved. These are discussed below. The *eclipsing variables* are a special case of binary star, which owe their special importance to the accident that the Earth is so placed that the components eclipse one another in their orbital motion. These also are discussed below.

The most authoritative catalogue of variable stars is that of Kukarkin, Parenago, Efremov and Kholopov, *General Catalogue of Variable Stars* (now with several supplements), in Russian, with inserts in English. The second edition lists 14,708 separate stars, including 9,855 pulsating (intrinsic) variables, 959 novae (including some other types of eruptive variable) and 2,763 eclipsing variables. The numbers discovered must be fairly strongly affected by observational selection.

5.2. Nomenclature of Variable Stars

Because the last capital letter used by Bayer in his system for star nomenclature was Q followed by the constellation name, Argelander chose to denote variable stars by the letters R, S, T, etc., followed by the genitive of the constellation name. When all the letters down to Z had been used, double-letter designations RR . . . RZ, SS, ST . . . SZ . . . ZZ were used, the second letter never being earlier than the first. Then similar sequences AA, AB . . . AZ, BB, BC . . . BZ are assigned as names of newly discovered variables. The letter J is always omitted and the last designation on this system is QZ. After this notations beginning V 335 are used as more variables are discovered in a constellation. This explains the somewhat odd names of certain variables such as RR Lyrae, AI Velorum, CC Eridani and so on. Stars with ordinary names, such as Delta Cephei keep these, but fainter ones, with, say, only Henry Draper numbers, get a variable designation as well. The system is apt to cause a certain amount of confusion and failure to recognise the same star under different names.

5.3. Observational Methods

An important contribution to knowledge of variable stars is still made by the amateur visual observer using relatively modest telescopic equipment. This is possible and necessary because to keep track of the vast numbers of known variable stars would more than tax the observational resources of all the world's professional observatories. Such bodies as the American Association of Variable Star Observers collect and collate tens of thousands of amateur observations each year. The traditional method of observation is the comparison by eye of the variable star with a series or sequence of comparison stars which appear in the same telescopic field and which have known apparent magnitudes. These provide a scale of brightness into which the observer fits the variable star at the moment of observation. The comparison sequence should consist of stars which are not variable themselves, which cover a magnitude range from above the maximum to below the minimum brightness of the variable, are roughly equally spaced in intervals of magnitude and have about the same colour as the variable. Nature rarely provides such ideal conditions, but an approximation is usually possible. The results are improved if the magnitudes of the comparison stars have been determined photoelectrically. Concerning accuracy it is difficult to say much of general validity. The results refer only to a single colour, that of the effective wavelength of response of the observer's eye, which varies from individual to individual and from night to night according to circumstances, such as, for example, the amount of background illumination provided by the moon. An average uncertainty of one or two tenths of a magnitude for the observer of average skill might be expected.

5.4. The Blink Microscope

Photographic methods are much in use for the study of variable stars. An instrument much in use for the discovery of variables is the blink microscope. It makes use of two plates of the same star field taken at different times with the same instrument, and depends on the principle that the two plates ought to be identical except for any variable stars which have changed brightness between the times of the two exposures. This is much harder to realise in practice than one might think, and for success the two plates to be compared have to be very carefully selected so that the corresponding images match very well throughout the magnitude range covered by the plates. If this is not done one is apt to arrive at the conclusion that all the stars on the plate are varying. Given a well-matched pair, the plates are mounted in the blink microscope which is an instrument permitting the operator to view corresponding areas of the two plates in rapid succession. Two optical systems with the same characteristics image corresponding areas of the plates in a single eyepiece on the same scale. In one form of the instrument the observer can switch rapidly back and forth from one plate to the other by twiddling a little lever: in another the

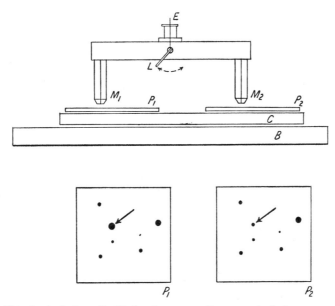

Figure V.1: Basic design of a blink microscope. Two matched plates are mounted on the carriage, C, and can be moved together over the base, B. Differential adjustments permit precise matching of the images. These are produced by the microscopes, M_1 and M_2, and are brought by anciliary optics to the common eyepiece, E. Movement of the lever, L (or illumination alternation) permits the plates to be seen in rapid succession with rapid variation of the variable star marked by an arrow.

two images are simultaneously present but the plates are illuminated alternately at a regular rate. If the match is good, and if the plates are so oriented and positioned that corresponding images are superposed (the blink microscope has screw adjustments on the plate stages for securing this condition), then the observer will see a steady field as the view alternates, with the exception that stars which have varied between the taking of the two plates will blink in and out. Properly used, the blink microscope is a most powerful means of picking out variable stars from fields containing, perhaps, thousands of images of constant stars.

5.5. Further Investigation

Once the variables have been marked down, any of the methods for determining magnitudes which are suited to the case may be used. These may be photographic, and the plates may be analysed by means of an iris-diaphragm photometer. In some cases double telescopes are used on variable star fields, so that simultaneous photographs of the same field through, for example, a yellow filter and a blue filter may be obtained. Each plate, whether single, or a member of a pair, will give a measure of magnitude in the appropriate wavelength range, corresponding to the time of mid-exposure, for all the variables measured on the plate. A comparison sequence, preferably photoelectric, and in two colours if necessary, is required for the reduction of the plate. Photographic photometry of variables is probably less accurate than photoelectric but has the advantage of providing data on a number of stars simultaneously if there is more than one variable in the field, in a form which can be analysed at leisure. Photoelectric methods though superior in accuracy permit observation of only one star at a time, and the lion's share of the work is done at the telescope. For stars of very short period, Walraven devised a method employing two similar telescopes on the same mounting each provided with essentially identical photoelectric equipment. One telescope was trained on the variable: the other diaphragm slightly offset on a nearby comparison star. Automatic switching from one equipment to the other was provided giving a nearly continuous record of the variations. Two identical sets of equipment are required for this technique, and the good fortune to find a suitable nearby comparison star.

5.6. Julian Dates

Variable star data consist of a series of measures of magnitude, and possibly colour, made at stated times. The latter are most conveniently expressed in terms of *Julian Date*. This system of reckoning counts the days from an arbitrary zero, chosen as noon, U.T., on January 1, 4713 B.C., sufficiently far in the past to ensure that negative numbers are never needed. The *Astronomical Ephemeris*, and similar works, provide tables of Julian Date for all ordinary dates up to A.D. 2000. To avoid errors of unity which might arise from the fact that ordinary dates are ordinal numbers, the tables list the number of Julian Days elapsed at noon, U.T., on fictitious dates, such as January 0, February 0, etc. For a time between Greenwich noon, on a given day D of a month, and noon on the following day, the Julian Date may be found as follows: Take the tabular figure for day zero of the same month, and increase this by D. To this add the decimal part of a day (the conversion is given in another table), corresponding to the interval of Universal Time elapsed since noon on day D. Thus for 1964 Jan 0, the number of Julian Days elapsed is 2 438 395. Whence the Julian Date for 1800 U.T. on January 13 is 2 438 408·2500 and for 0600 U.T. on January 14 is 2 438 408·7500.

If a star is observed on the meridian when the Sun is six hours past the meridian, the Earth and the Sun are at the same distance from the star. If the star is observed on the meridian at midnight, the Earth is nearer to the star than is the Sun by an amount not greater than the radius of the earth's orbit round the Sun. Light takes about 8 minutes to travel this distance. This is a negligibly small proportion of the time taken by light to travel from any star, but for stars of very short period variations in light time of this order are not negligible compared with the period. The shortest known period is 80 minutes for SX Phe, discovered by Eggen, and HD 199757, discovered by Churms and Evans, is nearly as short, at 97m. Particularly for short period variables, observation times must be corrected so that the time used in discussing the observations is the heliocentric Julian date, namely that time at which the light bearing the information would have arrived at the Sun. Corrections for light time to give heliocentric Julian dates from apparent ones are tabulated by Prager. (Figure V.2.)

The observational data on any variable star consists of a list of observations of some parameters, such as B and B-V, associated with a heliocentric Julian date for each separate determination. The annual disappearance of every star into daylight, vagaries of the weather, instrumental availability, and the fact that some kinds of observation are confined to moonless skies are all factors which combine to make the data list a thoroughly irregular one. In very many cases there will be some underlying period in which the phenomena described by the observations recur with greater or less exactitude. If this periodic time is P days, then the fractional part of the product: heliocentric J.D. $\times P^{-1}$ yields a number called the *phase* such that for an exactly periodic phenomenon the same observational values should always be found at the same phase. The most convenient way of representing data on variable stars is in terms of phase diagrams which are graphs in which phase is the abscissa.

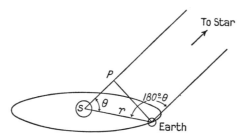

Figure V.2: If S is the Sun, the correction to be applied to the time of observation of a variable star from the earth is the light time corresponding to the distance PS, or $r \cos \theta$, where the angle Sun-earth-star $= 180° - \theta$.

Once the period has been found so that phases can be calculated most of the preliminary difficulties in the marshalling of the observations are over. The discovery of the period in any given case is a matter of drudgery, ingenuity, luck and skill The astronomer who has found a possible period always applies stringent tests to make sure that he has not arrived at a wrong value algebraically related to the correct one. Favourite examples of error are (i) the determination of a period which is a small multiple or submultiple (e.g. twice or a half) of the correct value; (ii) if the observations all occur near the same fraction of a day, and can be put on to a phase diagram with period P, then they can usually with equal plausibility be put on to a phase diagram based on period P', where $1/P' = n + 1/P$, where n is an integer. The difficulties are caused by the wide range of possible values of period, together with the fact that the problem of finding a period is not strictly a mathematical one. This remark is based on the fact that, leaving physical plausibility on one side, in the language of pure mathematics we can state the theorem: "Given any finite number of number pairs (parameter values and dates), then it is possible to find an infinite number of periods, most of them less than the interval between the two closest observations, in terms of which these arbitrary numbers can be represented as a periodic phenomenon."

5.7. The Cepheid Variables

Possibly the most celebrated of all variable stars, these take their name from the prototype star, Delta Cephei, of which the variability was recognised towards the end of the eighteenth century. The classical Cepheids are giant or supergiant stars of Population I occurring with a frequency which has been estimated as one per million of this population. They owe their variability to the fact that they pulsate: their variation is extremely regular and characteristic, and the periods of individual Cepheids are closely constant. The range of period is from about one and a half days to over 100 days, but the distribution of numbers of known Cepheids with period shows a pronounced maximum. For the Cepheids in the Galaxy the highest frequency of occurrence is at a period of about 4·2 days. The range of light variation is a magnitude or less. A general distinguishing feature of the Cepheids is that the rise to maximum light is much steeper than the fall from maximum to minimum. Most of the properties of Cepheids show a strong correlation with period. At both the shortest and the longest periods the curves of light variation are smooth, with the rise occupying some 20 to 30 per cent of the period. Near the middle of the range, however, the light curves are apt to show subsidiary humps, either before or after maximum light, or both. These are valuable for diagnostic purposes and have been made the basis of subdivision of the family into various subtypes. Efforts were made by Eggen, beginning in 1950 to divide the Cepheids into classes known as A, B, C, by analogy with the corresponding well-established divisions of curve form which apply to the RR Lyrae stars discussed below. In this case the divisions, a, b, c, were introduced many years ago by Solon I. Bailey, and have proved of great utility. The Cepheid divisions, though now often used, underwent some initial vicissitudes: for example, the Cepheids, WZ Sgr and T Mon, which have effectively superposable light curves, were originally placed in classes B and C respectively, but by 1957 had both been assigned by Eggen, Gascoigne and Burr to class A. It now seems reasonably clear that a differentiation of type can be made, and that, for example, the different types have a different relationship between the colour amplitude in a cycle of variation, and the logarithm of the period.

The spectral type of a Cepheid changes during the cycle, and is earlier at maximum brightness than at minimum, i.e. the surface temperatures are highest near maximum light. The mean spectral type is later for the longer period Cepheids, being mid-F for the shortest periods, and late G for the longest. Types at maximum light show less variation with period, and always lie within the F classification, being early F for periods between one and two days and late F for periods of the order of 40 days. Types at minimum light show a progressively greater range with increasing period, from late F for the short period Cepheids, to early K for those with periods of the order of 40 days. (Figure V.3.)

Because the phenomenon is one of pulsation the measured radial velocity of Cepheids varies through the cycle. In any individual case the curve of radial velocity variation is almost a mirror image of the light curve, with maximum and minimum brightness almost coincident with minimum and maximum velocity respectively. There is an empirical rule that the range of velocity variation is about 35 km/s per magnitude of range in photographic magnitude, or about 60 km/s per magnitude of visual range.

It will be appreciated that the measured radial velocity is a somewhat complicated average over the apparent disk of the star, in which the assumed variation of surface brightness from the centre to the edge of the disk, and projection effects along radii inclined to the light of sight, play an important part. The actual range of velocity of radial expansion and contraction of the star's surface must be higher than the range of the measured radial velocity. Even so, the phases at which maximum and minimum radii are reached can be inferred from the measured radial velocities. Minimum stellar radius will occur at the phase at which the measured radial velocity passes through its mean value going from positive to negative, and maximum radius at passage through the mean going from negative to positive. Minimum radius thus occurs only a little before maximum light, so that entry into a new cycle of variation has almost the character of an explosive outburst.

Many of these properties are illustrated by the prototype star, Delta Cephei

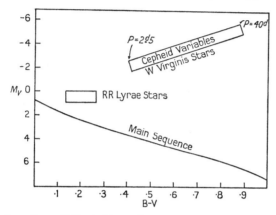

Figure V.3: Location of Cepheids and some other types of variable on the Hertzsprung-Russell diagram. Mean properties are indicated for variables.

(Figure V.4), which has a period of 5·366341 days, maxima and minima at apparent magnitudes 4·1 and 5·2, a spectrum varying between F5 Ib and G2 Ib, and a light curve in which the rise from minimum to maximum occupies 30 per cent of the period. The measured radial velocity ranges from −35 km/s to +5 km/s.

The literature dealing with Cepheids is far too extensive to be readily summarised, but we may note the papers of Joy on the northern Cepheids, and particularly on their velocity distribution, which have already been mentioned in the previous chapter. An excellent summary of Cepheid properties is given by Cecilia Payne-Gaposchkin in her book *Variable Stars and Galactic Structure*. Observations of Cepheids have been extended to the southern hemisphere in the last decade or so: the work of Stibbs on the velocities of the southern Cepheids has already been mentioned: in the photometric field we may note the work of Walraven, Muller and Oosterhoff, and of John B. Irwin.

The most important of all the Cepheid relationships was undoubtedly the discovery made in 1912 by Miss Henrietta Leavitt, that there was a linear relationship between the mean apparent magnitude of Cepheids in the Small Magellanic Cloud and the logarithm of their periods in days. The Large and Small Magellanic Clouds are the two nearest external galaxies and we shall meet them again later. At the time of Miss Leavitt's discovery the distance moduli of the Clouds were not known, though it was clear that the values must be large. However, whatever the correction for distance and extinction which might be needed to convert apparent magnitudes in the Small Cloud to absolute magnitudes, it would be the same for all members.

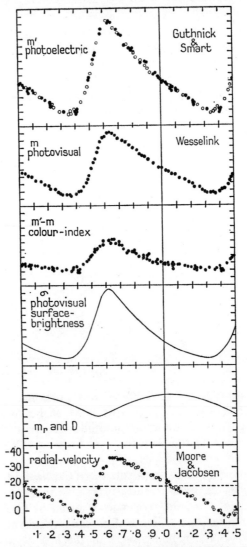

Figure V.4: This 1946 compilation of data on Delta Cephei by Wesselink shows that older observations are not to be despised. The photoelectric curve made with a photronic cell refers to 4400 Å: Wesselink's photographic curve to 5500 Å. The continuous curves show inferred variation of surface brightness and variation of radius apart from a scale factor. Vertical scale divisions are 0·1 magnitudes above and 10 km/s below. (By permission of Dr. Wesselink and the editors of the *B.A.N.*)

Thus the relation is equivalent to stating that there is a simple algebraic relation between the period of a Cepheid and its mean absolute magnitude. For the observer Cepheids seem to be ideally suited for the application of this fact in a wide variety of contexts. Cepheids occur widely: in our own Galaxy; in the Magellanic Clouds; and they are recognisable in many of the external galaxies which are near enough for individual stars to be resolved in them. Cepheids are intrinsically extremely bright, and can be observed at enormous distances. The properties of Cepheids permit them to be recognised from photometric data alone, so that they can be recognised for what they are even at apparent magnitudes too faint to permit other kinds of observation to be made.

To make full use of Cepheids we merely have to take the following steps: we must assume that the Cepheids found in different places have similar properties, and in particular follow the same period-luminosity law. We must determine the absolute magnitudes of a sample set of Cepheids in our own Galaxy. Then, wherever we find a Cepheid, we have only to determine its period to infer its absolute magnitude, and hence its distance modulus. In this way we can determine distances for all structures in which Cepheids occur: even if we cannot carry out the whole of this programme, we can still determine the distances of external galaxies in which Cepheids are found in terms of the unknown distance to the Small Magellanic Cloud.

The problem turns out to be far less simple than this optimistic catalogue might suggest. Cepheids occur very sparsely in space, and none of them is near enough to have a trigonometrical parallax of any evidential value. They belong to Population I and occur close to the galactic plane: to accumulate any considerable quantity of data Cepheids must be sought up to very considerable distances—of the order of 500 parsecs at least. Light paths of this length near the galactic plane always pass through regions where interstellar extinction is high. In the case of ordinary stars one might, with a measure of uncertainty, succeed in estimating what the corrections for interstellar extinction ought to be. In the case of Cepheids, however, the values to be adopted for intrinsic colours were at one time very uncertain, and even taking into account developments mentioned below, are still not known with satisfactory certainty. The possibility has even been mooted that the Cepheids in the two Clouds are not the same as each other, and different from those found in the Galaxy. Differences might be suggested by the facts that the periods of the most numerous Cepheids are 2·5 days for the Small Cloud, 3·8 days for the Large Cloud, as compared with 4·2 days for the Galaxy. This point has been hotly contested by partisans of the hypotheses of identity and of difference.

The literature on this topic is exceedingly complex and difficult to follow. We attempt to summarise some of the main ideas. Shapley discussed the available Cepheid results for the two Clouds in 1940 and found for the median photographic magnitude the result:

$$m = 17 \cdot 04 - 1 \cdot 74 \log P$$

where P is the period of a Cepheid in days. He converted this to absolute magnitudes on the assumption, now known to be wrong, that the distance modulus of the Clouds was 17·32 magnitudes. It is important to mention Shapley's work, because many of the later discussions have taken the form of attempts to determine a constant correction to his deduced absolute magnitude relation. However, even the question of the slope of the line is in issue, for, to take a recent example, Woolley and his associates have found for Cepheids at mean light in the Large Cloud the results, on the Johnson system:

$$B = 17{\cdot}86 - 2{\cdot}85 \log P: \quad V = 17{\cdot}22 - 2{\cdot}94 \log P$$

(apparent magnitudes), whereas for the Small Cloud, Arp found

$$B = 17{\cdot}74 - 2{\cdot}23 \log P: \quad V = 17{\cdot}24 - 2{\cdot}48 \log P$$

in which there has been some correction of zero point to allow for reddening. Arp has claimed that his investigations show that the stars in the Small Cloud are less abundant in metals than those in the Galaxy, but this has been resisted by spectroscopists such as Feast and Thackeray, who say that there is no spectroscopic evidence to support such a distinction. Although these disagreements between experts produce a certain sense of bewilderment, it must be recognised that there is a considerable scatter of all the observational data about the mean relationship in every case, and it may be that Cepheids have much more intrinsic scatter of properties than was at one time thought to be the case. This point has been emphasised in a note by Cecilia Payne-Gaposchkin in *Vistas in Astronomy*, No. 4, where magnitudes for Small Cloud Cepheids at minimum light are plotted against period. As Mrs. Payne-Gaposchkin points out, the usual style of plot relates the logarithm of period to an average or median magnitude: this style reduces the scatter in parameter values to a minimum. The plot of logarithm of the period against magnitudes at minimum emphasises the differences between different sorts of Cepheid, and suggests that the period-luminosity relation is really composed of a series of about six overlapping correlations, each slightly different for the various types of light curve distinguishable, with the differences most marked at minimum light.

It would carry us too far afield to pursue this contentious topic further. No doubt research now in progress will clear up the difficulties. Even so, it would be a mistake so to emphasise the points of disagreement as to give the impression that the period-luminosity law had ceased to be of value. So far as distance estimates are concerned it retains its value. In an application to, say, faint Cepheids in an external galaxy, the observational uncertainties are such as to outweigh the present lack of precision in the form of the law, and one cannot do better in this application than adopt the values given by Allen in *Astrophysical Quantities*, expressible as

$$\overline{M}_B = -1{\cdot}4 - 1{\cdot}9 \log P$$

where this defines the mean absolute photographic magnitude for a Cepheid of given period. This is the appropriate choice since any such investigation at the present time will probably be undertaken photographically. Although the value of the constant multiplier of $\log P$ differs considerably from some of the values found above, it must be remembered that the range in $\log P$ is only a little over unity so that discrepancies due to this cause are of the order of some tenths of a magnitude to half a magnitude. When it comes to distance moduli of extragalactic nebulae uncertainties in distance moduli of this order of size cannot, unfortunately, be regarded as very large. The relation quoted shows that a Cepheid with a period of rather more than a day is a giant star, while a 50-day Cepheid is intrinsically a very bright star indeed.

We have quoted a form of the period-luminosity law above involving both the slope of the curve and a zero-point constant. Following the original proposal of a period-luminosity law, further investigations produced various forms relating the apparent mean magnitudes of Cloud Cepheids to values of $\log P$. Arguments by Shapley produced a value of the distance modulus of the Clouds, and hence a relation between absolute magnitude and period. As we have already remarked, Shapley's value for the distance moduli is incorrect, and we shall explain this in more detail below. However, most investigations undertaken since doubts were cast on Shapley's result, have approached the problem on the assumption that the slope of the curve is correct for galactic Cepheids, and that what had to be done was to determine a corrected value of the additive constant. This is, perhaps, not too bad a method of work if we consider that the range in log P is fairly small, so that uncertainty in the value of its multiplier leads to uncertainties which are deplorable rather than disastrous. Moreover, in the range where Cepheids are most abundant, namely log P = 0·5 to 0·7 say, the three relations cited as examples do not produce differences in photographic magnitude (about 0·4 magnitudes covers them all) much outside observational uncertainty. The situation is far from clear, for as McVittie remarks in his *Handbuch* article, where he lists no less than eight different versions of the period-luminosity law, it is not always clear which of the original forms is being corrected by a given investigator.

Be this as it may, if the problem is seen as one in which only the additive constant is being corrected, the argument usually proceeds along the following lines: A given form of period luminosity law plus an allowance for absorption at so many magnitudes per kiloparsec puts the observed Cepheids at a certain set of distances. A change in the additive constant of the period luminosity law merely changes the scale of the map of the Cepheids on the galactic plane, near which most of them lie: a change in the assumed absorption has exactly the same effect, and so far as these two parameters only are concerned, any change in one can be exactly balanced by a change in the other. This is the nub of the problem, particularly since the concentration of the Cepheids to the plane produces a large extinction along their light paths to the Earth. What other data can be brought in to get us out of our dilemma? Several ways seem possible: if we knew the intrinsic colours of Cepheids of various kinds at various phases we could determine the amount of reddening, and if we knew the ratio of total absorption to selective absorption we could adjust the observed photometric data and so clear away the absorption difficulty. However, the intrinsic colours of Cepheids are not well known just because of the absorption difficulties, and it seems unsafe to apply methods like the Q-method to an unstable star. What about motions? Although Cepheids are all at large distances, some have tolerable values of proper motion, and many more, as the result of the work of Joy in the north and Stibbs in the south, have good mean radial velocities. As we have seen in the previous section, a knowledge of the radial velocities of a homogeneous group of stars enables us to determine a value for the solar motion with respect to the group, and then to interpret the proper motions as, on the average, a reflection of this solar motion. Since, on the way, individual or average parallaxes are produced, this should give us the answer to the problem. Again we encounter troubles. The argument from a solar motion with respect to a group of stars requires that the residual peculiar motions should be random: for the Cepheids, the distances are so large that all the data must have the effects of galactic rotation removed before they are analysed, and to do this properly we ought to know the distances of the stars and the appropriate value of the Oort constant A. Finally, even if new values for parallaxes are found from the analysis of the motions, values of absolute magnitude will still elude us, unless we can assess the interstellar absorption.

It is to be hoped that the reader is not now so confused as to feel that the problem is beyond solution. The case is an excellent example of the way in which an apparently simple problem can draw in more and more side problems which themselves require the solution of the main problem. Of course, some of the side problems may not need to be solved with the same precision as the main one, so that a good guess may do to begin with, followed perhaps by a later review in the light of the solution of the main problem.

As an example of this kind of procedure we may note the work of Raimond in 1954 who corrected the observed radial velocities for galactic rotation by adopting a value for the Oort constant typical of Population I; then he found a total solar motion of 22 km/s for the chosen group of Cepheids, with residuals which followed a Gaussian law, from which he drew confidence that he had removed systematic effects. In a companion paper Blaauw and Morgan used this value of the solar motion to represent the observed proper motions of 18 Cepheids, and from this derived a group parallax and hence a correction to the zero point of the period luminosity law, with, necessarily, a built-in assumption about the amount of interstellar absorption. They found a correction to Shapley's zero point of $-1\cdot35$ magnitudes, that their group of Cepheids lay at an average distance of between 300 and 400 parsecs, and that the photographic absorption was $0\cdot7$ magnitudes (but this might be in error by $0\cdot3$ magnitudes). Of the numerous discussions of zero point correction the extremes range from $-1\cdot74$ magnitudes by Kron to $-2\cdot53$ by Schmidt, so that the value is by no means yet agreed, and there is a good deal of room for further revision. A slightly cynical remark might be made to the effect that astronomers are now satisfied with zero-point corrections of this kind because they are of the same order of magnitude as that indicated by the discussion of the RR Lyrae stars (dealt with at length in later paragraphs). It is not so long since astronomers were satisfied with different results on the ground that they fell in with a quite different set of ideas about RR Lyrae stars.

Because of all the factors mentioned above there is a good deal of uncertainty about the value of the Oort constant for the Cepheids, itself bound up with estimates of distances of Cepheids. Thus Raimond took $A = 20\cdot0$ km/s/kiloparsec: Stibbs found $19\cdot5$: both are distinctly higher than the value for Population I found by Thackeray and Feast and higher still than the recent I.A.U. value.

Considering that Cepheids are members of Population I, it is somewhat surprising that, until relatively recently, it was a firmly held article of faith that Cepheids did not occur as members of the Population I galactic clusters. This idea was knocked on the head one night in 1955 when John B. Irwin, working as a visiting investigator at the Cape Observatory on southern Cepheids, looked into the eyepiece and saw that the variable S Normae was apparently in the galactic cluster N.G.C. 6087, and realised the significance of this fact. That it is not an accidental superposition has since been verified by radial velocity measurements. Irwin also found that U Sagittarii lay in the cluster M 25. Membership has been established from radial velocity measures of the Cepheid by Stibbs, and of the cluster members by Feast. In principle, if a Cepheid is a member of a cluster, its absolute magnitude can be well determined by fixing it on the Hertzsprung-Russell diagram in relation to the other members. For U Sagittarii this was done by Wallerstein, who found for this star (of period $6\cdot74$ days), a mean absolute photographic magnitude of $-3\cdot1$. This accords very well with the period luminosity-relation quoted above. There are some other cases of cluster membership, but the volume of material bearing on this crucial question remains small.

5.8. The RR Lyrae Stars

We now turn to the type of short-period, metal-weak, Population II variables, called after the prototype, RR Lyrae, which have periods ranging from a very few hours to just short of a day. Those in the general star field of the Galaxy have a solar motion in excess of 150 km/s, which places them in the high-velocity group with motion characteristics similar to those of the globular clusters. Variables which appear to be identical do occur in globular clusters in a small, well-defined region of the horizontal branches of their Hertzsprung-Russell diagrams. All the stars which occur in these positions are variables, and there is an obvious suggestion that the galactic RR Lyrae stars have originated from the debris of dispersed globular clusters. The fact of their occurrence in clusters led to their being given the name, still sometimes used, of *"cluster-type variables"*. In 1955, Helen B. Sawyer produced a second edition of her catalogue of variable stars in globular clusters. In N.G.C. 5139 (Omega Centauri) she lists 164 variables, and all but 27 of these have periods less than a day and belong to the RR Lyrae class. In M 3 (N.G.C. 5272), the great globular cluster in Canes Venatici, there are 187 variables, 174 of which have known periods, and all but two of these are less than a day. On the other hand, as the compiler remarks, "The actual frequency of variables . . . is at variance with common impressions that variable stars abound in globular clusters. Of 72 clusters . . . only 7 contain more than 50 variables each. . . . Three-quarters of the clusters contain less than 20 variables. It is rather surprising to note that the most frequent number of variables found in a globular cluster is one." There is thus a large range of real variation of incidence of RR Lyrae stars between one cluster and another.

As with the Cepheids, a vast store of information exists relating various features of RR Lyrae stars in a statistical way to each other. In the early years of the century, Bailey subdivided these stars according to the type of light curve which they exhibited, and his divisions have been confirmed and adopted by later workers. Those designated as belonging to Type a have an average amplitude of 1·0 magnitudes, show a very steep rise, a sharp maximum and a long flat minimum. Those in Type b also show asymmetrical curves, but have an amplitude of about 0·6 magnitudes. Those belonging to Type c have light curves of an almost sinusoidal shape and an amplitude of about 0·5 magnitudes. The average period for a Type c is about 0·3 days, roughly half that for the other two types. Other noteworthy features of the light curves are the tendency to the occurrence of bumps on the curves at particular phases, e.g. a weak hump just before maximum in Type c curves, and the occurrence of cyclic deviations from the mean curve in a well-defined secondary, or beat period (the so-called Blazhko effect). RR Lyrae stars may also show secular changes in period, but they are small, so that very long runs of observations, covering periods of the order of decades, are needed to define period changes, and in consequence there is difficulty in maintaining strict homogeneity of the observations over such a long period of time. Published results show comparable numbers with increasing, decreasing, and stationary periods.

Colours of RR Lyrae stars vary during the cycle: they are bluest at maximum light, values of B-V between 0·00 and +0·10 being common, and reddest near minimum light, typical values being in the range +0·40 to +0·50. Light variation is thus more marked in blue light than in yellow. The spectral type varies through the cycle: it is a little difficult to give numerical expression to this, since, strictly speaking, the original MK classification system did not provide for the metal-poor stars of Population II. Judging from the hydrogen lines one can say broadly, that spectra at maximum light run through the subdivisions of the A-class with increasing periods upwards from about a quarter of a day, and over the same range spectral types at minimum go from late A to mid-F. The uncertainties are considerable, and the closeness of correlation might be in dispute. A way of stating that the metallic lines are weak has been developed by Preston, who undertook the difficult task of estimating separate spectral types in terms of the absolute strengths of the Balmer lines and the metallic lines, the latter typified by the K-line of ionised calcium, or sometimes both by H and K. Hydrogen types are usually later than metal types, and if, at minimum light types A9 and A1 were found, Preston described this by the statement $\Delta s = 8$, i.e. the difference expressed in subtype steps. Evaluation of this parameter for an RR Lyrae star calls for a considerable degree of skill, and there are large uncertainties which might be reduced by a wider application of spectrophotometric methods. Preston found correlations between a number of properties and Δs, in particular that for RR Lyrae stars with Δs less than 2, the solar motion might be as low as about 50 km/s whereas for values over 5 it jumped to a value between 150 km/s and 200 km/s.

Considering the rapidity with which changes are taking place in the structure of RR Lyrae stars, it is an occasion for surprise that they should so often follow with relative closeness the correspondence between colour and type appropriate to non-varying stars. Among Type a variables a light increase in B of a magnitude or more can occur in less than an hour, so that this is an almost explosive phenomenon. It is just at the beginning of this phase that transient doubling of spectrum lines can occur, together with a species of ultraviolet flash. RR Lyrae stars like Cepheids, are pulsating, so that they show variable radial velocity, which it would appear is related to the light variation in the same way as in Cepheids, the relation being one of a variation of radial velocity of round about 90 km/s for a change of unity in visual magnitude. Although this has been established in some cases it would be misleading to suggest that the observations are anything like as clear-cut as in the Cepheid case. Particularly the shorter period RR Lyrae stars show very marked variations in period and light curve from one cycle to another. In some cases, after observations covering several hundred cycles, it has been possible to find some harmonic formula to represent these variations. In others the variations seem to have a random stochastic character. Only concentrated runs of observations are of any value, and to reconcile stray observations or series made a long time apart is usually impossible. In particular, unless radial velocity and photometric observations can be made simultaneously on different telescopes, it is often exceedingly difficult to establish the phases in terms of light curve which should be applied to radial velocity observations, even if these are no more than a day or two earlier or later than the photometric ones.

The mean absolute magnitudes of RR Lyrae stars are not strongly dependent on period, though there may be a slight increase in mean brightness with increasing period. There is an area of disagreement at the present time. There would probably be a general agreement that the mean relationship is of small slope and lies between $M_{pg} = 0$ and $M_{pg} = +0\cdot5$, and values nearer the latter are increasingly favoured. There remains an important degree of uncertainty. The RR Lyrae period-luminosity relation is definitely not a continuation of that for the classical Cepheids, although until relatively recently it was thought to be so.

Estimates of the absolute magnitudes of the RR Lyrae stars are necessarily indirect. Although distinctly fainter than the faintest Cepheids, they are still giants, and rare in space. A frequency of one in a million of Population II has been estimated. Trigonometrical parallaxes are only of indicative value. The star RR Lyrae itself, varies between apparent magnitudes 6·94 and 8·03 in a period of 0·56683735 days: there are variations in the magnitude at maximum, and secondary periods with lengths 72·37 and 108·55 times that of the primary period. The curve is of Bailey Type a with rise from minimum to maximum taking place in 19 per cent of the period. The spectral range is from A2 to F1. The radial velocity ranges from about −40 km/s to about −100 km/s with variations of the values both with the lines selected and from one group of cycles to another. (Figure V.5.) The best absolute magnitude

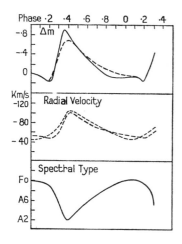

Figure V.5: Properties of the type star, RR Lyrae, after Pels-Kluyver, *B.A.N.*, **12**, 151, 1954. The light curve is not of constant form: two examples by Walraven are shown at the top. The velocity curve also changes. At centre, two examples by Struve and Blaauw, who also give the curve of spectral type variation. (By permission of the editors of the *B.A.N.*)

would be obtained for RR Lyrae itself if the contention of Sandage and Eggen mentioned previously, (on p. 135), were correct, namely that it belonged to a high-velocity co-moving group of stars typified by the high velocity star Groombridge 1830. The distance modulus would then be near 7 magnitudes (250 parsecs, or a trigonometrical parallax of $0''\cdot004$), far beyond the range of trigonometrical determination. For RR Lyrae stars in globular clusters, estimates of intrinsic brightness are obtainable from the relative positions of the RR Lyrae area on the Hertzsprung-Russell diagram and the lower part of the main sequence. Inconsistencies amounting to about half a magnitude are encountered here: if the globular cluster main sequences are identical in their lower parts then there must be a scatter in the magnitudes of the RR Lyrae mean magnitudes of about this amount: if all the RR Lyrae stars are identical, then the main sequences are not quite superposable. As with other types of object, statistical studies of the motions can throw light on the absolute magnitudes. The case of the RR Lyrae stars is somewhat less difficult than that of the Cepheids, because, since the RR Lyrae stars belong to Population II, they are not concentrated towards the absorbing regions of the galactic plane as the Cepheids are, and there is not the same range of intrinsic brightness. However, although the RR Lyrae distribution in space is much less flattened than that of the Cepheids, it does have the general property of star distribution in the Galaxy, that number density decreases outwards. This means that there are large numbers in the direction of the galactic centre in directions where absorption is not negligible. For example, there are more than 1,700 known variable stars, including almost all types, in the constellation Sagittarius where the centre lies, and hundreds of these are RR Lyrae stars.

From the historical point of view, one of the most important aspects of the discussion of the magnitude of RR Lyrae stars has been the destruction of the view held for many years that the RR Lyrae stars and the classical Cepheids formed a single period-luminosity sequence. The revision of ideas has made the Cepheids brighter than originally thought, by a change which approximately moved the period-luminosity law for them in the direction of increasing brightness, by about a magnitude and a half. This has been mentioned above, where it has been explained that the modification cannot, probably, be regarded as a simple shift. The implications have been far-reaching: the distances of a few extra-galactic objects depended directly on observations of classical Cepheids, while almost all very large distances had been estimated by methods which ultimately depended on this. The revelation of the error depended on a number of circumstances: first the extension of the main sequence of globular clusters to such faint stars that the position of the RR Lyrae stars in relation to the unevolved faint end of the main sequence could be judged: second, the bringing into use of two telescopes at about the same time, each large enough in its own field to extend observations in galaxies known to contain Cepheids to the expected magnitude level of the RR Lyrae stars. The matter was raised at the meeting of the Commission on Extragalactic Nebulae at the Rome meeting of the I.A.U. in 1952 by Walter Baade. He mentioned Sandage's work on the colour-magnitude diagram of M 3, which gave a good indication of the absolute magnitudes of the cluster type variables in that system on the basis of fitting the lower parts of the main sequences. Now classical Cepheids had been found in the Andromeda nebula and on the basis of Shapley's period-luminosity law, the distance modulus ought to be 22·4 magnitudes, so that RR Lyrae stars should be observable at an apparent magnitude of about 22·4 and this was expected to be within the range of the newly-installed 200-inch telescope. Baade reported that only the brightest stars of Population II, not the RR Lyrae stars, were visible at this magnitude level, both in the Andromeda nebula and in a neighbouring elliptical nebula at the same distance. Since the RR Lyrae stars are about 1·5 magnitudes fainter than the brightest stars of Population II, Baade assumed that they must occur in the Andromeda nebula at about apparent magnitude 23·9, and that since they were near absolute magnitude zero, this figure must represent the distance modulus of the system, which in turn would impute an error of 1·5 magnitudes to Shapley's Cepheid period-luminosity law. This change would have the effect of doubling all external distances dependent on Cepheid estimates, and would reduce the size discrepancy of our own Galaxy, which, up to that time, had appeared to be among the largest known systems. The point required to clinch the argument was to demonstrate observations both of RR Lyrae variables and Cepheids in the same system, i.e. so that the same distance modulus would apply, and to demonstrate that they did not form a single sequence. This was foreshadowed by Thackeray at Rome, reporting on first results with the 74-inch reflector at Pretoria on the Magellanic Clouds. Since these are at only about one-tenth of the distance of the Andromeda nebula, the problem could be solved with the smaller instrument, which was, however, the largest with which the Clouds were observable. In 1953 Wesselink and Thackeray found RR Lyrae stars of apparent magnitudes near 18·7 in globular clusters in both the Small and the Large Magellanic Clouds. This completed the differentiation between the two types of variable, and led to a revision of the distances of the Clouds from the figure of 25 kiloparsecs given by Shapley to about 44 kiloparsecs. As has been explained above, there still remains some area of disagreement, but the main outlines of the solution to this particular problem seem now to be settled.

An investigation in the RR Lyrae field which came into considerable prominence at the time, but which, in the light of new galactic parameter values may need reassessment, was that by W. Baade reported in the Stellar Populations Conference of the Pontifical Academy of Sciences in 1958. Baade obtained plates for variable star studies in the region of the globular cluster N.G.C. 6522, almost exactly in the direction of the galactic centre. The incidence of variable stars is enormous: Baade found 182 within 16′ of the cluster, i.e. in an area about the size of the full Moon, of which nearly half were RR Lyrae stars. The absorption in the line of sight was determined from the colour excess of the cluster as 2·75 magnitudes. This is an enormous value and would not need to be far wrong to alter many of the statistics. He put the cluster distance at 10·1 kiloparsecs, and the centre at 8·2 kiloparsecs, according to the figure then believed. He was then able to compute space densities of RR Lyrae stars at various points along the line of sight, the maximum occurring at the distance of the centre which he had adopted. Integration then gave him the total number of RR Lyrae stars in the Galaxy as of the order of 100,000 of which 20 per cent were within one kiloparsec of the centre, where the central density was expected to be about 16 of these variables per million cubic parsecs. Although the details of this investigation probably now require revision, the general conclusion as to total numbers and the degree of central concentration of these variables may not be too misleading.*

Another RR Lyrae problem which so far has not been solved, is the frequency distribution of periods. This is well brought out in a diagram of Helen B. Sawyer's. The most striking feature of her diagram which shows the occurrence of RR Lyrae stars of given period in globular clusters, is the almost complete absence of variables with periods near 0·44 days. For all globular clusters containing a fair number of these variables the mean periods for the a and b types lie either in the range from 0·51 days to 0·55 days, or in the range from 0·62 days to 0·65 days. There are peaks in Helen Sawyer's diagram near these values, and at 0·38 and 0·33 days. The last-named figure is that found for the variables near the galactic centre where it is the period of most frequent occurrence.

It is clear that there remain some very important problems in this field, and the explanation for this phenomenon of the segregation of periods may throw important new light on the origin, composition and evolution of globular clusters.

* A new discussion of the region, reducing the distance to N.G.C. 6522 and the absorption has been published by Arp (*Ap.J.*, **141**, 43, 1965).

5.9. Other Pulsating Variables

So many different types of variable star have now been recognised that even a fair proportion of professional astronomers, if not specialists in the field, would be unable to recite them all from memory, still less to enumerate all their properties. For the observer, the problem is posed as the discovery of a star with a variable magnitude, for which some classification has to be given. Even the discovery of a period, the light range, and even a light curve, will not always suffice for a classification to be made. Further information on colour, spectrum, radial velocity and so forth, may be essential. Even then, it will be found that stars are misclassified, and the literature situation still further confused by varying fashions in nomenclature for the same class of star.

The Beta Canis Majoris Stars (formerly known as Beta Cephei stars) are blue giants in spectral ranges B1-B3, and luminosity classes III-IV. They exhibit light variations with small amplitudes (range usually much less than a quarter of a magnitude) with variability of amplitude, in periods of a few hours, say 0·1 to 0·3 days. Not many of them are known, they presumably belong to Population I, and there is some kind of period luminosity relation which makes a star of the type with period one-seventh of a day have a visual absolute magnitude of about − 2, while one of a quarter of a day corresponds to about $M_V = - 3·5$. The stars thus lie above and to the right of the upper part of the Main Sequence for their mean B-V colours of − 0·2. This constitutes nearly all the simple information available about this class of star. Radial velocity measures have been made and the general conclusion is that the phase of maximum brightness corresponds to maximum compression (in contrast to the Cepheids), and that in most cases the brightness variations are mainly due to variation of surface temperature. Radial velocity observations can be immensely complicated. A common feature is the occurrence of two nearly equal periodocities causing long-term amplitude variations. When the amplitudes of these periodic terms are small a rather confused situation results, but they are not always so: in BW Vulpeculae there is only one period and the range is 150 km/s in a periodic time of 4h 49m, while in the star σ Sco one oscillation has a range of 15 km/s and the other a range of 110 km/s. In those stars with the larger velocity ranges at certain phases three different components of some lines are detectable, though never more than two simultaneously. One component will rapidly fade out and be replaced by another displaced relative to it, and as this fades out, the third component will appear. Each case requires very extensive observations and it is extremely difficult to obtain a clear picture. Modern ideas tend to represent the observations in terms of gas shells ejected from the surface in each cycle which fall back when their impetus is spent.

5.10. The T Tauri and Associated Stars

The T Tauri variable stars were first recognised as a class by Joy. They are always associated with nebulosity and absorbing clouds in the Galaxy, and have spectra in which there are many emission lines. There are extremely irregular light variations through a range of perhaps three magnitudes. On occasion the emission spectra clear away in some of these stars and an absorption spectrum rather like that of a normal dwarf can be seen. Radial velocity results are very confused. Herbig has advanced the view that these are extremely young stars and has associated them with the Herbig-Haro Objects. These are small clots of emission nebulosity with characteristic spectra found in the same type of interstellar structures as the T Tauri stars. Photographic evidence has been obtained of the formation of new Herbig-Haro objects. Although there are very great differences between the properties of these objects and the T Tauri stars, Herbig considers that they are linked, and may represent different evolutionary stages of the same object, through the similarities in their emission spectra. It seems possible that at a still later stage the T Tauri stars may lose their emission spectra and, completing the stage of Kelvin contraction become ordinary main sequence stars of the lower mass range. The classification of these stars is confused. According to Kukarkin the T Tauri stars are the later classes (from G to M) of stars with bright fluorescent lines of iron and forbidden lines of ionised sulphur and iron, and form a subclass of the wider RW Aurigae group covering a greater spectral range.

5.11. The W Virginis Stars

In Population II the dominant class of variable is the enormous class of RR Lyrae stars. Investigations by Arp published in 1955 showed up a group of stars occurring in globular clusters (and hence belonging to Population II) which have longer periods than the RR Lyrae stars, from 1·5 days upwards. These Arp called the "Type II Cepheids", possibly a not very happy choice of nomenclature since the important point is to differentiate them from classical Cepheids. In some ways these resemble Cepheids, but their light curves show many more humps than ordinary Cepheids, and the shape near maximum light sometimes shows a fairly long stretch in which the brightness, though not constant, shows only a fairly small range. Arp also noted several cases where alternate light cycles were not identical, so that the configuration would be repeated, not in the interval from one maximum to the next, but in twice this interval. Arp takes the view that in discussing these stars the correct value of period to adopt is the doubled one. Incidentally, a parallel phenomenon has been suggested in the case of RR Lyrae stars, where it has been suggested that the Type c stars are oscillating in the first overtone, while the Types a and b have the fundamental frequency. With this proviso (which does not affect his main conclusions) Arp derives a period-luminosity relationship for these stars which is of the order of one and a half magnitudes below that for the classical Cepheids, and hence not too different from Shapley's original law for the classical Cepheids. On the other hand the relation between type and absolute magnitude for the W Virginis stars follows the same trend and overlaps with that of the classical Cepheids. With this accepted we find a sequence of Population II variables which starts at periods of just over a day, with the Type II Cepheids and continues on to merge with the classes of variable known by their prototypes as W Virginis and RV Tauri stars. W Virginis is a supergiant variable with a range of 1·4 magnitudes, in the range F2 to G6 with emission lines, and a period of 17·27 days. As Kukarkin remarks it is a matter of considerable difficulty to distinguish stars in this group from classical Cepheids of similar period, and there may be misclassifications. RV Tauri stars are supergiants with comparatively stable light curves, and an amplitude of 3 magnitudes or less: they may show double waves. The periods are in the range from 30 to 150 days (RV Tauri has a period of about 78·7 days) and the spectral classes range from G to late K, being earliest near maximum brightness.

5.12. Some Short-Period Variables

Any attempt to cover all classifications of variable stars is likely to become tedious and obscure, or merely superficial. There are almost certainly too many subdivisions and certainly too many type names. One area of investigation which is a centre of some interest and difficulty is the problem of a number of very short-period stars which in spectral type and general behaviour are very like RR Lyrae stars. Periods are from 0·2 days downwards, but variability is often very erratic. Most of the stars in this group have previously had RR Lyrae classifications, and the principal reason for changing this is that the absolute magnitudes are wrong. Present opinion distinguishes two kinds: the δ Scuti stars, called after the prototype, which lie below the RR Lyrae stars, but still above the main sequence. The other kind are called Dwarf Cepheids and are several magnitudes below the main sequence. In this group belong the very short period erratic stars, like SX Phoenicis and AI Velorum, and possibly also Churms' star, HD 199757, which is much more regular. Types are in the late A or F region. It is very difficult to make classifications on photometric data alone, and parallax data are usually wanting or uncertain. There are, so far, only a handful of these stars known, and it may be premature to generalise about type characteristics.

5.13. Magnetic Variables

We select two groups of variable stars for which some generality of statement is possible. The first of these is the group of metallic-lined A stars, denoted as Am by spectroscopists. Their spectra include large numbers of metallic lines, especially those of silicon, strontium, chromium and rare earths such as europium, gadolinium and dysprosium. As ordinary visual variable stars they are not very striking: light variations are only of the order of 0·1 magnitudes and periods of some tens of days—in individual cases much shorter or longer. Their chief interest lies in the fact that they exhibit magnetic phenomena, and almost all information about magnetic stars is due to the work of H. W. Babcock in California during the last decade or two. It is, of course, truly remarkable that a star, composed of gas in violent motion, can exhibit the underlying regularity of molecular or quasi-molecular structure which enables it to exhibit a magnetic field. That this is possible has been known, however, for many years from the case of sunspot fields. The first magnetic star, 78 Virginis, was shown, in 1946 by Babcock to have a field of 1,500 gauss, the method used being to exhibit alongside each other spectra formed in oppositely polarised light, so that Zeeman effects would be revealed. Since then some dozens of magnetic stars have been found, the maximum field strength being 34, 000 gauss. The magnetic fields vary in strength with a period equal to that of the light variation. Babcock is of the opinion that all sharp-lined peculiar A stars show magnetic effects. Since it is thought that all A stars are in rapid rotation at rates sufficiently fast to blur the spectrum lines in any such star which is viewed from the plane of its equator it is conjectured that the sharp-lined stars are ones that are viewed almost from the direction of their poles of rotation, and that all peculiar A stars, whether broad or narrow lined are magnetic. A considerable literature exists on the nature of the magnetic variation, classification into various subtypes, attempts to provide a theory of the effect, and detailed spectral analyses of some individual stars. This last includes an assessment of the possibility that magnetic fields can produce anomalously high apparent abundances of certain elements for which the Zeeman effect is specially marked. The analyses include one by the Burbidges of the star α^2 Canum Venaticorum which is sometimes taken as the type star for this species.

5.14. The Long-Period Variables

The second example is the large class of long-period variables which lie in the period diagram on the long side of a rather miscellaneous group of semi-regular variables. It will be realised that although the present discussions were commenced by dividing stars into membership of Population I and Population II, the distinction between the two is not always clear cut. Old members of Population I have had time to undergo a considerable degree of evolution, at least for those which originally occupied positions fairly far up the main sequence. Thus, among middle-aged stars it is not always possible to divide populations in the simple way originally envisaged. The velocity characteristics do give some indication: for example, in the previous section, mention was made of the work of Woolley and Eggen in which the motions of the nearer stars were divided up according to the eccentricities of their galactic orbits. The resulting Hertzsprung-Russell diagrams suggested that the more eccentric the orbit, the older the star concerned was likely to be. Ideas of this kind have been applied in some sections of a very extensive study of the long period variables recently published by Feast. He concludes that they belong to all population types. The long-period variables most of which belong to the spectral classification Me, with emission lines due to hydrogen and some other elements have periods in the range from 80 to 1,000 days. They are giants, and Feast finds, in common with Osvalds and Risley, and Merrill and Wilson, that on the whole the stars with periods near 150 days are intrinsically brighter than those with longer periods; Feast, however, puts his stars in this period range frankly into the supergiants at luminosity classes Ib or Ib-II whereas the other authors make them somewhat fainter, in luminosity class II. At the longer periods the stars are less luminous and fall into the giant to mild supergiant classes. The light range of these stars is over 2·5 magnitudes and may go over 5 magnitudes. The type star is Omicron Ceti (Mira Ceti) which ranges from the second to the tenth (i.e. from easy naked eye visibility to invisibility) magnitudes with a period near 330 days. Because most of the long-period variables have spectral classifications well into the M spectral classification, the problem of radial velocity measurement due to the presence of bands and blends, and reconciliation of emission with absorption velocities is not easy. This is even more the case for the variables of classification S, some of which were also investigated by Feast.

5.15. The Explosive Variables

Light variations of a very irregular or catastrophic kind have been detected in many stars, and are capable of classification into many different types. The mechanisms of these outbursts must vary widely from one type to another in spite of qualitative similarities of behaviour. In some cases the explosive phenomena represent a total catastrophic reorganisation of the economy of a star, and can only occur once in its lifetime: in others there are outbursts which occur at random, and when they are over the star seems essentially unchanged and ready to undergo another outburst at some unpredictable time. If, in the latter case, the outbursts occurred regularly, the situation to all appearances would not be very different from that which applies to some of the regular variables already discussed. In this connection our custom of describing changes in terms of magnitudes, that is relative to the original brightness of the star, may be a little misleading. A change of two or three magnitudes in the brightness of a dwarf may represent a serious disruption of its economy, but, in absolute terms is insignificant in comparison with a similar change in a giant star.

In the dwarf range we begin with the UV Ceti and U Geminorum stars: the former are later M-type stars with emission lines, which, in a matter of seconds, at rare intervals, and quite irregularly, brighten up by from one to six magnitudes, and die down again in some tens of minutes. These are the so-called *flare stars* and derive their name from similar phenomena on the Sun which take place with a comparable time scale. In the solar case, the visual emission does not, fortunately for us, suddenly increase by a hundred times, but in other regions of the spectrum, possibly in the extreme ultraviolet, the proportionate increase may be large. Although the flare stars are dwarfs and their radii are relatively small, the time required for a light wave to traverse a distance equal to a diameter is still several seconds, so that considerations of interrelations between separated portions of the surface would make it seem likely that so rapid a phenomenon is associated in the flare stars, as in the case of the Sun, with a limited area of the surface. Since the star's surface is not seen as anything but a geometrical point, there is no direct evidence of this. However, in a recent note, Poveda, using evolutionary arguments, places the flare stars above the Main Sequence with types later than K1 or K2 and attributes the flare phenomena to the interplay of rapid rotation and a convective structure. This helps to explain the observation that in older clusters the earliest flare stars are of later spectral type.

The U Geminorum (or SS Cygni) stars, like a rather similar group, the Z Camelopardalis stars, are also dwarfs which, fairly quickly (in times of the order of one or two days) brighten up by several stellar magnitudes and then return to their former brightness in a time of the order of a week. Although these sporadic outbursts occur irregularly, for each U Geminorum star there is an average interval between outbursts which is characteristic of that star: these mean intervals lie in the range from 20 days to 2 years. The somewhat similar Z Camelopardalis stars are different in detail: for them the mean interval between outbursts is of the order of a month. The R Corona Borealis stars are very luminous and show irregular reductions in brightness of a variable duration.

5.16. The Novae and Supernovae

The rather hurried and superficial sketch in the preceding paragraphs enables us to clear away a wide variety of irregularly variable stars concerning which a vast quantity of observational data exists, but which at the moment tells no very coherent astronomical story, either for the observer or the theoretician. In contrast, the information concerning the classical eruptive variables, the novae, and in more recent decades, the supernovae, is capable of a more ordered exposition.

In defining what is meant by novae and supernovae we can hardly do better than quote directly from the English text of the introduction to the Russian *General Catalogue of Variable Stars*. This runs:

"Novae: Hot dwarfs with spontaneous increase in brightness by from 7 to 16 magnitudes in the course of from one to several dozens or hundreds of days, the brightness decreasing afterwards slowly, in the course of several years or decades, until the initial brightness is reached. Some novae show small light fluctuations at minimum. Near the maximum brightness an absorption spectrum is usually observed, similar to that of class A or F giants. After the maximum brightness has been attained, wide emission bands of hydrogen, helium and other elements with absorption components appear in the spectrum. Along with the decreasing brightness of the star, bright forbidden lines inherent to the spectra of gaseous nebulae appear in the complex spectrum. After the novae return to their initial stage the spectra of novae become continuous or similar to the spectra of the Wolf-Rayet star."

So much for the formal definition from the variable star observer's point of view, of what is now known as an "ordinary" nova. This requires a little amplification. First, the name "nova" arises from the fact that before the outburst the star which is to become a nova may be very faint, and either invisible or undistinguished among many thousands of other apparently similar faint stars. During the outburst it brightens up in a few days by a number of magnitudes, which, for the sake of illustration we take as 12, corresponding to an increase in light of about 60,000 times. This catastrophic increase may bring the star into prominence, by bringing it from, say, absolute magnitude $+ 5$ (approximately equal to the Sun) to about absolute magnitude $- 7$ or often distinctly brighter, that is to comparability with the brightest known ordinary stars. Any nova within 100 parsecs would, at maximum outshine Sirius (apparent magnitude $- 1 \cdot 6$), and any nova within 1,000 parsecs would be an easy naked eye object. The uncritical impression of a naked eye observer would be that a new star had been created where none existed before, and the name "nova" or "new star" is thus not inappropriate. Examples of naked eye novae are: Eta Carinae (1843), observed by Sir John Herschel;* Nova Perseii 1901, Nova Aquila 1918 and Nova Puppis 1942, all of which reached apparent magnitude brighter than $+ 1 \cdot 0$. Nova Pictoris, which was not quite as bright was discovered by an amateur astronomer walking in the streets of Beaufort West in South Africa. The length of the list is an indication of the frequency of occurrence of bright naked eye novae: Nova Puppis may have been a supernova, and if so belongs in a different part of this discussion.

More distant novae with fainter maxima are of course more numerous: the frequency of occurrence of novae in our Galaxy is difficult to determine since much depends on the assiduity of search and the capacities of the instruments used. Cecilia Payne-Gaposchkin in her *Handbuch* article quotes 150 known galactic novae, and for 80 of these data of some completeness are available. Allen gives as a rate of detection about 2 galactic novae per year. Arp, assiduously observing the Andromeda nebula (M 31) for over a year with the 60-inch telescope found about 26 novae per year. This should be a reasonable parallel with the true figure for our own Galaxy, for his search area was limited enough to be kept under good surveillance, and the difficulties of wide search area and great variation in obscuration which apply to our galaxy would not apply there. The figures indicate the rarity of novae: only by a fortunate accident will any information be available concerning a star which later becomes a nova. All data on absolute magnitudes of novae during their development must be derived indirectly, and the best information on the absolute magnitudes of novae is that provided by Arp's work, using the new distance modulus for M 31.

* Recent work by A. W. Rodgers and L. Searle suggests that Era Carinae is not a stellar object, and should probably be excluded from this list.

G

The classical physical account of a nova is as follows: some predisposing condition develops in a star, and the structure becomes potentially unstable. An explosive outburst takes place in which shells of gas are ejected from the surface with velocities in the range of 500 to 1,000 km/s. When these become optically thin, the absorption spectrum of the true stellar surface can still be seen through them. Recombination in the shells produces an emission spectrum, and any single region of a shell would produce a narrow-lined emission spectrum with the lines displaced according to the resolved part of the expansion velocity along the line of sight. The actual spectrum of a complete shell is a superposition of contributions having a large range of radial velocity. The nearest point has a velocity of approach relative to the central star equal to the expansion velocity; the farthest portion, seen right across the shell along a line of sight passing near the central star, has a relative velocity of recession equal to the expansion velocity. Other portions have relative radial velocities lying between these extremes. Superposition of the narrow-lined contributions from all these portions gives an emission spectrum consisting of broad bands, of which the width in kilometres per second approximates to twice the expansion velocity. The expansion behaviour of successive shells can sometimes be elucidated from a continuous series of observations of band-widths. The driving force for ejection of the shells is radiation pressure from the exploding star, and as the shells expand the radiation is diluted and the pressure falls, so that the expansion velocity decreases with time. The luminosity contribution from the shells also decreases, and that from the central star, itself possibly considerably altered, becomes steadily more important. The abnormal situation gradually dies away, and, after a period of months or years, the star may return to nearly its original brightness, though probably with an altered spectrum. It is reasonable to suppose that, the faster the ejection of the shells, the more quickly they will expand, and the more quickly will the light output decline. Thus Allen summarises the results in the form that, for a nova with an ejection velocity of 1,600 km/s the time of decline through three magnitudes is 10 days, whereas for an ejection velocity of 500 km/s it is 100 days. There is not much difficulty in giving a semi-quantitative account of the nova phenomenon, but in any individual case there may be important variations and there is considerable scope for profitable observations. As an example, Nova Herculis 1934, underwent a second outburst after a period of some months. From the character of the regions in which they occur, and the fragmentary data on the motions of novae, these objects have been assigned to Population II.

The problem of the kind of star likely to become a nova has exercised the ingenuity of generations of astrophysicists. It was once thought that all stars must pass through a nova stage, but the rate of occurrence of novae as compared with the total numbers of stars in galaxies, and their ages, has been adduced as evidence that this cannot be. However, calculations of this kind, based on the confrontation of very large numbers subject to a high degree of uncertainty, have often in the past been subject to drastic revision. It might probably be contended that the ordinary nova stage could be reached in any star as the result of exhaustion of the primary nuclear fuel, hydrogen, leading to a type of internal structure pregnant with the kind of instability required. As we shall see below, this type of argument may well be applicable to the super-novae, but in the case of ordinary novae recent ideas seem to be taking a different direction. The situation has been well summarised in an article by Kraft published in

April 1962. He uses the terminology "dwarf novae" for stars of the SS Cygni, U Geminorum and Z Camelopardalis groups, and points out that a considerable number, both of these stars and of ordinary novae have been found to be binary stars; that is, they are not single stars, but pairs of stars moving in orbits round their common centre of gravity under their mutual gravitational attraction. Such systems are discussed at length in the next chapter. In the present connection we note that the orbital periods of these nova binaries are very short indeed: for SS Cygni, 6 hours 38 minutes: for the Nova DQ Herculis, 4 hours 36 minutes: for Nova Aurigae 1891, 4 hours 54 minutes. Nova, T Coronae Borealis is a binary star, but with the long period of 230 days, while, at the other end of the scale, WZ Sagittae, also a recurrent nova, is a binary with a period of only 81·5 minutes. All these pairs have one feature in common, namely that the rotation periods are so short that the component stars must be in contact. Even in the case of the relatively long period of T Coronae Borealis, this is probably still true because the components consist of a hot dwarf and a red giant of large radius. Questions of stellar masses have been mentioned several times in passing, and will be discussed at greater length below: we remind ourselves that the theory of stellar evolution discussed in Chapter III is one of evolution at constant mass, and would be radically changed in any case where a mechanism of mass change existed. The Russian astronomer, Madame Massevitch believes that stellar evolution generally is accompanied by mass changes, but at the present time this does not seem to be a view which has won wide acceptance. In certain special instances mass changes have been considered: Deutsch has shown that red giant stars are losing mass; the ordinary nova stage may lead to the permanent loss of some mass from the stars affected. The possibility that the final graveyard of stellar evolution is represented by the white dwarfs with rather small masses poses the question of the way in which relatively massive stars might lose enough mass to reach this stage.

However, in the case of contact binaries we do have a mechanism of mass transfer available. The strong mutual gravitation will markedly distort both components from the spherical form which each would have in isolation. Theoretical arguments have been advanced which show how mass could be lost by the more massive star of a pair and gained by the less massive. In such a case there would be a serious alteration of structure which might lead to the state of instability required for the production of a nova outburst.

Novae (and supernovae) share with the Cepheids and RR Lyrae stars the important property of being recognisable with a high degree of certainty, purely photometrically, that is, by the observational methods which have the faintest limiting magnitudes. If the apparent magnitude of a nova (or supernova) at maximum light can be determined, then the occurrence of one in some system, such as an external

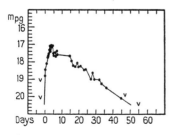

Figure V.6: Light curve for one of the novae found by Arp in the Andromeda Nebula: the constant surveillance maintained results in an unusually large number of pre-maximum observations. The v-marks indicate that the nova was then fainter than the indicated value. (After H. C. Arp, *A.J.*, **61**, 18, 1956, by permission of the authors and editors.)

galaxy, can be used as an excellent indicator of distance. So far, persistent nova searches have been carried out only in the Galaxy, the Andromeda Nebula, (Figure V.6), and less systematically, for the galaxies M 33 and the Magellanic Clouds. In the last three systems a total of 14 novae has been discovered. For the verification of very large distances, the discovery of the much rarer, but far brighter, supernovae, in extragalactic systems has proved more fruitful.

5.17. Types of Supernovae

Superficially, the supernova phenomenon resembles that of an ordinary nova. As in the former case, a star may be observed where none was before: its rise to maximum light is rapid, occupying no more than a few days: the initial decline may be fairly rapid, but a supernova may still not have decayed to its pre-outburst level after months or years. The phenomenon is on a scale so much greater than that of an ordinary nova that the final stages may not be stellar at all. Of 60 supernovae listed in a compilation by Zwicky, all occurred in extragalactic nebulae, and, at maximum light, the emission from the supernova was comparable with the total light from the galaxy in which it occurred. In spite of their enormous intrinsic brightness, most supernovae occur at such great distances that they are apparently very faint stars. To obtain a spectrum of a supernova in the restricted time available is usually a considerable technical feat. Those which have been obtained show emission bands, qualitatively similar to those produced by the ejection of gases in ordinary novae, but indicating velocities of ejection of the order of 6,000 km/s. Supernovae have been divided into two classes: Type I supernovae are weak in the near ultraviolet; Type II are strong there; Type II supernovae have more irregular light curves than Type I; Type I are intrinsically brighter at maximum and favour elliptical galaxies and the nuclei of spiral galaxies; Type II, which possibly occur with higher frequency, are found in spiral arms. These last features are the basis of the assignment of Type I supernovae to Population II and Type II supernovae to Population I. The nomenclature is somewhat unfortunate, and the certitude of some of the foregoing generalisations may leave something to be desired. According to van den Bergh, the photographic absolute magnitudes at maximum light are $-18 \cdot 7$ for Type I and $-16 \cdot 3$ for Type II. The frequency of occurrence of supernovae is of the order of one per galaxy per 500 years, and, with so many galaxies available, they are discoverable in fair numbers by the maintenance of an assiduous watch of the kind organised by Zwicky. Statistics of small numbers are notoriously tricky, but there is some suggestion that certain galaxies, such as N.G.C. 3184, 5236 and 6469 are exceptionally favoured, for each has had three supernovae since the beginning of the century.

A supernova almost anywhere in our own Galaxy would produce a star capable of outshining all others in the sky. An event so remarkable would be recorded even in the earliest times. Blurred by imprecision of observation and language, accounts have come down to us, of what are believed to have been supernova outbursts in the years 1054, 1572, and 1604, the last two being associated with the names of Tycho and Kepler. The remnants of the supernova of 1054 have been identified with the extraordinary gaseous object in Taurus, known as the Crab Nebula. This is still expanding at more than 1,000 km/s, yielding a measurable angular rate, leading to a well-determined distance modulus of $10 \cdot 3$ magnitudes. At maximum the supernova must have had an apparent magnitude of about -8, or some three or four magnitudes brighter than the planet, Venus, at its brightest, and six or seven magnitudes brighter than Sirius. The Crab Nebula is a strong source of radio waves, while its light shows a complicated pattern of polarisation, indicating the presence of strong magnetic fields within the cloud. A few other objects, for example a huge gaseous ring in Cygnus, have been identified as possible supernova remnants within the Galaxy, while there is also a large gaseous ring, some 420″ in diameter, either belonging to or in the foreground of the Large Magellanic Cloud. If the former is the case, this might also be a supernova remnant.

The supernova phenomenon has provided a rich field for theoretical investigation. Hoyle has summarised a system of ideas in semi-popular form in his *Frontiers of Astronomy* according to which the supernova phenomenon is an event occurring in the later evolutionary development of a giant star: at this stage, nuclear reactions occurring within the star have synthesised the heavy elements out of the lighter ones, and the star is suffering from a shortage of available nuclear fuels, such as hydrogen and even helium. The normal modes of energy production have been replaced by more complicated ones, and the star shows a high degree of stratification and element segregation. In a long technical paper by the Burbidges, Fowler and Hoyle, all possible nuclear reactions have been reviewed, with an important problem in mind. This is the problem of the origin of the heavier elements and their availability for incorporation into the structure of stars. The theoretical work of Burbidge, Burbidge, Fowler and Hoyle, shows that these heavy elements can only be synthesised in rather massive stars at a late stage of evolution. On the other hand they occur in stars which cannot themselves have synthesised these elements. The problem is thus to devise theoretical models in which these elements can be synthesised and later returned to the interstellar gas field so as to be available in material out of which new stars are created.

The scheme of synthesis provided by Burbidge, Burbidge, Fowler and Hoyle, together with the ejection process provided by supernovae (specifically of Type II), is thought to meet these requirements. The model for the supernovae of Type I, which are considered to have a different chemical composition, invokes other mechanisms involving the properties of degenerate (pressure ionised) matter.

The immediate pre-supernova structure is considered as unstable, and the outburst begins with a collapse of the star, during which large amounts of energy drawn from the star's gravitational store are made available. Matter is ejected into interstellar space, some with a velocity exceeding the velocity of escape from the star. The supernova gradually decays as the gaseous shells expand, and the residual star settles down to some new configuration concerning which there is practically no information at the present time. It has been suggested that the rate of decay of brightness after the outburst can be correlated with the half lives of certain of the heavy artificial radioactive elements.

Theoreticians have in recent years invoked the phenomena of supernovae to explain a considerable variety of phenomena. An ingenious example is the case of the runaway O-type stars, associated with the names of Blaauw and Zwicky. It is found that some ten per cent of the very earliest and brightest O-type stars have velocities of the order of 100 km/s with respect to other similar stars. This is very puzzling, since if these stars are very young they should reflect the velocity of the gas from which they were born, and as the low velocity dispersion of early type stars indicates, deviations of this order should simply not occur. The explanation proposed relies on the fact that there is a very high incidence of duplicity among early type stars (mentioned again below), but it is claimed that the runaway stars are all single. The runaway stars are thought to have begun as binary stars, and to have had a high velocity in their orbital motion. Then, it is contended, their companions have been so massive that they have run through a sequence of stellar evolution bringing them to the supernova stage in a very short time. The companions explode as supernovae of Type II, and it is assumed are completely dispersed. With their companions vanished, the runaways fly off into space with a velocity of the same order as that which they had when moving in an orbit.

5.18. Planetary Nebulae and other Gaseous Objects

The Crab Nebula has been mentioned as being identified with the remnants of a supernova explosion. It is to be expected that there will be a number of such objects occurring in our Galaxy, but they will be rare because of the rarity of occurrence of supernovae, and because they will be observable and identifiable only at relatively small distances. The modulus of the Crab Nebula is about 10 magnitudes (distance about 1,000 parsecs) and one might expect to encounter difficulty in the definite identification of a similar object at several times this distance. Thus although the field for recognition of galactic supernovae is the whole Galaxy, that for galactic supernova remnants is much more restricted.

The similarity between ordinary novae and supernovae has already been remarked: in both, gaseous shells are ejected and expand outwards from a central star with a speed which decreases with time. As in the case of supernovae, these shells have, in a few cases of ordinary novae, grown to a measurable angular diameter, so that a comparison of angular expansion rate and linear expansion rate enables an estimate of distance to be made. One would, therefore, expect ordinary novae to produce, in the course of time, gas clouds centred on a star, resembling miniatures of the observed supernova cases. It would also seem reasonable that because of the smaller scale and the lesser violence of the phenomenon, the remnants of ordinary novae would show much less complex structures. Because of the far greater frequency they would be expected to be much more numerous. There is a type of object known, which, at first sight, would seem to fit the bill exactly. These are the so-called "Planetary Nebulae". There is a very large variety of form, but the typical example consists of a very hot star of type O, with an absolute magnitude between $+1$ and $+6$, surrounded by a shell of gas showing an emission spectrum in which the Balmer lines of hydrogen, and the lines of neutral and ionised helium are prominent. The classic feature of the spectrum is, however, the occurrence of certain forbidden lines. These are lines corresponding to atomic transitions which in normal physical conditions are forbidden by the selection rules: they can, however, occur at conditions of very low pressure where the mean free path is so great that collisions are very rare. These are the conditions which obtain in planetary nebulae. The strongest lines are the pair, often known as N_1 and N_2 which are forbidden lines of doubly ionised oxygen at wavelengths 5,007Å and 4,959Å (before their identification by Bowen they were thought to be due to an unknown element, christened "nebulium" and are still sometimes so called); a forbidden doublet of singly ionised oxygen, usually seen as a single line at 3,727Å; and the forbidden pair of singly ionised nitrogen lines which occur on either side of Hα at 6,584Å and 6,548Å. Velocities of expansion of the gaseous shells can sometimes be inferred from curvature of the emission lines on high dispersion spectra. The study of the relative strengths of the emission lines, and their interpretation in terms of element abundance forms a vast subject which we shall not enter here. In some systems (e.g. the untypical system N.G.C. 6302) the red forbidden nitrogen lines are much stronger than Hα. In most systems the nebulium lines are in the ratio to the Balmer line of hydrogen, Hβ as $N_1:N_2:H\beta = 10:3:1$, but in some low-excitation systems (for example the unnamed system at 16h 13m·5, − 51° 52′), N_1 is much fainter than Hβ. The classical form of a planetary nebula is that of a spherical shell, with the exciting star at its centre. If the shell is very bright, then the central star will not be seen, and the nebula will appear as a circular disk. The diameters of the shells are in the range of tens or hundreds of thousands of astronomical units, and their emission spectra are excited by the far ultraviolet radiation from the central star. The basic theoretical account of the phenomena of excitation of the nebular envelope were given many years ago by Zanstra and Bowen. The most comprehensive list of emission lines in planetary nebulae is that of Aller, Bowen and Minkowski. Modern data on line strengths are being greatly improved by the technique of photoelectric scanning of planetary nebular spectra by Liller and Aller.

The name "planetary nebula" is possibly the most misleading of all astronomical nomenclature. It arose from the fact that the visual appearance of many of these objects closely resembles the disk of a planet, though it need hardly be said that in physical constitution and dimensions, and indeed in everything save superficial appearance, these objects have no resemblance or relation to planets.

Comparisons between the galactic distributions of planetary nebulae and novae have been made on several occasions, for example by Cecilia Payne-Gaposchkin in her book, *The Galactic Novae*, in 1957. There is, except possibly near the galactic centre, a close match between the numbers and distribution of the planetaries and galactic novae, with the former being about three times as numerous as the latter. The suggestion is that they belong to the same type of population, and, indeed, the high velocity dispersion of the planetaries based on radial velocity measurements favours assignment to an evolved population. The resemblance between the two distributions might be even closer if we took into account selection effects for discovery of novae in the Galaxy, and the numbers found by Arp in the Andromeda nebula, which would suggest that real numbers of novae should be much greater than those recorded.

There may indeed be a relation between the two classes, but modern opinion does not consider them to be successive stages in the evolution of the same objects. The dividing line is rather one of mass, with planetary nebulae being an evolutionary stage in some, possibly all, of the stars of masses below a solar mass. Expansion velocities in planetaries are low, about 20 km/s being typical: central stars are faint dwarfs, merging into the white dwarf range. Confusingly, there are some objects which are, or resemble, planetary nebulae, which have Wolf-Rayet stars as nuclei, and these would be assigned much higher luminosities than the normal nuclei of planetaries.

The current theoretical account makes the planetary nebulae a late product in the evolution of low mass stars with the envelope somehow ejected from the central star. After this happens the, now less massive, nuclear star follows a curved track on the

Hertzsprung-Russell diagram, first becoming bluer and brighter, and then declining both in temperature and absolute magnitude into the white dwarf range. Again, there is no telling yet whether all white dwarfs are so formed, or how the short-lived ejection phase occurs.

One point must be remembered: it has so far proved impossible to produce a satisfactory definition of a planetary nebula. Experts will argue about individual cases of gas clouds excited by a central star, in rare cases more than one, even for those near enough to be studied in detail. It is quite possible that some of the star-like objects classed as planetaries on the basis of their emission spectra might not be if they were near enough for structural details to be made out. These doubts are not trivial when it comes to statistics of distant planetaries near the galactic centre, or in the Magellanic Clouds.

In the first edition of *Astrophysical Quantities*, Allen gave the number of galactic planetaries as 136. Objective prism studies near the galactic centre by J. C. Duncan and A. Wilson, reported by Minkowski, pushed the number up to 371. The numbers of planetaries known continue to rise. Gum carried out a survey of Hα emission regions in the southern sky, and Henize also made a survey of which the results have apparently not yet been published. These last-named objects are not included in the catalogue of planetaries shortly to be published by Perek and Kohoutek of the Czechoslovak Academy of Sciences which is to include nearly 700 objects, including some new ones found by the compilers. Perek published a paper in 1963 in which he concluded that the planetaries belong to the disk population of the Galaxy and show no marked concentration towards the centre. In the same year, using essentially the same material, Minkowski and Abell published a paper of which the conclusion was that the distribution of the planetaries showed a marked concentration to the centre, and a pronounced, but moderate concentration towards the galactic plane. They therefore assigned the planetaries to Population II. The attribution is strengthened by such investigations as a recent one by O'Dell, Peimbert and Kinman which identifies an emission object in the globular cluster M 15, discovered many years ago by Pease, as a typical planetary nebula. Indications are that planetary nebulae may not be very long lived, and Minkowski in 1948 estimated an average lifetime of 30,000 years.

Reference was made above to the fact that the classical picture of a planetary nebula is that of a spherical shell or cloud surrounding a hot central star. A considerable variety of conditions is possible. In some cases the gas cloud is bright and dense, and the exciting star practically unobservable as in the case of the bright southern planetary N.G.C. 3918. In others the gases are faint and tenuous. In some cases the exciting star is easy to identify: in others it is so faint as to be identifiable only with difficulty. Cases occur, as in N.G.C. 3132, where a central star is easily seen, which, almost certainly, cannot be the exciting star, because it is of the wrong spectral type.

An immense amount of theoretical work on the excitation mechanism of planetaries has been done from the time of Zanstra and Bowen, to modern work such as that of Seaton and Shklovsky. The latter has given a formula for the absolute magnitude of a planetary nebula in the form $M = -1 \cdot 5 + 0 \cdot 8\delta$ where $\delta = m_* - m_n$, the magnitude difference between the exciting star and the nebula. The larger the value of δ the higher must be the temperature of the exciting star. Although formulae such as this and an earlier one by Berman are of great utility, it does sometimes happen that magnitude values calculated by their aid find their way into compilations of data as if they were the results of observation, and some care is needed in this respect.

The simple circular or spherical form is a grossly simplified representation of a planetary nebula. Large numbers of them exhibit convoluted, spiral or twisted forms of the weirdest imaginable character, and even some which seem to be simple will reveal extended faint ansae on long exposure photographs. The general topic of their forms and development would seem to be ripe for discussion.

Other relationships can exist between stars and gas clouds besides the processes of ejection taking place in novae and supernovae, and, if different, in planetary nebulae. These include the reflection of light as in the case of the gas clouds which surround the Pleiades stars; the stimulation of gas clouds as in diffuse or gaseous nebulae, as in the Orion Nebula and the Eta Carinae region; the relation which persists after the formation of a star from a gas cloud as in the O and T associations; the production of ejected streams of gas as in the double star Beta Lyrae; and the systematic ejection of gas from stellar surfaces, such as occurs, according to Deutsch, in the red giant stars. A particular phenomenon worthy of special remark is the production of what are called Strömgren spheres, or H II regions, where, a hot star being embedded in a gaseous cloud, usually very rich in hydrogen, produces round itself a volume which is approximately spherical, within which the hydrogen is ionised. The radius is quite sharply defined, for beyond this distance all the ionising radiation is absorbed. These objects are recognisable both in our own and other galaxies, and in the latter have in the past caused erroneous estimates of distance to be made, for they can be mistaken for stars.

REFERENCES:

General:
P. Ledoux and Th. Walraven, *Encyclopaedia of Physics*, Vol. 51, 353, Springer, 1958.
Data:
General Catalogue of Variable Stars, Kukarkin, Parenago, Efremov and Kholopov, Academy of Sciences of the U.S.S.R., Moscow, 1958. (Numerous Supplements.)
Light-Time Correction Tables:
R. Prager, *Kleinere Veröffentlichungen*, Berlin-Babelsberg, 12, 1932.
Cepheids:
Variable Stars and Galactic Structure, C. Payne-Gaposchkin, University of London, 1954.
A. J. Wesselink, *B.A.N.* No. 368, 83, 1946.
O. J. Eggen, S. C. B. Gascoigne and E. J. Burr, *M.N.*, **117**, 406, 1957.
Th. Walraven, A. Muller and P. Oosterhoff, *B.A.N.*, **14**, 81, 1958.
J. B. Irwin, *Ap.J. Supp.*, **6**, 253, 1961.
H. C. Arp, *A.J.*, **65**, 404, 1960.
R. v.d. R. Woolley, A. R. Sandage, O. J. Eggen, J. B. Alexander, L. Mather, E. Epps and S. Jones, *R.O.B.*, No. 58, 1962.
D. W. N. Stibbs, *M.N.*, **116**, 453, 1956.
G. C. McVittie, *Encyclopaedia of Physics*, Vol. 53, 445, Springer, 1959.
C. Payne-Gaposchkin, *Vistas in Astronomy*, Vol. IV, 184, Pergamon Press, 1961.

E. Raimond, *B.A.N.*, **12,** 99, 1954.

A. Blaauw and W. W. Morgan, *B.A.N.*, **12,** 95, 1954.

RR Lyrae Stars:

Helen B. Sawyer, *David Dunlap Pub.*, Toronto, Vol. II, No. 2, 1955.

Solon I. Bailey, *Harvard Annals*, **38,** 98, 1902.

A. H. Joy, *P.A.S.P.*, **67,** 420, 1955.

G. W. Preston, *Ap.J.*, **130,** 507, 1959.

H. Spinrad, *Ap.J.*, **130,** 539, 1959.

T. D. Kinman, *R.O. Bulletin*, No. 37, 1961.

M. Roberts and A. R. Sandage, *A.J.*, **60,** 185, 1955.

A. D. Thackeray and A. J. Wesselink, *Nature*, **171,** 693, 1953.

Beta Cephei (Beta Canis Majoris Stars):

Otto Struve, *P.A.S.P.*, **67,** 135, 1955.

R. M. Petrie, *J.R.A.S.*, Canada, **48,** 497, 1954.

T Tauri Stars:

G. H. Herbig, *Stellar Populations Symposium*, Vatican, 1958.

A. H. Joy, *Ap.J.*, **102,** 168, 1945.

W Virginis Stars:

H. C. Arp, *A.J.*, **60,** 1, 1955; *A.J.*, **62,** 129, 1957.

G. Wallerstein, *Ap.J.*, **130,** 560, 1959.

Magnetic Variables:

H. W. Babcock, "Stellar Atmospheres" (Vol. VI of *Stars and Stellar Systems*) (University of Chicago Press, 1960.

Long-Period Variables:

Paul W. Merrill, *Ap.J.*, **58,** 195, 1923.

M. W. Feast, *M.N.*, **125,** 367, 1963.

Novae and Supernovae:

C. Payne-Gaposchkin, *The Galactic Novae*, Amsterdam, 1957.

Articles by C. Payne-Gaposchkin and by F. Zwicky in *Encyclopaedia of Physics*, Vol. 51, Springer, 1958.

R. P. Kraft, *Scientific American*, April 1962.

W. Baade, G. Burbidge, M. Burbidge, F. Hoyle, W. Christy and W. A. Fowler, *P.A.S.P.*, **68,** 296, 1956.

Th. Walraven, *B.A.N.*, **13,** 478, 1957.

L. Woltjer, *B.A.N.*, **14,** 483, 1958.

G. Burbidge, M. Burbidge, W. A. Fowler and F. Hoyle, *Rev. Mod. Phys.*, **29,** 547, 1957.

Planetary Nebulae and other Gaseous Structures:

K. Wurm, *Encyclopaedia of Physics*, Vol. 50.

L. Aller, I. S. Bowen and K. Minkowski, *Ap.J.*, **122,** 62, 1955.

L. Perek and L. Kohoutek, *Catalogue of Planetary Nebulae*, Czechoslovakia. (In press.)

L. Perek, *Bull. Ast. Inst. Czechoslovakia*, **14,** 1963.

C. R. O'Dell, M. Peimbert and T. D. Kinman, *Ap.J.*, **140,** 119, 1964.

R. Minkowski and G. O. Abell, *P.A.S.P.*, **75,** 488, 1963.

W. Liller and L. Aller, *Proc.Nat.Acad.Sci.*, **49,** 675, 1963.

B. Strömgren, *Ap.J.*, **89,** 526, 1939.

VI
Binary Stars and Multiple Stars

6.1. The Binary Stars

A HIGH proportion of all stars is double or binary, by which is meant that pairs of stars can be recognised which are in motion under their mutual gravitational attraction. Systems of higher multiplicity are by no means uncommon, but the difficulties of adequate observation and discussion of triple and quadruple stars are often very severe. The astrophysical importance of these stars lies, first, in the fact that they provide the only direct approach to the problem of the determination of stellar masses: second, in the fact that a binary or multiple system can be regarded as a very small star cluster which can yield evolutionary information.

At one time multiplicity in stars was believed to be exceptional: it is now thought to be more the rule. In his Robert Grant Aitken Lecture in 1961, van de Kamp remarked, "According to Kuiper, ten arbitrary systems contain at least 18 individual stars. Among the 55 stars within 5 parsecs, including the Sun, 20 appear as members of visual binaries, while 6 are grouped in two triple systems. Of the remaining 29 single stars, at least 2 are unresolved binaries. Among the 20 brightest stars, there are 12 single, 5 double and 3 triple systems, yielding a total of 31 visible stars. In addition there are 5 spectroscopic binaries, bringing the total number of known components for the 20 brightest stars up to 36. If allowance is made for undiscovered binaries among single stars, it seems likely that binaries are more frequent than single stars." It has recently been conjectured that about 70 per cent of the B stars are double, and a random sample of twenty A-type stars yielded more than half double. For later type dwarf stars probably something like 20 per cent are easily shown to be double or multiple systems, and cases difficult of demonstration must increase the percentage considerably.

The nomenclature is apt to be rather loosely used. The word "double" strictly refers only to telescopic appearance, and states that the star in questions seems to have two components. If these turn out not to be physically related, i.e. if the appearance is produced by near coincidence of lines of sight to two stars at quite different distances, the term "optical double" will be used. If the components are physically related, by which is meant that there is gravitational interaction, the term "physical double" or more usually "binary" will be employed. The terms "visual double" or "visual binary" refer, rather loosely, to physical doubles of which the components are separately visible. The terms "spectroscopic binary", "interferometric binary", "astrometric binary" refer to stars which seem to be single but of which the binary character can be demonstrated by the physical methods implied by the adjectives. An "eclipsing binary" is a physical pair having the special (accidental) property, that as seen from the earth the components eclipse each other during orbital motion. Eclipsing binaries are thus light variables and as such have been briefly mentioned earlier.

The motion of two point-masses under their mutual attraction is such that the orbit of each is a conic section with the common centre of gravity at one of the foci of each conic. The two orbits relative to this point are identical except for a change of scale and a rotation through 180°. This is obvious from the fact that the two masses and their common centre of gravity remain collinear, and that the mass centre divides the line joining the two masses in a constant proportion. Geometry recognises the hyperbola, the parabola and ellipse as cases of conic sections. In the hyperbolic case the point masses approach from an infinite distance, interact, and recede. This is the case of a stellar encounter, discussed in a previous chapter, and not that of a binary star having a relatively permanent existence. A few cases of parabolic orbits of visual binaries have been computed, but their physical status, i.e. whether the eccentricity is precisely unity, or only very near it, is not clear. In almost all cases the plane in which the orbital motion takes place is inclined to the line of sight at some angle which is difficult to determine. The observer studies not the actual motion, but a projection of it: if the orbital plane is normal to the line of sight the real motion will be seen; if the orbital plane passes through the Earth, the stars will be seen to shuttle back and forth along a line. At intermediate inclinations circular orbits may be projected into ellipses or occasionally, even vice versa.

The periodic time, during which each star completes a circuit about the other, is a most important parameter. It is limited, probably, on the long side, by the consideration that the components of a binary must be sufficiently strongly bound not to be readily disrupted by chance encounters with field stars; on the short side by the fact that the shortest possible period is that of two stars rotating in contact. These considerations give an enormous physical range. Among wide pairs with long periods it is very unlikely that any useful information is available for a double star with a period of more than about 200 years, since double star astronomy has not existed long enough for it to be observed through a whole circuit. Deduction of physical parameters from observations of a limited arc of movement of a visual binary is notoriously the gateway to error. For less wide pairs, the orbital periods are shorter, but a star cannot be recognised as a visual double unless the angular separation between components exceeds a certain minimum. Thus, the shorter the period, the nearer a visual binary must be if it is to be detected, and the smaller the spatial volume available for search. The lower limit for detection of visual binaries seems to be about one year, and for this, only the nearest systems are available. Roughly speaking, the hunting grounds for the visual double star observer extend at most to one or two hundred parsecs, with periods less than about 200 years, with greatest preference in the range from 10 years to a century. Isolated examples transcend these limits. The limits for spectroscopic binaries are discussed later.

6.2. A Highly-Stylised Visual Binary

These ideas can be given quantitative expression by the case of two stars of masses M_1 and M_2 moving in circular orbits about their common centre of mass, with a distance a between their centres. If the individual orbital radii are r_1 and r_2, and the orbital velocities v_1 and v_2, and the orbital period P, we have

$$a = r_1 + r_2 \qquad\qquad r_1 M_2 = r_2 M_1$$

$$v_1 P = 2\pi r_1 \qquad\qquad v_2 P = 2\pi r_2$$

The centripetal forces are due to the gravitational attraction, so that

$$M_1 v^2{}_1/r_1 = M_2 v^2_2/r_2 = GM_1 M_2/a^2$$

where G is the gravitational constant.

These equations give

$$r_1 = GP^2 M_2/4\pi^2 a^2 \qquad\qquad r_2 = GP^2 M_1/4\pi^2 a^2$$

and by adding

$$4\pi^2 a^3 = GP^2(M_1 + M_2)$$

This is Kepler's third law. The equation remains true for elliptical orbits if a is given the interpretation of the sum of the semiaxes majores of the two orbits about the mass centre. The demonstration is then a little more complicated. The rule applies to the Sun-Earth system in which a is one astronomical unit, the sum of the masses effectively one solar mass, and P is one year. If these units are adopted, the equation becomes

$$M_1 + M_2 = a^3/P^2$$

Finally, if the separation between the components is expressed in seconds of arc as A, then, by definition $a = A/p$ where p is the parallax in seconds of arc, and we end with

$$M_1 + M_2 = A^3/p^3 P^2$$

where masses are in solar units and P is in years.

If the lower limit of observability of the separate components be taken as $A = 0''\cdot1$, and if the masses are comparable with the solar mass, we arrive at a lower observable limit given by $p^3 P^2 = 2 \times 10^{-3}$. At a distance of 10 parsecs, with $p = 0''\cdot1$, the lower limit of P is $1\cdot4$ years. At 100 parsecs it is 45 years. The argument will be modified in the case of high eccentricities when, in some parts of the orbit the separations will, if the inclination is favourable, be higher than those indicated here. The argument is adequate to illustrate the drive towards the observation of small angular separations, and the importance of relatively nearby stars. For circular orbits, with $p = 0''\cdot1$, the orbital velocity is 10 km/s, and the maximum velocity difference between components for an orbit observed edge-on is 20 km/s. If one star is so much brighter than the other that its spectrum is not seen, a variable velocity through this range is determinable with considerable certainty. For stars of equal brightness the lines would be double when one component was receding and the other approaching, but the resolution of the separate components is distinctly beyond the capacities of most stellar spectroscopes when the velocity difference is only 20 km/s. At a distance of 100 parsecs, each orbit in our limiting system has a radius of 5 astronomical units, the orbital velocity is just over 3 km/s and the velocity range of each component when the orbit is seen edge-on is about 7 km/s. Most observatories would find it difficult to disentangle this range of variation from uncertainties of observation.

6.3. Sirius as a Visual Binary

In the case of a few stars, transit circle observations have revealed oscillations of position resulting from orbital motion of stars with seen or invisible companions. The most celebrated is that of Sirius, for which orbital motion was detected before its faint white dwarf companion was detected visually. Sirius, an A1 V star, is at a distance of only 2·7 parsecs (parallax 0″·375), with apparent magnitude − 1·58 and absolute magnitude + 1·5. Oscillations in the position of the bright star were noted by Bessel from meridian observations before 1850, but the companion, which is fainter than apparent magnitude 8, was not discovered until 1862 by Alvan Clark. The latter is, of course, extremely difficult to observe because of the intense light of Sirius. The bright star oscillates through about 2″, and transit circle observations can establish this, the shape of the apparent orbit relative to the centre of gravity of the pair, and the period, which is 49·94 years. This information is not enough for a determination of masses. Observations of the apparent separation between the pair will give, using the known excursion of the primary star from the position of the centre of gravity, the ratio of the masses of the two component stars. After the transit observations have been duly corrected, with, in this case, a correction for parallax, this point should exhibit a uniform motion corresponding to the proper motion of the system, which, in this case, has the rather large value of 1″·324 per annum. The apparent orbit on the sky will be a projection of the real orbit, but the ratio of the distances of the components from the centre of gravity will be preserved in the projection. To find the individual masses, the semiaxes majores of the orbits of the individual stars about the centre of gravity must be found. The effect of projection on an elliptical orbit is that the times of maximum and minimum physical separation between the components, and the values of the distances between the components at these times, are not reproduced in the projected orbit. The methods by which the real shape and orientation of the orbit are found are discussed briefly below. Suffice it to say that, with one ambiguity, this can be done in the case of a well-observed double star orbit, and the value of the semiaxes found expressed in angular measure. In the case of Sirius the analysis yields a value of 7″·62 for the sum of the semiaxes majores of the two orbits, and shows that the orbits have the rather large eccentricity of 0·588. However, the formula given above applies independently of the eccentricity, so that using this value, and the quoted value of the parallax, the sum of the masses can be found. This total can then be distributed between the two components according to the ratio already found. Van de Kamp, using a slightly different value for the parallax (0″·379) has given values of 2·28 and 0·96 solar masses for the two components. It will be noted that, since the cube of the parallax is used in the formula, a slight uncertainty produces a relatively large error in the masses determined. Only the very largest parallaxes are known with enough precision to enable the values to be cubed without introducing a high degree of uncertainty. The dimensions of the companion of Sirius can be estimated from the fact that its spectrum, obtainable only with considerable difficulty, is that of a relatively hot star. The general course of the calculation is as follows: if we take the effective temperature of the surface to be about 8,000°K, while that of the Sun is 5,875°K, then each square centimetre of the surface of Sirius B emits a total radiation (according to the fourth power law) about 3·4 times as great as that of the Sun. This refers to the total emitted radiation, so in making a comparison between Sirius B and the Sun, appropriate, i.e. bolometric magnitudes, must be employed. The absolute visual magnitude of Sirius B is about 11·4, and the correction to bolometric magnitude on the adopted scale, is small. The bolometric absolute magnitude of the Sun has been given as 4·6, so that there is a bolometric magnitude difference between the two stars of about 6·8 magnitudes, that is, the Sun emits about 525 times as much radiation as Sirius B. Since the latter has a higher surface emissivity its surface must be about 1,800 times smaller than that of the Sun, i.e. its radius must be about 42 times smaller than that of the Sun (about 16,500 kms, or about $2\frac{1}{2}$ times that of the Earth), and, since its mass is effectively the same as that of the Sun its average density must be about 76,000 times that of the Sun, or about 106,000 times that of water. This feature of the white dwarfs was mentioned earlier: these enormous densities imply a totally different internal structure from that of ordinary stars. Although the exact figures might be open to modification there is no doubt that the order of magnitude is correct, and similar results are indicated for other white dwarfs, some of which are components of binary systems. It must be emphasised that the argument here is based on an adopted value for the effective temperature, and reference back to Chapter II, where this conception was introduced shows that for the establishment of an effective temperature scale, values of stellar radii must be known, i.e. the argument applied in the case of Sirius B must be reversed. We shall later come to the observational problem of determination of stellar radii from which this scale can be established.

6.4. Observational Methods

After this digression we may return to the determination of data on orbital motion of binary stars by transit circle observations. The cases in which this can be done are rather exceptional: besides Sirius one may mention Procyon, p Eridani, Alpha Centauri, and a few others.* In any case, transit observations of binary stars are liable to be somewhat less accurate than those of single stars, but they are of crucial importance because they provide data on motions relative to the centre of gravity of the system. Most double star observations yield data on relative motions of the components, permitting determinations of total mass to be made, but not of the separate masses of the components.

In general, observations of visual double stars entail, (i) the identification of the components, which is not always easy if they are nearly identical; (ii) the measurement of the apparent angular separation between the components; and (iii) the determination of the position angle of the fainter star relative to the brighter. This is reckoned as zero if the fainter star is north of the brighter, and increasing eastwards, i.e. position angles increase anticlockwise as seen on the sky (Figure VI.1). Each observation is associated with the time at which it was made: an accuracy of one-hundredth of a year is quite sufficient.

Three methods are in standard use: photography, visual measurement with a micrometer and measurement with an eyepiece interferometer. All require a long

* Volume I of the *Boss General Catalogue* discusses 25 instances with p Eridani misprinted a "p Eridani".

focus telescope, to give a good scale, and fair light-gathering power, say an aperture of 24 inches or more, though it cannot be denied that some notable double star observing has, in the past, been done visually by men such as Innes and Voûte with small telescopes. All double star observations require good or excellent atmospheric conditions of seeing.

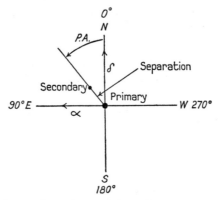

Figure VI.1: Position angle and separation of components of binary star as seen with the naked eye, related to coordinate directions.

One photographic method, applicable to fairly wide pairs, involves repeated exposures of the pair, possibly 50 or more in number, on the same plate, this being shifted between exposures to avoid overlapping. The east-west direction is marked by switching off the drive during one exposure and using the direction of trail as a reference. The best defined exposures are chosen for measurement. For both images to register, the blue magnitudes of the components must not be too unequal. A classic case is provided by Antares where the primary is a red supergiant, visually, but not photographically, much brighter than its blue companion. In a limited number of cases, useful results have been obtained from observation of separate images by photography. More generally, in researches in which van de Kamp has been the leading practitioner, photography has been used for the study of astrometric binaries. These are unresolved pairs in which movement of the centre of light of the astrometric binary can be detected by measurement of plates taken with much the same pre-cautions as those adopted in parallax work. Measures of the plates yield information on the movement of the centre of light with respect to selected comparison stars on the plate. If the fainter component is relatively so feeble that it contributes nothing to the image of the binary, the movement is that of the brighter (usually the more massive) star; when both contribute but are unequal in light and mass, the movement found is a reduced version of the movement of either star with respect to the centre of gravity; if the components are identical and unresolved, there is no movement. Analysis of the results is not entirely free of assumptions, but valuable results have been obtained, and, in all cases where the separate motions of the components with respect to the mass centre can be found, separate masses are determinable.

The vast majority of visual observations has been carried out by means of an instrument called the bifilar micrometer used at the eye-end of large refractors. In this instrument the separation of the two wires can be varied, and a reading of their separation made on a graduated drum, while the body of the instrument can be rotated into different position angles which can be read off from a scale. The principle of the method seems absurdly simple. The micrometer is rotated until a fixed wire at right angles to the movable pair lies along the line joining the two images: this gives the position angle. The wires are then adjusted in separation until each star image is bisected. This measures the separation. However, there is probably no branch of astronomy in which the gulf between what has to be done, and doing it successfully is so deep and so difficult to cross, as the art of double star observation. Star images are never quite stable even under the best conditions of seeing, and in practice to place a wire across the centre of an image may be almost as difficult as marking the mid-point of a live eel. The double star observer must always be actively conscious of what he sees, and know how much of it to register and how much to discount. There are optical defects in his own eyes and he turns his head, "eyes across" and "eyes parallel" to minimise their effects. He repeats his measures many times. He is especially careful to come to the telescope with no preconceived ideas of what he "ought" to see. In spite of all this, there is still room for surprises. Several cases are on record of discoveries of easy companions to bright stars which have been ob-served many times, possibly because all observers know that very bright stars often provide enough light to produce faint ghosts by reflections in optical surfaces, so that they automatically tend to discount faint companions of bright stars—but in a few cases the ghosts have been flesh and blood. Among the present masters of the double star art are van Biesbroeck in the north, and van den Bos and Finsen in the south, the last two named being successive Directors of the Johannesburg Observatory, which has become one of the most important centres for this work.

6.5. The Eyepiece Interferometer

Finsen especially is known for his application of the eyepiece interferometer to double star observation. If the objective of a telescope is covered by a diaphragm having two symmetrical parallel slits cut in it, it will be found that the image of a star in the focal plane consists of a symmetrical pattern of light and shade lying along a line perpendicular to the direction of the slits. The central fringe is bright and the side fringes decrease slowly in brightness on either side. A simple interferometric argument shows that the separation between bright fringes is (in angular measure) λ/D where λ is the wavelength of the light forming the pattern and D the separation between the slits on the objective. In practice immense advantages of instrumental construction and operation are gained by putting the slits, not at the objective but in the beam converging towards the focal plane: the parameter D then has the value corresponding to projecting the actual slits back on to the objective. Nor need the slits be narrow: they can be of considerable area, a marked advantage for conserving light, and of a number of shapes, of which a lune shape bounded by two sectors of equal circles is a favourite. The key feature which makes the replacement of the normal diffraction image of a star (central disk surrounded by diffraction rings) by the interferometric image advantageous, is that in the latter the separation of the fringes is greater. With the slits at the edges of the objective (an ideal attainable only if they had no area) a maximum theoretical gain of 2·44 times can be secured. An abbreviated account of the application to double star measurement is as follows: A single star produces a pattern of light and shade with the fringes separated by an angular distance determined by the separation between the interferometer slits. If the single star be replaced by two equal stars having an angular separation equal to the separation between the fringes, then with the lengths of the slits parallel to the line joining the two stars, the pattern observed will consist of alternate dark and light fringes as for a single star. This arises because the separate patterns produced by the two components are slightly displaced relative to each other in a direction perpendicular to their extension. If the slits are placed with their lengths perpendicular to the line joining the two stars, then the bright fringes due to one component will fall exactly into the spaces between the bright fringes due to the other component, and a uniform band of light will result. Thus as the slits are turned through 360° there will be two orientations when fringes are visible (separated by 180°) and two orientations when the fringes disappear. This sequence of appearances will verify the duplicity of the star (which will not be resolvable by direct vision) and will determine the position angle of the pair.

The assumptions made are, however, artificial. In particular it cannot be assumed that nature will oblige with a pair separated by exactly the correct angular distance. An interferometer with slits at a variable separation is a possibility, and Finsen has constructed one. He seems, however, to prefer in much of his work to use an interferometer with a fixed spacing and to determine the separation and position angle from a study of the appearances presented when the slits are turned through 360° in their own plane. He became adept at interpretation of the appearances from a long period of self training with artificial double stars. Suppose the double star has an angular separation greater than λ/D. With the slits parallel to the position angle of the pair, fringes will be clearly visible. As they are turned a situation will be reached such that the projection of the separation of the pair on the line perpendicular to the slits will attain the value at which the bright fringes from the one star will fall at the centres of the gaps in the pattern due to the other star. Since the star separation is now no longer assumed to match that of the slits, this will occur at some inclined position such that although the two patterns are in register along their lengths they will not be in register in the perpendicular direction. A characteristic zigzag pattern will be seen, and since the eye is extremely sensitive to detection of asymmetries a good determination of the position angle at which this occurs can be made. The zigzag pattern will occur four times in a complete rotation, corresponding pairs being separated by 180°. Two adjacent cases will correspond to the bright central patch of the pattern due to star A falling to the left of that due to star B, and that of star A falling to the right of that of star B. From the position angles at which these appearances occur, and the value of D, the position angle and separation of the pair can be found. An additional observation of fringe appearance is needed to remove an ambiguity of quadrant.

Additional important complications, which can only be mentioned, arise from the fact that starlight is not monochromatic, so that there is an effective value of λ with a spread on either side; from inequality in the brightness of the component stars of the pair—circumstances alter cases, but a limiting difference of about one magnitude applies in most pairs; from chromatic dispersion by the atmosphere, which, at relatively large zenith distances can distort the fringe patterns—Finsen has discussed this effect at some length.

The interferometer has, in Finsen's hands had great success: at the 26½-inch refractor at Johannesburg, micrometer observations stop near about two-tenths of a second of arc: interferometer measures go down to about half this value.

Printed double star catalogues which list observations are published under the names of Burnham, Aitken, Innes, Rossiter, Jouckheere and others. Newly published is the "Index Catalogue of Visual Double Stars" by Jeffers, van den Bos and Greeby (*Lick Observatory Pub.*, Vol. 21, 1963), which enables one to trace the source of all observations of all known visual doubles up to that time.

6.6. The Analysis of Double Star Observations

The specialists in this field have a great many special tricks and much technical "know-how" so that the present account is necessarily sketchy. If the period of a double star is short enough so that modern configurations repeat those of the past, there is usually not much difficulty in deriving the period. Difficulties arise in the case of doubles with very similar components, especially if at some epochs they are not separable, or if there has been a gap in the run of observations. Double star observations usually consist of statements of separation and of position angle of one star (usually the fainter) relative to the other. In the cases mentioned above there may be a risk of switching identities leading to ambiguity of quadrant, or even of setting the period at half its true value. Since in very many instances periods are longer than the lifetime of man, observations may have to be used long after the observers cease to be able to provide supplementary explanations.

Setting aside these difficulties we may suppose that for a given pair the observations provide data on relative positions of a secondary relative to a primary, each with its date, and that, by some least squares procedure the analyst can represent these by an ellipse for which the appropriate coefficients can be found. This ellipse is a projection of the true orbit from the physical orbital plane orthogonally on to the plane of the sky at the position of the star. To find the orbit in its own plane the analyst must determine the geometrical circumstances of projection, which are defined by three angles. The first of these is the inclination, which is the angle between the normal to the orbital plane and the line of sight. The inclination is zero when the orbit is seen truly in plan and $90°$ when the orbital plane passes through the Earth. From visual observations alone i cannot be determined without ambiguity: this is best illustrated by thinking of a circle drawn on a card and held at arm's length. If the top of the card is tilted towards the eye the circle projects into an ellipse for a given value of i. The projection has the same form if the top of the card is tilted away from the observer until the normal lies at the same angle to the line of sight.

In its own plane the orbit has the properties (determined from dynamical considerations) that the primary must lie at one focus of the orbit of the secondary and that the rate of description of areas by the radius vector must be constant. In its own plane the orbit is completely determined by the semiaxis major measured in seconds of arc, and the eccentricity e. To complete the specification we must define how this lies with respect to the line of sight and the plane of the sky which is normal to this. In specifying i we define how much the orbital plane is to be rotated to bring it to its real location. The direction in which this rotation takes place is defined by the line of intersection of the orbital plane and the plane of the sky, and this is defined by the position angle Ω of this line on the sky. Since this line of intersection lies in the orbital plane, it cuts the real orbit in two points which are called the "*nodes*" of the orbit. These are the points on the orbit at which, so to speak the secondary moves from behind a plane through the primary parallel to the plane of the sky and comes to the Earth side of this plane, and the point at which it passes from the Earth side to the farther side. The orientation of the orbit in its own plane is then determined by the angle between the line of nodes and the major axis of the orbit. The point at which the two stars are closest together is at one end of the major axis and is called the point of "periastron". The angle from the node to the point of periastron is called ω and when it is known the position of the true orbit in space is determined. Thus a complete specification of the elements is by the quantities P (the period), T (the time of periastron passage), e (the eccentricity), i (the inclination) and the two angles ω and Ω. The projection effects lead to the result that certain of these quantities are not determined unambiguously, but there is a set of conventions adopted by the I.A.U. in 1935 which are, unfortunately, not always adhered to in published results. These are, that i is taken between 0° and 90° when position angles increase with time: i is put in the second quadrant if they decrease. From visual observations only it is not possible to determine which is the ascending node (the one at which the secondary passes from being nearer the Earth than the primary) so, conventionally, Ω is taken to be less than 180° unless radial velocity observations are available to distinguish at which node the secondary has a positive radial velocity relative to the primary. If this additional information is available that value of Ω is taken which refers to the ascending node. The convention for ω is that it is measured in the direction of motion of the secondary from node to periastron; it may have any value from 0° to 360° and like Ω when only visual observations are available it is uncertain by 180°.

Formulae are available (they are, for example, set out by van den Bos in his contribution to Kuiper's compendium) relating the true and apparent orbits, and showing how, in the case of an orbit for which more than a whole revolution has been observed, the desired parameters can often be rather readily determined from a

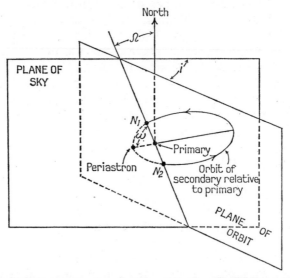

Figure VI.2: Defining parameters for the orbit of a visual binary star, with the conventions described in the text. N_1 is the ascending node, N_2 the descending node.

graphical plot of the best apparent orbit. However, in the more common case when the observations do not cover a complete circuit more elaborate methods are necessary for details of which reference must be made to van den Bos's article already mentioned. If the solution is to have any validity it is essential that a considerable arc should have been observed. In spite of the existence of these general formal methods, and of the formal apparatus for the correction by least squares methods of approximate estimates of the parameters, the finding of the best elements to

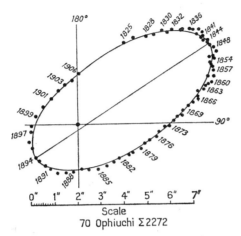

Figure VI.3: The orbit of the visual binary, 70 Ophiuchi. Mean positions for 78 years are represented by the ellipse corresponding to orbital period 86·70 years. This orbit was computed by Burnham, and more modern solutions (e.g. Strand, A.J., 1952) are available. The large separation permits astrometric study of the separate components, leading to a trigonometrical parallax of 0"·199, and masses of 0·90 and 0·65 in terms of the solar mass. (After *General Catalogue of Double Stars*, Part II, S. W. Burnham, 1906, by permission, Director of Publications, Carnegie Institution of Washington.)

represent a given set of observations is far from a simple matter. Experienced computers will often obtain better results as judged by their capacity to predict the future by relatively simple arguments in which experience and judgement of the observational skill of various measurers play the predominant roles, than by the machine-like application of general methods. The latest catalogue of 536 visual binary orbital elements is by Charles E. Worley, *Publications of the U.S. Naval Observatory, Second Series*, Vol. 18, Part III, 1963.

6.7. Stellar Masses and Dynamical Parallaxes

We have already remarked on the relation

$$M_1 + M_2 = a^3/p^3P^2$$

which emerges from the determination of the elements of a double star orbit, where M_1 and M_2 are the masses in solar units, a the semiaxis major of the relative orbit, expressed in seconds of arc, p the parallax, and P the period in years. In principle each solution gives the sum of the masses, but not with any accuracy unless the parallax is large and precisely known. In a case where the components were equal in all other respects, their masses might be assumed to be equal, and so be estimated from the above relation. If a preconceived relation between mass and luminosity be assumed, then estimates of the relative brightness may be used to partition the total mass and so lead to estimates of individual masses. However, as a matter of strict physical determination, only the total mass can be inferred with an uncertainty mainly determined by uncertainty in the parallax. The argument can be inverted. In its simplest form it can be stated in the following way: As will be seen later, there is reason to believe that stellar masses do not show a large range from the solar mass. If the left-hand side of the relation is put equal to 2, then a value for the parallax can be determined which is relatively accurate because the cube root of the observational and assumed quantities is involved. Thus, if the left-hand side were ten times as large as assumed, the error in p would be only by a factor of 2 roughly, and for smallish parallaxes, say, between $0''\cdot030$ and $0''\cdot010$ this represents a greater accuracy than is usually attainable by trigonometric methods. In more refined statements of the principle, the colour and spectral character are used to make closer estimates of the masses, and in such a case the *dynamical parallax*, as the result of the calculation is called, is much to be preferred to a trigonometric value for quantities even larger than the range indicated above. However, for such a method to be applicable an observationally-based relationship between mass and other stellar properties must have been established. We shall return to this point below.

6.8. Spectroscopic Binaries

We now turn to those double stars known as spectroscopic binaries in which the binary nature is established by the fact that the measured radial velocity varies during a definite periodic time. There is a possibility of confusion with pulsating variables, but, in many cases the latter can be recognised by the fact that variable velocity is accompanied by spectrum changes, or by the fact that the type of variation cannot represent orbital motion. Some cases of doubt remain.

If the brighter component of a spectroscopic binary is more than about two magnitudes above the fainter, in most cases only a single spectrum showing a variable radial velocity will be found. If the magnitude difference is small and the velocity range sufficiently high, both spectra may be detectable at phases of maximum velocity difference, so that the spectrum lines may for a time be seen as split into two components. Usually, a velocity difference of about 50 km/s is necessary for definite splitting to be observed, though this depends somewhat on the character of the spectrum. In some cases, although separate components cannot be measured, suspicions of the binary nature of the star may be aroused by the occurrence of fuzzy lines (unresolved pairs) at certain times. If one component is fainter than the other, its lines will usually be weaker, and fewer of them will be detectable, so that the brighter, or primary star will yield a much more accurate curve of velocity variation with time than the secondary or fainter star. It must be realised that, in the usual case, a spectroscopic binary presents the telescopic appearance of a single star, and that the spectrum of each component has the light from the other superposed on it. At maximum velocity separation the continuum of each tends to fill in the lines of the other, making them less visible and apparently less strong than if either spectrum could be seen separately.

Periodic times for spectroscopic binaries are relatively short, ranging from periods of the order of some hours (e.g. the old novae referred to in a previous paragraph), through periods of the order of a day, which can be reckoned as short for normal spectroscopic binaries; then come the vast majority, having periods in the range from about 3 days to 20 days, with relatively few examples extending to periods of the order of a year. Since the velocity variation is due to orbital motion the discussions of double star motions given above apply. The orbital velocity becomes small for longer periods and less easy to detect. Generalisations are difficult, but if the velocity of a single-lined binary (i.e. one showing only one spectrum) varies by less than about 20 km/s it begins to be difficult to separate real variations from accidental errors, particularly if observations from different observatories are involved, as they are apt to be in the case of rather long periods. Spectroscopic observers show a marked preference for systems with large velocity ranges and readily measurable lines.

An interesting question is whether there is any physical distinction between visual and spectroscopic binaries or whether the line is drawn by the visual and spectroscopic resolution of our equipment. Undoubtedly, if this were improved by a factor of ten, many spectroscopic binaries would be observable as visual pairs, and many visual pairs could be made to yield useful spectroscopic results. On the other hand there are general physical differences determined mainly by the fact that in spectroscopic pairs the separation between components is often comparable with the radii of the component stars, whereas this is not true for visual binaries. At these smaller separations various dynamic effects can evidently complicate the simple picture, for example mass exchange, and the existence of gaseous material between and around the components. This introduces a viscous retardation and tends to reduce orbital eccentricity. Among spectroscopic pairs those with the shorter periods, which must correspond to stars almost in contact, almost always have small orbital eccentricities. Even at the longer periods eccentricities as large as, say, $0 \cdot 5$, seem to be rare, whereas this type of value is common in visual binaries. In the case of visual binaries, however, the so-called period-eccentricity relation once thought to exist, has been shown to be a spurious effect resulting from observational selection.

6.9. Mass-Ratio in a Double-Lined Binary

In a spectroscopic binary which shows two spectra we can appeal to the condition that the mass centre, which will have a uniform translatory motion, divides the distance between the components inversely as their masses: therefore by differentiation with respect to the time and projection on the line of sight we have the result that the radial velocity of the mass centre (denoted by γ) divides the velocity difference between primary and secondary components in a constant ratio. We can write for the radial velocities at any time:

$$V_P = \gamma + f \cdot K_P$$
$$V_S = \gamma - f \cdot K_S$$

in which V_P, V_S are the radial velocities of primary and secondary respectively, f is a function of the time and of the orbital constants, and K_P, K_S are the semi-amplitudes of the velocity variations of primary and secondary during the orbital motion. Eliminating f, we find

$$V_P/K_P + V_S/K_S = \gamma(1/K_P + 1/K_S)$$

Also we have $K_S/K_P = M_P/M_S$ where the M's are the masses of the two components. Thus, a short way to find the systemic velocity and mass ratio is to plot primary and secondary velocities against each other (using only spectra where the two are properly resolved). This should give a straight line, of which the slope yields the mass ratio and the intersection with the line $V_P = V_S$ the systemic velocity. The plot of V_P against V_S is, of course, a segment of a straight line of limited length, extending between the points which mark the maximum velocity differences between the components, with the primary velocity relatively positive at one end and relatively negative at the other. The foregoing method is applicable only when both velocities are measurable with considerable accuracy. To determine the orbital parameters in other cases requires a determination of the complete velocity curve.

6.10. Variations of Radial Velocity

It is instructive to consider the kind of velocity variation which can occur in various geometrical circumstances. It should be noted that in all cases the measured radial velocity excursions involve multiplication of the physical velocity excursions by sin i, where i is the inclination of the orbit defined as for visual binary stars, and is such that for an orbit seen edge-on $i = 90°$. Consider the case of a circular orbit, with only one spectrum visible, and sin $i = 1$. When the brighter star is on the near side of the (invisible) secondary, its motion will be transverse, and the measured radial velocity will be equal to γ. A quarter of a period later the brighter star will be receding at its maximum velocity as it passes through the "plane of the sky" through the companion: a quarter period later the motion will be transverse and radial velocity will be back at γ, while at a quarter of a period later still the motion will be one of approach with the radial velocity at a minimum. In short, the velocity curve will be sinusoidal. In this curve the upward and downward lobes are equal; the upward and downward slopes are equal; the upward lobe is of equal width and equal excursion with the downward. In radial velocity curves of elliptic orbits at different orientations some or all of these equalities may become inequalities.

In the two examples shown we have an orbit of high ellipticity seen, in the first case (Figure VI.4), broadside on: in the second (Figure VI.5), end on. Corresponding points on the orbit round the mass centre and on the velocity curve, are marked.

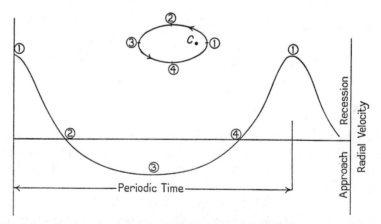

Figure VI.4: Radial velocity variation shown by star moving about mass centre, C, orbit broadside on, i.e. $\omega = 0°$.

We remember that near periastron (Point 1 in Figures VI.4 and 5) the orbital velocity is high and that the speed in the orbit rises sharply to its maximum value, and that at points symmetrically disposed about the major axis (e.g. Points 2 and 4) the orbital speeds are equal. Considering only the radial component we see that in Figure VI.4 the velocity has its maximum value at Point 1, falls quickly to zero at Point 2, and then, on the section of the orbit remote from the focus, falls slowly to a minimum at Point 3. Because the speed is low, this part of the orbit takes a long time to describe, so that the downward lobe is broader and less deep than the upward lobe. Each lobe is symmetrical in itself.

In Figure VI.5, the orbital velocity is transverse at Point 1 so that the radial velocity is zero. The orbital speed is high and swinging rapidly towards the observer, so that the radial velocity falls rapidly to a minimum at Point 2. Thereafter it rises slowly because the portion 2, 3, 4 of the orbit is described with low orbital speed. The radial

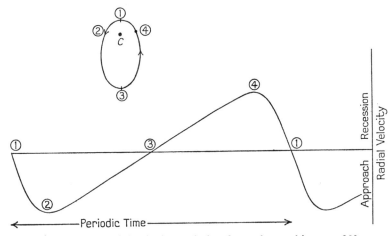

Figure VI.5: Radial velocity variation for end-on orbit, $\omega = 90°$.

velocity is zero at Point 3 because motion is then transverse. Pairs of points symmetrically disposed on the orbit about Point 3 yield values of radial velocity which are equal but of opposite sign. This follows because the orbital speeds are equal and so are the angles of inclination to the line of sight. The only difference is that in one case the velocity is one of approach, in the other one of recession. The final velocity curve has the saw-tooth form shown in Figure VI.5. If the orbit had been viewed end on from the direction of Point 1 rather than the direction of Point 3 the curve would be inverted, giving a rapid rise of radial velocity and a slow fall.

Saw-tooth radial velocity curves of the type shown in Figure VI.5 are strongly reminiscent of those produced by the pulsation of Cepheid variables. These were, for a time, interpreted erroneously as binary star curves, until the odd circumstance was noted that, if this interpretation were correct, then all the binary orbits were lined up pointing exactly away from the Earth.

6.11. Determination of Orbital Elements

All possible radial velocity curves of a star in orbital motion about a centre of mass have the common characteristic that there is one maximum and one minimum, and from the relative heights, widths, degree of asymmetry, and relative widths of the two lobes, the orbital parameters can be inferred. Indeed, most computers keep a set of standard curves handy and can get a good first approximation to the elements by inspection in a few minutes. The parameters which specify the physical orbit are the same as for a visual binary, but in calculating the velocity curve, for example, Ω does not enter because the position angle of the line of nodes can be changed without altering the radial velocities. The formula for radial velocity is

$$V = \gamma + K(e \cos \omega + \cos \overline{v + \omega})$$

(compare the formulae given above in the case of a double-lined binary). Here ω is the longitude of the ascending node measured from the node to periastron as in the visual binary case. In our two illustrative cases, $\omega = 0$ in Figure VI.4 and $= 90°$ in Figure VI.5. The quantities K and e are the half amplitude as the parameter v goes through $360°$ and the eccentricity of the orbit. The quantity v which would be measured as position angle in a visual binary seen face-on varies with time: it is called the *true anomaly* and, according to the theory of orbital motion is related to the eccentric anomaly, E, and the time t through the equations:

$$\tan \tfrac{1}{2}v = \sqrt{\frac{1 + e}{1 - e}} \tan \tfrac{1}{2} E$$

and

$$M = 360°(\phi - \phi_0) = E - e \sin E$$

The practice of different computers varies a good deal: we have chosen to define our observations in terms of phases, ϕ, which were defined at the beginning of this section: if the period in days is P, and the heliocentric Julian date of an observation is t, then ϕ is the fractional part of the product $P^{-1} t$, and ϕ_0 is one of the orbital constants which we have to evaluate. It is the phase of periastron at which E and v are zero.

The situation looks a little complicated but is not as bad as it looks: the astronomer who wants to solve the orbit of a spectroscopic binary star sets about the matter as follows: First he has observations of radial velocity at various times: the Cape practice is to obtain about a dozen observations scattered irregularly through a period of about 100 days, taking care that on one or two nights more than one observation is obtained so as to take care of the possibility that the period may be very short with the velocity changing rapidly during the course of a night. Each measure is associated with a heliocentric Julian date. Next, either a final or an approximate value of the period is found. This is done by guessing values of P and plotting the results on a phase diagram. If the points lie at random all over the diagram, the guess is a bad one. If they show signs of lying on the kind of curve required by orbital theory, small adjustments to the guessed value may produce a satisfactory answer. This part of the work is a combination of mother wit and good luck. The computer will pay special attention to points which look like maxima or minima, and try to get them to the same phase. He can, if the labour is not too heavy, systematically cover a range of periods with trials: there is a rule which states that, for observations covering N days he should space his shots at values of P^{-1} at equal intervals of $0·1/N$, so that for $N = 100$, the spacing in P^{-1} should be $0·001$. Thus, for observations scattered over 100 days, a systematic coverage of all trial periods from $P = 4$ to $P = 10$ days would take 150 trials, and the spacing is such that he would know if he drew a blank that the period could not lie in this range. This means a good deal of work, and the computer usually tries all kinds of tricks to narrow down the possible range of choice. Once he has some idea of the possible answer or answers he can make a detailed investigation near the suspected values to reach a final decision. If he has one or two observations made some years earlier, so that N is, say, 1,000 when these are included, then, on this broader range he can within a restricted run of periods, try shots spaced at intervals of $0·0001$ in P^{-1}. In most cases such an accurate value of the period can be found that it can be treated as exactly known in subsequent work. In some cases it will be impossible to decide between two alternatives, and then additional observations will be called for at time specially selected to differentiate between alternative possible periods. One favourite mistake is to pick a period which is twice or half the correct one, and a trial observation will soon show whether the velocity has the expected value or whether, for example, it is at a positive maximum when it was expected to be at a negative minimum. One difficult case is encountered when two spectra are observed, so nearly identical that it is impossible to distinguish which star is which from inspection of the plates. In such a case one plots, not individual values but the value of $|V_P - V_S|$ on the phase diagram. The correct period is one which produces a phase diagram in which this quantity (necessarily positive) has two maxima and two zeros, the latter resembling downward pointing cusps (Figure VI.6). When this has been achieved the two components can be identified, since all the relatively positive values in one lobe belong to

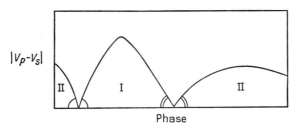

Figure VI.6: Phase diagram for $|V_P - V_S|$ for indistinguishable components. Lobes I and II must have equal areas: the angles at the "cusps" must be equal as marked.

one component which is the same star as that associated with all the relatively negative velocity measures in the other lobe. The separate values for the two stars can now be plotted.

At this stage we have the velocity curve, for one star in the case of a single-lined binary, for two stars in the case of a double-lined binary. In the second case the curve for the secondary component should be the same as that for the primary but turned upside down and drawn to a different scale. The number of measures of the secondary is often smaller than for the primary if the former is fainter, and they may not be as accurate.

Reverting to the case of a single-lined binary, the computer then examines the velocity curve, and from his stock of examples finds a set of elements which fit it as well as possible. He can usually estimate γ and K from inspection: he obtains ϕ_0 by shifting his trial curve left and right: the parameters e and ω are the important ones, and it is the shape of the curve which gives him the clue. With P known, and an adopted value of ϕ_0 he can compute ϕ from the time of observation, and hence obtain M. With an assumed value of e he can obtain v. This he does not need to calculate: tables produced by the Allegheny observatory produce the value from only a slight interpolation. The computation of $e \cos \omega + \cos \overline{v + \omega}$ is then straightforward and leads to a computed velocity which can be compared with the observed one. In favourable cases the residuals between observed and calculated values will not exceed 5 km/s at most, while for application of the method of variation of parameters the first trial ought to represent the observations with few, if any, residuals over 10 km/s. The method of variation of parameters is set out in detail in Aitken's *The Binary Stars*, and in the reports of individual computers. The basic idea is that the parameters of the trial solution represent the observations fairly closely: a system of proportionately small corrections to these parameters is sought which will improve the fit. If any one parameter is varied, e.g. if K is increased to $K + \Delta K$ then the change in computed velocity at any epoch is proportional to ΔK. For some of the parameters the factor of proportionality is a rather complicated mathematical function found by differentiating the expression for the computed velocity with respect to the parameter chosen. The complication arises because the differentiation has to be carried right through the series of equations used in computing the velocity at a given phase. The numerical values of these functions are found by inserting the trial values of the parameters. The total change at any epoch is the sum of the changes due to variation of each of the parameters. The computed value of total change, a linear function in the parameter changes $\Delta\gamma$, ΔK, Δe, Δ_ω, and $\Delta\phi_0$ (if the period is taken as known) is set equal to the residual for each observation, and the equations solved by the method of least squares. The aim is to find those values of parameter change which reduce the residuals as much as possible.

The practice of computers varies a good deal, and in some centres programmes for machine computation have been written. The general system of equations breaks down when the eccentricity is small, and computational methods for treating this case have been given by T. E. Sterne. In the most usual case of a single-lined binary with period fixed, the solution evaluates five unknowns—corrections to γ, K, e, ω and ϕ_0, which are usually handled as functions of these quantities rather than the quantities themselves. If the period is thrown in as an unknown as well, the total is six, and if there is a second component there are seven unknowns the additional one being the value of K for the secondary. For the secondary the value of ω is that for the primary increased by 180° and the shape of the secondary orbit is similar to that of the primary, so that no new unknowns are added on this score.

It may now be supposed that the constants for the system have been found.

Figure VI.7: Radial velocity variations in double-lined spectroscopic binaries as observed, and as inferred from the derived orbital elements.

(a) HD 6619, components nearly identical, orbital eccentricity, 0·22. (b) HD 155555, components nearly identical, circular orbits. (By permission of the Astronomer Royal.)

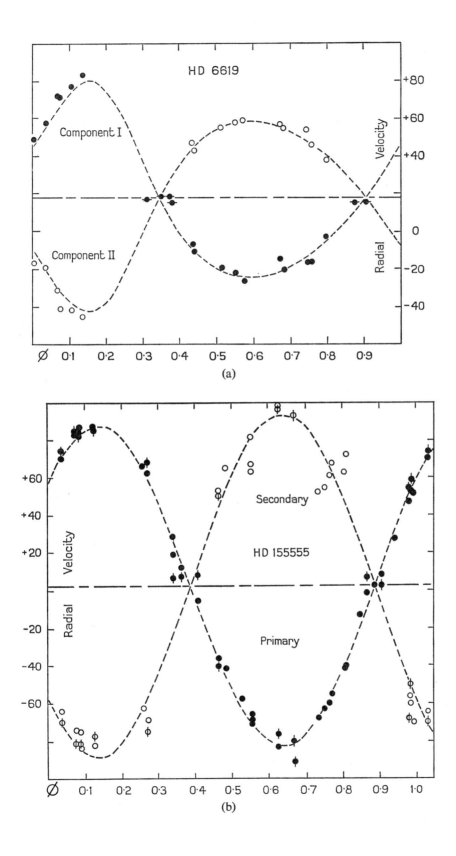

(a)

(b)

Dynamical theory gives the results

$$a_1 \sin i/K_1 = a_2 \sin i/K_2 = 1{\cdot}375 \times 10^4 P(1 - e^2)^{1/2}$$

$$M_1 \sin^3 i/K_2 = M_2 \sin^3 i/K_1 = 1{\cdot}039 \times 10^{-7}(K_1 + K_2)^2 P(1 - e^2)^{3/2}$$

where suffixes 1 and 2 refer to primary and secondary, the parameters K are in kilometres per second, P is in days, and M_1 and M_2 are masses in solar units. The quantities a_1 and a_2 are semiaxes majores of the orbits of the two components and are in kilometres. It is reasonable that this should be so, for, in the simplified case of $\sin i = 1$, $e = 0$ the value of K would be the speed in a circular orbit and this would only have to be multiplied by P to give the circumference.

In the case of a single-lined binary the only information obtainable is in the form of the mass function, a rather complicated function of the component masses for which the numerical value can be found, but which is of rather little use in throwing light on the system. Double-lined binaries are thus of far greater interest, and great efforts are made to get some kind of clue concerning the invisible secondary: if the elements for the primary have been found, even a single spectrum line on a single occasion from the secondary is, theoretically, enough to establish K_2, and so, greatly to enhance the information derived.

A solution of a double-lined spectroscopic binary establishes the mass ratio of the components, and, if spectral classifications for them can be derived from the joint spectrum, this can provide useful information on the run of stellar masses in different parts of the Hertzsprung-Russell diagram. The individual masses remain uncertain by the factor $\sin^3 i$ which cannot, in general, be found from the analysis of a spectroscopic binary. In certain circumstances, for example, the case of eclipsing binaries, mentioned below, values of $\sin i$ can be estimated. If results for many binaries are available they can be treated in a statistical way by assuming a random distribution of orbital planes, and the mean value of $\sin^3 i$ for random orientation can be used. The same arguments apply to the orbital dimensions. The values of $a \sin i$ give a good indication of the general dimensions of spectroscopic binary orbits: they naturally tend to be smaller for shorter periods but the general run is from 1 to 20 million kilometres with many cases about the middle of this range. There must be a good deal of observational selection owing to the natural tendency to favour clear-cut cases.

Most observatories concerned with radial velocity work produce solutions for spectroscopic binaries, and the results are noted in works such as the *Mount Wilson General Catalogue of Radial Velocities*. A *Bibliography on Spectroscopic Binaries* is in preparation by D. Ya. Martynov of the Kazan Observatory. So far the first six hours of right ascension have been published, and contained 529 entries, which should give an indication of the existing volume of data. However, new discoveries are continually being made, and, for example, at the time of writing, the Cape workers using the Radcliffe reflector have 70 spectroscopic binaries on their books, most of them new discoveries, only a few of which can be intensively investigated at any given time. To an increasing extent the computation of orbital elements is being adapted to electronic computer methods. No doubt in the near future complete programmes covering all stages from period determination to production of corrected elements will be available.

6.12. Stellar Masses

At the beginning of the discussion on binary stars it was stated that they provide the only method of determining stellar masses. At this stage in a long road it seems that the hopes of using visual binaries are blocked in all but a few cases by uncertainties in parallaxes, while spectroscopic binaries are blocked by lack of information concerning the value of sin i. The number of cases in which it is possible to determine the masses of the components of a binary or multiple star without recourse to some assumption which might be open to challenge is very small. The various types of case can be easily enumerated. That where there is a good visual orbit and a large and well-determined trigonometric parallax has already been remarked. If there is a good visual orbit and the components are far enough apart for separate observation photometrically and spectroscopically, a satisfactory photometric parallax can sometimes be obtained. If there is a good visual orbit and separate radial velocities or the radial velocity difference can be observed, this result can be combined with the visual orbital elements. Even if the parallax is not known the value of the product of the parallax and the velocity difference between the components can be calculated, so that, in principle, the parallax can be found from a measure of radial velocity difference. This was done successfully by Wesselink for Alpha Centauri, for which it was predicted that, in 1952 the radial velocity difference between the components would attain a maximum value near 13 km/s. A velocity difference of this order would not produce on the spectral dispersions in general use, a doubling of the lines in the spectrum if the components were observed as a single star image. Fortunately in the case of Alpha Centauri the components could be observed separately, and the lines of each are very suitable for radial velocity measurement. The velocity difference was successfully measured and a good value of the parallax inferred. In this case, of course, excellent values of trigonometrical parallax are available. There are a considerable number of other cases where, at particular epochs the velocity difference between the components of visual double stars may be expected to be high enough to be measurable. These usually occur in cases where the orbital eccentricity is fairly high. The difference attains a considerable value when the components are at their smallest physical separation (near periastron) for those systems in which this also happens to occur near nodal passage. These stars are at these special times visible in most cases only as an unresolved or very close pair, and cannot be separated on the spectroscope slit. To get a measure of radial velocity difference requires that the spectrum lines be split into two components, demanding high spectroscopic dispersion and spectrum lines narrow enough to show the effect. These requirements are rather stringent, but Dommanget has drawn attention to a number of systems in which these favourable circumstances are likely to occur.

The problem might also be solved by measuring the separate velocities of components of double stars with good visual elements at various epochs round the orbital cycle. The results have usually been disappointing. The velocity differences are usually so small that they tend to be swamped by observational errors. This is particularly the case when modern observations have to be combined with observations made, possibly, half a century earlier. The results derived then depend critically on a discussion of the systematic errors of radial velocity programmes undertaken by a variety of observers at widely different times and with totally different instruments and techniques. Wesselink in his study of Alpha Centauri endeavoured to combine his own observations made in 1952 with radial velocity observations made in 1904 by Lick, and in 1909–15 by the Cape, in order to derive the mass-ratio of the components. Here he obtained a much less clear-cut result, and the difficulty is generally of this kind. It is perhaps suitable at this point to interpolate a remark of a theoretical difficulty, which can lead to practical errors if it is not kept in mind. There is a difference of practice between visual double star observers and spectroscopists. Visual double star observers always record the position of the secondary relative to the primary. Spectroscopic data give radial velocities of one or both components which can be reckoned as excursions relative to the velocity of the centre of gravity of the system.

Good values of parallax of a visual binary can be obtained from spectroscopic data if the visual binary belongs to a cluster or can be assigned to a moving group of which the spatial velocity has been established.

In the case of a double-lined spectroscopic binary the mass-ratio of the components can be established, often with considerable accuracy. If it can be assumed that there is a functional relationship between luminosity and mass, in which there are disposable constants to be determined, it is often possible to use mass-ratio data, supported by estimates of relative brightness of the components, to assist in the evaluation of the constants.

If the inclination of the system can be derived in the case of a double-lined spectroscopic binary, the separate masses can be found. This is sometimes possible in the case of eclipsing binary stars which are discussed below, though these are often much less productive of useful information than might be expected.

In the case of stars of higher multiplicity it is sometimes possible to construct special arguments adapted to particular cases which yield information on the masses of the components.

It should, in any case, be remembered that in close binary stars there is a possibility of exchange of mass between the components. A star which has had its mass changed through this mechanism will have had an evolutionary history different from that of a single star, and it may be dangerous to apply results derived in such cases to the generality of stars.

6.13. The Mass-Luminosity Relation

In his book, *The Internal Constitution of the Stars* Eddington discussed many years ago the character of a relation made plausible by contemporary studies of stellar structure, between the masses of the stars and their luminosities. The latter were expressed by the total energy output from their surfaces, that is, by their bolometric absolute magnitudes. Eddington thought in terms of a single mass-luminosity relation which he established mainly by the discussion of the few impeccable determinations of stellar masses made up to that time. This relation approximated to the form $L \sim \text{Mass}^3$, from which it is clear that although there is a vast range of luminosities to be found among the stars, the range of masses is much more restricted. A range from about 100 solar masses to one-hundredth of a solar mass should include all but a minute proportion of stars: the vast majority are included in a much more restricted range, from 10 solar masses to 0·1 solar masses. Use has already been made of this general conclusion at several places in the foregoing text.

The topic of the mass luminosity relation has been taken up by numerous authors since Eddington's time. Clearly since the present theory of stellar evolution is one at effectively constant mass, but with varying luminosity, it follows that among stars of different ages there will be a variety of luminosities for stars of the same mass.

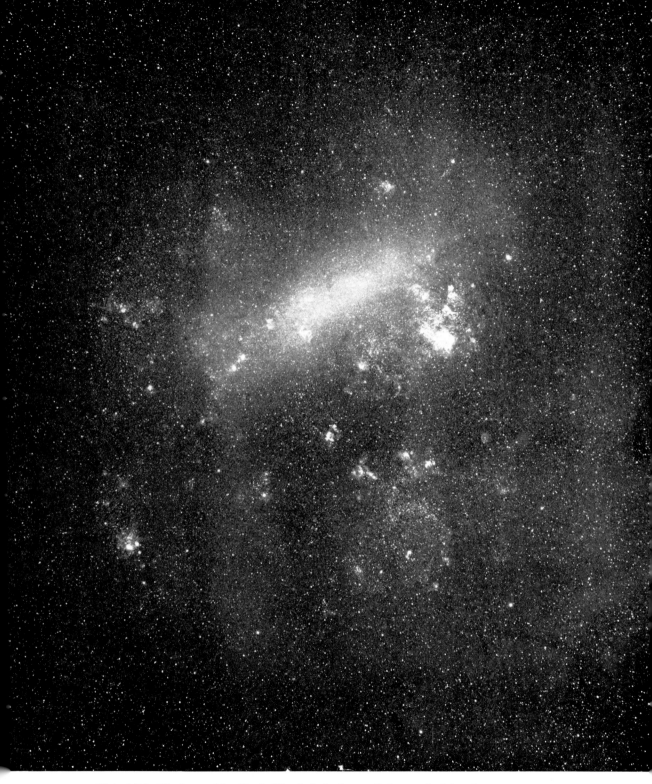

Plate 34(a). The Large Magellanic Cloud. In hydrogen light, emphasising the
gas distribution. (By permission of Dr. Karl G. Henize.)

Plate 34(b). Through a broad-band red filter, emphasising the star distribution.
(By permission of Dr. G. de Vaucouleurs.)

Plate 35(a). Detail of the Large Magellanic Cloud. S Doradus with accompanying
nebulosity and globular clusters. (By permission of Dr. A. D. Thackeray.)

Plate 35(b). The great looped nebula surrounding 30 Doradus.
(By permission of Dr. A. D. Thackeray.)

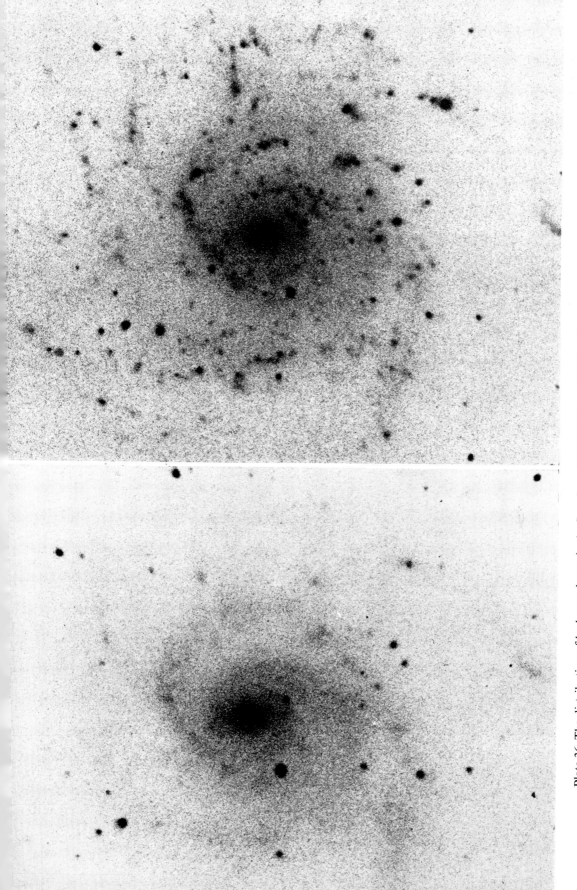

Plate 36. The distribution of hydrogen knots in the Sc galaxy, NGC 5457 (= M 101). (a) A red photograph through a broad band-pass filter. (b) Through an interference filter centred on Hα and showing the hydrogen clouds. (Photographs by G. Courtès, by permission of the Director, Haute-Provence Observatory.)

Plate 37. Types of galaxies. (a) Normal spirals. (b) Barred spirals.
(By permission of Mount Wilson and Palomar Observatories.)

Plate 38. NGC 300, a late-type spiral is a member of the Local Group. (By permission of H.M. Astronomer at the Cape.)

Plate 39. NGC 1097, a large southern spiral classified by Sandage as SB b(s), i.e. there is a bar, the arms are fairly open and do not spring from a ring structure. (By permission of H.M. Astronomer at the Cape.)

Plate 40. NGC 1365, a magnificent southern barred spiral covering about $12' \times 7'$. (By permission of H.M. Astronomer at the Cape.)

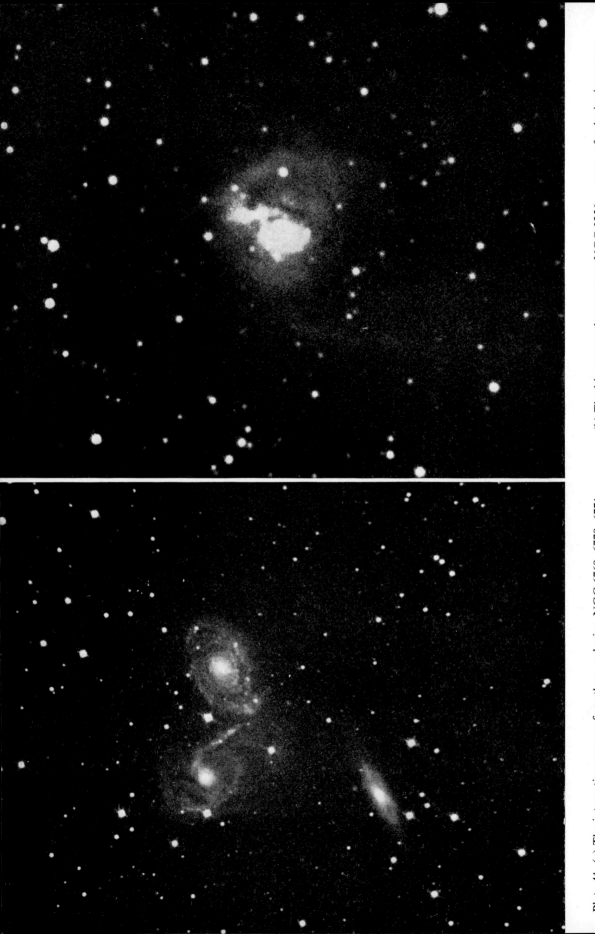

Plate 41. (a) The interacting group of southern galaxies, NGC 6769, 6770, 6771. (By permission of H.M. Astronomer at the Cape.)

(b) The bizarre southern system NGC 3256, a group of galaxies in contact. (By permission of H.M. Astronomer at the Cape.)

Plate 42. NGC 1553 is a striking S 0 southern galaxy.
(By permission of Dr. A. D. Thackeray.)

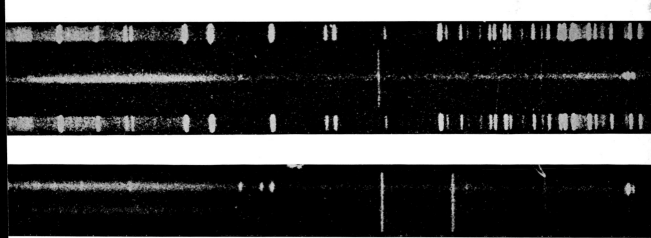

Plate 43. (a) Spectrum of NGC 1614 showing nebular emission lines of hydrogen and forbidden nitrogen in the red (*far right*), and night sky lines crossing the whole dekker. (b) Spectra of NGC 1741 A, B, showing also, in the former, emission lines of forbidden oxygen and of hydrogen near the continuum (*at left*). (By permission of Dr. G. de Vaucouleurs.)

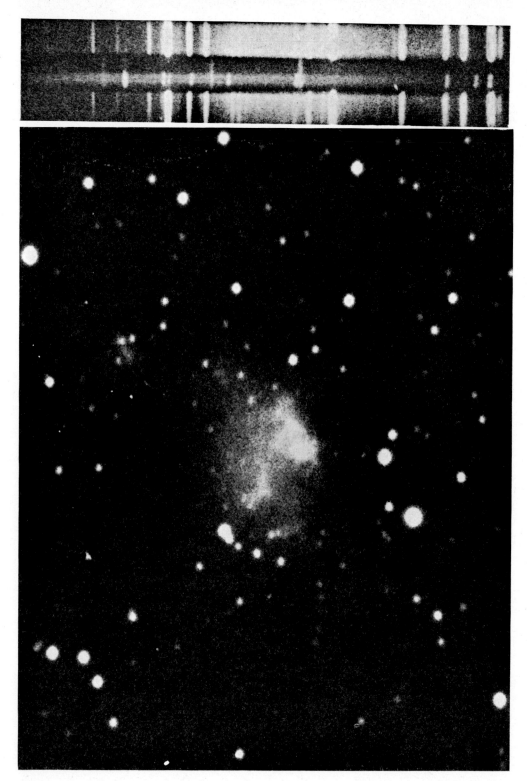

Plate 44. IC 4662, a gaseous object receding at only 375 km/s from the Sun, shows rapid rotation by the inclined lines in its emission spectrum. Long lines which are not inclined are from terrestrial sources, (mercury lamps). (By permission of H.M. Astronomer at the Cape.)

Plate 45. NGC 5128, the Centaurus radio source.
(By permission of Mount Wilson and Palomar Observatories.)

Plate 46. NGC 1316, a giant elliptical with dust lanes, marks the Fornax radio source.
(By permission of H.M. Astronomer at the Cape.)

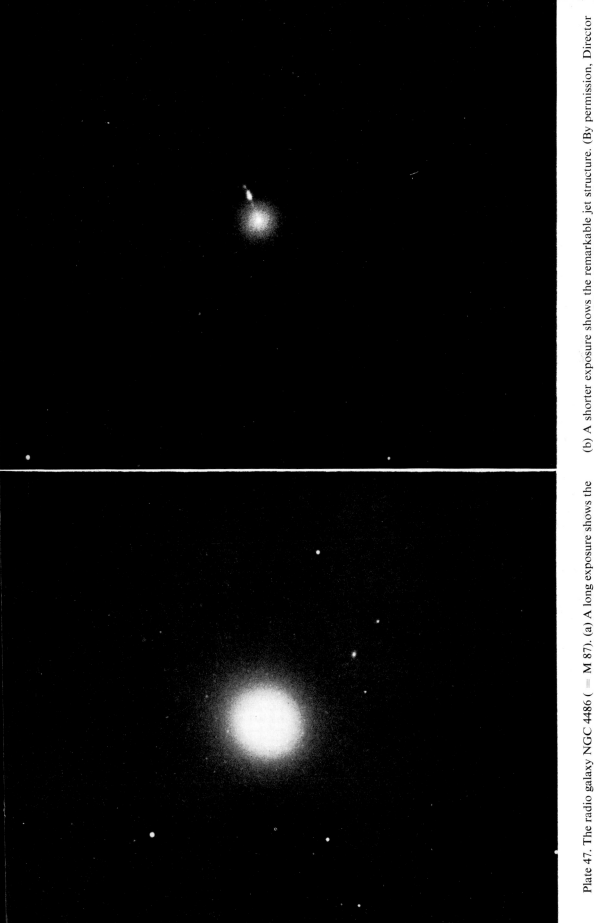

Plate 47. The radio galaxy NGC 4486 (= M 87). (a) A long exposure shows the outer parts and attendant globular clusters.

(b) A shorter exposure shows the remarkable jet structure. (By permission, Director of the Lick Observatory.)

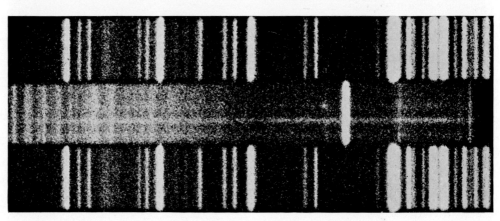

Plate 48. *Above*, the distant radio galaxy 3C 295, in Boötes, photographed with the 200-inch telescope. *Below*, a spectrum: wavelengths increase from about 3600 Å at left to about 6400 Å at right. Most of the features are of terrestrial origin. The sole feature originating in the galaxy is the dot just to the left of the very strong emission line. This is interpreted as 3727 Å displaced from the ultraviolet to the green by the enormous recession velocity, then the largest known. (By permission of Mount Wilson and Palomar Observatories.)

However, in the case of such evolved stars an adjustment can be made in the light of evolutionary ideas to give the luminosity corresponding to the point of departure from the main sequence. In a recent study Eggen has discussed 228 visual binaries for which orbits are available. It is an index of the difficulties encountered in this work that Eggen classifies only 46 of these orbits as of first quality, and it does not follow that all of these will yield good mass determinations or cover the whole gamut of stellar masses. Eggen finds that there are two distinct mass-luminosity relationships. One applies to young stars of Hyades-Pleiades type, for which the masses are approximately described by the relation

$$M_B = 3 \cdot 6 - 5 \cdot 25 \log (\text{mass})$$

where M_B are absolute bolometric magnitudes. This approximates to the relation $L \sim (\text{mass})^2$ and for a mass equal to that of the sun gives a bolometric magnitude about $1 \cdot 8$ magnitudes brighter than the Sun.

Stars described by this relation go all the way from bright blue stars with $B - V = -0 \cdot 15$ and $M_V = -1 \cdot 0$ to faint red dwarfs with $B - V = +1 \cdot 7$ and $M_V = +13 \cdot 0$. Eggen states that these stars have galactic orbits of relatively small curvature, i.e. they have always been at about their present distance from the galactic centre, and that they are characterised by a higher helium content than the members of the other mass-luminosity relation. This is called the Sun-Sirius relation, because these stars are members. It gives a relation approximating to $L \sim (\text{mass})^3$ and appears to terminate, with no stars brighter than $M_V = +2 \cdot 0$. Eggen's relation for these can be given as $M_B = 4 \cdot 64 - 7 \cdot 40 \log (\text{mass})$ (though it may not be precisely linear). There are difficulties connected with the theoretical representation of these results, for, at the present time, theoretical models would give a more rapid variation of luminosity with mass.

6.14. A Highly-Stylised Eclipsing Binary

If the inclination of a binary star orbit is given by a value not too far removed from $\sin i = 1$, and if the separation of the component stars is not too large compared with their diameters, then, as seen from the Earth, the components will eclipse each other during each revolution. This is not an intrinsic property of the system: all binaries would be eclipsing if their orbital planes passed sufficiently near the Earth. Even so, there is a preferential tendency for eclipsing binaries to show rather complex features because the probability of eclipse increases markedly for systems for which the separation between the stars is small compared with the sum of the component diameters. For such close systems the components are liable to be distorted from the spherical form and additional causes of variation in the total light of the system are present over and above the effects of the eclipses. We shall return to this point later. For the time being we consider a highly-stylised case stripped of all its complications.

Consider two stars of masses M, luminosities L, radii r, moving in circular orbits of radii a about their common centre of gravity in a period P with $\sin i = 1$. All these symbols are given suffixes 1 and 2 as appropriate, to distinguish the two stars. In these circumstances each component will eclipse the other centrally when the line of centres passes through the Earth as it will twice in each revolution according to the assumptions adopted. Suppose $r_1 > r_2$. Outside eclipse the total luminosity of the system will be $L_1 + L_2$. When star No. 1 eclipses star No. 2, the light of the latter

H

will be totally cut off, and the luminosity of the system will be reduced to L_1. In the usual magnitude terms of photometric measurement this will correspond to a reduction by $2 \cdot 5 \log_{10}(1 + L_2/L_1)$ magnitudes, i.e. $0 \cdot 75$ magnitudes if the stars are of equal luminosity, and more than this, if, as can happen, the smaller star is the more luminous. For analytical purposes it is usually best to get the observations plotted in terms of relative luminosity and phase once the period has been found. When star No. 2 eclipses star No. 1, and is fairly in front of it, the total light of the system will be $L_2 + (1 - r_2^2/r_1^2) L_1$, because the light from the larger component is reduced by the loss of that area covered by the smaller.

As viewed from the Earth, the light of the system just begins to fall off when the two star disks appear to be externally tangential. This occurs when the line of centres and the line of sight are inclined to each other at an angle θ_p, where $\sin \theta_p = (r_1 + r_2)/(a_1 + a_2)$. If the line of centres is rotating in space at a uniform rate, taking the periodic time P to turn through $360°$, the total duration of each eclipse (star No. 1 by star No. 2 or vice versa) is $\theta_p P/180$ if θ_p is expressed in degrees. Totality begins and ends when the star disks are in a position of internal tangency. This occurs when the line of sight is inclined to the line of centres at an angle θ_t, where $\sin \theta_t = (r_1 - r_2)/(a_1 + a_2)$, and the duration of each total or annular phase is $\theta_t P/180$. The orbital velocities are $2\pi a_1/P$, $2\pi a_2/P$ so that if radial velocity observations are available, the amplitudes of the radial velocity variations give the orbital dimensions and the masses. This is in line with previous remarks since we are assuming that $\sin i = 1$.

Figure VI.8 shows the light curve for the highly simplified case in which the orbits are exactly circular, the inclination precisely $90°$, the stars are fairly far apart compared with their diameters, and they have disks of uniform brightness. The smaller star has been taken, for diagrammatic convenience as the brighter and less massive of the pair. Nothing as simple as this ever does occur. Presented with such a light curve the analyst would note the equal spacing of eclipses as indicating that the eccentricity was small: the flat-bottomed minima on the light curve would show that the star discs were uniform and that the eclipses were total and annular. The widths of the total and partial phases would give the proportion between the star dimensions and their separations. This is as far as could be gone using only photometric data. Spectroscopic data would also give the actual linear dimensions in kilometres of the stars and the orbit, and the stellar masses. Both spectra must be observed to make this possible. For questions of identification of components it is useful to remember that the component which has been eclipsed will next pass through velocity minimum (i.e. for a circular orbit it will have maximum velocity of approach one-quarter of a period after it has been eclipsed).

In principle eclipsing binaries give an immense amount of information, namely, luminosities, masses and radii as well as orbital parameters. In practice, for the reasons surveyed below, it is usually difficult to obtain all this information. In one respect, however, principle and practice coincide: in order to solve for the parameters of an eclipsing binary system the analyst must usually make some preliminary assessment of the nature of the system and estimate rough values of various constants. Preliminary guesses are then improved by comparing observations with predictions and making adjustments to the constants. The whole process has not yet been reduced to a machine programme, but programmes have now been written by, for example, Huffer and Collins, for the improvement of instrumental constants by iteration in the case of eclipses which are total and annular. It is a measure of the intricacies of the problem that provision for up to 21 iterations is written into the programme.

The complications may be briefly listed.

(i) The inclination is not 90° so that the eclipses are not central. Still further deviations, the limit depending on the relative dimensions of stars and separation, will make the eclipses partial. There will then be no intervals of constant brightness within the eclipses. The shoulders of the minima are not the crude straight lines of

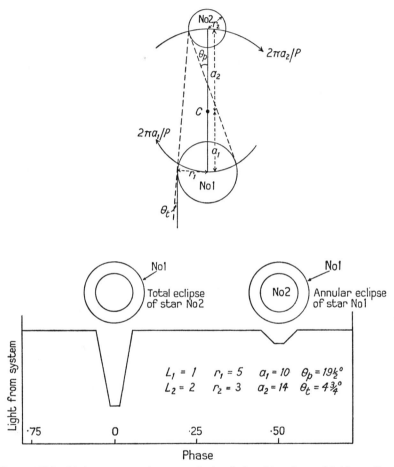

Figure VI.8: Light curve and geometrical relationships for a highly stylised eclipsing binary.

Figure VI.8 (they are not precisely so even in the highly-stylised case). Extensive tabulations of curves for different parameter values are to be found in J. E. Merrill's Princeton *Tables*.

(ii) The components are not usually of uniform surface brightness, but exhibit the phenomenon of "darkening to the limb" already mentioned in connection with the Sun. The light loss in an annular eclipse of a larger star by a smaller increases towards mid-eclipse when this effect is present.

(iii) If the components are separated by a distance less than some ten diameters, or if they are actually in contact, the stars will be distorted by mutual gravitational attraction, and will approximate to ellipsoids if the separation is not too small. Such configurations show marked darkening towards the limb and marked differences of total brightness with aspect. Thus, even when there is no eclipse (the value of i is not sufficiently near to 90°) the brightness of such a pair will vary as the line of centres rotates with respect to the observer. This type of variation, often approximately sinusoidal, when superposed on the light curve of a pair which actually do eclipse, converts the between-eclipse constant-light intervals of Figure VI.8 into continuously varying curves. It is often possible to estimate the extent of this effect and to remove this from the light curve before analysis (a process known as "rectification") so that one is left with the equivalent light curve for spherical stars.

The configurations of close binary systems under their mutual gravitation have been studied by Kopal, who shows that there is a certain surface, called the Roche equipotential, shaped in section like a figure eight with unequal lobes. These surfaces are such that no mass particles moving inside the surfaces under the influence of the two star masses, can ever cross them. Each star must lie within its own surface. If neither fills its surface, the system is called detached: if one does, the system is semi-detached. Contact binaries each fill their surfaces and are thus pointed at their join. In such complicated systems there can be exchange of matter or loss of matter from the system, probably triggered off by forces other than gravitational ones. There is a preference for matter to be lost in this way from the points of axial symmetry— the top and bottom of the eight, and the cross-over point, and the outer extremity of the smaller loop of the eight is the favoured point. Material lost from here will have a zero velocity, and may either accumulate or leak out in a kind of gaseous trail, forming a spiral round the two stars. This type of phenomenon occurs in Beta Lyrae and similar stars. The presence of gas streams alters the photometric picture and complicates the spectra by the transient appearance of emission features.

(iv) If one component is a large star of low surface brightness, and the other a small star of comparable luminosity, so that its surface brightness is high, a difficult observational situation may arise. When the small bright star is eclipsed there will be a deep minimum. When the annular eclipse of the larger star takes place only a small fraction of its area may be lost, so that the depth of the secondary minimum may be very small. Sometimes it may be too small to be measurable: if it is measurable, even with photoelectric methods the errors of observation may bear too high a proportion to the depth of the minimum to yield a useful result. If the secondary minimum is not observable, it is impossible to discriminate on photometric grounds alone between two interpretations: one is that the minima are equal and two of them occur in a time equal to the periodic time: the other is that the secondary minimum is not observed, and the period must be chosen so that only one measurable minimum occurs in an interval equal to the periodic time. Radial velocity measurements can discriminate between these two cases.

(v) Radiation emitted by one of the component stars falling on the surface of the other can produce enhanced radiation from the affected area, as if this radiation had been reflected from it. This *reflection effect* also causes distortion of the light curve. All the foregoing effects can only be properly evaluated if the orbit can be solved, and the orbit can only be solved with certainty if these disturbing effects are first identified and corrected.

(vi) The star may turn out to be of higher multiplicity—a triple or more—which still further confuses the physical picture. This is not unusual. Eclipsing binaries are divided into three different groups as set out below. These are called after certain type stars, but each of the actual type stars is a member of a system of higher multiplicity.

To sum up: in very many practical cases the brightness of an eclipsing binary varies continuously, and shows few of the clear-cut features of our stylised example. In very many cases definitive solutions are difficult or impossible. Radial velocity data are frequently obscure, because spectrum lines are broad and show no resolution. In a few cases analyses do yield definitive results. These are of inestimable value for they are among the rare sources of information on radii and masses and form the observational basis of the major part of our information about effective temperatures.

The observational reference source for eclipsing binaries is the *Finding List* of Koch, Sobieski and Wood published in 1963. This contains 1,266 items. This is fewer than the 2,763 cases in the *General Catalogue of Variable Stars*, but most of those in the *Finding List* have had some work done on them, and lacunae in the observational data are marked for the guidance of observers. Technical accounts of the computation and analysis of light curves, with all their manifold complications are to be found in the works of H. N. Russell and of Z. Kopal noted in the references. There is a valuable catalogue of orbital elements of eclipsing binary stars produced in 1956 by Z. Kopal and Martha B. Shapley.

6.15. Types of Eclipsing Binary

Eclipsing variables are usually divided into three categories called after the type stars, Beta Persei (Algol), Beta Lyrae and W Ursae Majoris. The Beta Persei type are those which most closely resemble our stylised example. They have spherical or only slightly ellipsoidal components and, outside eclipse, the light variation is small. The

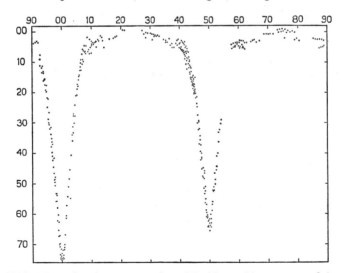

Figure VI.9: Photoelectric measures from Washburn Observatory of the Algol-type eclipsing binary, U Ophiuchi, period 1·677 days. (After C. M. Huffer and Z. Kopal, *Ap.J.*, **114**, 1951, by permission of the authors and the editors of the *Astrophysical Journal*.)

range of period is very large (the *General Catalogue of Variable Stars* quotes from 0·2 to 10,000 days). As we have remarked the secondary minimum is sometimes not observable. The type star is of apparent magnitude 2·0, with the depths of the minima being 1·3 and 0·1 magnitudes. The period is 2·8673285 days and the spectral type B8 V. As has been remarked, the type star turns out not to be typical, for it is at least a triple, and many puzzles remain. From the name of the star, an Arabic reference to a demon, one may infer that the variability of this object which is readily detectable with the naked eye must have been known in ancient times. The eclipses last for 9 hours but within eclipse there is no period of constant light.

The Beta Lyrae type have ellipsoidal components and neither between eclipses nor within them is there any interval during which the light is constant. A secondary minimum is always observed, periods are mostly in excess of one day, spectral types are early and light variations less than about 2 magnitudes. Beta Lyrae has been the object of most intensive studies, for, like some other eclipsing binaries it shows extremely complicated phenomena which arise from the fact that there is an extended gaseous atmosphere surrounding both components which is set into a complex régime of motion and excitation by the two component stars. The period is 12·93016 days but as with many eclipsing systems shows variability.

The W Ursae Majoris stars are binaries with very ellipsoidal components almost in contact. There is no period of constant light, the spectra are usually in the range F-G, the periods usually less than one day, the minima nearly equal and usually not over 0·8 magnitudes deep. The shortest possible period for a binary is, of course, that which will apply when the components are in contact, and this is approximately the situation for the eclipsing binaries of this group. The type system consists of two F 8 peculiar stars having a total apparent magnitude of 8·5, with eclipses, which are total, of depths 0·7 and 0·6 magnitudes respectively. These last 2 hours in a period of revolution of 0·3336384 days. There is evidence that both the light curve and the period are variable, a result which is not surprising in a system with such strong and complex dynamical interaction between the components.

Data for masses and radii for the three type stars are included by Gaposchkin in a list of 81 systems for which solutions have been published. It must be recognised that some of these might be challenged by later workers as not taking all the complexities into account, but they provide a useful guide to the quantities involved:

	Period	Masses		Radii		Spectra	
β Per	2·867	4·7	0·9	2·6	2·9	B8	G0
β Lyr	12·925	9·7	19·5	19·2	13·8	B8	F8
W UMa	0·333	0·8	0·6	1·2	1·1	F8	F8

The eclipsing binaries are an irreplaceable source of basic information, but, although one feels reasonably safe in using information on masses, radii, etc., in other contexts, when it is derived from wide Algol-type systems, one is never quite sure whether the mere fact that a star is a member of a close binary system does not automatically imply that there is something exceptional about it.

6.16. Other Methods of Determining Stellar Radii

There are several other methods of estimating stellar radii applicable to a limited number of cases. They are of special value because they provide alternative lines of approach to the problem, and usually confirm the results obtained from eclipsing variables. One is of a more theoretical nature than most of those previously admitted and is applicable, possibly with considerable reservations, to pulsating variables. Radial velocity observations can be used to estimate the rate of expansion of the surface at any moment, and integration of these figures yields a value for the change in radius during a cycle, expressed in kilometres. If this is accompanied by a change in magnitude and a change in effective temperature as estimated from the change in spectral type, then, if it can be assumed that throughout the cycle the relations between parameters are those which would apply to an equilibrium configuration, an estimate of the radius can be made. The magnitude change, converted to change in bolometric magnitude, gives the proportional change in total luminosity. To achieve this by a certain linear change in radius requires that this linear change be a certain proportion of the original radius, and so the latter can sometimes be found.

Arguments based on effective temperatures show that red giants and supergiants must have enormous diameters, in extreme cases up to some 400 million kilometres. Approximate relations for linear and angular diameters were given many years ago. If R is in solar units $\log R = 0 \cdot 82I - 0 \cdot 20 M_v + 0 \cdot 51$ where I is colour index. For angular diameters $\log d'' = 0 \cdot 82I - 0 \cdot 20\, m_v - 2 \cdot 52$. For those stars such as Antares, Arcturus, Aldebaran and Betelgeuse, which are not at too great distances, the computed diameters should correspond to angular diameters of the order of a few hundredths of a second of arc. Efforts to measure these angular diameters were made at Mount Wilson many years ago by means of an interferometer in principle no different from that used in double star measurement but on a vastly greater scale. If each stellar disk were regarded as close double star consisting of the right and left halves of the disk, a measure might be obtained with slits on the objective at distances between about 8 and 24 feet apart. Since these separations are greater than the diameter of any instrument available at the time this work was done by Pease in 1920, he replaced the slits by two mirrors running along a beam mounted across the aperture of the 100-inch telescope and feeding the light from the two mirrors into fixed plane mirrors which fed it into the telescope. A separation of the two mirrors was sought which caused the fringes to disappear. Pease secured positive results on seven stars, the largest being Mira Ceti (giant variable) at maximum, at $0'' \cdot 056$ and Betelgeuse at $0'' \cdot 047$, and the smallest angular diameters measured being those of Arcturus and Aldebaran, both at $0'' \cdot 020$. The agreement with theoretical calculations was very good, but the method proved very difficult to work, particularly because of the problems of maintaining instrumental stability in the long beam carrying the mirrors, and it has not been tried since.

In a very few cases stars of large angular diameter lie in parts of the sky where from time to time they will be occulted by the Moon. Normally when a bright star is occulted by the dark limb of the Moon it appears to the eye to disappear instantaneously. A high speed photoelectric record shows that in fact there are usually oscillations in brightness caused by diffraction of the starlight at the lunar limb even when the angular diameter of the star is negligible. If the star has a perceptible angular diameter, say of the order of $0''\ 040$, the star will disappear in a time of the order of $0 \cdot 1$ seconds, the actual figure depending on the rate of apparent motion of the Moon against the star background and on the position of the point at which the occultation takes place in relation to the vertex of the relative motion of the Moon and the stars. Most of the work on this topic was undertaken in South Africa and angular diameters were determined for Antares and μ Geminorum. One point of controversy was the effect of irregularities on the lunar limb on the results, but it now seems clear from this work and from photoelectric observations of occultations made in the U.S.A. and Japan for geodetic purposes that these are of relatively slight importance.

However, as in most of astronomy, these "special occasion" methods of limited applicability tend to be replaced by improved general ones based on different physical principles. Starting originally with an application in radio astronomy, Hanbury Brown and Twiss showed that there should be a correlation between the times of arrival of photons at two receivers separated by a certain base-line, which depended on the length of the base-line and the angular diameter of the source. They then realised that this was applicable to visual light, and, in 1956 using a trial instrument in which the two receivers were two phototubes at the foci of two searchlight mirrors, demonstrated that the expected correlation was found in the case of Sirius and that it corresponded to an angular diameter of $0''\cdot0068$, the computed value being $0''\cdot0063$. A working version of this instrument is now in operation at Narrabri in Australia. This represents an extremely important advance and will lead to direct measurements of quantities so far only known by inference, and to the determination of experimental values of effective temperatures for a considerable number of stars.

6.17. Stars of Higher Multiplicity

It was remarked earlier that duplicity in stars is now recognised to be far more common than believed at one time. So, among recognised binary stars, systems of triple and higher multiplicity are being recognised as far from uncommon. The analysis of any individual case is apt to turn into a considerable piece of research, especially since systems of higher multiplicity can exhibit such a variety of physical manifestations that each case is effectively unique and demands *ad hoc* methods. Stars of higher multiplicity obviously also present a great opportunity for increasing our stock of rare data. As an example a brief account is given of a system in which the present author has a special interest. This is the star, *p* Velorum, a visual binary with a good orbit—$P = 16\cdot00$ years according to van den Bos, though a revision by Finsen may make it a few tenths of a year longer; components of apparent magnitudes $4\cdot5$ and $5\cdot3$, with a semiaxis major in the relative orbit of $0''\cdot316$ and an eccentricity of $0\cdot70$. The parallax is round about $0''\cdot030$, and with these parameters, near the node in the visual system the relative radial velocity between the components is about 35 km/s. The expected values were quoted in the form of product of relative radial velocity and parallax so as not to prejudge the value of the latter. The separation between the pair is always so small that the spectroscopists do not see the system resolved on the spectroscope slit, so their spectra are a mixture of all the components in this system. We say "all" and not "both" because one of the visual components is a spectroscopic binary and there is good reason for believing that it is the visual primary and not the secondary. The spectroscopic binary has an orbital period of $10\cdot2104$ days, and an eccentricity (distinctly on the high side for a spectroscopic binary) of $0\cdot56$. The two components of the spectroscopic binary are narrow-lined stars (a subgiant fairly early F and a later main-sequence F probably fit the bill as well as any choice) and they have values of K of $43\cdot3$ and $53\cdot6$ km/s so that the mass ratio in the spectroscopic pair is pretty exactly fixed. The parameters for the visual orbit ought to give the total mass in the system (sum of all three stars) but we are up against the usual difficulty that the trigonometrical parallax is not exactly enough known to stand the strain of being cubed. Now there is another feature of this system still to be taken into account, namely that the spectroscopic pair is in orbital motion in its character of visual primary in the optical pair. The value of γ for the spectroscopic pair is thus not constant, and, in fact we can fairly easily derive from observations made over a number of years the value of γ at any time. This is the radial velocity of the spectroscopic pair in its orbital motion round the centre of gravity of the whole system. Now comes a point which is characteristic of the difference in approach of the observer of visual double stars from that of the spectroscopist. The former usually works in terms of the relative motion of a pair and in particular of the motion of the secondary relative to the primary. The latter works in terms of motion relative to the centre of gravity, and, in particular, if he cannot pick up the spectrum of the secondary, in terms of the motion of the primary only, relative to the centre of gravity. Reconciliation of the two kinds of data requires extreme care, and provides a fertile field for errors of sign.

If in the present case we call the masses of the components of the spectroscopic pair M_1 and M_2 and that of the visual secondary M_3 the visual orbital data give the radial velocity of M_3 relative to M_1 and M_2 together. The values of γ in, say, different years, derived for the spectroscopic pair show the motion of the centre of gravity of M_1 and M_2 relative to the centre of gravity of all three components. If the orbit is a good one, the two variations should be proportional and from this we can find a value for the ratio of M_3 to $M_1 + M_3$ as a simple number if we trust the trigonometrical parallax, but involving this value as an unknown if we do not. It is wiser not to. Success, in the form of a determination of all three masses with no debatable assumptions, still eludes us. We still have another shot in the locker. The spectrum of p Velorum consists of a superposition of all three individual spectra. If we could get a velocity for star No. 3, the visual secondary, we should be home and dry, for this would give an independent determination of $(M_1 + M_2)/M_3$, not involving the parallax. Comparison with the previous determination which still contained the value of the parallax would give an excellent value for this quantity, and then out would come all three masses. As it is, the sign of the factor reconciling the curve of γ with the visual double star curve of relative radial velocity tells us which is the ascending node in the visual orbit, while if we found the masses in the way sketched above we should also get $\sin i$ in the spectroscopic orbit and be able to construct a complete spatial model of the whole system.

Well, then, why not measure the velocity of the visual primary? The snag is that this star is of earlier type than the other two: it shows in the joint spectrum only through its very broad hydrogen lines. It may actually be underluminous, because very broad hydrogen lines are a mark of low luminosity, and since they are broad in the joint spectrum they would be of far greater strength in the spectrum of Star No. 3 seen on its own. However, they are quite unsuitable for an attempt to measure velocity particularly because the lines of the spectroscopic binary fall near their centres and thoroughly confuse the picture. So far, this is the end of the line, for a careful search for some measurable line which might belong to Star No. 3 has had no success. We can resolve the whole system if we are willing to guess at the mass of any one of the stars from its spectrum, but this is not the same as making a solid determination of all three masses. There is one curious feature about this system which may have to be taken into account in many systems of higher multiplicity. The spectroscopic orbit is very eccentric so that the velocity separation between this pair changes from about zero to 150 km/s and back to zero in a time of 2 days. At certain critical phases the velocity separation is changing by nearly 10 km/s per hour. Now the visual orbit is quite large, and during some years we may have the spectroscopic pair on the remote side of the visual orbit: in others on the near side. The situation is analogous to the motion of the Earth round the Sun, and we have seen that for all variables we ought to correct observation times to the time at which the light would arrive at the Sun. In this case the difference in time of arrival of the light from the spectroscopic pair at the Sun will vary by about an hour depending on whether the spectroscopic pair is on the far side or the near side of the visual orbit. We have to put in a correction for this, for we cannot afford to have the epochs of maximum velocity separation wandering about by an hour: in order to do this we first have to have a solution for the system, so that getting the correction in requires a process of successive approximation; we first make a solution without the correction, this gives us the value of the relatively small correction with all the needful accuracy, and then make a second solution from the corrected data.

These are simply an example of the kind of complications presented by systems of higher multiplicity. They are both difficult problems and opportunities for gaining rich rewards.

REFERENCES:

General:
P. van de Kamp: (Robert Grant Aitken Memorial Lecture), *P.A.S.P.*, **73**, 389, 1961. Also "Visual Binaries", *Encyclopaedia of Physics*, Vol. 50, 187, Springer.
Orbit Computation; Visual Binaries:
W. van den Bos, "Astronomical Techniques", Vol. II of *Stars and Stellar Systems*, University of Chicago,
Eyepiece Interferometer:
W. S. Finsen, *Popular Astronomy*, **59**, 399, 1951.
Catalogues of Orbits:
Charles E. Worley, *Publications of the U.S. Naval Observatory*, Second Series, Vol. 18, Part III, 1963. ("Visual Binaries".)
Alan H. Batten (in preparation), *Spectroscopic Binaries*.
J. Dommanget, (with O. Nys), "Catalogue d'Éphémérides des vitesses radiales . . . des étoiles doubles . . ." (*Communications*, R. Belgian Obs., B, No. 15, 1967).
Z. Kopal and Martha B. Shapley, "Catalogue of the Elements of Eclipsing Binary Systems", *Jodrell Bank Annals*, Vol. 1, 141, 1956.
D. Ya. Martynov, *Catalogue of Spectroscopic Binaries*, Soviet Academy of Sciences, Moscow, 1961 (and subsequent).
Calculations and Techniques:
"Tables for True Anomaly": Frank Schlesinger and Stella Udick, *Allegheny Publications*, Vol. 11, No. 17, 1912.

Th. Sterne, *Proc. Nat. Acad. Sci.*, **27**, 175, 1941 (spectroscopic binaries of small eccentricity).

J. E. Merrill, "Tables for Solution of Light Curves of Eclipsing Binaries", *Princeton University Observatory Cont.*, No. 23, 1950.

H. N. Russell and J. E. Merrill, "The Determination of the Elements of Eclipsing Binaries", *Princeton Cont.*, No. 26, 1952.

Z. Kopal, *Eclipsing Variables*, Harvard, 1946; *Close Binary Systems*, Chapman and Hall, 1959.

C. M. Huffer and George W. Collins, "Computation of Eclipsing Binaries by Computing Machines", *Ap.J.*, Supp. **7**, 351, 1962.

Catalogues and Finding Lists:

H. Jeffers, W. van den Bos and F. Greeby, "Index Catalogue of Visual Double Stars", *Lick Obs. Pub.*, Vol. 21, 1963.

R. H. Koch, S. Sobieski, and F. B. Wood, "A Finding List for Observers of Eclipsing Variables", *Pub. Univ. Pennsylvania*, Astronomical Series, Vol. 9, 1963.

Mass-Luminosity Relation:

"Colours and Space Motions of 228 Visual Binaries", O. J. Eggen, *A.J.*, **70**, 19, 1965.

Stellar Diameters:

Earliest reference to the work of Hanbury Brown and Twiss, *Nature*, **178**, 1046, 1956.

VII
The Galaxy and the Galaxies

7.1. The Galaxy

THE system which we see on the sky as the Milky Way is not unique; observations of other systems having properties in common have helped towards an understanding of our own system. These other objects, known as extragalactic nebulae or galaxies, or sometimes by other names, are discussed in more detail below. Most of them are very remote, and only three of them, the two Magellanic Clouds and the Andromeda nebula, are large enough or bright enough to be visible to the naked eye. For any elucidation of their properties astronomy has had to wait for the installation of telescopes giving both large scale and large light-gathering power, and for the development of radio astronomy.

The Galaxy reveals many of its features to the naked eye or to slight telescopic aid, but here the difficulty is that of seeing the wood for the trees. The Sun is a member star of this system, not as badly-placed a coign of vantage as it might be had it been near the centre of the system, but still at none too good a position for gaining a general impression of galactic structure.

However, there are one or two quite direct ways in which a general impression can be obtained fairly easily. Early thinkers like Thomas Wright and the elder Herschel argued nearly two centuries ago that if stars were intrinsically not very different from each other (a grossly incorrect assumption but not so bad as to invalidate the conclusion) then merely studying the distribution of stars of given apparent magnitudes should give a model of spatial structure. On any given area of sky the bright stars would be placed nearest, and fainter ones at greater distances, so that a spatial model could be constructed. On this basis Wright proposed a crude model known as the "grindstone" universe, from its shape, and Herschel's result was rather similar. In the latter case, the Sun was placed at the centre of the Galaxy, and the regions near the galactic plane which are obscured by interstellar material were considered to be empty of stars. Herschel's model thus had a series of empty fissures running through it and pointing towards the Sun, but in other respects it provided a surprisingly accurate crude description of the Galaxy. Modern researches have been almost entirely directed towards the problems of taking account of the inherent diversity in brightness of the stars, and of allowing for the effects of interstellar absorption. A striking demonstration of the nature of our Galaxy, approximating in appearance to the view which might be had by an astronomer in intergalactic space, was provided by a photograph taken by A. D. Code and T. E. Houck using an all-sky camera. This is the type of equipment used in auroral studies: an ordinary camera photographs the reflected image, comprising the whole sky, produced in a highly curved convex mirror. The most striking of these photographs showed the Milky Way belt with the galactic nucleus at the centre: this shows as a more or less oval region of brightness with the rest of the Milky Way forming a flattened nearly plane belt about the nucleus, and with a black zone of obscuring material dividing the whole symmetrically. The structure thus incorporates three elements: a highly flattened plane distribution of gas and dust, a less flattened distribution (the disk) of stars, and a nucleus approaching a spherical form. What did not appear was the much less luminous practically spherical system of stars known as the halo having the spherical form associated with the Population II objects. The resemblance to many external galaxies was so striking that there could be no doubt of the essential identity of structure between the two.

Much of the work discussed in the previous chapters has contributed towards a better understanding of problems of galactic structure. Early systematic work, such as that undertaken by Seares and van Rijn was concerned with the infinitely laborious task of evaluating the mean distribution of stars in the sky according to position and apparent magnitude, and these basic statistics will be found tabulated in their papers or in abbreviated form in reference works such as Allen. An illustration of the gigantic scale of this enterprise is afforded by their result that the number of stars in the sky down to the twenty-first photographic magnitude is 890,000,000 or 1,000,000,000 down to the twentieth visual magnitude. This type of investigation represents an extension of the general star counting methods of Herschel, and leads to important results on the general distribution of matter and light in the galaxy. Between the time of this work and the present, the number of investigations on the distribution of stars and other objects in the Galaxy has been legion. As a general tendency more recent investigations have turned towards the study of specialised classes of object which could be used as indicators of special structural features. The account of the super-posed systems shown on the all-sky photographs merely underlines what has already been found in many other researches. At the centre is a nucleus of spherical form and high star density; the absorbing clouds of dust and gas are concentrated towards the galactic plane; Population I stars show a flattened distribution and Population II stars a more nearly spherical one. All this has been pieced together from studies of distributions and motions of various classes of objects.

The B-type stars are intrinsically bright and can be used to map out the Population I structure: it was in order to do this that the MKK system of stellar classification first came into being. The underlying argument is as follows: Bright Population I stars are recently born from gas, so that their distribution must indicate the gas distribution in the galaxy at the present time or in the recent past. In other galaxies, as we shall see below, the old stars of Population II have a relatively smooth distri-bution and provide a gently varying background. Embedded in this, and providing the most striking features of the appearance of other galaxies are the bright young stars of Population I and associated luminous clouds of gas and dark lanes of dust. In the majority of cases these striking features show evidence of spiral structure which are used in the classifications of various kinds of galaxy. The all-sky camera can show how the Galaxy would seem to an external observer in its own plane: it cannot show the appearance seen face-on. It was hoped that a study of the distribution of individual O and B stars and of associations of early type stars would reveal this distribution. A great deal of work has been done on the latter which can be found by consulting the lists of clusters and associations published by the Czech astronomers. Numerous investigations on individual stars have been undertaken. One of the most recent is that by a group headed by Mrs. Vera C. Rubin which studied data on the distribution of 1,440 early type stars lying within about 3 kiloparsecs of the Sun, for which complete information was available. The spatial distribution of these stars shows a tendency to favour a number of distinct lines, but, by themselves, these stars do not cover a sufficiently large proportion of the Galaxy to delineate its general structure. When this has been established by other methods, it

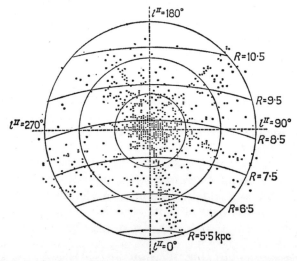

Figure VII.1: Projection on the galactic plane of 1162 early-type stars from computed distance moduli. The Sun is central, concentric circles are of radii, 1, 2, 3, kiloparsecs, and arcs represent distances from the galactic centre with the old value of solar distance of 8·2 kiloparsecs. (After Rubin *et al.*, by permission of the authors and the editors of the *A.J.*)

seems that the O and B stars provide supporting evidence. Radial velocity studies by the Rubin group favour a distance to the centre of 10 kiloparsecs.

The most illuminating information on the distribution of Population I objects in the Galaxy has come from studies of the distribution of gaseous clouds by the methods of radio astronomy. The interpretation of this data has depended to a considerable extent on the use of a model of the Galaxy incorporating all available observational data, including the assumption of values of the Oort constants and the variation of circular velocity with distance from the galactic centre. Such a model was constructed by Maarten Schmidt in 1956. In studies of the rotation of an extra-galactic system, a parallel to our own Galaxy, Wyse and Mayall had found it necessary to represent the mass distribution as a series of superposed or intermingled distributions. Schmidt followed their lead and represented the mass distribution in our own Galaxy by a series of spheroidal distributions of varying density. The behaviour of these separate distributions is linked through the fact that the members of each move in the gravitational of all. All the distributions are rather strongly flattened, so that they approximate to disks. In section they are ellipses, with c denoting the semiaxis minor, and a the semiaxis major. For convenience Schmidt used a mass unit equal to $2 \cdot 32 \times 10^5$ solar masses. In terms of this unit Schmidt derived a model composed mainly of four non-homogeneous spheroids, as follows:

(i) Population I objects, including gas: for this $c/a = 0 \cdot 02$, total mass in the above units, 18,500;

(ii) F-M stars: $c/a = 0 \cdot 07$: total mass = 81,800;

(iii) High velocity F-M stars: $c/a = 0 \cdot 16$ (i.e. even this is a strongly flattened system). Total mass = 43,600;

(iv) Unknown objects. For these, $c/a = 0 \cdot 07$ and total mass = 160,300.

In addition to these Schmidt found it necessary to introduce a series of 9 homogeneous spheroids having various values of a, for which the total algebraic mass was − 3,000 units. These adjustments, some of positive mass, some negative (i.e. in these cases the mass distribution lay below that given by the four basic elements) were necessary to represent observed variations in the circular velocity. The model, complicated though it is, is probably much simpler than the complexities of the actual structure. The total mass of the model is $0 \cdot 7 \times 10^{11}$ solar masses, and it is remarkable that it should include so high a proportion of masses of unknown objects.

Schmidt's model sought to represent a Galaxy in which the circular velocity at the Sun was 217 km/s, with the escape velocity 70 km/s higher than this, with a distance from the Sun to the centre of $8 \cdot 2$ kiloparsecs. The Oort constants in the solar neighbourhood were taken as $A = 19 \cdot 5$ km/s, $B = -6 \cdot 9$ km/s. With the introduction of new values for all the foregoing parameters a revision of the model becomes necessary, and, at the time of writing, is understood to be in progress. The figures for total mass and its apportionment will thus be changed, but probably not by an order of magnitude. The total mass may thus be taken as near 10^{11} solar masses.

7.2. Radio Astronomy and the Distribution of Neutral Hydrogen

It is not the intention of the present work to attempt to give a general account of radio astronomy, which should be left to specialists in this field. It is a field in which progress is being made by leaps and bounds, until the total body of knowledge bids fair to rival that of optical astronomy. In reality the two sciences supplement one another, and we shall concern ourselves only with those topics which bear upon the relations between the two. It is now well known that radio waves in the form of random noise can be detected from a variety of astronomical objects, including the Sun, certain concentrated sources in the Galaxy, such as the Crab nebula, supernova remnants, and from large numbers of external galaxies. The incident flux and variation with frequency are different at different wavelengths, and the nature of the radiation sources has provided fuel for discussion and controversy. One case of line emission is well established[*]: this is the emission from neutral hydrogen at a wavelength of $21 \cdot 1$ cm (1,420 MHz) whose existence was first suggested by van de Hulst in 1945. It arises from a hyperfine structure (spin) transition in the hydrogen atom and is exceedingly weak: the density of interstellar hydrogen is, by terrestrial standards

---

[*] Four line-frequencies due to the OH molecule have recently been observed but the physical picture is so rapidly developing and so confused that the topic cannot be pursued here.

extremely low (less than 1 atom per cc) but the total mass of hydrogen in the Galaxy is vast (round about 4×10^9 solar masses) and this is enough to permit the radiation to be detected. Much of the work has been undertaken by means of large paraboloidal antennae, either steerable or fixed in the meridian, of diameters of $7 \cdot 5$ metres upwards.

Observational methods and techniques of reduction have varied considerably, and vast resources of ingenuity have been expended on this work: the underlying ideas are, however, relatively simple. The Galaxy is rotating: the hydrogen in the Galaxy rotates as well, to a first approximation at the circular velocity at any distance from the centre. The hydrogen clouds will produce line emission: the total incident flux will give a clue as to the number of atoms responsible, and the frequency at which the maximum intensity occurs will indicate the relative radial velocity of the emitting cloud, since this will be displaced by Doppler effect. In the vast majority of cases a plot of incident flux against frequency as received from a given direction will not consist of a single peak. If observations are made, as in effect they have been, by allowing the frequency to vary steadily through a range about the undisplaced value of 1,420 MHz, the incident flux received will show usually a number of peaks. Each of these may be supposed to correspond to a mass of gas moving with a given radial velocity. If, as in Schmidt's model, we have a plot of circular velocity against distance from the centre, then it is a relatively simple matter to decide at what distance a mass of gas must lie if it has the circular velocity appropriate to its position and produces a given observed radial velocity. However, in the case of a vast series of observations such as those reported by Muller and Westerhout in 1957, and published along with discussions by various colleagues, the task of interpretation becomes a herculean one, owing to the occurrence of ambiguities and the necessity of relating observations made at a large number of points throughout the Milky Way region. Suppose, for example, there is a ring of gas of circular form rotating about the galactic centre at a central distance less than that of the Sun. Then a line of sight which cuts this ring will do so in two points, and contributions with the same radial velocity will be received from the farther and nearer points of intersection (Figure VII.2). If the ring of gas is a torus of constant cross-section, then a little scanning in galactic latitude will help to separate the farther source from the nearer, because it will have the smaller angular range in latitude. If these artificial assumptions concerning uniformity of distribution are abandoned, then the presence of peaks on the

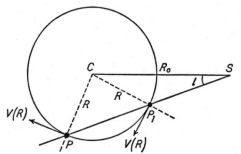

Figure VII.2: S is the Sun: C the Galactic Centre. If a torus of gas, or a series of gas clouds, is moving at distance R from the centre with the circular velocity, $V(R)$, the observed radial velocity along a line of sight, SP_1P is $V(R) \cdot R_0 \sin l/R$. Observation of a given value puts the source at P or P_1, and further data are needed to resolve the ambiguity.

profiles, after they have been subjected to laborious processes of correction to remove instrumental effects, permit the analyst to assume that the line of sight cuts a number of gas clouds for each of which there may be an alternative position. These ambiguities can be resolved by consideration of the variation of results in latitude and comparison of adjoining regions of the Milky Way. In the end the jigsaw puzzle has been solved and a model produced showing that there are concentrations of hydrogen following fairly well-defined lines in the galactic plane. They are not perfectly continuous and they appear to show occasional branching and they strongly resemble the kind of spiral structure which is observed in many external galaxies. Information based on work in the north, originally at Leiden, but later at other centres, and in the south from Sydney, has given a coverage of the whole Milky Way with the exception of the regions of the centre and anti-centre within which the differentiation of intensity peaks by the separation produced by differential radial velocity ceases to apply. The analysis is not entirely dependent on an assumed model for the variation of circular velocity with distance from the centre, for observations of the 21-cm line can themselves contribute significantly to knowledge of this variation. It can readily be seen that if a rotating ring of gas is observed lying within the solar distance from the centre, then the maximum radial velocity

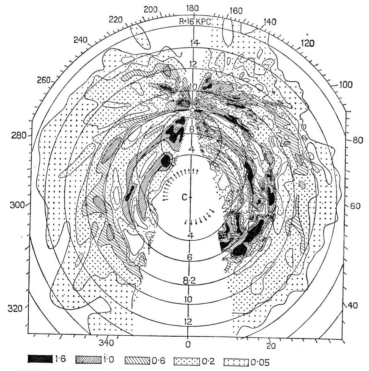

Figure VII.3: Distribution of hydrogen in the galactic plane according to 21-cm observations made by the Leiden Observatory (Northern Milky Way) and the Radio Physics Laboratory, C.S.I.R.O., Sydney (Southern Milky Way). The galactic centre is at C, the Sun at S. Distances from the centre are in kiloparsecs (old scale), and the density of hydrogen atoms, indicated by shadings, is in numbers per cm³. (By permission of Professor J. H. Oort.)

will occur for a line of sight tangential to the ring. Some difficulties of interpretation arise if the ring is not continuous, but useful results can be obtained.

The leading features found from observations at 21 cm are first, data on the general density of neutral hydrogen, which gives values of the order of 1 atom per cc for the denser parts and a general average in the galactic plane of round about 0·5 atoms/cc. The extension perpendicular to the galactic plane is small, and the radial limit is about 15 kiloparsecs from the centre. The densest parts of the gas define a number of somewhat irregular and not perfectly continuous tubes, which, by analogy with what will be met in spiral extragalactic systems are called "arms". The Sun lies on the inner edge of an arm extending from the direction of Cygnus past the anti-centre and into the Orion association. This has been called the Orion arm which can be followed round in the direction of decreasing longitudes for almost half a circuit.*
At about 10·5 kiloparsecs from the centre starting roughly in the direction of the association near h and χ Persei is another arm which has been called the Perseus arm. Starting at a galactocentric distance between 6 and 7 kiloparsecs is the Sagittarius arm which, followed in a clockwise direction as seen from the north galactic pole (this is the direction of rotation of the system) appears to curve into smaller distances from the centre. This is relevant to a topic mentioned in more detail later, namely, the question of the direction of rotation of galaxies relative to the sense of the spiral arms in them. The above result suggests that the Galaxy has a spiral structure and that the arms trail in the rotational motion. However, it must be acknowledged that the spiral character of the Galaxy cannot be so marked as that in some external galaxies, and that the conclusion concerning the direction in which the arms separate along their length is dependent on whether or not a general expansion of the system is assumed. Systematic deviations of the arms from the local circular velocity would require the arm structure as found in the surveys noted here to be replaced by another having a different spirality. Thus although the general picture of arms spaced about 2 kiloparsecs apart, each having a width of about 0·8 kiloparsecs and a maximum density of neutral hydrogen of about 1·5 atoms per cc can be regarded as well established, the details may yet demand some modifications.

The topic of general expansion was brought into prominence by the discovery of a gaseous arm near the centre and at about 3 kiloparsecs from it (the "3 kiloparsec" arm) which is expanding at the rate of about 53 km/s. This is part of a complex structure which seems to exist right at the galactic nucleus, where there may be a small (on the scale of the Galaxy), rapidly-rotating structure of radius less than about 400 parsecs, with a surrounding ring of radius about 600 parsecs separated from it. As we shall see, similar strange phenomena have been picked up right at the very centre of a number of other galaxies, and they may imply the existence of a small, massive, rapidly-rotating inner nucleus, and possibly an inflow of intergalactic gas down the axis to provide the observed gaseous outflow evidenced by the 3-kiloparsec arm.

An enormous amount of work on radio emission in the Galaxy has been under-taken by many investigators, in the first place in Britain, Holland and Australia, but later in the U.S.A., France and elsewhere. It must suffice to say that three

* Dr. S. V. M. Clube has recently demonstrated, however, that attributing circular motion to gas clouds which deviate from this pattern could lead to the erroneous delineation of non-existent arms of nearly circular shape.

mechanisms of radiation are recognised. First, the line radiation of neutral hydrogen clouds at temperatures of the order of 100°K, which has been discussed at some length above. Then, free-free transitions of electrons in hot ionised hydrogen clouds at temperatures of the order of 10,000°K produce what is known as "thermal" radiation. Sources are effectively a continuous distribution concentrated towards the Milky Way plus localised intense sources which have been identified in many but not all cases with emission regions of optical gaseous nebulae in the Galaxy. Synchrotron radiation is produced by the motion of very high velocity electrons (relativistic electrons) moving in magnetic fields. A number of localised sources are known. These include the Crab nebula, a supernova remnant, exhibiting features such as polarisation which indicate the presence of magnetic fields. A similar correlation has been established with other known cases of supernova remnants, and probably a high proportion of what are called Class I sources (radio sources within the Galaxy) are of this type. This particular problem is bound up with the question of the existence of magnetic fields, both localised and general, in the structure of galaxies, and we shall return to it later.

7.3. External Galaxies

Enough has been said to make it clear that our own Galaxy is not a unique object. Enormous numbers of objects in the same general classification can be detected in the sky. The nomenclature has evolved gradually, and not altogether happily, over a period of rather more than a century. It was recognised as early as the time of Sir William Herschel that in addition to individual stars and clusters in the sky, there were also objects of perceptible angular diameter, many of them of very low surface brightness. They were at first all accorded the blanket name of "Nebulae" (the Latin word for "clouds") but at a fairly early stage an attempt was made to classify them into different types. It was at this stage that names such as "planetary nebulae" were introduced. The real nature of these objects was not realised until relatively recently. The basic modern distinction between extended objects of small linear dimensions which are features of our own Galaxy, and extended objects of galactic dimensions which seem no larger because they are at enormous distances, was settled only relatively recently. Even in the twenties this topic could form the subject of lively controversy between Shapley and Curtis.

Our present subject is the latter class of nebulae. They are objects of dimensions and population comparable with our own Galaxy, separated one from another by vast distances of effectively empty space, and containing, as features of their structure, clouds of gas of various kinds which in our own Galaxy are also accorded the name of "nebulae". These objects have been distinguished by a variety of names such as "extragalactic nebulae", "external galaxies" and so on: the term "island universes", possibly the best descriptive term yet invented, has fallen into disuse. Official usage now calls them "galaxies", but this seems an unfortunate choice since the term for our own system is "the Galaxy" and the writer finds himself continually forced into the use of rather clumsy locutions to make clear whether our own or some other system is meant.

Because of the variety of forms and types a condensed description to serve as a definition is somewhat difficult to give. We can say that a galaxy is an effectively isolated system comprising stars, gas, dust and all the other components mentioned in previous paragraphs. Its total mass will be of the order of 10^{11} solar masses, and the same figure will give the approximate number of stars in the system. The proportion of gas and dust may be anything from practically zero up to the order of one-quarter of the mass. The average distance between galaxies is of the order of 200,000 to 500,000 parsecs, and the average largest diameter of an individual system is about 30,000 parsecs for the largest specimens. There is a considerable range of dimensions and integrated magnitudes: the largest specimens have absolute magnitudes approaching − 20, but smaller examples with dimensions down to only some 2 or 3 kiloparsecs will be round about 5 magnitudes fainter and contain fewer stars and correspondingly smaller mass. The quotation of an average value for distance between systems is complicated by the fact that galaxies show a marked tendency to occur in clusters, and, quite apart from this, the occurrence of pairs, triplets and other small groups, showing physical interaction is common.

Almost all the single systems and many which belong to groups, show, as does the Galaxy, a plane of symmetry dividing the system into two practically identical halves, and, perpendicular to this, an axis of symmetry which may be presumed to mark the axis about which the rotations of the system take place. Most systems show some degree of flattening towards the diametral plane of symmetry: this may be slight or so extreme that at least in its outer parts the galaxy approximates to a thin disk. There may be a well-defined nucleus of less flattened form at the centre (where the axis of symmetry cuts the diametral plane), and, on the average, both star density and brightness decreases in all directions outwards from this. However, it must be recognised that although galaxies often show well-marked and rather simple geometrical properties, they are not just geometrical figures but dynamic structures of immense antiquity in which the accidents of evolution have produced local variations of form in even the most symmetrical of examples.

7.4. The Classification of Galaxies

Galaxies show a great variety of forms and some properties are correlated with type. The classification introduced by Hubble during the twenties and early thirties was so successful that no generally accepted alternative has yet been devised, although the reforms introduced by Sandage in the *Hubble Atlas of Galaxies* and the proposals of de Vaucouleurs are likely soon to produce a generally adopted change. Hubble's system had the cardinal advantage in any classification system that the number of categories was not large, and that it was not particularly difficult to apply, so that different authors would not disagree on the classification of a given object. It did not make the mistake of trying to put too much of a description into the category of classification: systems of classification which do this are all too apt to lead to the enumeration of the material only as a series of individual objects and not as members of well-defined categories.

7.5. Elliptical Nebulae

It is therefore worth while briefly to recapitulate the Hubble system. He began with the *Elliptical Nebulae*. These are objects in which the curves of equal brightness (isophotes) were concentric ellipses, of similar shape and orientation showing practically no detail, but only a smooth distribution of brightness. The general type was divided into subclasses by numbers denoting the apparent ellipticity of the isophotes, defined by the expression $10(a-b)/a$ where a and b are the apparent major and minor axes. The observed subdivisions ran from E0 to E7: the first named are therefore circular in outline, while the classification E7 refers to a form in which the minor axis is only 30 per cent of the major. The latest classifications of the ellipticals sometimes showed a lenticular form in which the extremes of the apparent major axis showed corners or even short spindle-like extensions. It has to be recognised that since classes were assigned on apparent form some misclassification must result, e.g. the case of a highly-flattened elliptical being classed as E0 because it happens to be turned pole-on towards the Earth. Hubble showed, and it has been verified by later workers, that the variation of brightness over an elliptical nebula is such that along any radius, it follows the rule $I = I_0(r/c + 1)^{-2}$ where r is the distance and c is a scale parameter. The quantity c is not constant from one radius to another, but is constant along the chosen radius: in other words, if one isophote is an ellipse, all succeeding isophotes are concentric and similar ellipses and can be plotted from a knowledge of any one: alternatively the rule means that by a simple scale change along the minor axis, the isophotes of all elliptical nebulae can be transformed into circles with the same distribution. This formula, actually introduced into astronomy in 1913 by Reynolds in connection with the brightness distribution in the nucleus of the Andromeda nebula, begins to break down at very great distances from the centre. A number of other nebular nuclei which would strongly resemble ellipticals if the arms were removed, seem to show the same brightness variation. Whether the variation is represented by this analytical form or by others such as that of de Vaucouleurs, this almost universal similarity is very curious and does not seem to have been the object of theoretical investigation. The limit of axis ratio observed at E7 is also an interesting feature, probably connected with considerations of dynamical stability. The nature of the elliptical nebulae was cleared up by the technical feat of Baade, mentioned in a previous chapter, in which he succeeded in resolving into individual stars one of the ellipticals found as a companion to the Andromeda nebula. Thus ellipticals are thought to be composed entirely of Population II stars. A fair proportion of them show in their spectra the forbidden emission doublet at 3,727Å, which is unexpected unless the lines originate in numerous planetary nebulae. Many nebulae which might be classed as ellipticals do have exceedingly faint outer arm structures which can be revealed in long exposure photographs in favourable cases.

7.6. Spiral Nebulae

In Hubble's system the remaining objects were classified by the spiral structures which they exhibited. This feature has already been mentioned in connection with the Galaxy. In very many galaxies one or more pairs of arms, or occasionally single arms, can be discerned starting near the centre and winding outwards. In some cases these are very open and continuous and are extended in what seems to be empty space, so that the whole nebula may resemble the letter S written in italics, with only a slight thickening and brightening of the central part to mark the nucleus. In others, the arms may be marked by a series of discontinuous blobs of brightness, either masses of gas or bright Population I star clusters, showing several quite tightly wound turns, the spiral structure being seen against a background of more or less continuous brightness provided by the Population II components of the galaxy. In such cases the striking detail may be enhanced by the obvious presence of dark obscuring material, sometimes in the form of discrete clouds, sometimes in the form of dust arms. In others, as has already been mentioned above, the nucleus may be a bright object resembling an elliptical nebula, and the arms may be very faint. Deviations from a true spiral form are common, and a further feature often encountered is the presence of a fairly faint practically continuous isolated ring of luminous material enclosing the whole system.

Hubble classified this material in fairly broad categories, though, according to Sandage's introduction to the *Hubble Atlas*, Hubble himself was preparing a revision towards the end of his life. He distinguished two classes of spiral: those in which the arms seemed to spring from the nucleus of the galaxy (the normal spirals) and those in which the arms seemed to spring from the ends of a straight bar structure having the nucleus at its centre (the barred spirals). These two general categories were distinguished as S, and SB respectively. Each category was subdivided according to the closeness of winding of the arms into subcategories a, b, and c, the terms "early" and "late" being applied respectively to the first and last subdivisions. These terms did not necessarily have any temporal significance in the process of evolution of galaxies which must necessarily be taking place. Hubble would classify a normal spiral with closely wound arms showing several turns as Sa. A system in which the nucleus was much less prominent, with the arms showing less than a whole turn and being more opened out and marked more by star clusters than by gas clouds would be classed as Sc. The latter would then be called a late-type spiral, and since it seems hard to imagine how in the evolution of galaxies the latter structure might turn into the former, the idea that the late type spiral could evolve out of the early type seems not unjustified.

Recent developments in the system of classification have taken two forms. First, a new major class called the S0 systems has been introduced to form a bridge between the ellipticals and the spirals. Secondly, attempts have been made to categorise more narrowly the variety of observed forms. The S0 galaxies are symmetrical systems resembling ellipticals which show some incipient structure and thus depart from the completely smooth light distribution of the true ellipticals. These developments can take the form either of the greater flattening characteristic of the spirals, or the development of spindle-shaped extensions or by the occurrence of a bright lens surrounded by a fainter envelope, or by the first indication of dark lanes in an otherwise amorphous structure. It will be clear that many of these objects would have been classified by Hubble as ellipticals, and those late ellipticals noted by him as having lenticular or spindle forms would now go into the S0 class.

Although greater precision may be expected by the replacement of the Hubble system, the present situation, where we are confronted by the not entirely consistent systems of Sandage, de Vaucouleurs, Morgan and van den Bergh is not altogether happy. The astronomer now presented with a photograph of a new nebula no longer has the certainty of the Hubble system, and no generally agreed scheme of classification yet replaces it.

At the beginning of the *Hubble Atlas*, Sandage gives an account of nebular classification in which at certain points he relies heavily on unpublished notes left by Hubble. It therefore seems correct to call this the Hubble-Sandage scheme of classification.

It begins with the elliptical nebulae which run from E0 to E7, where the axis ratio is 3:1. Then the scheme splits into two branches respectively called S0 and SB0 with subclasses, 1, 2, 3. In the former as we move along the subclasses, a dark internal ring develops. In the latter a rudimentary bar develops often in the form of ansae formed along a line not at right angles to the major axis of the nucleus. The S0 nebulae are the precursors of the normal spirals and the sequence goes on through Sa, Sb, Sc, a sequence characterised by a greater degree of openness of the arms, an increasing tendency towards discontinuity and towards the replacement of gas clouds by resolved stars clusters. This is a feature only detectable on large-scale photographs of the nearer and brighter systems. The S sequence may itself be regarded as bifurcated, for the distinction may also be drawn between S(s) systems in which the arms spring from the nucleus, and the S(r) systems in which the arms originate as tangents to a ring structure. The barred spirals are characterised by a central bar passing through the nucleus, and the degree of development is specified by the three subclasses SBa, SBb, SBc, with again a subdivision into (s) and (r). There is a considerable class of irregular galaxies in many of which there is a high degree of resolution into stars or star-like objects and no definitely recognisable arm structure. The Hubble-Sandage system puts these at the end of the S sequence and in some cases recognises a transition stage defined as Sd. In addition, there are a considerable number of galaxies which do not fit perfectly into their nearest categories, and these are described as peculiar. Peculiarities often occur in members of multiple systems where there is evidently some gravitational interaction at work, but many interesting isolated systems occur. The system of classification is best illustrated by examples, some of which are shown in the accompanying photographs. In the nature of things it can never be perfectly precise, for the classification system aims to give a spatial description of an object such as might be examined from every angle in the case of an object small enough to be held in the hand. In the real case our view is limited to a single aspect and the spatial structure has to be inferred. Moreover, classification based on photographs taken with a large instrument is bound to be more precise than one based on results from a smaller instrument, or alternatively, the classification of more remote objects undertaken with any telescope becomes progressively less precise. Aspect effect is particularly important in the case of systems seen edge on, in which the spiral structure is invisible and the nebula has the appearance of a long streak with a bulge of brightness at the centre marking the nucleus and in many cases a dark line dividing the system lengthwise. This marks the plane on which the absorbing material lies.

Other recent work on classification includes that by de Vaucouleurs whose system involves placing the observed object on a polar diagram in which distance from the centre represents what might be called "degree of development", i.e. E0 systems are at the middle and systems with open arms and a high degree of resolution at the periphery. The normal spirals are called SA, the barred SB, and the (r) and (s) categories of the Hubble-Sandage system divide each into two. There are thus four radial lines describing the pure members of these types while the intermediate areas are available for intermediate forms.

The work of S. van den Bergh attempts to classify galaxies not only by Hubble types but in terms of luminosity as well. Undoubtedly galaxies show a wide range of dimensions and intrinsic luminosity, so that terms such as supergiant and dwarf become appropriate. These categories can be distinguished in galaxies which are members of the same cluster, while for isolated systems the measured radial velocity, as explained below, provides a guide to distance and enables the distinction to be drawn. This particular aspect does not seem to have been widely taken up along the lines proposed by this author. His system lays some stress on peculiar features encountered in pairs and groups of galaxies.

The chief point of W. W. Morgan is the lack of correlation between spectrum and structure and he has sought to establish a classification system illustrated by a collection of photographs in which two parameters are used: one is the Hubble class, denoted S, B, E and I for normal spirals, barred spirals, ellipticals and irregulars; the other is what Morgan calls the "form family" with categories such as, L for systems of low surface brightness, and N for those with small brilliant nuclei, and certain others.

7.7. Catalogues of Galaxies

It has been mentioned in a previous section that the first attempt at a nebular catalogue was made by Charles Messier, a cometary observer, who published a list of 103 nebulous objects and clusters as a supplement to the *Connaissance des Temps* for 1784. About 30 of them are external galaxies, and the numbers which he assigned them are still in use. We have already met Messier numbers in connection with globular clusters, since at the time of the compilation the essential distinction between these objects and the extragalactic nebulae (which have their own attendant globular clusters) was not realised. An example of a common use of a Messier number for an extragalactic object is the designation of the Great Nebula in Andromeda as M 31. Further cataloguing work was undertaken in the north by both the Herschels, while that in the south was undertaken by the younger, Sir John Herschel, during his stay at the Cape of Good Hope (1834-8). In 1888 Dreyer produced his *New General Catalogue of Nebulae and Clusters of Stars*, comprising 7,840 objects. The majority of these are extragalactic, though lists of members of population categories in our own Galaxy, such as star clusters, planetary and gaseous nebulae are also included. Supplements rather oddly known as *Index Catalogues* were published in 1895 and 1908. Designations in these catalogues are by NGC or IC numbers, and since all the real Messier objects are included, one also finds, for example, M 31 referred to alternatively as NGC 224.

A catalogue confined to extragalactic nebulae brighter than the 13th apparent magnitude was produced by Harlow Shapley and Adelaide Ames in 1932. The entries are mostly NGC and IC objects, and the additions are few. It contains 1,249 objects and was a very useful general guide to the brighter galaxies all over the sky.

This has now been superseded by the *Reference Catalogue of Bright Galaxies* produced by G. and A. de Vaucouleurs. This lists 2,599 galaxies brighter than the 14th magnitude, and assembles in one place the accumulated information on structures, magnitudes, colours and radial velocities. There are still a good many gaps in available information: for example, photoelectric B magnitudes are given for only 873 of the galaxies in the catalogue. One of the most useful functions of the catalogue will be to guide future work on the brighter galaxies.

How far it is reasonably possible to catalogue galaxies all over the sky is questionable. A comprehensive catalogue down to the 15th magnitude has been mooted, and might contain some 50,000 galaxies. The *National Geographic Sky Atlas* consists of a series of plates taken with the Palomar Schmidt which, in the original version covered the whole sky down to declination $-30°$. This has now been extended. Objects with a limiting magnitude of 21·1 in blue light, and 20·0 in the red are recorded, and enormous numbers of galaxies can be picked out. In many ways the survey prints are as rich a field for investigation as the sky itself. Vorontsov-Velyaminov has produced from it a catalogue of pairs and higher order systems showing interaction. Abell has identified on it no less than 2,712 rich clusters of galaxies, of which 1,682 have been chosen for special study. According to Abell 1,224 of these have membership between 50 and 79 galaxies each, and the largest one has a membership of over 300. Sky studies are likely to proceed by intensive investigation of sample areas because of the very large numbers of objects involved. Thus, for example, Zwicky and his colleagues have produced surveys of the galaxies and clusters of galaxies in particular areas, which will be of value for statistical purposes.

The apparent distribution of galaxies on the sky is influenced by the presence all around us of our own Galaxy, and in particular by the presence of the gas and dust layer near its central plane. This produces a somewhat irregular zone (the *Zone of Avoidance*), around the sky, about 20 degrees broad within which nebulae are seen only exceptionally. These rather rare glimpses of outer space are possible because the obscuring material is not continuous, but occurs in discrete clouds. For example, about 30 degrees east of the galactic centre is a region quite near the plane in which the distant extragalactic systems NGC 6215 and 6221 can be seen through quite rich star fields. In this direction the line of sight crosses most of our Galaxy and passes between the 4-kiloparsec arm and the 7-kiloparsec arm delineated in the Sydney radio surveys. Apart from these rather small-scale irregularities, the general run of absorption produced by the material in our Galaxy has been represented by the expression $0·25$ (cosec $b-1$) magnitudes, where b is the galactic latitude corresponding to the line of sight.

7.8. Methods of Observation of Galaxies

The primary method of recording an external galaxy is that of direct photography with a suitable telescope. The nearer galaxies appear as extended objects of low surface brightness and in order to photograph them successfully instruments with small f-numbers must be used, following the discussion in Chapter II. At the same time the good resolution afforded by a large linear scale is desirable, and with the attainment of this condition goes the large aperture which gives a faint limiting magnitude for the registration of point sources. These conditions explain the outstanding importance of large aperture instruments having focal lengths as short as possible, of which the leading example is the Palomar Schmidt telescope.

Programmes of direct photography yield positional data for galaxies. From these studies of their distribution can be made, and clusters of galaxies identified if the photographs reach a sufficiently faint limiting magnitude. According to Abell second order clusters of galaxies, that is, clusters of clusters, can be identified. A number of recondite statistical studies of the distribution of galaxies have been made, for example by Neyman and Miss Scott.

Direct photography permits the nearer systems, for which detail can be discriminated, to be classified according to their types. Small groups of galaxies showing dynamical relationships can be identified. Superposition of photographs taken with different filters has been used to reveal the distribution of various types of object within nebulae.

In the very nearest galaxies individual stars can be identified. In favourable cases their nature can be discriminated, and ordinary novae, Cepheids or RR Lyrae stars identified. At maximum, supernovae are intrinsically so bright as roughly to equal the total brightness of the galaxy in which one occurs. The occurrence of supernovae and their brightness variation can therefore be observed in galaxies by the use of direct photography, coupled in this last case by assiduity of search and a measure of good fortune.

If the plates are photometrically calibrated it is possible to measure densities and to convert these to the surface brightness which produced them. In this way the variation of brightness over the nebula can be measured, and lines of equal brightness (isophotes) can be drawn. Executed point by point all over the image of a galaxy, this process is extremely tedious, and there is now a move towards the construction of machines which will automatically make the measurements and reduce them to real intensities, and thereafter draw the isophotes. In the case of the larger systems the measurements have been carried out photoelectrically by allowing the nebular image to trail through the field at a known rate.

A general conclusion from these studies, whether undertaken photographically or photoelectrically, is that the extent of the nebulae is always several times larger than the extreme dimensions which can be rendered visible on a photographic print. This sometimes makes it difficult to utilise the results. The outermost parts of the galaxy are very extended but very faint, so that their contribution to total luminosity is represented by a large sky area multiplied by a small, and usually rather uncertain brightness. The product usually represents a sensible fraction of the total light and is progressively more uncertain the farther out one goes. It is usually less difficult to handle this problem when the measures are made photoelectrically. Measures of this kind can, in some cases yield good values of dimensions of galaxies. Since galaxies have no definite boundaries these usually have to be expressed in the form of the angular dimensions (usually of an ellipse) within which some fraction, say a half, of the total luminosity is produced. The luminosity integral ought, also, to yield the total brightness of the galaxy, but for extended systems and photographic measurements, the convergence difficulties mentioned above can make the result uncertain. An important point is that for more distant systems, of smaller angular dimensions the whole nebula can be included in the diaphragm of a photoelectric photometer at the same time, or the whole image can be included in the diaphragm of an iris-diaphragm photometer, and the entire object treated as a single source. Even if a little light does spill over, measures with diaphragms of different sizes can be made and an empirical rule for correcting for the contributions of the outlying parts devised. There is thus some risk that the integrated magnitudes of nearby systems will be less accurately known than those of more remote ones. This is insidious, because the nearer systems, in which stars or other details can be recognised enable distance estimates to be made for these galaxies. These then should yield estimates of linear dimensions and integrated brightness for galaxies of various types. For more remote systems, of which the type can be recognised, the adopted values of dimensions and integrated magnitudes derived from studies of nearer systems of similar type will be used to estimate distances for these more remote systems.

Direct photography may profitably be undertaken with various combinations of filters and photographic emulsions. One set of choices gives an approximation to U, B, V photometry. Another, worthy of special mention, is the employment of interference filters transmitting only a few Ångstroms band-width at a selected mean wavelength. A useful choice of wavelength coincides with the red H-alpha line of hydrogen, undisplaced for gaseous structures within our own Galaxy and displaced judiciously to the red for a selection of extragalactic nebulae with velocities of recession not too large. This technique has been much exploited by G. Courtès and is capable of revealing the distribution of hydrogen in a variety of structures. To separate fully the features due to hydrogen from those of the nearby continua of stars, the interference filter picture should be compared for differences, with a second exposure of the same region made through an ordinary gelatine filter with wide bandpass and the same mean wavelength of transmission.

A photographic method for the determination of integrated magnitudes of galaxies which is mentioned even in relatively recent literature is that of the schraffierkassette or "jiggle camera". In this equipment the plate is oscillated over a range of some tenths of a millimetre in both directions by means of motor driven sewing-machine cams. Each image, whether of a star or a nebula is converted to a uniform rectangle for which an integrated magnitude can be derived by the measurement of photographic densities. Calibration is from stars of known magnitude on the same plate. This method gets over the difficulties produced by spread of light in nebular images and the extremely sharp intensity peak near the nuclei.

To a large extent photographic methods are being replaced by photoelectric ones. As has been explained, results found with diaphragms of different sizes can be extrapolated to give total intensities. For faint systems, integration methods are used, notably by workers such as Baum. For the faintest systems, integration times of many hours have been used, reaching magnitudes beyond the photographic limit. The determination of magnitudes and colours is of the greatest importance and handsomely repays the technical difficulties which have had to be overcome.

7.8. Radial Velocities of Galaxies

Radial velocities of galaxies are determined from the Doppler shifts shown by their spectra. If galaxies resemble our own Galaxy they will be in rotation and different parts of a nebular image will yield different values of velocity. We begin however with the general problem of obtaining spectra in the integrated light of galaxies and the determination of their systematic motions of translation in the line of sight. Because the nuclei of galaxies are by far their brightest parts, the spectra obtained from the integrated image are those of the nuclei.

The overwhelming need in extragalactic spectroscopy is to conserve light and to make the spectra as bright as possible. Dispersions are small: values in the region of 300 to 400Å/mm are adequate for the main spectral features to be distinguished and radial velocities measured.

The considerations which govern the speed of spectrographs were discussed in Chapter II. The conclusion was that the f-number of the camera should be as small as possible. In spectrographs used for extragalactic spectroscopy, the f-number is invariably less than 1·0, and very much smaller values have been attained. In general, camera optics are of the Schmidt type, and f-numbers as small as 0·65 have been achieved with miniature Schmidt cameras of conventional pattern. These instruments are extremely difficult to adjust because their depth of focus is practically zero. Improved instrumental stability and still smaller f-numbers can be achieved by a variety of stratagems. These include solid Schmidt designs in which all the optical surfaces of the camera are figured on various faces of a single piece of ultraviolet glass. If this is maintained at constant temperature the relative positions of the various optical surfaces are fixed rigidly relative to each other. Another device employed is that of oil immersion of the photographic emulsion and the last optical surface. This is the reverse of the oil-immersion objective in microscopy, and in both cases the substitution of an oil of suitable refractive index for air permits more extreme optics to be used.

The photographic surfaces used to record the spectra whether plates or film are, in these spectrographs, quite minute. Plates may be used if the focal surface is plane: if it is not, film may be forced to the correct shape. Difficulties have been encountered with the use of the latter if there are sharp changes in humidity causing changes in dimensions of the film base during exposure. Whichever is used, problems of handling scraps of plate perhaps no more than a centimetre square, or pieces of film no larger than a flake of confetti, can be severe. There are surprisingly few spectrographs in use for extragalactic spectroscopy—almost certainly less than a dozen in the world—and each is a highly individual piece of equipment. Their very small f-numbers make them extremely fast for recording emission lines, and the intensity of these lines in the recorded spectrum is not affected by the slit width used. Thus with a rather narrow slit the velocity of an emission object can be measured with considerable accuracy, say, with a probable error of only 10 km/s if there are several emission lines, or in the region of 50 km/s if there are only one or two. The emission lines most commonly used for the measurement of radial velocities of galaxies or of emission knots in them are the close pair due to forbidden oxygen at λ 3,727Å, the "nebulium" lines, N_1 and N_2 already mentioned in connection with planetary nebulae, and the Balmer lines. This is for the photographic region: others are of importance if panchromatic emulsions are used.

The density of the continuous spectrum of an extended object increases when the spectrograph slit is opened, though at the cost of a loss of resolution. In many cases the choice is between no spectrum at all, and one where only the strongest lines, notably the H and K absorption lines of ionised calcium, can be detected. A remarkable proportion of all radial velocities of galaxies depends on measures of these two absorption lines only. There is a reduction in scale from the plane of the slit to the emulsion surface. The factor is equal to the ratio of the f-number of the camera to the f-number of the telescope, and, for the type of instrument we have been discussing this may lie between one-fifth and one-tenth. It is thus often possible to open the spectrograph slit very wide indeed—up to possibly half a millimetre—while keeping the projected slit width not too much above the resolution of the rather coarse-grained very high speed emulsions used. The latter may be reckoned as being in the neighbourhood of 40 microns. The accuracy of measurement of extragalactic radial velocities, using absorption lines, and excluding the very nearest systems, is represented by probable errors in the range from about 25 km/s to about 150 km/s.

An important point connected with the spectroscopy of faint extended sources is that once a typical galaxy of a certain species is observable, say by the introduction of a spectrograph of a certain speed, then other similar galaxies even at considerably greater distances will also be accessible to observation. The reason is simple. If a galaxy is removed to twice its present distance, its total light will be diminished four times, and so also will the area of its image, so that the surface brightness will be unchanged. The argument ceases to be valid when the distance of the galaxy becomes so great that it can no longer be treated as an extended object. The meaning to be attached to this is that the major proportion of the light is included within the spectrograph slit. This feature also sets a limit to the useful slit width, since, once the whole nucleus is included in the slit, the light gain to be secured from opening it wider is slight.

Sources of data on the translatory radial velocities of galaxies are to be found, for the brighter specimens, in the de Vaucouleurs catalogue. For the northern galaxies the principal large source of information is the compilation by Sandage of the observations made over many years by Hubble, Humason and Mayall. Other notable contributions have been made by Thornton Page and Minkowski, while the Burbidges and their colleagues have undertaken extensive researches on the internal motions in galaxies. The field is relatively unexplored in the south. The principal contributions have been made by de Vaucouleurs and by Shobbrook at Canberra, and by Evans and his colleagues using the Radcliffe reflector at Pretoria, South Africa.

7.10. The Electronic Camera

An important new development which may perhaps alleviate the chronic shortage of light afflicting the nebular spectroscopist and other types of research into very faint objects, is the introduction of the electronic camera devised in France by Lallemand and Duchesne. The normal photographic process consists in the formation of an image on an emulsion, followed by chemical development. It is found that

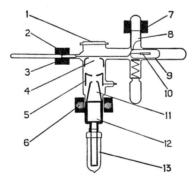

Figure VII.4: The electronic camera. The highly evacuated glass envelope receives light through the window, (1). The magnetic coil, (2), with iron core, (3), pulls the photo-cathode into the operating position, (4). The electrodes of the electron optical system are (5) and (11). The dark slide and plate-changer are operated by the magnetic coils, (6). The photocathode, (10), is initially in the ampoule, (9), which is broken by the hammer, (8), manipulated by the coil, (7), and then drawn into the operating position. (12) is the plate magazine, and (13) a Dewar flask with liquid air. (After Lallemand, Duchesne and Walker, *P.A.S.P.* **72**, 270, 1960, by permission of the authors and editors.)

approximately 100 quanta are needed to produce one developed grain on the emulsion. Normal emulsions also show non-linearity of response, and possess a threshold such that stimuli below this produce no response. These topics have been mentioned in connection with photographic photometry in Chapter II. The principle of the electronic camera is that the light image is formed, not directly on a photographic plate, but on a light-sensitive semiconducting layer coated on the inside of a small sealed, evacuated glass vessel. The incident quanta produce photoelectrons which are emitted from this surface, and are accelerated and focused within the vacuum by the application of electrostatic fields and the use of electromagnetic lenses. These cause the visual image to be reproduced as a pattern of electrons on a photographic plate of the type known as a nuclear emulsion which is employed in cosmic ray studies. These have the property of producing a developable grain for each incoming particle and they are therefore linear in their response. In spite of some losses incurred in the process of stimulation of the photosensitive layer, it is in principle possible to effect an overall gain in terms of grains per incident photon of nearly one hundred times. This would correspond to an effective increase in aperture of ten times. The instrument has been employed on the 120-inch telescope at Lick Observatory, California and at the Haute Provence Observatory in France. At the former an important result was the demonstration from spectral observations of the existence of a rapidly-rotating very small central region in the middle of the nucleus of M 31, which thus parallels the discoveries of high-speed rotation in the inner nucleus of our own Galaxy made by the radio astronomers. The electronic camera is thus an instrument of enormous promise, but it must be recognised that its operation poses the most formidable problems of technique and the installation of equipment for the production of high vacuum more reminiscent of a physics laboratory than an observatory, and of a standard of cleanliness usually only found in an operating theatre. The sensitive surface is specially prepared for each night's exposure, and although each equipment now permits a total of some half dozen different exposures, usually far more than enough for the extremely difficult objects which are observed, nevertheless the demands on specialised manpower and resources are so severe that the technique is unlikely to be widely adopted in the immediate future. Work on development of somewhat similar image intensification equipment is being carried on elsewhere, for example by McGee in London, and there seems little doubt that eventually these methods will become part of the ordinary armoury of the astronomer.*

This completes a preliminary sketch of the methods of observation of galaxies. In short we may assume that for the nearer galaxies an analysis of stellar content, distribution of brightness and translatory and rotational velocities may be available. For the more remote ones, values of integrated magnitude and colour and translatory radial velocity may be determinable. The data will be coupled with information concerning the distribution of galaxies on the sky, and in particular their aggregation into clusters and groups, and with the statistics of their allocation into different nebular types.

---

* Image tubes have now come into use at several observatories, e.g. at Kitt Peak, Arizona, where C. R. Lynds is obtaining spectra of faint galaxies in quite short exposure times, limited only by the general light of the night sky. Because of greater convenience of operation they will probably supersede the electronic camera.

7.11. The Distances of the Galaxies

We have already touched on various aspects of this problem in the previous chapter. Cepheids are the distance indicators and we may take their absolute magnitudes and the period luminosity law either from the discussion of proper motions or from the cases of the five Cepheids which occur in galactic clusters. Kraft obtained the relation for absolute visual magnitude at mean light $M_V = -1 \cdot 67 - 2 \cdot 54 \log P$. In a discussion of the distance scale Sandage adopts this and reviews the evidence for distances of the nearest galaxies based on Cepheids. The idea of observing Cepheids in other galaxies and using their apparent magnitudes for the determination of distances seems simple enough. It originated in the small Magellanic Cloud. It has been applied to the Large Magellanic Cloud. Apart from these the number of cases of discovery of Cepheids in external galaxies is rather small.* The examples cited by Sandage in which there is a photoelectric calibration, are: M 31, where 20 Cepheids give a modulus of 24·2 magnitudes after allowance for absorption: IC 1613, a resolved irregular system in which over many years Baade found some 60 Cepheids yielding a modulus of 24·2 magnitudes: and M 33, a large Sc system in Triangulum which also is found to have a modulus of about 24·3 magnitudes. These are practically the only systems in which studies of individual variables have led to firm values of distance moduli. Variables have also been found in large numbers in the dwarf systems in Sculptor and Fornax and it is possible that certain of the other nearby systems might yield results.

From this point outwards other criteria must be used. In his address to the Santa Barbara Symposium on External Galaxies, Sandage dealt with them in some detail. The brightest star in a Galaxy or the mean of a small number of the brightest may be used to estimate its distance on the assumption that the brightest stars in our own galaxy and in the Large Magellanic Cloud have absolute magnitudes near − 9·3. However it is sometimes difficult to be sure that the black spot on the negative of a galaxy really is a star and not a cluster or some other non-stellar object. There is also a suggestion that dwarf galaxies contain fewer or no super-supergiant stars. A galaxy must be fairly near for individual stars to be distinguishable, but Sandage finds moduli for two or three systems other than those listed above, going out to a modulus between 27 and 28. This means that the brightest stars in these galaxies have apparent magnitudes past the 18th magnitude. The normal novae, based on Arp's study of novae in the Andromeda nebula, and compared with a discussion by Schmidt-Kaler of galactic novae give a mean absolute magnitude at maximum of near − 9·0 in the blue: these are thus, potentially, useful distance indicators but not likely to give a greater range than bright stable super-supergiants. Globular clusters in external systems, though recognisable, and giving a mean integrated photographic absolute magnitude of round about − 9·2 are not good distance indicators because there is a considerable intrinsic scatter, and there are possibly real differences from one galaxy to another. Although not intrinsically much, if at all, brighter than the brightest stable stars or ordinary novae at maximum, globular clusters would have the advantage of being distributed round a galaxy in a way which makes them fairly easily recognisable for what they are, and their almost spherical distribution means that they are often seen well clear of the main part of the image of the galaxy to

* This is no longer true. See for example Miss Swope and the late Walter Baade, *A.J.*, **70**, 212, 1965, where 263 Cepheids and other variables are discovered in M 31.

which they belong. Possibly the most promising criterion is afforded by the H II regions which can be picked out on monochromatic photographs in which only one or another of the Balmer lines is recorded. Sandage estimates the linear diameter of the largest H II regions in a galaxy to be about 245 parsecs on the basis of studies in M 33 and the Large Magellanic Cloud. Sérsic prepared a histogram of the diameters of H II regions in M 33 where he found a few large ones and a large number less than about 20 parsecs in diameter. Measures of H II regions in other galaxies permit distance moduli up to almost 31 magnitudes to be estimated. While all these methods show a satisfactory accordance a knowledge of the history of the subject should correct any tendency to over-confidence for it is only a few decades ago since the evidence seemed to point quite satisfactorily to very different values of distances.

This point is best brought out from a discussion of what is certainly the most accurate method for the determination of *relative* values of large distances. This is the observed fact that there is a strong correlation between measured radial velocities of galaxies and magnitude, in the sense that the fainter the galaxy the larger the velocity of recession. For velocities of recession below, say, 5,000 km/s the situation is fairly straightforward and can be dealt with in simple terms. The average galaxy of the 12th magnitude is receding at about 1,600 km/s, while for the average galaxy of apparent integrated magnitude 13·5 the measured velocity is just about double this. For the lower end of the scale the mean line is consistent with the idea that velocity of recession is proportional to distance. This is consistent with the figures given above because doubling the distance of an otherwise identical object increases its apparent magnitude by 1·5 magnitudes. There is a considerable scatter about the mean line for two reasons: first, as we have already noted, particularly when considering the classification system of van den Bergh, there is a considerable range in integrated magnitudes of galaxies between the very large giant systems and the faint dwarf systems. This is demonstrated with perfect readiness on photographs of groups of nebulae where one cannot believe other than that they are relatively close to each other in space, but yet some are large and bright and others small and faint. Further, in addition to their systematic velocities of recession the galaxies all have individual or peculiar components of motion. The errors of determination of velocity can also be considerable—a formal probable error of between 50 and 100 km/s for a single determination must usually be regarded as acceptable, and these errors inflate the scatter produced by the real range of peculiar motions. If we accept the existence of a relation between velocity of recession and distance as an empirical fact, we shall be able to use it for the estimation of distance of any system whose velocity we know provided that this velocity exceeds the range due to peculiar motions and provided we can calibrate the relation from independent determinations of distance of systems having large velocities. In practice it would be unwise to attempt to estimate relative distances from velocities of recession much less than 500 km/s to 1,000 km/s, but beyond this they can be regarded as good. The determination of distance moduli and integrated absolute magnitudes for the nearest systems and some way beyond is thus of the greatest importance for the calibration of the relatively easily established velocity-magnitude relation as a velocity-distance relation. At the present time the best established value for the relation between velocity and distance (the Hubble constant) is 100 km/sec/megaparsec, so that, on the basis of the remark made above the distance of the average galaxy of the 12th apparent magnitude is about 16 megaparsecs. For this the modulus is 31 magnitudes and the integrated absolute magnitudes average out at about − 19, which is thought to be approximately correct. From the literature one might easily form the impression that the last word had been said on the velocity-distance relation but one should be warned by the fact that only a decade or two ago astronomers found themselves quite satisfied with a value of the Hubble constant more than five times as large as the present one. The change is partly due to the revision of the period-luminosity law for Cepheids, and partly to other factors, such as the realisation that what are now known to be H II regions in galaxies were in the past taken for single stars.

In constructing a velocity-magnitude relation out of raw data we have to apply a number of corrections. A correction is applied to remove the effect of the rotation of the Sun round the galactic centre. This is based on a circular velocity as judged by the nearest galaxies of about 300 km/s (rather higher than the value used in galactic studies, but the precise figure is not very important). The formula giving the correction to integrated magnitude for absorption of light in passage through our own Galaxy has already been noted: low latitudes are best avoided because of additional local absorption irregularities.

In his discussions of extragalactic radial velocities in 1956 Sandage had a fair density of measures up to 10,000 km/s for galaxies at about the 16th magnitude, and thereafter a few special points reaching a maximum of about 60,000 km/s, or about one-fifth of the velocity of light. Since that time efforts have been made to push up the limiting value, and at the present time the largest measured red-shift appears to be one due to Minkowski which has a value of 0·46 of the velocity of light.* When large shifts of this kind are considered the photometric aspects of the problem have to be re-examined with the utmost care. In ordinary stellar spectroscopy the effect of a Doppler shift is to move the whole spectrum by a very small amount. For large velocities, the spectrum is shifted bodily through a considerable displacement, and its colour characteristics totally changed. For example, in the case of Minkowski's object, the ultraviolet line at 3,727Å is transported right into the green at 5,448Å, and the ordinary visual continuous spectrum, if it were observable, would be found in the near infra-red. Even for velocities which are only a fraction of this extreme example, the changes of colour and of magnitude are considerable, and discussions of observations which neglected this effect would be quite misleading. Measures of radial velocity and of magnitude which are combined in the construction of a velocity distance relation are both subjected to corrections which are much more severe for the latter. If the intrinsic colours of nebulae at all distances are the same for nebulae of the same structural type, the apparent colours which will be observed for different velocities of recession can be computed. It seems now certain that there is no systematic change in intrinsic colour with distance. At one time the opposite opinion was held. It was thought by Stebbins and Whitford that there was a progressive change in intrinsic colour of elliptical nebulae at greater and greater distances. Since progressively more remote nebulae are observed in the light of a more and more remote past, this was for a time held to be evidence of an evolutionary change in intrinsic colour of the elliptical nebulae. Nowadays the progressive change in measured colour of nebulae of a given type with increasing Doppler shift is used as a

* Recent developments mentioned in the final section of this chapter have now overtaken this limit.

I

means of making photoelectric determinations of velocity. This has been done, particularly by Baum, using very long integration times for the observation of very faint objects, and red-shifts of a number of very remote galaxies have been found in this way.

In an earlier chapter it was noted that supernovae occurring in galaxies had a magnitude at maximum light about the same as the integrated magnitude of an average galaxy. They are thus visible at all distances at which galaxies themselves can be detected visually: in any individual galaxy they are rare, but, in the enormous numbers of galaxies accessible to observation in the largest telescopes, there can hardly be a moment at which some one of them does not include a supernova. To keep a watch on all is impossible, but supernovae are discovered sporadically, and then provide both an indication of the distance of the galaxy in which they occur, and a little more information on the maximum brightness attained in these outbursts.

7.12. The Expanding Universe

It is not necessary to embark on too lengthy a discussion of the strange observational fact that all the galaxies appear to be receding from us. The phenomenon has been widely discussed often in a glare of publicity, by numerous eminent astronomers. Some scientists at one time found the unvarnished observations so repugnant to good sense that they tried to interpret them as other than physical velocities.* It is now clear that the fact that all the galaxies are receding from our own does not endow our particular space vehicle with any special importance. In a general expansion every observer, to no matter which galaxy he is attached, will see all the others receding from him, and a statistically linear relation between radial velocity and distance will result. Attempts to account for this theoretically have been numerous: Einstein's General Theory of Relativity produces equations governing the behaviour of point masses in a universe such that a particular range of solutions describes just such an expansion. Milne produced a theory of kinematical relativity in which the expansion found a ready kinematic explanation, namely that any system of moving points confined originally to a small volume will in time segregate themselves with the fastest moving objects farthest away. It is not clear what physical mechanism for the origin of the original configuration was envisaged. Lemaître, the Belgian cosmologist has produced a theory of an exploding primaeval atom (sometimes referred to as the "big bang theory") in which an original massive particle exploded so that we now see the relics of this cataclysm. An important feature of this type of theory is that the mathematical parameter known as the curvature of space changes as the matter expands, so that the original "atom" not only contained all matter, but so to speak wrapped space time around itself. The so-called Steady State Theory advocated by the school of Hoyle, Bondi and Gold maintains that the grand aspect of the universe remains unchanged not only with change of the observer's position but is also unchanging with time.† The demonstration of the erroneous nature of the Stebbins-Whitford effect removes one observational obstacle to the steady-state theory.

---

* This possibility cannot be entirely ruled out: a discussion by Westervelt for example predicts a red-shift arising from the gravitational disturbance due to a light pulse emitted from a remote object. If correct, this would make red-shift measurement a precise rather than a statistical means of determining large distances.

† Most of the supporters of this theory now seem to have abandoned it, but it occupied a major portion of the energies of many astronomers for years.

Since the matter contained in the universe is being spread out with the expansive motions this involves creation of new matter in space, though not in such densities as are likely to be observable in the foreseeable future. Bondi has made an interesting point in this connection involving the explanation of what is known as Olbers' paradox. This may be put in the following form: if we imagine space to be infinite and filled with galaxies having, for the sake of argument, the same uniform surface temperature all over each, these galaxies being scattered about at random, then any line of sight must, sooner or later intersect a galaxy, and along that line we shall see a patch of surface brightness which, as we know, is independent of its distance. Why then, in the conditions assumed do we not see a surface having the average surface temperature of a galaxy wherever we look in the night sky? Why then is the whole night sky not dark as it is, but covered with a uniform brightness due to innumerable galaxies at all kinds of distances? Bondi puts his finger on the particular feature that makes this so, as the fact that the universe is expanding so that the remoter objects are less bright because their spectra are progressively shifted to the red with increasing distance. In other words, he claims that we can have an immediate and elementary appreciation of the consequences of the expansion of the universe.

All theoreticians working in this field have faced the baffling question as to what is to happen if the linear velocity distance law continues to hold until the velocity approaches that of light. Recent work with the 200-inch telescope already mentioned has pushed the velocity measures out to almost half the velocity of light, and, after numerous corrections have been applied, it appears as if the relation between apparent integrated bolometric magnitude of a galaxy and the red shift still has the form $m_{bol} = \text{const.} + 5 \log z$ where z is the measured red-shift, $d\lambda/\lambda_0$, produced by the velocity. Now, for velocities of the order of 100,000 km/s the different cosmological theories predict that the relation between $\log z$ and bolometric magnitude should show a slight curvature. The curves for the three cases of the steady-state cosmology, the Euclidean case, and the case of an exploding universe with no significant gravitational deceleration all show a curvature such that the observed velocity should be less than the value given by a straight line: the case of an expanding universe which will later collapse again gives a straight line or a line with a slight upward curve. So far as evidence now goes the latter appears to represent the observations best. However, with observational techniques so subtle, and arguments so close reasoned, there is still room for debate. On the observational side Holmberg has claimed that the red-shift results for clusters of nebulae show systematic effects with respect to nebular type and apparent magnitude, and although the observers have been inclined to contest this rather hotly, it will not do to be too dogmatic. It has also been remarked that the present values for the Hubble constant and for the curvature of the relation give an age for the universe from the time when all the matter in it was very concentrated which is rather small. The original calculation on this point was made with a higher value of the Hubble constant than is now thought to be true, and possibly a higher value for the curvature of the velocity distance relation, but even so, with modified values the figure seems to be in the range of 10^{10} years, or not really beyond the figures used for ages of the oldest clusters. When much higher values of the Hubble constant were fashionable, the contradiction was even more marked, and this was probably one of the mainsprings in the formulation of the steady-state theory, in terms of which the universe has either no age or an indefinitely large one.

7.13. The General Properties of Galaxies

The discussion above on the implications of the red-shifts has carried us away from the fact that the red-shift relation is for a wide range of magnitudes a most useful method for the estimation of nebular distances. With suitable corrections, not usually very uncertain for medium-distance objects we are now able to cite statistics for a number of fairly typical galaxies. In brief these are as follows:

Relative numbers; Ellipticals comprise 13 per cent of the brighter galaxies; the apparent incidence of different subtypes is about constant up to E4 and then falls off; the real incidence when projection is taken into account makes E0 ellipticals the most common with a steady reduction for more flattened systems. Lenticular galaxies form 22 per cent, and spirals of various kinds 61 per cent. The remainder are made up of irregular galaxies and peculiar galaxies of which the last named form less than 1 per cent of the whole.

Total luminosities: There is a considerable range within each type class. Some giant ellipticals exceed absolute photographic magnitude -21, but most normal ones known are near -20. Dwarf ellipticals are known down to about -14, and one must exercise considerable caution in interpreting relative numbers at different luminosities, since clearly there will be a marked selection effect working against the faint ellipticals except at very small distances. The range in spiral galaxies is about the same: the integrated absolute magnitude of the Andromeda nebula is just short of -20 and that of the Galaxy has been estimated as a little fainter. Spirals as faint as -16 have been noted. Irregular galaxies of the Magellanic Cloud type (absolute magnitudes for the Large and Small Clouds have been estimated as -18 and -16) run down to about -14 and fainter irregulars down to about -13.

Dimensions: These go approximately with total luminosity and run down from a diameter of about 25 kiloparsecs for the largest systems to about 2 kiloparsecs for the smallest. The interpretation of figures is difficult since current ideas would make the Galaxy larger than the maximum quoted above, but a determination of dimensions made by an astronomer on the Andromeda nebula might give a lower value since the surface brightness at the solar distance is very low.

Colours: The Colours show a progression along the type sequence giving $B - V = 0·9$, with a wide scatter, for E nebulae and somewhat below $0·7$ for the later type spirals. The Magellanic type systems are bluer still with a $B - V$ colour a little less than $0·5$. For the ellipticals Baum has noted that the colour indices show a progression with absolute magnitude, being near $0·6$ for the dwarf systems (i.e. near the globular cluster values) and increasing up to $0·9$ for visual integrated absolute magnitudes brighter than about -16. A considerable amount of work has been done on the construction of theoretical models of elliptical galaxies composed of varying proportions of different kinds of star, to match the observed colour distribution found in six-colour photometry.

Spectra: Spectral types of the different forms show the kind of run to be expected from the colours. Ellipticals and early spirals are mainly late G in appearance with the H and K lines strong. Later type spirals and irregulars have earlier spectra, even running into mid-A types. However, classification among fainter systems tends to be difficult because of the low dispersions necessarily employed. There is some suggestion of broadening of lines due to internal motions, and a particular series of galaxies studied by Seyfert showed in their nuclei all the stronger lines found in planetary nebulae but broadened, corresponding to turbulent velocities in the emitting gases of some thousands of kilometres per second. The forbidden oxygen pair at λ 3,727Å occurs fairly frequently in the spectra of galaxies showing no particular visual distinctive features. As has been previously remarked, some 20 per cent of ellipticals show this (for them) surprising feature, and the proportion increases until in the irregulars it is of almost universal occurrence. The Burbidges have found hydrogen emission in a considerable number of galaxies and have used their observations of radial velocity in studies of mass distribution.

7.14. The Rotation of Galaxies

In many galaxies the nucleus is surrounded by a flat, relatively thin, disk-like structure, in general outline circular, incorporating numerous bright knots, dark lanes and often, a spiral structure. The system requires to be in rotation if it is to persist for any length of time. Viewed face-on it presents to optimum view all the details of its disk structure, but nothing can be determined concerning its rotation since this provides no radial component of motion. Times of axial rotation are all so long that detection of rotation by proper motions transverse to the line of sight is impossible. Viewed edge-on, the system becomes a streak with a central bulge and a diametral division. All rotational motions now present themselves as components of radial velocity, but detail concerning the structure of the system is now almost completely lost because of foreshortening effects. The galaxies most profitable for study are those seen at a high inclination (the official technical meaning of this word is the angle between the equatorial plane of the galaxy and the plane of the sky). Now the disk appears as a very elongated ellipse and some of the detail in the plane of the disk can be glimpsed. The major axis of this long ellipse marks the intersection of the equatorial plane with the plane of the sky through the galaxy's nucleus. One half of this axis will appear to be receding because of the rotation of the nebula, and the other half approaching. Knots on this line which lie in the disk of the galaxy will yield measured radial velocities which are compounded of the systematic motion of the galaxy (exemplified by the radial velocity of its nucleus) together with a quantity representing the orbital speed of rotation. Since the inclination of the system is high and since the line of sight is perpendicular to the long axis of the projected ellipse, the measured velocities will differ only slightly from the true ones. If V_0 is the radial velocity of the nucleus, and V_r the measured radial velocity at some point on the major axis of the projected ellipse, then the circular velocity V_c is given by

$$V_c \sin i = V_r - V_0$$

where, in the case assumed, $\sin i$ is very nearly equal to unity.

The variation of circular velocity with distance from the centre of a galaxy can be studied by taking spectra of features along the major axis already defined, and plotting them against distance from the centre. If the galaxy is relatively small and the spectrograph has a long slit, a single exposure may suffice, since the spectrum lines for a carefully oriented slit may show a tilt from one end to the other. For larger nebulae or shorter slits, a number of exposures of selected features may be required.

As usual this is all somewhat idealised: many nebulae are just sufficiently unsymmetrical to make it less than easy to specify exactly the major axes we have so lightly defined. Many will present inviting knots or other bright features which are not quite along this axis. Now the measured radial velocity must be increased by some component of transverse motion if we are to find the circular velocity. Quite a small off-axis displacement corresponds to a large linear displacement along the line of

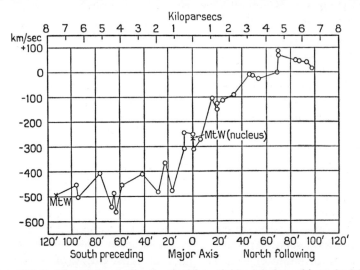

Figure VII.5: Observed rotational velocities of 32 emission objects in M 31. (After N. U. Mayall, Publications of the Observatory of Michigan, Vol. X, 1951, by permission.) Note that the angular scale remains unchanged, but the linear distance scale at the top is changed by the revision of the cosmic distance scale.

sight in the conditions of severe foreshortening which we have assumed. Difficulties of geometrical interpretation which can be severe in simple cases and almost insuperable for very asymmetrical nebulae, can present themselves. In particular, nebulae do have structure, often irregular, which brings knots and clusters to considerable distances from their equatorial planes. The observer can only locate these on the projected image, and he may run into trouble if he puts them in his model in the equatorial plane itself. Measures which are based on emission lines will in general refer to the gaseous component of the galaxy, and there is reason to believe that these structures do lie near the plane and that, in general, the gas moves approximately in circular orbits. Absorption spectra give the motions of clumps of stars, and here we have to think of the possibility that they may have motions in their galaxy far removed from circular orbits: since the hard-pressed observer usually goes for bright concentrated clusters it may usually be assumed that his observations refer to rather young luminous stars with near circular motions, but there can be no absolute guarantee of this. For one reason or another, the results usually show very considerable scatter, but a standard velocity picture which applies to the less complicated cases emerges. Near the centre, the relation between velocity and distance is roughly linear, as if the nucleus were rotating as a solid body. Some of this simplicity may be illusory, for, as we have remarked, both in the case of the Galaxy and M 31, there appears to be a very rapidly rotating inner nucleus which would produce a velocity distance curve with a sharp peak in it. This feature is so small that it is likely to be missed in any but the largest systems most favourable to its detection. The Burbidges found a somewhat analogous phenomenon in the system NGC 1097, where the emission lines showed a sharp break just at the nucleus. Apart from this complication the curve continues outwards until a point is reached at which the circular velocity is a maximum. It then falls back towards the base-line provided by the mean velocity of the system along a curve which is asymptotic to the base-line. The general picture is easy enough to interpret. The motion of the nucleus or a considerable part of it, approximates to that of a rigid body: beyond this the motion resembles that of the planets round the Sun in which the linear velocity falls off steadily with increasing distance. The way in which the circular velocity varies with distance provides a means of determining the gravitational field at each point from the acceleration inferred from the circular velocity and the radius of the orbit. From this information on the distribution of mass in the galaxy may be found, and from the value for very large orbits estimates of total mass may be made. H. W. Babcock investigated the Andromeda nebula in 1939 and, carrying the observations out to about twice the nebular dimensions shown on photographs by using small knots of emission nebulosity, he derived a rotation curve giving a maximum circular velocity near 350 km/s. His observations, and their own observations of M 33 were discussed a little while later by Wyse and Mayall, and they found it necessary to represent the distribution of mass by a number of superimposed ellipsoids, a technique of representation later followed, as we have seen, by Schmidt in his model of the Galaxy. In recent years, in addition to large nearby systems to be mentioned individually later, the major research on rotation of galaxies has been undertaken by the Burbidges and their collaborators and data on rotation have been obtained and analysed for some two or three dozen systems using a very short focus long slit spectrograph. The method is a very powerful one, for in many cases a single exposure will yield a velocity curve from the deformation of the H-alpha line, and although a single measure of one line at each point leaves a good deal of room for observational uncertainty, repetitions usually tie the curve down fairly certainly.

So far this discussion has been couched in general terms, for although many of the older observations remain perfectly valid, changes in the adopted value of the distance scale and of the Hubble constant have seriously changed the deduced values of the parameters. The effect is not difficult to see: if the Hubble relation with a constant H is used to determine distance this will be taken as V_0/H megaparsecs, so that the adopted total luminosity for a given apparent magnitude will be proportional to V_0^2/H^2. If a knot remote from the centre is observed to have circular velocity V_c, the mass interior to this radius r, i.e. effectively the whole mass of the galaxy, will be taken to be proportional to $V_c^2 r$, or, regarding the angular distance and circular velocity as known observational quantities, the mass will be taken proportional to $V_c^2 V_0/H$. Thus inferred masses obtained by this method will increase as the adopted value of H decreases, and the ratio of mass to light in solar units will be proportional to H. If the distance modulus is found by other methods as in the case of nearby galaxies such as M 31 the value of H will not enter explicitly, but if the estimated distance is doubled by any argument, the luminosity will increase by four times and the linear scale will be doubled, leading to a doubling of the inferred mass and a halving of the mass to light ratio.

With the present adopted scale for the universe, masses of galaxies are in the range from about 10^{10} to 10^{11} solar masses, with higher values for giant systems and lower for dwarfs. Ratios of mass to luminosity in solar units range downwards with type from possibly as high as 100 for ellipticals to round about 2 to 4 for the later type resolved systems. The distinction is reasonable enough regarded in the light of the characteristics of populations: the mass-luminosity relation shows that a population of young individually massive bright stars radiates far more strongly per unit mass than a population of older and less massive stars. In any discussion of this kind the role of the light-weight feeble stars is to contribute mass without a proportionate contribution to luminosity.

Discussions of the rotation of galaxies also play an important part in settling an important question connected with the spiral structure of galaxies. The question is, in which direction do galaxies rotate with respect to their spiral structure? Do the spiral arms trail or lead in the rotation? Since the phraseology is sometimes a trifle obscure, we may say that we here understand by the phrase "trail in the rotation" the following situation. The galaxy is presumed to rotate carrying its spiral structure with it. If an observer fixed in space and observing the spiral arms as they pass him decides that the distance between the arms at his position is increasing as a result of the rotation, then we call this a situation in which the arms trail.

There has been much argument over this, and a powerful supporter of the theory that the arms lead in the rotation has been B. Lindblad. The problem is not an easy one to settle. In the case of the Galaxy the spirality is not particularly strongly marked, and might be upset as to its sense by a hypothesis of a general expansion which could not be disproved on the basis of existing 21-cm radiation radio observations. In an external galaxy it is often not difficult to decide which part of the galaxy is receding as the result of axial rotation and which approaching relative to the nucleus. It is more difficult to decide which edge of the long ellipse which the galaxy presents to view is the nearer. Here a well-known optical illusion is encountered: the un-critical viewer always unconsciously adopts the standpoint on looking at a picture of a galaxy that the top edge is the one remote from him: he automatically assumes that he is looking "down" on to the flat surface of the disk. It is easy to demonstrate that this is an illusion by turning the photograph the other way up: the viewer will now assume that the edge which he previously thought the more remote is now the nearer. More careful examination of nebular photographs will show that, even in many apparently closely symmetrical cases there are differences in appearance between regions on the minor axis of the projected image on opposite sides of the nucleus. These are mainly produced by differences in the apparent distribution of obscuring matter. Now, as is well known, the gas and dust layer is relatively very thin and when a nebula is seen exactly edge-on (inclination of 90°) this material is seen as a narrow dark band projected on the entire image and crossing in front of the nucleus. Here there is no difficulty about distinguishing which side of the nebula is which, since only one is seen, and the spiral structure is so foreshortened that it has disappeared. At somewhat smaller inclinations the interpretation has been open to debate. One argument says that obscuring material will only be visible if it lies in front of a bright portion of the nebula: where it lies in front of empty space it is not seen. Therefore in such a nebula if the sides are distinguishable then the nearer must be the one showing more obscuring material. There is a distinct difference in appearance between the two sides of the Andromeda nebula and by this criterion the preceding side is the nearer. The same is true of the great southern spiral NGC 253 where the north-preceding side shows much more obscuration than the other. The alternative argument by Lindblad says that the opposite effect would occur if the dark material were distributed so as to lie always on the inner curvature of bright arms. It has proved extremely difficult to find cases where the inclination is high, the spiral structure is unequivocally shown, and the sense of the inclination can be determined without ambiguity. The argument is not finally settled, but an important point made by de Vaucouleurs is that, whichever answer is correct, it appears to be always in the same one. It is certain that arms do not sometimes lead and sometimes trail, but are all of one kind, and the consensus is in favour of the latter, namely trailing arms.

7.15. The Origin of Spiral Arms

The problem of the origin of spiral arms has provoked lengthy discussions, so far without producing a generally accepted conclusion. The observational features which present the most difficulty may be briefly reviewed: spiral arms often, but not always, show a high degree of symmetry between opposite pairs, in regard to shape, degree of resolution into stars, and even the occurrence of large star clusters at roughly corresponding positions on opposite arms. Corresponding points are about as completely isolated from each other in the physical sense as it is possible to imagine. One is compelled to the feeling that the arms have followed some generally parallel course of physical evolution leaving room for a good many local accidents of development. Spiral structures occur in enormously varied environments: sometimes the arms are rich in gas, sometimes they are marked more by the stellar population: sometimes the spiral structure is embedded in a rich population in a disk, in others the arms extend out into what looks like empty space. Whatever may be the mechanism for the development of spiral arms it is one of very great generality and certainly requires no special conditions for its operation. One may also argue from the frequency of occurrence of spiral arms in different galaxies that in any individual case the spiral arms must be relatively long-lived. This has two consequences: one is, that although the arms are fairly closely marked by young stars, the underlying mechanism which produces the arms must be of much greater antiquity, and in all probability results from some aspect of the behaviour of the gas out of which these young stars have been born. The second feature is that the circular velocities in galaxies vary with distance from the centre, and it is easy enough to see that the consequent shearing motion might be expected to draw out a spiral arm into a filament wrapped round and round the galaxy in a time corresponding to only a few rotations, that is, in a time of the order of a few hundred to a thousand million years. In other words, it is extremely hard to see why differential rotation does not rapidly destroy all semblance of spiral structure.

Theoretical attempts to explain spiral structure have been made along a variety of lines. P.O. Lindblad has used a computer to calculate the subsequent history of a series of point masses originally revolving in the form of a number of concentric rings around a centre of mass, taking into account the consequences of gravitational interactions between these point masses, supposed to typify stars. Spiral structures are produced which are sometimes leading and sometimes trailing, though none are very long-lived.

Modern theories of spiral arms lay stress on the importance of interstellar magnetic fields. The optical observations date from 1949 when Hiltner and Hall independently reported results of polarisation measures on the light from stars. The effects were most marked in the light from distant stars near the galactic plane of which the colours showed most evidence of interstellar reddening. The direction of polarisation was usually parallel to the galactic plane. Theoretical studies, some already mentioned, led to the postulation of interstellar particles of a needle-like form aligned by the action of an interstellar magnetic field. A number of theoretical workers, such as Hoyle and Ireland, and L. Woltjer have invoked this postulated magnetic field as an agency capable of preserving the structure of a spiral arm against the dissipative forces of differential galactic rotation, and have demanded fields of the order of 3×10^{-5} oersteds. The verification or disproof of the existence of such fields has lain in the field of radio astronomy and has provoked much controversy. The effect sought has been the Faraday effect of the rotation of the plane of polarisation of polarised radiation in the radio astronomy domain due to passage through a medium with a certain electron density in a certain magnetic field. Just as in the optical case the polarisation effects are not characteristic of the stellar sources but of the medium through which their light has passed, so, in the radio case, the radiation from strong radio sources external to the Galaxy can show how this has been changed during the final stages of its journey. The sources concerned emit synchrotron radiation, that is, they emit by the mechanism operative when very rapidly moving electrons, with velocities close to that of light, are moving in a magnetic field, in this case the magnetic field of the remote source. Synchrotron radiation is polarised in a plane normal to the magnetic vector in the source. This plane will be rotated, if the theoretical account of the radiation source is correct, by Faraday effect within the Galaxy. The original plane of polarisation of the radiation is unknown, but the magnitude of the Faraday effect is dependent on the wavelength of the radiation, and its presence and sign can be demonstrated by measurements of the plane of polarisation of radiation from external sources at different wavelengths. Recent work reported in a summary article by Berge and Seielstad, shows that the effect has been found and for a sufficient number of external sources shows the expected dependence both on galactic longitude and latitude, and defines a magnetic direction through the Sun's position running along a spiral arm through longitudes 70° and 250°. What is unexpected is that the sense of the magnetic vector is in one direction in the material just north of the galactic plane and in the reverse direction in the material just south. Whether these results will be accepted remains to be seen. As matters stood previously the theoreticians were insistent on requiring a general interstellar magnetic field in the Galaxy in excess of 10^{-5} oersteds, while some observers, although granting the presence of such fields in limited regions such as supernova remnants, wished to set much lower limits to the interstellar field. The decision has extensive implications, since theoreticians such as Woltjer have required fields high enough to trap high speed cosmic ray particles within the limits of the galaxy, and to provide the mechanism for the emission of synchrotron radiation from our own system.

7.16. Clusters and Groups of Galaxies: The Local Group

We have several times mentioned the strong tendency for galaxies to occur in clusters or groups. Our own Galaxy appears to belong to such a group for there exists a number of galaxies, probably about twenty of them, which are rather close to our own system. The brightest members are the Large and Small Magellanic Clouds, the Andromeda Nebula (M 31 = NGC 224) and the Triangulum Galaxy M 33 (= NGC 598). The Andromeda nebula has two satellite elliptical system forming with it a small close group just as the Magellanic Clouds do with the Galaxy. One of these, M 32 = NGC 221, appears 24 minutes south of the nucleus of M 31 and is superposed on its spiral structure. The other, NGC 205, the first elliptical to be

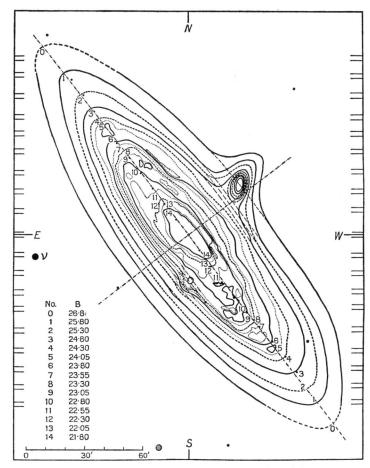

No.	B
0	26·8:
1	25·80
2	25·30
3	24·80
4	24·30
5	24·05
6	23·80
7	23·55
8	23·30
9	23·05
10	22·80
11	22·55
12	22·30
13	22·05
14	21·80

Figure VII.6: Photoelectric isophotes of M 31 in blue light (B). Declinations of scans are marked on the margins: a few bright stars are shown. The size of the scanning hole is shown by the hatched disk. The units are magnitudes/sec.^{2}, and the small closed isophotes of the nearby elliptical nebula, NGC 205 are levels 4, 6, 8, 10 and 14 in these units. (After G. de Vaucouleurs, *Ap.J.*, **128**, 465, 1958, by permission of the author and editors.)

resolved by Baade, lies about 35 minutes north-west of the nucleus of M 31. According to Holmberg both these systems are of about 9th photographic magnitude. NGC 6822 is a little fainter, and IC 1613 somewhat fainter still (m_{pg} = 10·0 according to Holmberg). Both are irregular Magellanic type systems resolved into stars, the former at a rather low galactic latitude (− 20°) and therefore likely to be rather heavily obscured. Two other systems, NGC 147 and NGC 185 are normal ellipticals and have magnitudes between 10 and 11 and another, somewhat fainter, is the Wolf-Lundmark system in Cetus. Perhaps the most remarkable objects in the Local Group are the systems known as the Sculptor and Fornax systems which are classified as dwarf ellipticals. They are each resolved into stars and are certainly more than a degree across. They have an extremely low surface brightness and no well-defined edges or structure except for a general ellipticity indicated by star counts which give, according to Shapley for the Sculptor system nearly 3,000 stars down to the 19th magnitude in the central square degree. Four more dwarf ellipticals, two in Leo and one each in Ursa Minor and Draco have been found on the Palomar Sky Survey by Harrington and A. G. Wilson. Variable stars of various kinds have been detected in NGC 6822, IC 1613 and in large numbers in the Sculptor and Fornax systems. The term "Local Group" is not very precisely defined, and membership, often judged on the smallness of the measured radial velocities, is somewhat uncertain. Further members may include the three spirals IC 10, IC 342, and NGC 6946 all with small velocities, two irregular systems in Leo and Sextans and possibly even the very resolved extensive system of about the ninth magnitude, NGC 300. The resolved low-velocity system IC 5152 is another candidate for membership.

It will be noticed that the list of certain members of the Local Group contains only three spirals (the Galaxy, M 31 and M 33), 5 ellipticals, 6 dwarf ellipticals and 4 irregular systems. The numbers are small, but it should not surprise us that there are more of the intrinsically faint systems found than are detected in more remote groups. As A. G. Wilson puts it, probably two-thirds of the population of the local group is composed of elliptical galaxies and two-thirds of these are dwarf specimens. It sounds a little Irish, but it is worth noting that of the five "normal" ellipticals, three are classified as "peculiar".

For the four brightest members of the Local Group de Vaucouleurs has given a compilation of data as follows:

	LMC	SMC	M 31	M 33
(i)	6°·25	2°·6	71′	24′·2
(ii)	10°·6	4°·6	185′	56′·3
(iii)	0·705	0·84	0·92	0·94
i		27°	65°	77°	55°
m_T	0·63	2·79	4·36	6·27
$(B-V)_T$	0·55	0·50	0·91	0·55
$m - M$	18·8	18·7	24·3	24·2
M_T	− 18·2	− 15·9	− 19·9	− 17·9
log M	10·1	9·4	11·57	10·23
M/L	5·5	7 ±	25	7·4
HI/M	0·08	0·2 ±	0·012	0·06

The photometric data are all based on photoelectric measures. Line (i) gives the length of the major axis of the isophote including half the light of the system and represents a dimension somewhat less than would be obtained on a photographic of moderate exposure. Line (ii) is the same dimension out to a surface brightness corresponding to a star of the 25th magnitude per square second of arc, and line

(iii) is the proportion of total light contained within this isophote. Here we approach the extreme dimensions of the systems. The inclination (as defined above—other usages are found elsewhere) is the quantity i. m_T is total apparent photographic magnitude (Johnson's B) and B-V the total colour. $m - M$ is the apparent distance modulus and M_T the total absolute magnitude. log **M** gives mass in solar units and **M/L** the mass to light ratio in solar units. HI/**M** is the proportion of the mass represented by neutral hydrogen found from radio investigations.

Little further needs to be said concerning these systems unless we wish to enter into great detail. The Large Magellanic Cloud shows a bar structure marked by stars and gaseous material running roughly from south-east to north-west, and about three degrees in length. Hydrogen emission regions are scattered about all over the field, but the most conspicuous and strongest of these is the 30 Doradus nebula which lies just to the north of the eastern end of the bar. The next most conspicuous associations and gaseous structures lie about 3 degrees north of the centre of the bar. Although at first sight the Large Cloud only exhibits a structure capable of description in spiral terms by a fairly remote extrapolation from the observations, nevertheless de Vaucouleurs has done so and has produced a good deal of evidence to support his case. Superposed direct photographs taken with a short focus camera show structures more reminiscent of the spiral, and reveal what appears to be a connection with the Small Cloud. De Vaucouleurs has also analysed the motions of gaseous objects in the Large Cloud and has interpreted them in the sense of a rotation about a line through the centre of the bar in an almost east-west direction. Support for this has been given not only by an analysis of star velocities by Thackeray, but also by radio observations by Hindman, McGee and others, reported by Kerr, which gave a rotation for the Large Cloud about a centre roughly coinciding with the one found by de Vaucouleurs and Thackeray. The newest radio observations show a hydrogen envelope embracing both Clouds. The spiral nature of the Large Cloud thus seems clear and demonstrates that in systems seen from particular aspects, spiral structure may be there even though the special circumstances of projection make it hard to distinguish. Other examples of concealed spiral structure provided by fairly bright galaxies are the cases of NGC 55 and NGC 2188. In both these cases the structure is rather highly resolved and seen nearly edge-on, and in all probability one arm is brighter than its opposite number, so that the total effect is of a bar structure with a rather curious variation of brightness along it.

The Small Cloud is also rotating, and the rather imprecise mass estimates come from observations of this. Among the very bright galaxies the two Magellanic Clouds are at present attracting the most attention, for at a distance of only ten per cent of that of the Andromeda nebula, corresponding detail becomes observable with a far smaller telescope in the former case. The general area of effort may be described as an attack on the general problems of the population structure of the two Clouds, leading to a comparison between the Clouds and with the Galaxy. This covers a wide variety of researches, ranging from the basic observational problems of the determination of exact magnitudes and colours, the establishment of the period luminosity law for Cepheids and RR Lyrae stars, populations of clusters—indeed the whole gamut of problems already tackled for the Galaxy, to theoretical questions concerning the origin, chemical content, stability, and so forth, of our two nearest neighbour galaxies.

7.17. The Local Supergalaxy

In the whole sky there are only five galaxies brighter than the 6th photographic magnitude: the only one of them not mentioned so far is NGC 5128 which will be dealt with in the discussion of radio sources. Between the 7th and 8th total magnitude there are 7 systems, all but one southern objects: of the 11 galaxies in the next magnitude interval, the majority are northern sky objects. There are about 60 galaxies down to the 10th magnitude. The distribution of the relatively bright or near galaxies is far from uniform: most of the members of the Local Group are south of the galactic equator, and of those that are not, several are quite close to it. In the north there is an immense group of moderately faint galaxies running across the sky in a band from Ursa Major, through Canes Venatici and into Coma and Virgo. On the charts of the Skalnaté Pleso Sky Atlas where the brighter galaxies are marked in red the red ellipses marking the galaxies form a great band across the charts. In fact the distribution is reckoned as belonging to a number of clusters since the measured radial velocities fall into groups near particular mean values. Thus, for example, the Ursa Major Cloud has a mean recession velocity of 1,040 km/s, the Virgo cluster a velocity of 1,222 km/s, and the Coma cluster the completely different value of 6,645 km/s. On plates taken with the 48-inch Schmidt the membership of the last named cluster is estimated by Zwicky at nearly 11,000 galaxies. In the south, nothing at all comparable exists, but there is a group of rather bright galaxies (including for example NGC 55, 253, and 300) and groupings of bright galaxies in Eridanus and Fornax, and extending down towards the position of the Large Magellanic Cloud. The term "Local Supergalaxy" was coined by Shapley to indicate that the nearer galaxies, including the Local Group, formed part of a larger aggregate, and de Vaucouleurs has discussed this in more detail and concluded that the latter is an outlying part of the Virgo Cluster system. The supergalaxy is thought to be a roughly ellipsoidal system with minor axis in the direction $l^{II} = 47°$, $b^{II} = +6°$ (i.e. $\alpha = 19^h$, $\delta +15°$). De Vaucouleurs has represented the observed radial velocities in terms of a rotation of the whole supergalactic system about the centre of the Virgo cluster, coupled with a general expansion.

7.18. Clusters of Galaxies in General

With the work of Abell the tendency to clustering of galaxies has been well-established as a general observational phenomenon, and he has further claimed that a tendency for clusters to be aggregated in second-order systems can be detected. That many clusters existed was well recognised a long time ago, and, for example, much of the work on red-shifts has been done, both spectroscopically and photoelectrically, by observations of the mean value for objects in clusters. The particular point made by Abell is that in all probability every galaxy belongs to some kind of cluster. Statistical investigations aimed at permitting the real distribution of galaxies in clusters to be delineated have been undertaken by Elizabeth Scott and Neyman, and this bears upon questions of the origin and permanence of clusters of galaxies. Not surprisingly a good deal of disagreement has shown up, connected with the problems of definition and identification of clusters. If there are many clusters all at different distances and overlapping on the sky, how is a cluster to be defined, and to which cluster ought a given galaxy to be assigned? This affects such questions as the existence of higher-order clusters, where Zwicky does not concur with Abell, and on membership of clusters, where, for example, in the Coma cluster, the membership figure given by Zwicky is much higher than that agreed to by others. Only by rather recondite statistical methods are we likely to be able to disentangle the effects of accidental aggregates from those of real clustering when such vast numbers of entities as individual very faint galaxies are considered.

With brighter galaxies the problems are not so difficult, for here one has to deal with relatively small numbers of objects well separated from other similar ones and standing well out from the background of the general run of faint objects. Considerable numbers of small groups, some showing evidence of gravitational interaction are known, and when radial velocities are available these groups can be analysed so as to yield opinions on the masses of the components and the stability of the group by means of a proposition known as the virial theorem. To express the matter in very crude terms, this theorem can be used to answer the question: "Given the spacing and relative velocities of a number of galaxies forming a group, is there enough mass in all the members to hold the group together, or is it dispersing?" A very general form of the theorem has been given by Chandrasekhar: Limber has given a good exposition of the subject and notes that one form of the theorem is that for stability of a cluster of galaxies we must have

$$2T + E = 0$$

where T and E are the total kinetic and potential energies of the system, and the time-average of the quantities is understood. The equation is basically a tensor equation and for a cluster of galaxies the axis along which the corresponding component is to be made zero can be chosen as the line of sight, so that the observed radial velocities can be introduced into the formulae directly. Computation of the potential energy term involves a good many assumptions connected with passing from the projected dimensions to the real ones. Various authors adopt different techniques, but basically it can be said that, if a cluster contains some three or four galaxies, if their individual radial velocities, types, and if possible, magnitudes, are known, then a fair shot can be made at applying the virial theorem. It seems odd that so many uncertainties can be tolerated, but in a great many cases, no matter what the assumptions may be, the clusters of this sort are found to be unstable by a very large margin. This point seems first to have been made in connection with four galaxies called the M 81 group by Ambartsumian, who found a situation of instability. A considerable number of other cases has been discussed by the Burbidges. Instability has been found in most cases, or rather, the mass of the galaxies and of any intergalactic matter which might be present would have to be made altogether larger than is now thought reasonable to ensure stability. The lines of approach are clear enough: in a few cases rotation studies have given masses for individual galaxies in groups; sample values for mass-to-light ratios are available for other similar galaxies; classification into giants or dwarfs on van den Bergh's system can be attempted; the mean radial velocity gives distance modulus; the measured magnitudes lead to absolute magnitudes. Thus the data for a general order of magnitude calculation are available, and instability is usually deduced by a factor of between one and two orders of magnitude. Thus the investigators in this field are breaking into new ground concerning the life-history of groups and clusters of galaxies, and facing new problems. One of these is that if these groups are all breaking up, how has the supply been renewed? The answer is not known, though some workers, such as Lemaître contend that there is a two-way exchange from field galaxies into groups and out of groups into the general field. Related to this topic is the discovery especially by Zwicky and by Vorontsov-Velyaminov of numerous cases, but forming a small proportion of the whole, of pairs or groups of galaxies connected by bridges, possibly of gaseous material, which sometimes span dimensions of space equal to several galaxy diameters. At present the whole topic of the dynamics of such bridges seems completely open.

7.19. Galaxies as Radio Sources

Within our own Galaxy are radio sources of various kinds: the line emission of neutral hydrogen; the synchrotron radiation associated with magnetic fields and thermal radiation. It is not surprising therefore that normal galaxies should be sources of radio waves, though there is still dispute concerning some of the mechanisms involved. However, just as our own Galaxy is a source, so are others. Some galaxies, such as the Magellanic Clouds and the Andromeda system have been studied in great detail, and it has been possible to demonstrate rotation and to determine total masses and the proportion of mass which is gaseous. Results for some of the brighter galaxies have been included in the table above. Data for some hundreds of galaxies are now available, and workers in this field have defined a radio index, analogous to a colour index, in which the radio emission at 158 Mc/s is used to define a radio magnitude and compared with the photographic magnitude. It is found that the spiral systems are the strongest radio emitters compared with their light intensities (radio index near 1·0) while systems like the Magellanic Clouds and NGC 55 are weaker, with an index near 3·0. Much of the data on early type galaxies is still in the form of limiting values. Normal elliptical galaxies and S0 systems are such weak emitters that in general the values of index given for them are lower limits. Total emission from spirals varies with size and inclination. In general each individual spiral shows an internal structure in the radio source. The distribution on the sky is composed of two parts: a disk component which is relatively concentrated, surrounded by an enormous halo of dimensions of the same order of size as the greatest extent reached in optical photometric studies. For example, M 31 which has been intensively studied, produces 90 per cent of the total intensity at 158 Mc/s from a halo measuring $10° \times 7°$ to the 1 per cent contour line, which is of elliptical form centred on the optical galaxy. Magellanic type systems do not have these enormous powerful halos.

Known external galaxies and known sources such as supernova remnants within the Galaxy account for a considerable number of the known radio sources. These are catalogued in various ways: the I.A.U. designations are of the form 04 N5A, by which would be understood in an obvious code, a position at 04 hours R.A., in the Northern Hemisphere, at a declination of 50-60 degrees, the source being the first discovered in this sky area. Alternatively one has detailed catalogues such as the revised 3 C catalogue of sources which contains some three or four hundred sources in a declination range going from the north pole to just south of the equator. An important field of research is the optical identification of radio sources and, at one time, when the resolution of radio equipment was less than it is now, this used to proceed along the lines of taking a long-exposure optical photograph of the area where the radio source had been found, and picking out the oddest looking object which appeared on the plate. This kind of technique was mainly motivated by the fact that the radio telescope could not distinguish between one object and another in quite a large visual field, and neither the optical nor the radio astronomers had any idea what they were looking for. The situation has now vastly improved: a number of galactic sources has now been identified: for example, within the Galaxy 00 N6A is the supernova remnant of the phenomenon of 1572: 05 N2A is the Crab Nebula supernova remnant. The source 05 S0A is the Orion nebula and 18 S1A is M17, the Omega nebula. A fairly large number of bright sources have been identified with normal galaxies, as has already been explained, and the Local Supergalaxy and clusters of galaxies are detectable. However, in addition to these normal galaxies are a number of cases where it is clear that the radio emission is enormously greater than would be expected from the visual evidence. For example the source 19 N4A is the second strongest in the whole sky, and is one or two orders of magnitude more

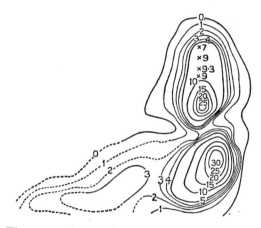

Figure VII.7: The extent of the Centaurus A radio source (NGC 5128), at 31 cm (960 MHz). The central source has been subtracted to show the pair of sources above and below often found in these systems. The extent of the diagram from top to bottom is 10°, some hundred times the dimensions on a photograph. (After J. G. Bolton and B. G. Clark, *P.A.S.P.*, **72**, 33, 1960, by permission.)

intense than the Andromeda source depending on the wavelength in which this is measured. There is no bright galaxy in this position, but an identification was eventually made with an extremely faint object of the 15th photographic magnitude which was found by Minkowski to have an extraordinary spectrum showing numerous emission lines with a mean velocity just short of 17,000 km/s. The structure appears to consist of two galaxies in collision, although the mechanism of emission is not clear. The same mechanism was invoked in other cases: for example, the strong radio source in Centaurus has been identified with the galaxy NGC 5128, a system of quite extraordinary form, apparently consisting of a more or less normal giant elliptical galaxy crossed by a band of dark absorption. The interpretation was made in terms of a collision between an elliptical galaxy and some later-type system containing a large amount of absorbing matter, but doubt was cast on this by the velocity observations of Evans and Harding, later confirmed by the Burbidges, which showed that there was no serious difference between the radial velocities of the two components of the system. More detailed studies of the radio source have shown that it extends almost in a north-south direction for some 8 degrees with very elongated isophotes. The optical shape is much less elongated and its major axis is about 20 degrees tilted with respect to the radio pattern major axis. This source when examined with high radio resolution shows a feature which is common, namely that the inner structure shows duplicity with the most intense radiation coming from two regions roughly symmetrically disposed about the centre. The peculiar elliptical galaxy NGC 4486 which has a bright "jet" of material, the light of which is polarised, protruding from its centre for some 1,500 parsecs, coincides with the Virgo A source 12 N1A. Both these systems are of the genre of giant ellipticals with something odd about them: but there is no regularity in this: the Fornax A radio source 03 S3A is identified with the galaxy NGC 1316 which looks like an elliptical with the very first beginnings of a pair of dust arms. The source is a strong one, but the galaxy finds a place among the normal S0. The theory of synchrotron radiation put forward by Shklovsky and Ginzburg is the present favourite one to account for these strong radio sources but nobody knows for certain what the mechanism is. Many of the possibilities were rehearsed by Ambartsumian in his invited address to the Berkeley meeting of the I.A.U., but many of the most attractive ideas do not fit the observed facts. In other cases there has been an appeal to a concatenation of supernova outbursts. Considerable interest has been aroused by two recent developments: one is the discovery by Sandage and Lynds that the galaxy M 82, an irregular system, which is a radio source having the same type of slow variation of flux density with frequency which characterises 05 N2A, the Crab Nebula source, must have been the scene of an immense explosion some one and a half million years ago. This is thought to have involved a total mass of material which might be as great as five or six million solar masses. The exact significance of this discovery remains to be evaluated, but it is evidently the kind of phenomenon which the theoreticians have been looking for, even though a proper understanding of it may take a long time. The phenomenon has certain parallels with the discovery that five of the sources in the C 3 catalogue are very remote objects which are certainly not typical galaxies, for they look just like stars. A few spectra have been obtained which show unexpected emission lines and very large red-shifts, corresponding in the case of source 3C 295 to a velocity of nearly half that of light, have been found. The problem is, if these are not galaxies, where do their enormous energies come from? Speculations by Hoyle and Fowler follow the line of postulating a condensation not of normal stellar mass, but something of the order of some millions of solar masses. The energy required might then be found from a dramatic collapse of one of these structures. If this line of argument is correct, then similar explosive situations might be invoked to provide the radio energy even from galaxies which are exceptional sources. The problem presented by these new observations brings us into a region which is so far completely speculative.

It had been realised for some time that there existed in the universe a great many radio sources whose radio efficiency was so great as to outstrip by far the emission of any galaxy in the visual region. It therefore followed that observations of strengths and numbers of weak radio sources provided a means of reaching much farther out into space than is at present provided by optical methods. It does not particularly matter what the nature of these sources may be, as long as they are scattered throughout the depths of space. Just as in the case of visual stars, in any star field the remote giants outnumber the weaker nearby sources, so in the radio case, the number of relatively nearby sources which occur among the weaker ones must be a vanishingly small proportion of the whole. There is some debate as to what constitutes a source in this sense, for a certain number of extended sources, due either to objects within the galaxy or to clusters of galaxies, do occur. Even so, if the universe were static and Euclidean and the observational equipment perfect, the number N of sources with flux density greater than S would be given by the relation

$$\log N = \text{constant} - 1 \cdot 5 \log S$$

Statistics of counts of sources of given strength might therefore be expected to yield information about the large-scale structure of the universe by the determination of the observed relation between N and S. The results involve much argument and are not capable of indicating which world model is correct, but according to M. Ryle, they do indicate that the steady-state model does not fit the observations. By way of riposte to this, Hoyle and Narliker have proposed something of a modification of the steady-state theory in which the so-called perfect cosmological principle remains true on the grandest of scales, but that locally there is a large-scale deviation from perfect uniformity. Whether this hypothesis, which suggests that the true steady-state universe only begins to apply just beyond the distance to which the observations have penetrated, will be found intellectually convincing remains to be seen. What is certain is that there are still vast fields of astronomy where the liveliest of debates can still be carried on.

7.20. Quasi-Stellar Radio Sources

Since the main part of this chapter was drafted, revolutionary developments have taken place in the study of extragalactic radio sources. These have been so rapid that any summary is likely to be rendered obsolete before it can be printed. Nevertheless a brief exposition of the leading facts must be attempted.

The most important first step was the introduction of much improved accuracy in the determination of the coordinates of radio sources, notably at the Owens Valley Radio Observatory where two 90-foot steerable paraboloidal antennae can be used at various separations as an interferometer. Accuracies of the order of 10 seconds of arc in both coordinates are now attainable. Matthews and Sandage were able to identify three radio sources each having radio diameters of less than 30 seconds of arc, namely 3C 48, 3C 196 and 3C 286, with objects of stellar appearance except for faint wisps of nebulosity. The photometric data in the optical range are remarkable. Values of V, B-V and U-B for 3C 196 are 17·79, 0·57, and − 0·43. For 3C 286 they are 17·25, 0·26, − 0·91. That is, by ordinary stellar comparisons these objects have an enormous ultraviolet excess, and probably do not radiate like black bodies. The only similar colour combinations are those of old novae. The brightest member of the trio, 3C 48 is fainter than the 16th magnitude, with a B-V colour a little greater than 0·4 and U-B near − 0·60. The extraordinary feature of this object is that its brightness varies by some four-tenths of a magnitude and that variations of some hundredths of a magnitude can occur in V and in the colours in a matter of 15 minutes. This indicates that the diameter of the source of visible light can be traversed by a light wave in about this time. These objects might have been taken to be some kind of very extraordinary star in our own galaxy but for the fact that they have very strange spectra. These have now been successfully interpreted as showing immense displacements to the red. Considerable numbers of quasars, as these objects have now been named, have now been identified. Maarten Schmidt has recently discussed five of them in which emission lines have been identified. For example, in the source 3C 9 the Lyman alpha line has been shifted from the far ultraviolet at 1,216Å to the ordinary photographic range at 3,666Å. This is the largest observed red-shift, and for it $z = (\lambda - \lambda_0)/\lambda = 2 \cdot 012$. A remark may be interpolated here that in the ordinary form of the Doppler formula used for the measurement of radial velocities which are small compared with that of light, a value of z in excess of unity would be impossible. However, using the accurate relativity formula for the case where there is no transverse motion $z = (1 + x)(1 - x^2)^{-1/2} - 1$ where $x = V_r/c$, so that this value of z can be obtained with $x = 0 \cdot 8$ approximately.

Visual absolute magnitudes have been estimated as in the neighbourhood of -25 or -26, that is some two magnitudes brighter than ordinary galaxies. Limits which can be set to angular diameters indicate that the linear dimensions of these objects must be small. A discussion by Greenstein and Schmidt in 1964 of the sources 3C 48 and 3C 273 put optical and radio radii for the former at less than 2,500 parsecs, and for the latter, less than or equal to 500 parsecs. An H II region in the centre of no more than a few parsecs in radius would have to contain some 10^5 or 10^6 solar masses of hydrogen.

The enormous energy outputs observed, possibly uncertain by several orders of magnitude, but certainly between 10^{40} and 10^{45} ergs/sec for many of the quasars, present physical problems of the utmost difficulty. These immense energy outputs correspond to the conversion into energy of large quantities of mass: for 3C 273 Greenstein and Schmidt cite a figure of 500 solar masses in a thousand years, possibly by the nuclear fusion of 10^5 solar masses of hydrogen to helium. Discussion brings up the possibilities that these objects are relatively short-lived, and that large masses of material are concentrated in very small volumes of space. A mechanism discussed in the last case is that of gravitational collapse in which the material density is so high that the gravitational forces between the various parts of the configuration override any possible countervailing pressures. This view was put forward by Hoyle and Fowler in 1963, but objection has been taken to it, and several authors have appealed to the occurrence of large numbers of supernovae as the possible energy sources.

After this manuscript was finished, a paragraph was added reporting the claim by Sandage that, in addition to quasars, a class of blue point-galaxies could be identified at enormous distances, somewhat resembling quasars, but without their radio emission. This claim now seems to have been disproved. Development in the quasar field proceeds apace, without, as yet, any real enlightenment. Interest concentrates on their light variability (3C 273 being a prime example), on their dimensions, for which smaller and smaller figures are being found, and on their spectra and velocities. It now seems common for quasars to show more than one spectrum associated with different velocities, possibly by absorption en route, but Maarten Schmidt has been quoted as saying, "If you get an impression of uncertainty about the state of knowledge of quasars, you are right. That is what the situation is." (*Time*, April 7, 1967.)

REFERENCES:

The Galaxy:

D. W. Sciama, *The Unity of the Universe*, Faber, 1959 (historical account of early models).

F. H. Seares, P. J. van Rhijn, M. C. Joyner and M. L. Richmond, *Ap.J.*, **62,** 320, 1925 (beginning of series on star counts).

Vera C. Rubin and six others, *A.J.*, **67,** 491, 1962 (kinematics and distribution of early stars).

M. Schmidt, *B.A.N.*, **13,** 15, 1956 (model based on contemporary values of parameters).

Hydrogen Surveys at 21 cm wavelength:

H. C. van de Hulst, C. A. Muller, and J. H. Oort, *B.A.N.*, **12,** 117, 1954.

C. A. Muller and G. Westerhout, *B.A.N.*, **13,** 151, 1957.

J. H. Oort, F. J. Kerr and G. Westerhout, *M.N.*, **118,** 379, 1958 (combination of Dutch and Australian observations).

R. D. Davies and D. R. W. Williams, *Nature*, **175,** 1079, 1955.

E. F. McClain, *Ap.J.*, **122,** 376, 1955.

(Last two on 3-kiloparsec arm.)

Catalogues, Charts, Photographs:

A. Bečvář, *Skalnaté Pleso Atlas* and Companion Volume, Academy of Sciences of Czechoslovakia, Prague, 1956, 1959.

A. Sandage, *The Hubble Atlas of Galaxies*, Carnegie Institute of Washington, 1961.

J. L. E. Dreyer, *Mem. R.A.S.*, **49,** Pt. I, 1888 (the NGC); **51,** 185, 1895; **59,** 105, 1908 (the two parts of the Index Catalogue).

H. Shapley and A. Ames, *Harvard Annals*, **88,** No. 2, 1932.

G. and A. de Vaucouleurs, *Reference Catalogue of Bright Galaxies*, University of Texas, 1964.

E. Hubble, *The Realm of the Nebulae*, Oxford Press, 1936 (this contains a description of Hubble's original classification scheme).

Classification (in addition to above references, see also):

W. W. Morgan, *P.A.S.P.*, **70,** 364, 1958; **71,** 394, 1959.

W. W. Morgan and N. U. Mayall, *P.A.S.P.*, **69,** 291, 1957 (spectra).

S. van den Bergh, *Pub. David Dunlap*, Vol. II, No. 6, 1960.

G. de Vaucouleurs, *Encyclopaedia of Physics*, Vol. 53, 281.

General Data Sources:

Most individual references can be found through the de Vaucouleurs' *Reference Catalogue*. Note as a general source of radial velocities.

M. L. Humason, N. U. Mayall, and A. R. Sandage, *A.J.*, **61,** 97, 1956.

Electronic Camera:

A. Lallemand, M. Duchesne and M. F. Walker, *P.A.S.P.*, **72,** 76 and 268, 1960.

General Reference (distance scale, cosmological discussion, etc.):

I.A.U. Symposium, No. 15 (Santa Barbara, 1961); *Problems of Extragalactic Research*, ed. G. C. McVittie, New York, 1962.

See also F. Hoyle and A. Sandage, *P.A.S.P.*, **68,** 301, 1956.

Rotation of Galaxies:

   H. W. Babcock, *Lick Obs. Bull.*, No. 498, 1939.

   N. U. Mayall and L. Aller, *Ap.J.*, **95**, 5, 1941.

   A. B. Wyse and N. U. Mayall, *Ap.J.*, **95**, 24, 1941.

   H. C. van de Hulst, E. Raimond, and H. van Woerden, *B.A.N.*, **14**, 1, 1957 (from 21 cm observations).

   M. Burbidge, *I.A.U. Symposium*, No. 15, for summary and references to numerous papers on rotation by Burbidge group.

Spiral Arms and Magnetic Fields:

   B. Lindblad, *Stockholm Annals*, **14**, No. 3, 1942.

   F. Hoyle and J. G. Ireland, *M.N.*, **122**, 35, 1961 (previous references cited).

   Glenn L. Berge and G. A. Seielstad, *Scientific American*, **212**, 46, 1965.

Local Group:

   Magellanic Clouds: The literature defies condensation: See especially A. D. Thackeray, Vol. 2, *Advances in Astronomy and Astrophysics* and *I.A.U. Symposium*, No. 20; *The Galaxy and the Magellanic Clouds*, Australian Acad. Sci., 1964.

   G. de Vaucouleurs, *Ap.J.*, **128**, 465, 1958.

   Paul W. Hodge, *A.J.*, **69**, 853, 1964 (and previous references).

Clusters and Groups:

   G. Abell, *Ap.J.*, *Supp.*, **3**, 210, 1958.

   J. Neyman and E. L. Scott: see e.g., *I.A.U. Symposium*, No. 15.

   F. Zwicky, *Encyclopaedia of Physics*, Vol. 53.

   F. Zwicky, E. Herzog and P. Wild: *Catalogue of Galaxies and Clusters of Galaxies*, Vol. I, Cal. Tech., 1961.

   Problems of Stability and Virial Theorem: Conference Report, *A.J.*, **66**, 533, 1961.

Radio Sources:

   J. L. Pawsey, *Ap.J.*, **121**, 1, 1955 (nomenclature).

   A. S. Bennett, *Mem. R.A.S.*, **68**, 163, 1962 (revised 3C Catalogue).

   I. S. Shklovsky, *Russian Ast. J.*, **30**, 15, 1953.

   S. P. Maran and A. G. W. Cameron (ed. by), *Physics of Nonthermal Radio Sources*, N.A.S.A., 1964.

   C. R. Lynds and A. R. Sandage, *Ap.J.*, **137**, 1005, 1963.

   M. Ryle and R. W. Clarke, *M.N.*, **122**, 349, 1961.

   M. Ryle and P. F. Scott, *M.N.*, **122**, 389, 1961.

Quasars. Numerous references include:

   T. A. Matthews and A. R. Sandage, *Ap.J.*, **138**, 30, 1963.

   J. L. Greenstein and M. Schmidt, *Ap.J.*, **140**, 1, 1964.

   M. Schmidt, *Ap.J.*, **141**, 1, 1965.

   M. Schmidt, *Ap.J.*, **141**, 1295, 1965.

Index

Note: Objects in particular constellations are listed under the nominative of the name, e.g. for RR Lyrae, see Lyra. Italic figures refer to plate numbers.

A (Oort constant), 142
A-type stars, 84
A.A.V.S.O., 158
Abell, G. O., 188, 235, 256, 264
Aberration, 8; constant of, 8
Absolute magnitude, 91, 92; bolometric, 92, 114; Cepheids, 168; galaxies, 246; globular clusters, 241; novae, 179; RR Lyrae stars, 171; supernovae, 182
Absorption, interstellar, and reddening, 107
Absorption lines, 51
Abundance of elements, 89
Age parameters, 122
Ages of clusters, 123
Air Almanac, 23
Aitken, R. G., 189, 206
Aldebaran, 217
Alexander, J. B., 139, 154, 187
Algol, 215
Allegheny Observatory, 45
Allen, C. W., 46, 140, 166, 179, 180, 223
Aller, L. H., 90, 185, 188, 264
Alter, G., 104, 111
Altitude, 1
Amateur observers, 158
Ambartsumian, V. A., 135, 257
Ames, Adelaide, 234, 263
Andromeda nebula, 113, 172, 179, 181, 182, 222, 231, 234, 253; Cepheids in, 241; novae in, 179, 181; physical parameters, 254; radial velocities of features, 248; radio source, 258; rotation of nucleus, 248
Ångström unit, 50
Angular diameter of stars, 217
Annual parallax, 34, 133
Anomaly, 204
Antapex, solar, 132

Antares, 217, 218, *12*
Apex, solar, 42, 132
Aphelion, 22
Apogalacticon, 147
Apparent magnitude, 54, 91
Apparent place, 33
Aquila, 179
Arcturus, 217
Argelander, F. W. A., 39, 158
Aries, First Point of, 4
Arms, spiral, 228, 250, 251; Orion, 228; Perseus, 228; 3-kpc arm, 228
Arp, H. C., 111, 112, 124, 125, 166, 175, 179, 181, 187, 188, 241
Asiago Observatory, *24*
Associations, 121; expanding, 135; O-associations, 122; T-associations, 121
Astrographic project, 40
Astrolabe, impersonal, Danjon, 30, 46, *4*
Astrometric binaries, 190, 194
Astronomical Ephemeris, 5, 160; Explanation to, 34
Atkinson, R. d'E., 33, 114
Atmospheric refraction, 14, 75
Auriga, 175; 181; Nova Aurigae, 181; RW Aurigae, 175
Autumnal equinox, 5
Avoidance, zone of, 235
Axis, declination, 6; polar, 6
Azimuth, 7, 16; error, 15
Ažusienis, A, 54

B (photometry), 57 *et seq.*; (Oort constant), 144 *et seq.*
B-stars, 84, 143, 224
Baade, W., 113, 125, 172, 188, 231, 241, 253

Babcock, H. W., 176, 188, 249, 264
Bailey, S. I., 162, 171, 188
Bailey types, 169
Baker-Nunn camera, 72
Baker-Schmidt camera, 72
Baking (of emulsions), 70
Balmer discontinuity, 51
Balmer series, 49, 82, 86
Bappu, M. K. V., 88
Barred spirals, 232, 233
Basic solar motion, 145
Batten, A. H., 220
Baum, W. A., 63, 111, 112, 237, 244
Bayer, J., 39, 158
Beaufort West, 179
Bečvář, A., 263
Becker, W., 67, 89
Bennett, A. S., 264
Berge, G. L., 252, 264
Bernstein, S., 153, 155
Bessel, F. W., 192
Besselian Day Numbers, 34
Besselian Year, 34
Betelgeuse, 217
Bethe, H., 115
Bifilar micrometer, 193, 194
Binary stars, 189 *et seq.*; astrometric, 190, 194; catalogues, 199, 220, 221; interferometric, 190, 195; novae as, 181; orbital parameters, 191
Binary stars, eclipsing, 157, 190, 211 *et seq.*; finding list, 215, 221; types of, 215
Binary stars, spectroscopic, 200 *et seq.*; bibliography of, 208; catalogue of orbits, 220; mass ratio in, 201; orbital elements, 203, 204; velocity curves, 202, 203

Binary stars, visual, 191 *et seq.*; analysis of observations, 197; catalogues of orbits, 199, 220; masses of components, 211; observational methods, 193 *et seq.*; orbital elements, 197, 198; Sirius as, 192

Blaauw, A., 124, 135, 136, 154, 168, 171, 183, 187

Black body, 47, 48

Blanketing, 101

Blanketing line, 102

Blazhko effect, 169

Blink microscope, 42, 158

Bolometric absolute magnitude, 92, 114

Bolometric magnitude, 93, 157

Bolton, J. G., 259

Boltzmann, L., 47, 80

Bondi, H., 244

Bonn Observatory, 40

Bonner Durchmusterung, 40

Bottlinger, K. F., 148

Bowen, I. S., 184, 185, 188

Branch, horizontal, 113

Break-off point, 113, 118

Bridges, intergalactic, 258

Bright Galaxies, Reference Catalogue, 234, 263

Brouwer, D., 25

Brown, R. Hanbury, 218, 221

Burbidge, E. Margaret, 122, 125, 177, 183, 188, 239, 247, 248, 249, 257, 259, 264

Burbidge, G. R., 120, 122, 125, 177, 183, 188, 239, 247, 248, 249, 257, 259

Bureau International de l'Heure, 27

Burnham, S. W., 199

Burr, E. J., 162, 187

c-characteristic, 99

Caesium clock, 20, *2*

Calcium, 52, 82; H and K lines of, 107; interstellar lines of, 78, 145

Calibration, photographic, 67

Camelopardalis, Z, 178, 181

Camera, all-sky, 223; Baker-Nunn, 72; Baker-Schmidt, 72; electronic, 239; jiggle, 237; Schmidt, 69, 71, 72, 104, 235, 238

Cameron, A. G. W., 125, 264

Camm, G. L., 143, 145, 155

Campbell, W. W., 89

Canes Venatici; α² Canum Venaticorum, 177

Canis Major; β Canis Majoris, 157, 174

Canopus, 53

Cape Observatory, 40, 45, 46, 54, 130, 168, 208, 209

Cape of Good Hope, 15

Cape Photographic Catalogue (CPC), 40

Cape Photographic Durchmusterung (CPD), 40

Carbon-Nitrogen-Oxygen (CNO), cycle, 115

Carina; η Carinae, 179

Carte du Ciel, 40

Cassegrain spectrograph, 73

Catalogues, galaxies, 234, 263; radial velocities, 79, 208; star clusters, 104; variable stars, 157, 215

Catalogues, stars; binary, 199, 220, 221; bright, 40; durchmusterung, 39, 40; parallax, 46; positional, 27, 40, 46; spectral, 40

Celestial, equator, 1; latitude, 1; longitude, 7; pole, 1; sphere, 1

Centaurus A (radio source), 259; α Centauri, 193, 209; parallax of, 209; ω Centauri, 111, 169

Cepheid variable stars, 143, 162, 165, 181, *22*, *24*; absolute magnitudes of, 168; in clusters, 168, 241; in M 31, 241; in Small Magellanic Cloud, 163; intrinsix colours of, 167; period-luminosity relation, 165, 166; properties of, 162; See also Cepheus

Cepheids, dwarf, 176

Cepheus; β Cephei stars, 174; δ Cephei, 157, 162, 163, 164; η Cephei, 134

Cetus; o, (Mira), Ceti, 157

Chalonge, D., 64

Chandrasekhar, S., 117, 118, 120, 122, 125, 152, 155, 257

Christy, W., 188

Churms, J., 160

Circle, great, 1; small, 1; transit, 10 *et seq.*, *1*

Circular velocity, 140

Circumpolar stars, 2

Clark, A., 192

Clark, B. G., 259

Clarke, R. W., 264

Clemence, G. M., 46

Clocks, caesium, 20, *2*; pendulum, 19; quartz, 19; Shortt, 19

Cloud, Ursa Major, of galaxies, 256

Clouds, Magellanic; see Magellanic Clouds

Clube, S. V. M., 228

Cluster parallaxes, 106

Clusters of galaxies, 230, 252, 256

Clusters, open, 104

Clusters, star, 103; ages of, 123; catalogue of, 104; Coma, 107; dynamics of, 151; interstellar absorption and reddening, 107; magnitudes and colours in, 103; motions, 105. See also Clusters, galactic; Clusters, globular

Clusters, galactic, 103, 104; Cepheids in, 168, 241; Coma, 107; h and χ Persei, 103, *13*; Hyades, 103, 104, 105, 119, 133, 134, 139, 211; κ Crucis, *15*; NGC 2362, 108, 109; Pleiades, 103, 104, 108, 110, 134, 152, 211, *14*; Praesepe, 103, 104, 108, 110, 134; Scorpio-Centaurus, 134; Ursa Major, 107, 134, 139

Clusters, globular, 111, 117, 149, 152, *16*; absolute magnitudes of, 241; Hertzsprung-Russell diagram of, 112; M 3, 118, 169; M 5, 112; periods of variables in, 173; velocity dispersion in, 152; ω Centauri, 111, 169; 47 Tucanae, 111, 153, *16*

Cluster type variables; see Lyra, RR Lyrae stars

Coal Sack, 127

Code, A. D., 223

Coffeen, Mary, 152

Collimation error, 16

Collins, G. W., 212, 221

Colour excess, 92, 109

Colours, of Cepheids, 167; in clusters, 103; See also Stars: Photometry

Colour temperature, 49

Coma (optical aberration), 68, *5(b)*; (constellation), 107, 134

Conde, H., 89

Constants, aberration, 8; astronomical, 46; Hubble, 242, 245, 249; nutation, 10; Oort, 142, 143, 144, 147, 168, 224; plate, 38; precession, 10

Constellations; see under individual names

Content, metallic, 118, 119, 124

Contour, of spectrum line, 86

Contraction, Kelvin-Helmholtz, 119, 120

Coordinates, altazimuth, 7; ecliptic, 7; equatorial, 3 *et seq.*; galactic, 128; standard (astrometric), 37, 38

Cordoba Durchmusterung (CoD), 40

Core, of spectrum line, 86

Corona Borealis: Nova T Coronae Borealis, 181; R Coronae Borealis, 178
Coudé spectrograph, 78
Counts of stars, 223
Courtès, G., 237
Cousins, A. W. J., 58, 89
Cowling, T. G., 114, 117
Crab Nebula, 182, 183, 184, 225, 229, 260, *26*. See also Radio sources: Supernovae
Crux; κ Crucis, *15*
Culmination, 2; lower, 3; upper, 3
Curtis, H. D., 229
Curve of growth, 88
Cycle, CNO, 115
Cygnus, 228; SS Cygni, 178, 181; 61 Cygni, 134

Daguerrotype, 54
Danjon, A., 30, 33
Darkening to limb, 49, 50
Date, Julian, 160
David Dunlap Observatory, 46
Davies, R. D., 263
Day numbers, 34; Besselian, 34; independent, 34
Day, sidereal, 4
Declination, 3, 13
Declination axis, 6
Deeming, T. J., 155
Delhaye, J., 136
Delta Cephei; see Cepheids: Cepheus, δ Cephei
Density, mass, in Galaxy, 150; photographic, 65
Dependences, 44
Deutsch, A. J., 181
de Sierra, A. C., 89
de Vaucouleurs, Antoinette, 234, 263
de Vaucouleurs, G., 89, 230, 231, 232, 233, 234, 239, 251, 253, 254, 256, 263, 264
Diagram, Hertzsprung-Russell; see Hertzsprung-Russell diagram
Diameters, angular, of stars, 217
Diffraction grating, 74
Direct photography, 68
Dirty ice, 108
Disk, of Galaxy, 223
Dispersion, of velocities, 133, 138; in galactic clusters, 151, 152; in Galaxy, 150; in globular clusters, 152; nearby stars, 140
Distance modulus, 92
Distances, of galaxies, 241. See also Absolute magnitude: Parallax

Distribution, Cepheids, 165; neutral hydrogen in Galaxy, 227; OB stars, 224; planetary nebulae, 186; RR Lyrae stars, 173; stars in Galaxy, 223
Dominion Astrophysical Observatory, 90
Dommanget, J., 220
Doppler-Fizeau effect, 72, 82, 243
Double stars; see Binary stars
Dreyer, J. L. E., 234, 263
Drifts, stellar, 136
Duchesne, M., 239, 263
Duflot, Madeleine, 124
Durchmusterung, 39; Bonn, 40; Cape Photographic, 40; Cordoba, 40
Dust, interstellar, 108; polarisation by, 108
Dwarf, Cepheids, 176; red, 96; stars, 95; white, 102
Dynamical parallaxes, 199, 200
Dynamics of clusters, 151

Early type stars, *10*
Earth, rotation of, 2
Ebert, R., 120
Eccentricity, 198
Eclipsing binary stars, 157, 190, 211 *et seq.* See also Binary stars
Ecliptic, 4; obliquity of, 4
Eddington, Sir A. S., 114, 156, 210
Edmondson, F. K., 155
Efremov, Yu. I., 157, 187
Effect, Doppler-Fizeau, 72, 82, 243; intermolecular Stark, 82; reflection, in binaries, 214; Stebbins-Whitford, 243, 244; Zeeman, 176
Effective temperature, 48
Eggen, O. J., 42, 102, 124, 125, 134, 135, 143, 148, 149, 154, 155, 160, 162, 171, 177, 187, 211, 221
Einstein, A., 244
Eichner, L., 67
Element abundance, 87
Electronic camera, 239
Elliptical nebulae, 113, 230; isophotes, 231; numbers, 246. See also Galaxies
Ellipsoid of velocities, 136, 137; from nearby stars, 139; from radial velocities, 138
Emden, R., 114
Emission spectra, galaxies, 238; planetary nebulae, 184
Encounter, stellar, 152, 190
Energy generation, in stars, 114

Ephemeris, The Astronomical, 5, 160; Explanation to, 34
Ephemeris Time, 24, 26, 46
Epoch, 33
Epps, Elizabeth, 187
Equation, of the Equinoxes, 24; of Time, 22
Equator, celestial, 1; galactic, 127
Equatorial mounting, 6
Equinoxes, 4; autumnal, 5; equation of, 24; vernal, 4, 9
Equipment, photoelectric, 60
Equivalent width, 86
Eridanus: p Eridani, 193
Errors, of transit circle: azimuth, 15; clock, 18; collimation, 16; division, 18; flexure, 14, 18; level, 13, 15; pivot, 18
Escape velocity, from Galaxy, 148
Escape of stars, from clusters, 151 *et seq.*; from Galaxy, 149
Essen, L., 20, 25, 46
Euclidean universe, 245
Evolution, stellar, 116, 123
Evans, David S., 160, 239, 259
Excess, colour, 92, 109; ultraviolet, 101
Excitation, 80; temperature, 88
Expanding associations, 135
Expansion of the universe, 242
Explosive variables, 177. See also Novae: Supernovae
Exposure meters, 75
External galaxies, 229, 230. See also Galaxies
Extinction and reddening, 92, 110, 143
Extragalactic spectroscopy, 238
Eyepiece interferometer, 194, 195, 196

Fabry, Ch., 64
Factor, parallax, 43
Faraday rotation, 252
Feast, M. W., 124, 140, 143, 145, 146, 153, 154, 155, 166, 168, 177, 188
Fehrenbach, Ch., 79, 89, 124
Field stars, 103
Filters, interference, 70
Finsen, W. S., 195, 196, 218, 220
Fizeau, H., 72, 82, 243
FK3, FK4, Catalogues, 27, 40, 46
Flamsteed, J., 39
Flare star, *24*
Flexure, error of transit circle, 14, 18; of spectrograph, 75
Focal ratio, 70
Forbidden lines, 184
Fornax system, 254
Foucault test, 68

Fowler, W. A., 115, 122, 125, 183, 188, 260
Function, luminosity, 118

GC, catalogue, 40
Galactic, clusters, 103, 104. See also Clusters; coordinates, 128; equator, 127, latitude, 128; longitude, 128; poles, 127
Galaxies, 111, 222, 229; absolute magnitudes of, 246; Andromeda, 172, 179, 181, 182, 222, 231, 234, 253; Andromeda, novae in, 179, 181; Andromeda, parameters of, 254; Andromeda, radio source, 258; Andromeda, rotation of nucleus, 248; Andromeda, velocities of features in, 248; barred spiral, 232, 233; bridges, intergalactic, 258; Bright Reference Catalogue, 234; catalogues of, 234; classification, 230; clustering, 230, 252; cluster, Coma, 256; cluster, Ursa Major, 256; cluster, Virgo, 256; distances of, 241; elliptical, 113, 230, 254; elliptical, isophotes, 231; elliptical, numbers, 246; elliptical, properties, 246; emission lines in spectra, 238; external, 229, 230; Fornax, 254; Hubble expansion, 242; hydrogen emission, 247; inclination, 247; Index Catalogues, 234; instability of groups, 257; Local Group, 252; Local Supergalaxy masses, 249; New General Catalogue, 234; normal spirals, 231, 232, 233; obscuring matter, 231; observations of, 235; Olbers' paradox, 245; parameters, 230; photometry, 236; proper motions from, 43; properties, 246; quasi-stellar, 262; quasistellar sources (quasars), 261; radial velocities, 237; radio sources, 258; rotation of, 247; Sculptor, 254; Seyfert, 246; spectra, 246; spectroscopy, 238; supergalaxy, 256, supernovae in, 182, 236; variables in, 236. See also Magellanic Clouds
Galaxy, The, 104, 111, 127, 165, 182, 222, 225, 229; arms of, 228; clusters in, 103, 104; dimensions of, 172; hydrogen in, 225, 226, 227, 250; magnetic fields in, 252; mass density of, 150; motions per-

pendicular to plane in, 150; nucleus, 223; OH molecule in, 225; rotation of, 140, 226; rotation from proper motions, 143; structure, 127
Gaposchkin, Cecilia Payne-, 163, 166, 179, 187, 188
Garfinkel, B., 46
Gascoigne, S. C. B., 143, 162, 187
Gases, kinetic theory of, 152
Gemini: μ Geminorum, 218; U Geminorum, 178, 181
Generation of stellar energy, 114
Giant stars, 97, 98, 99
Gill, Sir D., 16, 54
Ginzburg, V. L., 260
Gliese, W., 98, 99, 102, 124, 130, 139, 150, 154
Globular clusters, see Clusters, globular
Globules, 121, 17
Gold, T., 244
Gradient, photometric, 62
Grating, diffraction, 74; objective, 55
Great circle, 1
Greeby, Frances M., 197, 221
Greenstein, J. L., 102, 125, 262, 264
Greenwich Observatory, 40, 45, 1
Greenwich Sidereal Time, 5
Griffin, R. F., 78
Groombridge 1830, 134
Groups, moving, of stars, 134
Growth, curve of, 88
Guiding, 7
Gum, C., 154
Guthnick, P., 164
Gyldenkerne, K., 63, 85, 89

H (line of calcium), 107; interstellar, 78, 145
Haffner, H., 67
Half width, 86
Hall, J. S., 251
Halley, E., 153
Halo, 148, 223
Hamburg Observatory, 40
Harding, G. A., 259
Haro, G., 122, 175
Harrington, J. P., 254
Harvard Observatory, 83; HR catalogue, 97, 100
Hartmann, G., 76
Haselgrove, C. B., 123
Haute Provence Observatory, 80, 240, 8
Heckmann, O., 105, 106, 125
Heliocentric, Julian Date, 160; positions, 33
Helmholtz, H. von, 119

Henry brothers, 54
Henry Draper catalogue (HD), 40, 158
Herbig, G. H., 119, 122, 175, 188, 18
Hercules, 112, 130; globular cluster, M 13, in, 112; Z Herculis, 134
Herschel, Sir J. F. W., 54, 179, 234; Herschel's Jewel Box, 15
Herschel, Sir W. F., 222, 223, 229, 234
Hertzsprung-Russell diagram, 92, 106, 110, 112, 117, 119, 122, 136, 148, 154, 156, 168, 171, 177, 208; of galactic clusters, 107, 123; of globular clusters, 112, 123; of nearby stars, 94
Herzog, E., 264
High velocity stars, 130, 147, 148
Higher multiplicity stars, 218
Hill, E. R., 155
Hiltner, W. A., 251
Hindman, J. V., 255
Hipparchus, 9, 53
Hodge, P. W., 264
Holmberg, E. B., 253
Horizontal branch (HR diagram), 113
Houck, T. E., 223
Hour Angle, 3, 4
Hoyle, F., 122, 123, 125, 183, 188, 244, 252, 260, 262, 263, 264
Hubble constant, 242, 245, 249
Hubble, E., 230, 232, 233, 239, 263
Huffer, C. M., 212, 215, 221
Humason, M. L., 239, 263
Hyades, 103, 104, 105, 119, 133, 134, 139, 211
Hydrus: β Hydri, 134
Hydrogen, Balmer discontinuity of, 51; Balmer series of, 49, 82, 86; density in galaxies, 227; emission lines in galaxies, 247; H II regions, 242; neutral in galaxies, 225; radio emission (21-cm) from, 225, 226, 227, 228, 250

Ice, dirty, 108
Image tubes, 240
Images, star, 65, 5
Incidence, stellar multiplicity, 189
Inclination, binary orbit, 198; galaxy, 247
Independent Day Numbers, 34
Index Catalogue, Double Stars, 197, 221; nebulae and clusters, 234
Index, colour, 55

Indus: ε Indi, 134
Innes, R. T. A., 194
Instability, groups of galaxies, 257
Instrumental profile, 87
Intensity, residual, 86
Interference filters, 70
Interferometer, eyepiece, 194, 195, 196; stellar, 217
Interferometric binaries, 190, 195. See also Binary Stars
Intergalactic bridges, 258
Intermolecular Stark effect, 82
"Internal Constitution of the Stars", 114
International Astronomical Union (IAU), 198
Interstellar absorption and reddening, 107
Interstellar dust, 108; polarisation by, 108
Interstellar lines, 78, 145
Intrinsic colours, of Cepheids, 167
Invariable plane, 9
Ionisation, 81; potentials, 82; temperature, 88
Ireland, J. G., 252, 264
Iriarte, B., 124
Iris-diaphragm photometer, 67, 160, 7
Irwin, J. B., 163, 168, 187
Isophotes, 230; of Andromeda nebula, 253; of elliptical nebulae, 231

Jacobsen, T. S., 164
Jaschek, C., 89
Jeans, Sir J. H., 120, 156
Jeffers, H. M., 197, 221
Jiggle camera, 237
Johnson, H. L., 57, 59, 83, 89, 105, 106, 108, 109, 111, 124, 125, 165
Johannesburg (Union, Republic), Observatory, 195, 197
Jones, Susan, 187
Joy, A. H., 143, 163, 167, 174, 188
Joyner, Mary C., 263
Julian Date, 160

K-line (calcium), 78, 107, 145
K-term, 145, 146
Kahn, F. D., 120
Kapteyn, J. C., 54
Keenan, P. C., 83, 89
Kellman, Edith, 83, 89
Kelvin, Lord, 119, 175; Kelvin-Helmholtz contraction, 119, 120
Kenya, 15
Kepler, J., 182; third law of, 191

Kerr, F. J., 255
Kholopov, P. N., 157, 187
Kinetic theory of gases, 152
Kinman, T. D., 155, 188
Kitt Peak National Observatory, 240
Knuckles, C. F., 105, 125
Koch, R. H., 215, 221
Kohoutek, L., 188
Kopal, Z., 214, 215, 220, 221
Kraft, R. P., 180, 188, 241
Kron, G. E., 57, 59, 153, 155, 168
Kuiper, G. P., 46, 93, 102, 124, 189, 198
Kukarkin, B. V., 157, 175, 187

Labrecque, J. J., 46
Lacerta: 10 Lacertae, 135
Lallemand, A., 239, 263
Large Magellanic Cloud; see Magellanic Clouds
Later type stars, 11
Latitude, celestial, 7; galactic, 128; geographical, 1; variation of, 13
Leavitt, Henrietta S., 163
Ledoux, P., 156, 187
Leiden Observatory, 54, 227
Lemaître, G., 244, 258
Leningrad, 15
Level error, of transit circle, 13, 15
Lick Observatory, 46, 209, 240
Light year, 35
Liller, W., 185, 188
Limb, 50; darkening to, 49, 50
Limber, D. N., 121, 257
Lindblad, B., 131, 141, 250, 251, 264
Lindblad, P. O., 251
Line, contour, 86; profile, 86; wings, 86
Lines, spectral; see Spectral lines
Local Group, galaxies, 252
Local Sidereal Time, 5
Local standard of rest, 130
Local supergalaxy, 256
Long period variables, 177
Longitude, celestial, 7; galactic, 128; geographical, 5, 6
Luminosity, 54; relation to stellar mass, 210; ratio to mass in galaxies, 250; relation with Cepheid period, 165, 166
Luminosity function, 118
Lundmark, K., 254
Luyten, W. J., 102, 125, 154
Lynden-Bell, D., 149, 155
Lynds, C. R., 240, 260, 264
Lyra: β Lyrae, 214, 215: RR Lyrae, 135, 157, 171; RR Lyrae

variables, 149, 162, 169, 181, 23, 24; absolute magnitude, 171; distribution, 173; periods, 173; secular changes of periods, 169; spectral types, 170

M 3 (cluster), 118, 169
M 5 (cluster), 112
M 13 (cluster), 112
M 31; see Andromeda nebula: Galaxies
M 33 (galaxy), 182, 254
MK classification system, 83, 85
MKK system, 83
McClain, E. F., 263
McCormick Observatory, 45
McCrea, W. H., 120, 125
McGee, J. D., 240, 255
McVittie, G. C., 167, 187, 263
Magellanic Clouds, 163, 164, 165, 166, 182, 222, 241, 242, 253, 255, 258; Cepheids in, 163, 166; distance modulus, 254, 255; hydrogen in, 254; rotation of, 255; supersupergiants in, 241
Magnetic fields, in Galaxy, 252
Magnetic variables, 176
Magnitudes, 53; absolute, 91, 92; absolute bolometric, 92, 114; absolute, of Cepheids, 168; absolute, of galaxies, 246; absolute, of globular clusters, 241; absolute, of RR Lyrae stars, 171; absolute, of supernovae, 183; apparent, 54, 91; bolometric, 93, 157; and colours in clusters, 103; photographic, 54; photovisual, 54
Main Sequence, 93, 95, 104
Maksutov, D. D., 72
Maran, S. P., 264
Markowitz, W., 25
Martynov, D. Ya., 208, 220
Mass, density in Galaxy, 150; of galaxies, 249; luminosity ratio in galaxies, 250; luminosity relation for stars, 210; ratio in binary, 201; stellar, 118, 199, 208, 209; from visual binaries, 199, 211
Massevitch, Alla G., 181
Mather, Linda, 187
Matthews, T. A., 261, 264
Maxwell, J. C., 153
Mayall, N. U., 153, 155, 224, 239, 248, 249, 263, 264
Mean places of stars, 33
Mean Sun, 22
Mean Time, 23
Measurement of spectra, 76

Meridian, 2; passage, 2
Merrill, J. E., 221
Merrill, P. W., 177, 188
Messier, Ch., 111, 234
Metal content, of stars, 118, 119, 124
Meters, exposure, 75
Micrometer, bifilar, 193, 194
Microphotometer, 87
Microscope, blink, 42, 158
Middlehurst, Barbara, 46
Milky Way, 104, 111, 127, 222. See also The Galaxy
Miller, W. C., 70
Milne, E. A., 244
Minkowski, R. L., 185, 188, 239, 243, 259
Mira Ceti, 157, 177
Mirror transit, 33
Model of Galaxy, 225
Modulus, distance, 92
Molecules: OH in Galaxy, 225; TiO in stars, 52
Moon, 24, 53
Moore, J. H., 164
Morgan, W. W., 57, 83, 89, 108, 109, 125, 135, 168, 187, 232, 234, 263
Motions, cluster, 105; nearby stars, 130; orbital, 36; peculiar, 130; perpendicular to galactic plane, 150; proper, 35, 40, 41, 126; proper, affected by galactic rotation, 143; proper, referred to galaxies, 43; solar, 130, 131; systematic, 133; velocity ellipsoid from, 139
Mount Palomar Observatory, 72, 104, 235
Mount Wilson Observatory, 113; General Catalogue of Radial Velocities, 79, 208
Mounting, equatorial, 6
Moyls, B. N., 154, 163, 226
Muller, A., 187
Muller, C. A., 263
Multiplicity in stars, 189 *et seq.*; higher, 218

N 30, catalogue, 40
Nadir, 1; observations of, 13
Narrabri, 218
Narrow band photometry, 63
National Geographic Society Sky Survey, 72, 235, *19*
National Physical Laboratory, 20, *2*
Naval Observatory, U.S., 40
Nearby stars, Hertzsprung-Russell diagram, 94; motions of, 130, 139

Nebula; see galaxy, planetary nebula
Nebulium lines, 184
Neutral hydrogen, 225
New General Catalogue of Nebulae and Clusters of Stars (NGC), 234
Newton, Sir I., 9, 24
Newtonian, focus, 71; spectrograph, 237, 238
Neyman, J., 235, 256, 264
Nicholson, S. B., 93, 124
Nitrogen; see CNO cycle
Nodes, 197
Nomenclature, radio sources, 258; stars, 39; variable stars, 158
Nordström, Helge, 154
Norma, *27*; S. Normae, 168
Normal spirals, *37*
North Polar Sequence, 57
Novae, 157, 178, 179, 180, 181, 200; in Andromeda nebula, 179, 181; binary nature of, 181; Nova Aurigae, 181; — Aquilae, 179; — DQ Herculis, 181; — Herculis, 180; — Persei, 179; — Pictoris, 179; — Puppis, 179; — T. Coronae Borealis, 181. See also Supernovae
Nucleus, galactic, 223
Numbers, Day, 34
Nutation, 8, 10; constant of, 10
Nys, O., 220

O-stars, distribution, 224; spectra, 84
O (oxygen): CNO cycle, 115; forbidden lines of, 184, 238; OH molecule, 225
Objective grating, 55
Objective prism, *8, 9*; radial velocities from, 79
Obliquity of ecliptic, 4
Obscuring material in galaxies, 231
Observational determination of R.A., 17
Observations, of galaxies, 235; of nadir, 13
Observatories: Allegheny, 45; Asiago, *24*; Bonn, 40; Cape, 40, 45, 54, 130, 168, 208, 209; Cordoba, 40; David Dunlap, 46; Dominion Astrophysical, 90; Greenwich, 40, 45, *1*; Hamburg, 40; Harvard, 83; Haute Provence, 80, *8, 9*; Herstmonceux, 46, *1, 3*; Johannesburg, 195, 197; Kitt Peak, 240; Leiden, 54, 227; Lick, 46, 209, 240; McCormick, 45; Mount Palomar, 72, 104, 235;

Mount Wilson, 113; Pulkovo, 15, 40; Radcliffe, 130, 143; Smithsonian Astrophysical, 46; Sproul, 45; U.S. Naval, 40; Yale, 40, 45; Yerkes, 45. Note: Researches credited to names of individual authors do not always cite the observatory name as well.
Observers, amateur, 158
Observers, American Association of Variable Star, 158
Occultations, 25, 217
O'Dell, C. R., 188
Off-axis aberrations, 68
Ohlsson, J., 128
Olbers' paradox, 245
Oort, J. H., 141, 142, 145, 155, 167
Oort constants, 142, 143, 144, 147, 168, 224
Oosterhoff, P. Th., 163, 187
Opacity of stellar atmosphere, 49
Open clusters, 104
Orbital motion, correction for, 77; parameters of, 197; of spectroscopic binary, 204. See also Binary Stars
Orion, *24*; Orion arm, 228
Osvalds, V., 133, 154, 177

Page, T. L., 239
Parallax, 34, 126; of α Centauri, 209; annual, 34, 133; cluster, 106; dynamical, 199, 200; factor, 43; secular, 131, 133; trigonometric, 43, 46; trigonometric, catalogue of, 46
Parenago, P. P., 157, 187
Paris, 54
Parry, J. V. L., 46
Parsec, 35
Passage, meridian, 2
Pawsey, J. L., 154, 264
Payne-Gaposchkin, Cecilia, 163, 187, 188
Pearce, J. A., 143
Pease, F. G., 217
Peculiar motion, 130
Peimbert, M., 188
Pels-Kluyver, H. A., 171
Perek, L., 188
Perfect, D. S., 29, 46
Periastron, 198
Perigalacticon, 147
Perihelion, 22
Period, of binary stars, 190, 198; Cepheids, 162; finding, 161; long, variables, 177; luminosity law for Cepheids, 165, 166; RR Lyrae stars, 171; RR Lyrae stars in clusters, 173

Perseus, arm, 228; II, association, 136; h and χ cluster, 103, *13*
Petrie, R. M., 72, 76, 134, 154, 188
Pettit, E., 93, 124
Phase, 161
Phoenix: SX Phoenicis, 160
Photocentre, 36
Photography, astronomical, 36; baking of emulsions, 70; calibration, 67; catalogues by, 40; density, 65; densitometry, 66; direct, 68, 235; emulsions, 68; filters, 68, 70; plate constants, 38; sensitometer, tube, 64; zenith tube (PZT), 27, *3*
Photometer, iris diaphragm, 67, 160, *7*; photoelectric, see Photometry; types of, 67
Photometric, gradient, 62; sequences, 56
Photometry, narrow-band, 63; photoelectric, 57 *et seq.*; of galaxies, 236, 253; pulse counting, 63; reductions, 61; traces, *6*; variable stars, 160
Photometry, photographic, 54 *et seq.*; variable stars, 158. See also Photography
Places, apparent, 33; mean, 33
Planck, M., 48
Plane, galactic, 127; motions perpendicular to, 150; invariable, 9
Planetary nebulae, 184
Plaskett, J. S., 143
Platt, J. R., 108, 124
Pleiades, 103, 104, 108, 110, 134, 152, 211, *14*
Pogson, N., 53, 55
Point, turn-off (break-off), 113
Pole, celestial, 1; galactic, 127
Polar axis, 6
Polar Sequence, North, 57
Polarisation, 252; by interstellar dust, 108
Population, disk, 223; halo, 148, 223; type I, 113, 140, 143, 148, 231; type II, 113, 148, 231
Position angle, 193, 194; relation to coordinate directions, 194
Positions, heliocentric, 33
Potentials, ionisation, 82
Poveda, A., 178
Prager, R., 161, 187
Praesepe, 103, 104, 108, 110, 134
Precession, 8, 9, 10; constant of, 10
Preston, G. W., 170, 188
Prism, objective, *8, 9*; radial velocities from, 79
Procyon, 193

Profile, instrumental, 87; spectrum line, 86
Proper motion, 35, 40, 41, 126; effect of galactic rotation, 143; referred to galaxies, 43; used for velocity ellipsoid, 139
Proton-proton chain, 115
Przybylski, A., *12*
Pulkovo Observatory, 15, 40, 46

Q-method, 167
Quasars, 261

Radcliffe Observatory, 130, 143
Radial velocities, 72, 126; catalogue, 79, 208; of galaxies, 237; limiting magnitude, 74; by objective prism, 79; photometric method, 78; velocity ellipsoid from, 138
Radiation, synchrotron, 229, 252
Radii, of stars, 217
Radio astronomy, 225; Andromeda nebula, 258; Centaurus A, 259; Faraday rotation, 252 Fornax source, 254; galaxies, 258; hydrogen in galaxies, 247; nomenclature of sources, 258; observations of 21-cm line; OH molecule, 225; quasars, 261; structure of Galaxy from, 225 *et seq.* See also Crab Nebula
Raimond, E., 168, 187, 264
Ratio, focal, 70; mass, in spectroscopic binaries, 20; mass-luminosity in galaxies, 250
Rectification, 214
Reddening, interstellar, 92, 110, 143; absorption and, 107
Redman, R. O., 58
Reference Catalogue of Bright Galaxies, 234
Reflecting telescopes, 71
Reflection effect, 214
Refracting telescopes, 71
Refraction, atmospheric, 14, 75
Relation, mass-luminosity, for stars, 210; period-luminosity for Cepheids, see Cepheids
Relaxation time, 152
Residual intensity, 86
Rest, local standard of, 130
Reynolds, J. H., 231
Richmond, Myrtle, 263
Right Ascension, 3, 5; observational determination of, 17
Risley, A. M., 133, 154, 177
Roberts, M., 188
Rodgers, A. W., 179
Roman, Nancy G., 134, 154

Rosino, L., *24*
Rosseland, S., 156
Rotation, Earth, 2; Faraday, 252; galactic, 140, 226; galactic, from B-stars, 143; of galaxies, 247; of Magellanic Clouds, 255; rapid, in galactic nuclei, 248
Roy, A. E., 117
Rubin, Vera C., 224, 263
Runaway stars, 183
Ruprecht, J., 104, 111
Russell, H. N., 92, 114, 215, 221
Ryle, Sir M., 261, 264

S-stars, 177
Sadler, D. H., 46
Sagittarius, 127, 172, 228; WZ Sagittarii, 181
Saha, M. N., 81
Sandage, A. R., 111, 112, 113, 117, 118, 122, 124, 149, 155, 171, 172, 187, 188, 230, 232, 233, 239, 241, 242, 243, 260, 261, 262, 263, 264
Sartorius photometer, 67
Saturation, photographic density, 67; spectral line, 82
Sawyer, Helen B., 169, 188
Schatzman, E. L., 102, 124
Schilt, J., 67
Schilt photometer, 67
Schlesinger, F., 43, 44, 46, 220
Schmidt, B., 71
Schmidt camera, 67, 71, 72, 104, 235, 238; Palomar, 72, 104, *19*
Schmidt, M., 168, 224, 226, 249, 262, 263, 264
Schmidt's model of the Galaxy, 225
Schmidt-Kaler, Th., 241
Schönberg, M., 117, 118, 120, 122, 125
Schraffierkassette, 65, 237
Schwarzschild, M., 122, 153, 155
Sciama, D. W., 263
Scorpio, 127
Scorpio-Centaurus cluster, 134
Scott, Elizabeth L., 235, 256, 264
Scott, P. F., 264
Sculptor system, 254
Scutum: δ Scuti stars, 176
Seares, F. H., 223, 263
Searle, L., 179
Seaton, M. J., 186
Secchi, A., 83
Secular changes, RR Lyrae stars, 169
Secular parallaxes, 131, 133
Seielstad, G. A., 252, 264
Sensitometer, tube, 64

Sequences, photometric, 56; North Polar, 57; Main, in H-R diagram, 93, 95, 104
Series, spectral, 49
Sérsic, J. L., 242
Seyfert galaxies, 246
Seyfert, K., 246
Shapley, H., 111, 165, 166, 167, 172, 173, 175, 229, 234, 254, 256, 263
Shapley, Martha B., 215, 220
Shklovsky, I. S., 186, 260, 264
Shobbrook, R., 239
Sidereal Day, 4
Sidereal Time, 4, 23; Greenwich, 5; Local, 5
Sirius, 36, 53, 102, 193, 211, 218; as visual binary, 192; companion, 102, 192, 193
Skalnaté Pleso Atlas, 256
Small circle, 1
Small Magellanic Cloud; see Magellanic Clouds
Smart, W. M., 46, 154, 164
Smith, H. M., 46
Smithsonian Astrophysical Observatory, 46
Sobieski, S., 215, 221
Solar; see Sun
Sources, radio; see Radio Astronomy
Spectral lines, 51: absorption, 51; Balmer, 49, 82, 86; emission in galaxies, 238; forbidden, 184; hydrogen, 21-cm, 225; interstellar calcium, 107, 145; nebulium, 184
Spectral series, 49, 82, 86
Spectral types, 83, 84, 85; of Cepheids, 162, 163, 164; of β Canis Majoris stars, 174; of RR Lyrae stars, 170, 171; early, 10; late, 11
Spectra of galaxies, 246
Spectrographs, Cassegrain, 73; coudé, 78; flexure of, 75; Newtonian, 237, 238; speed of, 74, 238
Spectrophotometry, 85, 86; parameters, 86, 87
Spectroscopic binaries, 190, 198 et seq.; bibliography of, 208; catalogue of, 220; orbital parameters, 204. See also Binary Stars
Spectroscopy, extragalactic, 238
Sphere, celestial, 1
Spinrad, H., 188
Spiral arms, 250, 251; in Galaxy, 228; Orion, 228; Perseus, 228; 3 kpc-arm, 228
Spiral galaxies, barred, 232, 233;

normal, 231, 232, 233. See also Galaxies
Spitzer, L., 153
Sproul Observatory, 45
Standard coordinates, 37, 38
Standard of rest, local, 130
Stellar associations, 121
Stars, angular diameters of, 217; associations of, 121; B-stars, 143, 224; binary, see Binary Stars; counts of, 223; drifts, 136; dwarf, 95; early type, 11; encounters of, 152, 190; energy generation in, 114; escape of, 149; evolution of, 116, 123; field, 103; flare, 24; giant, 97, 98, 99; halo, 148; high velocity, 130, 147, 148; images of, 65, 5; late type, 11; magnitudes of, 53; masses of, 118, 199, 208, 209; Mira stars, 133, 157, 177; motions of nearby, 130; moving groups of, 134; nearby, 139; nomenclature, 39; O-stars, 224; origin of, 119, 120, 121; Przybylski's, 12; radial velocities, 208; radii of, 217; runaway, 183; S-stars, 177; streaming, 136; subdwarf, 100, 101, 149, 12; subgiant, 99; super supergiant, 241; supergiant, 99; systematic motions, 133
Stark effect, intermolecular, 82
Steady state theory, 244
Stebbins, J., 57, 59, 93, 243
Stefan, J., 47, 93
Stefan-Boltzmann law, 47
Sterne, T., 206, 221
Stibbs, D. W. N., 143, 155, 167, 168, 187
Stoy, R. H., 58, 89
Straižys, V., 54
Strand, K. Aa., 199
Stream, of stars, 136; two-stream theory, 137
Strömberg, G., 139, 154
Strömgren, B., 63, 85, 89, 114, 124, 188
Strontium, 83
Structure of Galaxy, 127; from 21-cm line, 226, 227. See also The Galaxy
Struve, O., 171, 188
Subdwarfs, 100, 101, 149, 12
Subgiants, 99
Sun, 53, 211, 222, 228; Mean, 22; spectral type, 84; solar antapex, 132; solar apex, 42, 132; solar motion, 130, 131; solar motion, basic, 145
Super supergiants, 241
Supergalaxy, 256

Supergiants, 99
Supernovae, 157, 181, 182, 25; in galaxies, 182, 236; magnitudes, 182; types, 182; supernova of 1054 A.D., 26. See also Crab Nebula
Swope, Henrietta H., 241
Sydney, 227
Synchrotron radiation, 229, 252
Systematic motion of stars, 133

T-association, 121
T-Tauri stars, 121, 174
Taurus: RV Tauri, 176
Temesváry, S., 120
Temperature, colour, 49; effective, 48; excitation, 88; ionisation, 88
Test, Foucault, 68
Thackeray, A. D., 82, 83, 89, 124, 143, 145, 146, 153, 155, 166, 168, 173, 188, 255, 264
Thomas, D. V., 46
Time, 18 et seq., 46; Ephemeris, 24, 26, 46; equation of, 22; Greenwich Sidereal, 5; Local Sidereal, 5; Mean, 23; relaxation, 152; Sidereal, 4, 23; Universal, 22
Titanium oxide, 52
Titus, J., 143, 146, 155
Transit, 2
Transit circle, 10 et seq., 46, 1; errors of, 15 et seq.
Transit, mirror, 33
Tropical Year, 26
True anomaly, 204
Trumpler, R. J., 138, 154
Tube, image, 240; Photographic Zenith, 27, 3; sensitometer, 64
Turn-off point, 113
Twiss, R. Q., 218, 221
Two-stream theory, 137
Tycho Brahe, 182
Types, Bailey, 169; supernovae, 182. See also Spectral Types

UBV photometry, 58 et seq.
Udick, Stella, 220
Ultraviolet excess, 101
Unit, Ångström, 50
Universal Time, 22
Unsöld, A., 89
Ursa Major: W Ursae Majoris, 215; Cloud of galaxies, 256; star cluster, 107, 134, 139
U.S. Naval Observatory, 40

V; see UBV photometry
van Biesbroeck, G., 195
van Bueren, H. G., 106, 125

van de Hulst, H. C., 124, 225, 263, 264
van de Kamp, P., 189, 194, 220
van den Bergh, S., 182, 232, 233, 242, 257, 263
van den Bos, W. H., 195, 197, 198, 199, 218, 220, 221
van Rhijn, P. J., 223, 263
van Woerden, H., 264
Vanýsek, V., 104, 111
Variable stars, 156; American Association of, Observers, 158; catalogue of, 157, 215; cluster type, 169; in galaxies, 236; long-period, 177; magnetic, 176; Mira, 133, 157, 177; nomenclature, 158; photo-electric observation of, 160. See also Binary Stars: Cepheid Variable Stars: Dwarf Cepheids: Long Period Variables; Lyra (RR Lyrae): Magnetic Variables: Scutum (δ Scuti): Virgo (W Virginis Stars)
Vega, 130
Vela: p. Velorum, 218
Velocity, circular, 140; dispersion, 133, 138; in globular clusters, 152; ellipsoid, 136, 137; ellipsoid of nearby stars, 139; ellipsoid from radial velocities, 138; of escape, 148; radial, see, Radial Velocities
Venus, 183
Vernal Equinox, 4, 9

Virgo: Cluster of galaxies, 256; W Virginis stars, 157, 175
Virial theorem, 257
Visual binary stars; see Binary Stars
von Hoerner, S., 120
von Weizsäcker, C., 115
Vorontsov-Velyaminov, B. A., 235, 258
Voûte, J., 194
Vyssotsky, A. N., 131, 145, 149, 154

Walker, M. F., 239, 263
Wallerstein, G. N., 168, 188
Walraven, Th., 59, 143, 160, 163, 171, 187, 188
Washington, 40
Wayman, P. A., 150, 155
Weaver, H. F., 89, 138, 154
Wellgate, G. B., 46
Wesselink, A. J., 56, 89, 124, 143, 164, 173, 187, 188, 209
Westerhout, G., 154, 226, 263
Westervelt, H., 244
White dwarfs, 102
Whitford, A. E., 59, 93, 243
Width, of spectrum line, 86
Wien's law, 48, 50
Wild, P., 264
Wildey, R. L., 125
Williams, D. R. W., 263
Williams, E. G., 58
Williams, Emma T. R., 145, 149

Willstrop, R. V., 63
Wilson, A. G., 254
Wilson, R. E., 79
Wilson, O. C., 88, 124, 152, 177
Wings, of spectrum line, 86
Wolf-Lundmark system, 254
Wollaston, W. H., 30
Woltjer, L., 124, 188, 252
Wood, F. B., 215, 221
Woolf, N. J., 124, 125
Woolley, Sir R. v.d. R., 125, 135, 150, 151, 153, 154, 155, 165, 177, 187
Worley, C. E., 199, 220
Wright, T., 222
Wurm, K., 188
Wyse, A. B., 224, 249, 264

Yale University Observatory, 40, 45, 46; Bright Star Catalogue, 40
Yates, G. G., 63
Year, Besselian, 34; Light, 35; Tropical, 26
Yerkes Observatory, 45

Zanstra, H., 185
Zeekoegat, 80
Zeeman effect, 176
Zenith, 1
Zenith distance, 2
Zenith Tube, Photographic, 27, 3
Zone of avoidance, 235
Zwicky, F., 182, 183, 188, 235, 256, 257, 258, 264, 25